UNIVERSITY OF
WOLVERHAMPTON
KNOWLEDGE ▪ INNOVATION ▪ ENTERPRISE

M

Harrison Learning Centre
City Campus
University of Wolverhampton
St. Peter's Square
Wolverhampton
WV1 1RH
Telephone: 0845 408 1631
Online Renewals: www.wlv.ac.uk/lib/myaccount

Modern Thinkers on Welfare

Edited by

Vic George
The University of Kent at Canterbury

and

Robert Page
University of Nottingham

PRENTICE HALL
HARVESTER WHEATSHEAF

London   New York   Toronto   Sydney   Tokyo   Singapore
Madrid   Mexico City   Munich

First published 1995 by
Prentice Hall/Harvester Wheatsheaf
Campus 400, Maylands Avenue
Hemel Hempstead
Hertfordshire, HP2 7EZ
A division of
Simon & Schuster International Group

Typeset in $10\frac{1}{2}$/12pt Erhardt
by PPS Limited, London Road, Amesbury, Wilts.

Printed and bound in Great Britain by
T.J. Press (Padstow) Ltd

Library of Congress Cataloging in Publication Data

Modern thinkers on welfare / edited by Vic George and Robert Page.
    p. cm.
  Includes bibliographical references and index.
  ISBN 0-13-353864-8
  1. Public welfare—Philosophy. I. George, Victor. II. Page,
Robert M.
  HV51.M62 1995   94-42493
  361—dc20   CIP

British Library Cataloguing in Publication Data

A catalogue record for this book is available from the British Library

ISBN 0-13-353864-8

---

1 2 3 4 5   99 98 97 96 95

Contents

Contributors

Floya Anthias	Professor of Sociology, University of Greenwich
Norman Barry	Professor of Politics, University of Buckingham
Michael Cahill	Principal Lecturer in Social Policy, University of Brighton
Nicholas Deakin	Professor of Social Policy and Administration, University of Birmingham
Hartley Dean	Reader in Social Policy, University of Luton
David Denney	Reader in Social Policy, Roehampton Institute, London
Mary Evans	Professor of Women's Studies, University of Kent
Vic George	Professor of Social Policy, University of Kent
Robert A. Gorman	Professor of Political Science, University of Tennessee
Ian Gough	Professor of Social Policy and Political Economy, School of Social Policy, University of Manchester
Michael Kenny	Lecturer in Politics, University of Sheffield
Adrian Little	Lecturer in Politics, Nene College, Northampton
Stewart Miller	Lecturer in Social Policy, University of Kent
Robert Page	Lecturer in Social Policy and Administration, University of Nottingham
Robert Pinker	Professor of Social Administration, London School of Economics
David Reisman	Senior Lecturer in Economics, University of Surrey
Daniel Ritschel	Assistant Professor, Department of History, University of Maryland, Baltimore County
Richard Silburn	Senior Lecturer in Social Policy and Administration, University of Nottingham
Jim Tomlinson	Reader in Economic History, Department of Economics, Brunel University
Paul Wilding	Professor of Social Policy, University of Manchester
Fiona Williams	Professor of Applied Social Studies, University of Bradford

John Williams	Professor of Economic History, University of Wales, Aberystwyth
Karel Williams	Reader, Department of Accountancy, University of Manchester
Anthony Wright	Labour MP for Cannock and Burntwood

Preface

One of the most entertaining distractions for sports *aficionados* is to be invited to select one's greatest team or most prolific player. Once decided, such selections are likely to be the topic of heated discussion and debate among other fans. For example, there is unlikely to be unanimity among English football fans about what constitutes the best 'post-45' team. Many would no doubt include Bobby Moore, Johnny Haynes and Jimmy Greaves in their all-star XI, but the remaining selections are likely to be less clear cut, reflecting diverse estimations of the relative worth of particular players.

Similar disputes are likely to arise in academic selections of key or influential thinkers. In terms of this volume, the selection of, say, Hayek, Keynes, Beveridge, T.H. Marshall and Titmuss is likely to be uncontroversial, whereas some of the other selections may find less support. In arriving at our selection of modern thinkers on welfare, we decided to choose writers from varied ideological traditions in an attempt to capture the diversity of welfare thought – a decision which inevitably meant that we had to omit a number of influential writers. For example, it would have been possible to fill a volume of this kind solely with writers of a democratic socialist persuasion, although it must be noted that even specialist perspectives of this kind are far from unproblematic as Kenneth Morgan's volume on *Labour People* (Oxford: Oxford University Press, 1992) demonstrates (luminaries such as Crosland were omitted from the collection). We believe that all the thinkers selected for this volume have made distinctive contributions to debates about welfare, and we are grateful to all our contributors (not least Michael Cahill, who stepped in at the last moment to fill a gap in Part VI) for providing such stimulating essays.

Vic George and Robert Page

Introduction: Thinking about welfare in the modern era

Vic George and Robert Page

This volume is about *contemporary* ideologies of welfare as reflected in the work of nineteen modern thinkers on welfare. Debates on these issues have a much longer history, and it is useful to remind our readers of this. Equally important is to remind our readers of the composite source of welfare – the market, the family, philanthropy and the state – and how this has changed over the years.

This chapter, therefore, discusses four interrelated themes: the concept of welfare, evolving ideological debates on welfare, the emergence of state welfare and the current challenge to state welfare. To these four, we have added a fifth: the academic study of welfare within the intellectual environment of the new academic subject of social policy and administration.

The concept of welfare

Like many other social science concepts, the notion of welfare has been defined and interpreted in a number of diverse ways. It is not only slippery and difficult, but, as Barry observes, promiscuous as well, for it 'attaches itself somewhat indiscriminately to other moral and political ideas' (Barry, 1990: 6) with the result that it becomes even more complex. Essentially, however, the notion of welfare refers to the well-being of individuals. In ordinary language this covers, in the first place, the satisfaction of the individual's needs.

Disagreements inevitably arise as to both the number of these needs and the level of their satisfaction. The more comprehensive approaches will examine the notion of welfare within the framework of a hierarchy of needs. This will include not only material but psychological or emotional needs. A person's welfare, for example, includes not only such material needs as food, housing, clothing and holidays, but also a feeling of individual security from physical attack as well as a sense of belonging to a community. Vice versa, the more restrictive definitions will confine themselves to material needs met at basic levels (see Doyal and Gough, 1991).

1

Defined in broad terms, the notion of welfare inevitably involves issues of distributional justice. Women in advanced industrial societies, for instance, may feel aggrieved that as a group their welfare suffers because of their inferior position *vis-à-vis* that of men. Black people in these societies may experience similar feelings as a result of prejudice, discrimination and their generally disadvantageous position compared with that of white people. However defined, the notion of welfare raises the well-known thorny issues of how it will be measured and by whom. A series of indicators based on objective data may tell a different story from a measurement based on the views of individuals.

Clearly, the source of people's welfare is of paramount importance to them not only for reasons of security and reliability, but also because different sources carry different social labels. Over the years, individuals have sought to satisfy their welfare through the market, the family, charitable organizations and the state. For reasons which are beyond the scope of this introduction, market satisfaction has always been highly esteemed, while satisfaction through voluntary or charitable organizations has carried a certain degree of social opprobrium and disapproval. State-provided welfare is of a mixed nature, depending primarily on the test of eligibility. Where it can be established that the individual has contributed directly or where it is acknowledged that society will benefit from the service, no stigmatization is attached to service recipients. Where, however, service delivery is akin to charitable services, recipients are treated with degrees of social disapproval similar to clients of charitable societies.

The different ideologies discussed in this book all emphasize the importance of individual welfare satisfaction, but they define welfare and its sources differently. The more one moves from the right to the left of the political spectrum, the wider the definition and the greater the acceptability of state-provided welfare becomes, as the following chapters will make clear.

The evolving debate on welfare

It is important to acknowledge that in previous periods the attainment of welfare was seen as strictly a matter for individual resolution. Individuals were expected to maximize their own welfare through various forms of legitimate market exchange. The idea that spontaneous self-interested activity of this kind would be at the expense of the collective good was rejected by Classical Liberals such as Adam Smith (Reisman, 1982). According to Smith, unfettered individualism would lead towards a state of economic equilibrium in which labour, land and capital were combined in the most effective way to satisfy consumer demand. He acknowledged that the equilibrium pertaining at any given time might fail to satisfy the tenets of distributive justice but believed that the attainment of the latter required charitable activity rather than state interventionist strategies which would merely hinder economic efficiency. However, Smith's adherence to *laissez-faire* was not absolute. He recognized that a thriving market system might not satisfy all the desires of citizens. For example, a citizen might desire a 'good' which required a 'collective' solution, such as the eradication of poverty. Clearly, Smith believed that there were a number of genuine, albeit limited, public goods. Importantly, the provision of such public goods was not based on any notion of redistribution, as is demonstrated by Smith's support for compulsory education on the grounds that it enables 'individuals to acquire those elementary moral principles on which a commercial order depends' (Reisman, 1982: 21).

Although Smith accepted the case for public goods, he continued to reject the idea that there existed collective, as opposed to purely individual, forms of welfare. Public provision was merely a means of meeting certain individual satisfactions. As Barry notes, 'In the tradition of methodological individualsm . . . there is no such thing as a collective social welfare function which is not logically reducible to statements about individuals' (Barry, 1990: 51).

The idea that 'welfare' has a collective dimension over and above individual preferences is most clearly associated with the New Liberal thinking of T.H. Green and Hobhouse in the late nineteenth and early twentieth centuries (Freeden, 1978). Departing from the Classical Liberal tradition, Green promoted the idea that there was a common good which amounted to something more than aggregated individual satisfactions. He contended that the attainment of this goal was possible only if all citizens were provided with sufficient opportunities for self-realization – a state of affairs which would transpire only if there was a shift from 'negative' to positive liberty. As Barry points out, from this perspective society was no longer to be equated with a 'set of individuals bound together by common rules but lacking a common purpose', but rather was to be viewed as an organism which was 'held together by social bonds that transcended contractual relationships' (Barry, 1990: 34). Green's attachment to positive liberty led him to press for modest forms of state intervention, such as factory, health and employment liability legislation and educational reforms, provided that it could be demonstrated in each case that this would promote the common good (Harris and Morrow, 1986).

Like Green, Hobhouse (who is often regarded as the most influential liberal thinker of the age) was also committed to the pursuit of the common good, but he was prepared to countenance more wide-ranging forms of state intervention in order to achieve this outcome. In essence, Hobhouse was prepared to refashion liberty in order to promote welfare. Hobhouse laid great store on the notion of progress, which he equated with increased individual self-realization – a process which could be demonstrated by citizens' growing acceptance of the inextricable link between their own personal well-being and the welfare of others. This shift from 'impulsive' lower-order pursuits to 'rational' higher-order activity was, for Hobhouse, the mark of social progress.

The state had a vital role to play in the creation of this more advanced 'altruistic' society, although Hobhouse was keen to distance himself from that variant of Fabianism which seemed prepared to promote state intervention with little, if any, regard to the impact that such policy would have on human advancement.

Accordingly, he rejected all forms of intervention which were based solely on considerations of social efficiency. State action was to be a means for social harmony – never an end. As he remarked:

> Mere reform of machinery is worthless unless it is the expression of a change of spirit and feeling. If the change from individualism to socialism meant nothing but an alteration in the methods of organising industry, it would leave the nation no happier or better than before. (quoted in Collini, 1979: 67)

Hobhouse believed that the state could function in a disinterested way and could facilitate the development of a more humane society in a number of ways. First, it could intervene in the industrial sphere to ensure that the superior economic power of many employers was restricted in ways which would make it impossible for them to impose highly disadvantageous work 'contracts' on vulnerable employees. To this end, Hobhouse advocated legislative measures or initiatives (such as extending the jurisdiction of the Wages Board) to ensure that fair practices became more widespread.

Second, Hobhouse was sympathetic to municipal 'gas and water' initiatives. Although support for ventures of this kind did not signify a distinctive break with traditional liberal orthodoxy (which had long accepted the need for public control in the case of natural monopolies), Hobhouse's enthusiasm for such developments is noteworthy. He welcomed any extension of public provision in spheres where demand was 'constant and predictable' and where consumers were virtually 'unanimous in the quality of provision demanded' (Dennis and Halsey, 1988: 80). In such circumstances, Hobhouse favoured the introduction of 'stable, bureaucratic, non-innovative, utterly reliable' public services. Moreover, he lent his support to community developments such as the provision of hospitals, parks, libraries and transport, provided that private operators were not prevented from offering alternative services.

Third, Hobhouse believed that the state should provide material assistance for those who were unable to secure a 'market' income because they were providing 'community' services. For instance, Hobhouse believed that state allowances should be provided for widowed or deserted mothers on the grounds that they were performing one of the most valuable public services – namely, creating a secure and stable home environment for children. For Hobhouse, contributions of this kind were of far greater importance for social well-being than paid employment alternatives. Similarly, Hobhouse favoured the introduction of old-age pensions, which he believed should be regarded as a form of deferred pay – not as a hand-out or dole. Such pensions were to be seen as a reward for the low wages which workers had been forced to subsist on during their period of employment.

Fourth, the state should intervene on paternalistic grounds in cases where it could be demonstrated that 'inaction' would result in the continuation of debased patterns of living. Like Green, Hobhouse believed that state intervention was perfectly justifiable in such circumstances, provided that there was a clear opportunity to improve the life of the individual concerned.

New Liberal thinking of this kind served to underline the fact that purposeful kinds of government intervention could actually enhance the level of welfare within society. Previously, it had been commonplace to assume that collectivism would undermine social welfare by interfering with the free play of market forces. Now, it was being argued that non-intervention rather than intervention was undermining welfare. The type of intervention required for the enhancement of welfare was to extend far beyond a modest increase in the range of public goods: nothing less than decisive action designed to alleviate the unmet needs of citizens and foster communitarianism was deemed necessary. Interventionism and horizontal redistribution were now to be regarded as legitimate ways to promote welfare in a capitalist society.

Ideologies of the left naturally accepted this type of state intervention and much more. Fabian socialists, according to Thane,

> were convinced of the incapacity of the free market significantly to diminish poverty and inequality. They placed their faith instead in social ownership, economic planning and extensive measures by central and local government to provide institutional and other relief to prevent and cure poverty due to unemployment, old age, sickness and other causes of need. (1982: 16)

Government planning, state ownership and public provision on a large scale were the foundation stones of Fabian socialism of this period. What obviously separates Fabian and other socialist groups from the New Liberals is not merely their greater acceptance of state collectivism, but their belief that capitalism had to be supplanted by socialism for the maximum realization of human welfare. In other words, the private ownership of the means of production and the free operation of the market had to be socialized.

Although it would be misleading to suggest that the era from 1880 to the early 1940s was marked by some form of linear progression from individualism to collectivism (Harris, 1993: 11–13), it is undeniable that there was a greater appetite for state intervention during this period from all political quarters, albeit for a complex range of economic, social and political factors (Fraser, 1984). Welfare capitalism began to be seen as superior to *laissez-faire* capitalism by a widening array of theorists and politicians.

The emergence of the collectivist state

All our ideologies accept that the period from the 1870s to the late 1930s witnessed a gradual but steady rise in state intervention in social affairs in all industrial societies. By the end of the nineteenth century, many European countries had introduced legislation against industrial injuries; by the outbreak of the First World War, many had passed legislation for retirement pensions and health insurance; and by the outbreak of the Second World War most had introduced insurance schemes against unemployment. By this time, the foundations of the welfare state had been firmly laid.

In the case of Britain, it has been argued that the period between 1880 and 1920 was characterized by a growth of legislative innovation – most notably the Liberal reforms in the period from 1906 to 1911, which saw the introduction of both old-age pensions (1908) and National Insurance (1911) – whereas the following two decades were an era in which the fiscal consequences of reform and the 'costs' of the First World War came home to roost (Pierson, 1991: 117). By the end of the 1930s, the UK had a patchwork of social services of varying quality and generosity which hardly added up to a welfare state, but which formed the foundations of what was to follow.

In the case of Sweden, one witnesses a steady advance in collectivist provision from the late nineteenth century onwards, in response to the impact of industrialization and mass emigration. The first social insurance bill was initiated in the early 1880s and a modest old-age pensions scheme was introduced in 1913. The most significant changes occurred, however, in the 1930s – a decade which saw the election of a Social Democratic-led government (1932) which was firmly committed to social reform. Reforms included new housing programmes, maternity services and benefits, enhanced pension payments and the extension of holiday entitlements to all workers (Olsson, 1990). It was during this period that the historic compromise between capital and labour was forged. As Pierson explains:

> This celebrated 'historic compromise' ensured that capital would maintain intact its managerial prerogatives within the workplace, subject only to guarantees on rights to unionization, and capitalist economic growth would be encouraged. At the same time, the Social Democratic government would pursue Keynesian economic policies to sustain full employment and use progressive taxation to reduce economic inequality and promote provision for collective needs, such as education, health and housing. (Pierson, 1991: 122)

In Germany, legislation against industrial accidents was introduced in 1871, followed by health insurance protection in 1889, retirement pensions in 1889 and unemployment benefit in 1927. Bismarck's concern that the rising tide of socialist ideas should not be allowed to take deep roots in the working class was a major factor behind the introduction of the early legislation. The provision of state benefits was seen not as a socialist measure, but as an antidote to the advance of socialism.

Even in Tsarist Russia, where serfdom had not been abolished until 1861, the first welfare measures were introduced during the years immediately prior to the Bolshevik Revolution of 1917. Nevertheless the breadth and scope of these measures were extremely limited, and the emerging working class was almost driven to overthrow a regime which by oppression, neglect and inaction made itself vulnerable to socialist ideas (Rimlinger, 1971). The marchers to the Tsar's

Winter Palace in 1905 presented a petition which was humility personified and yet totally ignored.

> 'Your Majesty! We, the workers and citizens of St Petersburg, our wives, children and parents, have come to Your Majesty to beg for justice and protection. We are all paupers, we are oppressed and overburdened with work; we are often insulted for no reason, we are not regarded as human beings, but are treated as slaves; we suffer and we have to bear our sufferings silently.' (Rimlinger, 1971: 246)

In the United States, which has often somewhat inaccurately been portrayed as the last bastion of residualism, the introduction of the New Deal in the 1930s represented the most significant step forward in terms of the acceptance of a role for collectivism in the promotion of human welfare. Prior to this period, American welfarism was underpinned by an extremely strong individualistic ethos, which retained its pre-eminence despite the adverse impact of industrialization on familial welfare structures. Although there were some minor reforms in the early part of the twentieth century – workman's compensation and aid to widows with dependent children – there was little sign of any major collectivist advance. According to Sullivan (1992) the absence of collectivist initiatives can be explained by 'state' resistance to federal reforms, the buoyancy of the voluntary sector, the fragmentation of the working class and the advance of occupational welfare particularly among the larger corporations.

The New Deal had both an economic and a social dimension. In terms of the former, the government established planning forums in which state officials and businessmen could map out future economic developments, and also recommended the introduction of consultation procedures at shop-floor level so that employers and employees could discuss industrial relations matters, wage rates and other conditions of employment in a more constructive way. In the case of the Social Dimension, Roosevelt introduced unemployment compensation, national old-age pensions and grants in aid to the states for assistance programmes for dependent children in need, the blind and the elderly. The main beneficiaries of the New Deal were the middle class, the organized working class and farmers (Handler and Hasenfeld, 1991).

These and other country profiles illustrate most clearly that the days of *laissez-faire* capitalism were over and that state welfarism was on the march in all industrialized societies.

The 'golden era' of the welfare state, 1945–75

During this brief interlude, it came to be generally accepted that the state should be the main provider of welfare, either directly through the provision of services or indirectly through the maintenance of full employment. Discordant voices that emphasized the market or the individual as the main agent of welfare were politically marginalized and ignored. It was a period which was characterized by broad political support for the mixed economy, the pursuit of economic growth and the promotion of full employment; and a dominant and ever-expanding role for the state as both a funder and provider of welfare services (Deakin, 1994). All the main political parties in most advanced capitalist societies accepted that the state had the ability, the resources and the moral duty to promote the collective welfare of its citizens.

Although it is possible to contest the argument that all advanced western nations accepted equally the need for both a mixed economy and state welfare provision in the period from 1945 to 1975 (Esping-Andersen, 1990), one trend is indisputable – the steady (1950s) and then dramatic (1960–75) rise in public and social expenditure as a proportion of national income among all OECD countries during this time (see Table 1). Even in the USA and Japan, which are considered residual welfare states, social expenditure as a proportion of GDP doubled during the period 1960–75. This proportional increase in social expenditure must also be seen within the context of an expanding economy in all these countries. During the decade 1950–60, the average annual growth in GNP in the seven major OECD countries was 4.4 per cent, while for the period 1960–73 it was 5.5 per cent (Pierson, 1991: 131). It is also worth noting that a similar trend took place in the Soviet Union, even though the relevant statistical evidence is less reliable and less comprehensive (George and Manning, 1980). Faced with such statistical evidence, it is difficult not to conclude that collectivism had ousted individualism as the guiding principle in state affairs during this period – a truly remarkable trend in historical terms. It was, however, a short-lived triumph, as we shall see below.

The challenge to the welfare state

By the mid-1970s, the universalist welfare state was being subjected to intensive scrutiny of a negative kind from both the left and the right of the political spectrum. It became fashionable on the left to argue that the welfare state had entered a period of 'fiscal' or 'legitimation' crisis (O'Connor, 1973; Gough, 1979; Mishra, 1984; Offe, 1984; Taylor-Gooby, 1985). Other writers of the left criticized the welfare state because of its failure to reduce class, gender or race inequalities (Wilson, 1977; Townsend, 1979).

From the right, it was claimed that high levels of public expenditure and provision created an 'overload' for democratic governments that undermined their political legitimacy (Brittan, 1975; King, 1976). It was further argued that the dramatic rise in public expenditure undermined economic growth by creating disincentives to work, to save and to invest (Bacon and Eltis, 1976).

Though the critiques of the left and the right were similar, they were diametrically opposed in terms of their remedies. The left saw the solution in more socialist measures or, more cautiously, in reining back further expenditure until economic growth returned. The right prescribed heavy doses of public

Table 1   Social expenditure as a proportion of GDP (%)

	1960	1975	1980	1985
Australia	9.5	17.6	17.3	18.4
Austria	17.4	23.4	26.0	28.8
Belgium	n.a.	28.7	33.9	35.8
Canada	11.2	20.1	19.5	22.6
Denmark	9.0	27.1	35.1	33.9
Finland	14.9	21.9	22.9	22.8
France	14.4	26.3	30.9	34.2
Germany	17.1	27.8	26.6	25.8
Greece	n.a.	10.0	12.6	19.5
Ireland	11.3	22.0	23.8	25.6
Italy	13.7	20.6	23.7	26.7
Japan	7.6	13.7	16.1	16.2
Netherlands	12.8	29.3	31.8	30.7
New Zealand	12.7	19.0	22.4	19.8
Norway	11.0	23.2	24.2	23.5
Portugal	n.a.	n.a.	17.3	n.a.
Spain	n.a.	n.a.	15.6	15.2
Sweden	15.6	27.4	33.2	32.0[1]
Switzerland	8.2	19.0	19.1	20.5[1]
United Kingdom	12.4	19.6	20.0	20.9
United States	9.9	18.7	18.0	18.2
OECD average[2]	12.3	21.9	23.3	24.6

Notes:
[1] 1984.
[2] The OECD average figures are the unweighted averages excluding Portugal and Spain for all years and Belgium and Greece for 1960.
Source: OECD, 1988; data from OECD Social Data Bank. From: A. Cochrane and J. Clarke (eds) (1993), *Comparing Welfare States*, London, Sage, p. 243.

expenditure cuts, a programme of privatization and the 'rolling back' of the frontiers of the state wherever possible.

In this conflict of ideas, it was the critique and proposals from the right that won the day, simply because they better fitted the prevailing material conditions of the period. Declining international growth rates coupled with oil price rises meant that public expenditure was being increasingly financed through public borrowing. While such a solution could be maintained in the short term, it could not be sustained indefinitely – as the Labour Government in the UK found to its cost in the late 1970s when the IMF forced it to reduce public expenditure levels in order to restore 'confidence'. The election of Reagan in the USA and Thatcher in the UK provided the first governments determined to implement the New Right approach to dealing with the economy and the welfare state. It was an approach that gained substantial acceptance, so that even governments of the left in several countries during the 1980s adopted it, albeit unwillingly.

In a period of ten years, we witnessed the spectacle of the reassertion of individualism over collectivism as the dominant method of providing human welfare. It has, however, been argued that this triumph is more rhetorical than real, for levels of public expenditure have remained stubbornly unchanged during the 1980s, even in countries with right-wing governments (see Tables 1 and 2).

Table 2   Public expenditure as a proportion of GDP (%)

	1970	1975	1980	1989
UK	38.8	46.6	44.9	41.2
USA	31.6	34.6	33.7	36.1
Japan	19.4	27.3	32.6	31.5
Germany	38.6	48.9	48.3	45.5
France	38.5	43.4	46.1	49.4
Italy	34.2	43.2	41.7	51.5
Canada	34.8	40.1	40.5	44.6
Total	32.3	37.7	38.4	38.7

Source: OECD, *Economic Outlook*, no. 51, June 1992, table R15.

The resilient welfare state?

What are the prospects of the welfare state in the future? On one hand, some commentators have argued that the British welfare state has managed to withstand hostile government overtures during the 1980s and 90s quite well, and that public support for social service provision remains strong (Glennerster, 1991; Le Grand, 1991; Taylor-Gooby, 1991; Green and Lucas, 1992; Sullivan, 1992; Lowe, 1993). Similar comments have been made for other welfare states on the basis of the level of public or social expenditure.

Others, however, point to the numerous changes made by governments in the 1980s which had downward effects on levels of social provision. Social expenditure grew because of demographic, social or labour market factors which increased service demand, rather than because of improvements in the social services (Johnson, 1990; Wilding, 1992). According to Mishra (1990) these conflicting evaluations may result in part from differing evaluatory criteria. He suggests that an unwarranted concentration on public expenditure trends or developments in mainstream education, health or social security programmes may lead to over-optimistic assessments about the resilience of the welfare state. In contrast, if the welfare state is defined as 'the institutionalization of government responsibility for maintaining national minimum standards' (Mishra, 1990: 34), it is possible to argue that New Right policies have been highly successful. The commitment to full employment has been abandoned, the numbers in poverty have risen sharply, concern with income and wealth inequality has been abandoned, and a significant shift from universalism to selectivity has occurred.

Importantly, Mishra contends that even those public welfare services which currently enjoy the widest level of public support, such as education and health care, may (given the highly contingent nature of citizens' welfare allegiance (Taylor-Gooby, 1985, 1987, 1990)) decline in popularity if the standard of provision declines to a level which encourages middle-class 'exit' to the private sector (Goodin and Le Grand, 1987). Certainly, the fact that New Right ideas have begun to influence the policy agenda in countries which have come to be regarded as bastions of welfare (Sweden, Denmark, Norway) seems to give credence to Mishra's views (Olsson and McMurphy, 1993; Gould, 1993a, 1993b). Moreover, the intellectual advantage lies still with the New Right in welfare matters, although the left is gradually reformulating its pro-welfare state ideas and may come to mount a successful challenge.

If the current brief historical review of debates on welfare suggests anything, it is that neither the market nor the state by itself can guarantee the welfare of all citizens. It is only when the two work together that welfare is achieved, and the real debate is what kind of partnership between the two can best achieve this. Political and economic as well as ideological factors will determine the nature of this partnership, and inevitably it will vary from one country to another.

The changing shape of social policy and administration in the UK

Not surprisingly, the various challenges to the welfare state have been reflected in the development of the academic study of social policy and administration in the United Kingdom. Although it has a 'history' which can be traced back to at least the beginning of the twentieth century (Pinker, 1971; Bulmer *et al.*, 1989), it can be argued that this area of academic enquiry has become firmly established as a reputable social science only since the mid-1960s – a period in which the subject increased in size, as measured by: student numbers and new courses; influence in the sphere of policy making; relevance in tackling some of the pressing issues of the period, such as homelessness and poverty; the theoretical, conceptual treatment of policy issues; and the attempt to look at issues in comparative terms.

In its early days, the subject was dominated by those who subscribed to what Baker (1979) has termed the 'social conscience thesis'. They believed that social policy reflected the benevolence of citizens and that its evolutionary expansion to its current high level owed much to 'a widening and deepening sense of social obligation' (Baker, 1979: 178) and a greater understanding of human need. The acceptance of this thesis reflected the underlying concerns of what Wilding (1983) described as traditional social administration, a subject that tended to be 'pragmatic and practical rather than theoretical and speculative' (Mishra, 1981:

3–4), and focused on specific problems within society with the aim of resolving them by purposeful forms of state intervention.

Although it would be inaccurate to suggest that the assumptions of the social conscience thesis were unanimously accepted in the 1950s and 1960s (see Saville, 1957/8; Titmuss, 1968: ch. xi), it was only the emergence of more theoretical approaches to social policy in the 1970s and early 1980s which effectively challenged the dominance of this approach (Pinker, 1971, 1979; George and Wilding, 1976; Ginsburg, 1979; Gough, 1979; Room, 1979, Taylor-Gooby and Dale, 1981). Publications of this kind have enriched and transformed the subject matter of social policy, and there is now a real diversity of both theoretical and ideological approaches in welfare thinking, making it more akin to other social science subjects.

It is difficult to predict how the subject will evolve in the light of prevailing economic, social and political change. However, it does seem likely that there will be a continuing retreat from 'Fabianism', a greater interest in international developments, and a more thoughtful debate about the relative merits of universalism and diversity (Williams, 1992) and the role of the market within the social services (Deakin and Page, 1993).

Conclusion

Ideologies of welfare are both analytical and normative. They attempt to explain both how the welfare of citizens is being met and what the ideal way of providing welfare should be. In their normative sense, they highlight and exaggerate the differences between them, for they aim to influence and attract followers. They are often couched in general and vague terms that are susceptible to more than one interpretation. They nevertheless provide different ways of looking at the world as it is and as it should be. The chapters that follow will furnish numerous examples of this.

Welfare ideologies are espoused by political parties, but it is very rare indeed that political parties adhere strictly to their ideology when in power. A host of other factors – economic, social, electoral – intervene to influence government policy. Ideologies are largely utopias: politics is largely the art of the possible. The first four ideologies covered in this volume range from right to left, while the other three fall outside this political continuum. The choice of ideologies presented in this volume is partly a reflection of the authors' views on welfare debates, but it is also in line with other lists of welfare ideologies in the social policy literature. Recent and not so recent claims that the end of ideological debates has arrived and that only public and party-political consensus remains are illusory. Ideological differences will always exist, although their depth will vary from one period to the next.

References

Bacon, R. and Eltis, W. (1976) *Britain's Economic Problem: Too few producers*, London: Macmillan.

Baker, J. (1979) 'Social conscience and social policy', *Journal of Social Policy*, 8, 2, pp. 177–206.

Barry, N. (1990), *Welfare*, Milton Keynes: Open University Press.

Brittan, S. (1975), 'The economic contradictions of democracy', *British Journal of Political Science*, 5, 1, pp. 129–59.

Bulmer, M., Lewis, J. and Piachaud, D. (eds) (1989) *The Goals of Social Policy*, London: Unwin Hyman.

Collini, S. (1979) *Liberalism and Sociology*, Cambridge: Cambridge University Press.

Deakin, N. and Page, R. (eds) (1993) *The Costs of Welfare*, Aldershot: Avebury.

Deakin, N. (1994) *The Politics of Welfare* (revised edn), Hemel Hempstead: Harvester Wheatsheaf.

Dennis, N. and Halsey, A.H. (1988) *English Ethical Socialism*, Oxford: Clarendon.

Doyal, L. and Gough, I. (1991) *A Theory of Human Needs*, London: Macmillan.

Esping-Andersen, G. (1990) *The Three Worlds of Welfare Capitalism*, Cambridge: Polity.

Fraser, D. (1984) *The Evolution of the British Welfare State* (2nd edn), London: Macmillan.

Freeden, M. (1978) *The New Liberalism: An ideology of social reform*, Oxford: Clarendon.

George, V. and Manning, N. (1980) *Socialism, Social Welfare and the Soviet Union*, London: Routledge and Kegan Paul.

George, V. and Wilding, P. (1976) *Ideology and Social Welfare*, London: Routledge and Kegan Paul.

Ginsburg, N. (1979) *Class, Capital and Social Policy*, London: Macmillan.

Glennerster, H. (1991) 'Social policy since the Second World War', in Hills, J. (ed.), *The State of Welfare*, Oxford: Clarendon, ch. 2.

Goodin, R. and Le Grand, J. (eds) (1987) *Not Only the Poor*, London: Allen and Unwin.

Gough, I. (1979) *The Political Economy of the Welfare State*, London: Macmillan.

Gould, A. (1993a) *Capitalist Welfare Systems*, London: Macmillan.

Gould, A. (1993b) 'The end of the middle way?' in Jones, C. (ed.), *New Perspectives on the Welfare State in Europe*, London: Routledge, ch. 8.

Green, D.G. and Lucas, D. (1992) 'Private welfare in the 1980s', in Manning and Page (1992), ch. 3.

Handler, J.F. and Hasenfeld, Y. (1991) *The Moral Construction of Poverty*, London: Sage.

Harris, J. (1993) *Private Lives, Public Spirit*, Oxford: Oxford University Press.

Harris, P. and Morrow, J. (eds) (1986) *T.H. Green: Lectures on the principles of political obligation and other writings*, Cambridge: Cambridge University Press.

Johnson, N. (1990) *Reconstructing the Welfare State*, Hemel Hempstead: Harvester Wheatsheaf.

King, A. (1976) *Why is Britain Becoming Harder to Govern?* London: BBC.

Le Grand, J. (1991) 'The state of welfare', in Hills J. (ed.), *The State of Welfare*, Oxford: Clarendon, ch. 2.

Lowe, R. (1993) *The Welfare State in Britain Since 1945*, London: Macmillan.

Manning, N. and Page, R. (eds) (1992) *Social Policy Review 4*, Canterbury: Social Policy Association.

Mishra, R. (1981) *Society and Social Policy* (2nd edn), London: Macmillan.

Mishra, R. (1984) *The Welfare State in Crisis*, Brighton: Wheatsheaf.
Mishra, R. (1990) *The Welfare State in Capitalist Society*, Hemel Hempstead: Harvester Wheatsheaf.
O'Connor, J. (1973) *The Fiscal Crisis of the State*, New York: St James.
Offe, C. (1984) *Contradictions of the Welfare State*, London: Hutchinson.
Olsson, S.E. (1990) *Social Policy and Welfare State in Sweden*, Lund: Arkiv.
Olsson, S.E. and McMurphy, S. (1993) 'Social policy in Sweden: the Swedish model in transition', in Page, R. and Baldock, J. (eds), *Social Policy Review 5*, ch. 12.
Pierson, C. (1991) *Beyond the Welfare State?*, Cambridge: Polity.
Pinker, R.A. (1971) *Social Theory and Social Policy*, London: Heinemann.
Pinker, R.A. (1979) *The Idea of Welfare*, London: Heinemann.
Reisman, D. (1982) *State and Welfare*, London: Macmillan.
Rimlinger, G. (1971) *Welfare Policy and Industrialisation in Europe, America and Russia*, New York: Willey.
Room, G. (1979) *The Sociology of Welfare*, Oxford: Blackwell and Martin Robertson.
Saville, J. (1957/8) 'The welfare state: an historical approach', *New Reasoner*, 3, Winter, pp. 5, 6, 11, 12–17, 20–4.
Sullivan, M. (1992) *The Politics of Social Policy*, Hemel Hempstead: Harvester Wheatsheaf.
Taylor-Gooby, P. (1985) *Public Opinion, Ideology and State Welfare*, London: Routledge and Kegan Paul.
Taylor-Gooby, P. (1987) 'Citizenship and welfare', in Jowell, R., Witherspoon, S. and Brook, L. (eds), *British Social Attitudes: The 1987 Report*, Aldershot: Gower, ch. 1.
Taylor-Gooby, P. (1990) 'Social welfare: the unkindest cuts', in Jowell, R., Witherspoon, S. and Brook, L. (eds), *British Social Attitudes: The 7th Report*, Aldershot: Gower, ch. 1.
Taylor-Gooby, P. (1991) *Social Change, Social Welfare and Social Science*, Hemel Hempstead: Harvester Wheatsheaf.
Taylor-Gooby, P. and Dale, J. (1981) *Social Theory and Social Welfare*, London: Edward Arnold.
Thane, P. (1982) *Foundations of the Welfare State*, London: Longman.
Titmuss, R.M. (1968) *Commitment to Welfare*, London: Allen and Unwin.
Townsend, P. (1979) *Poverty in the UK*, London: Penguin.
Wilding, P. (1983) 'The evolution of social administration', in Bean, P. and MacPherson, S. (eds), *Approaches to Welfare*, London: Routledge and Kegan Paul.
Wilding, P. (1992) 'The public sector in the 1980s', in Manning and Page (1992), ch. 2.
Williams, F. (1992) 'Somewhere over the rainbow: universality and diversity in social policy', in Manning and Page (1992), ch. 11.
Wilson, E. (1977) *Women and the Welfare State*, London: Tavistock.

Part I

The New Right

Introduction

Anti-collectivist ideas dominated government policies throughout the nineteenth century. They remained highly influential during the early decades of this century, although they were increasingly challenged by the rising tide of collectivist thought. It was, however, the recession of the 1930s that marked the end of the supremacy of anti-collectivism. It was not just socialists who demanded government intervention on a large scale, but such establishment figures as Macmillan in the UK with his call for a middle way and Roosevelt in the USA with his New Deal policies. Keynes' theories of government intervention to get the economy out of recession were the intellectual forces that provided the rationale for active state intervention in capitalist societies. The Second World War and Beveridge's call for state provision to create a fairer capitalist society added another dimension to the relevance of welfare capitalism. State intervention in terms of both regulation and provision became the accepted method of government throughout the world during the three decades following the end of the Second World War. Government expenditures grew very substantially, so that by the mid-1970s they consumed 50 per cent or more of the gross domestic product in many advanced industrial countries.

If the recession of the 1930s marginalized right-wing ideology, the recession of the late 1970s signalled its reinstatement. Keynes' ideas of managing the economy were now being seen as the root cause of the new economic malaise. A return to market principles was, it was now argued, the only way to stop and reverse the economic stagflation that threatened the living standards of so many affluent countries. Hayek's and Friedman's ideas and warnings, which went unnoticed and even ridiculed for decades, came not only to be taken very seriously, but to be revered by world leaders such as Reagan and Thatcher. The writings of these two authors, which span more than half a century, jointly bring out the essentials of the New Right ideology very satisfactorily.

The advanced welfare state, according to the New Right, is unacceptable in both economic and political terms. It is inefficient because its taxation policies weaken the incentives to work, invest and save; its employment of large numbers of professional, skilled and unskilled workers creates a scarcity of labour for the private sector and creates strong trade unions in the process; its monopolistic services are not open to the winds of competition; and its creation of an army of state beneficiaries destroys individuals' will to look after themselves and their dependants. In brief, high levels of public expenditure were now seen as the root cause of the economic difficulties that some advanced industrial countries were experiencing.

In political terms, the welfare state undermines the freedom of the individual through its taxation and regulatory policies. Potentially, it is, in Hayek's phrase, the 'road to serfdom'. For all these reasons, a return to a residual welfare state where market principles reign supreme, and where the family and voluntary societies play a much more active role, is the only way to protect both individual freedom and economic prosperity. Attempting a middle course will only muddy the waters, for, in Friedman's view, one cannot be a supporter of both equality and liberty.

Tomlinson's account of Hayek and Barry's discussion of Friedman bring out as objectively as is possible in such debates the strengths and weaknesses of New Right ideology. The experience gained from right-wing government in so many countries during the 1980s shows that reducing welfare provision may increase the freedom of higher groups in society, who benefit from paying lower taxes, but it has the opposite effect on other groups, whose standard of living suffers. Improvements in economic growth do not necessarily benefit all groups in society alike, as New Right dogma claims. The 'trickle down' effect did not take place, and the lower decile of income distribution in the UK was relatively worse off at the end of the 1980s than at the beginning of that decade.

The events of the 1980s are another reminder that one needs to look at the distributional effects of economic, fiscal and social policies not in global national terms, but in a desegregrated form that takes into account the experiences of different income groups, various ethnic groups, women versus men, and other such structural dimensions. The rise in unemployment, income inequality, poverty and homelessness during the 1980s was in large or some part the inevitable result of the pursuit of New Right policies by governments. Disinterested observers may rightly disagree on the degree of blame that should be attributed to New Right theories, but they cannot totally exonerate them.

Perhaps the greatest contribution of New Right thinking during the 1980s was to reassert two commonsense ideas that were somewhat forgotten during the boom years of the 1950s and 1960s: first, that efficiency is important not only in the private but also in the public sector of society; and second, that governments cannot go on borrowing indefinitely beyond their capacity to repay, in order to finance ever-expanding public services. There comes a time when this is no longer possible and when social policy may have, for a while, to assume a subsidiary role to economic policy.

1 Hayek

Jim Tomlinson

Brief biography

Fredrick August von Hayek was born in Vienna in 1899 and died in Freiburg
in 1992. After a short period as a 'mild Fabian', he was strongly influenced by
the work of economists like Carl Menger (1840–1921), a founder of the Austrian
school of economics. In the 1920s and 1930s, Hayek's work was mainly in the
area of theoretical economics; in 1931 he published *Prices and Production*, and
shortly after became a professor at the London School of Economics. In the
1930s he was engaged in major economic controversies with Keynes and his
co-workers and with advocates of socialism, but from the 1940s especially he
moved into broader areas of social philosophy. This was signalled by the
publication in 1944 of his most famous book, *The Road to Serfdom*. In 1949 he
moved to the USA, and in 1960 he published his most important book, *The
Constitution of Liberty*, followed in the next decade by the three volumes of *Law,
Legislation and Liberty* (1973, 1976, 1979). In 1974 he was awarded the Nobel
prize for economics. In the 1970s and 1980s he also published topical pieces on
issues such as inflation and unemployment: for example, *A Tiger by the Tail:
The Keynesian legacy of inflation* (1978a). He died while much better known and
popular than during most of his life, especially because of his influence on the
New Right in the USA and UK, and in the ex-communist countries of eastern
Europe. For recent discussions of Hayek's work, see Barry (1979), Kukathas
(1989), Gray (1986), Gissurarson (1987) and Tomlinson (1990).

Hayek's economic and social policy

Hayek was, above all, a theorist. Most of his economic work is at an extremely
high level of abstraction, and the same would be true of most of his broader

works in social theory. While much of Hayek's work is polemical, it is polemic conducted mainly on a theoretical plane.

Some of the early economic writings of Hayek do not have a direct bearing on his later social theory. For example, *Prices and Production* (1931) and *The Pure Theory of Capital* (1941) are largely concerned with issues which have little interest outside debates in high theory. But other works in that period produced economic arguments which were to resonate through the whole of his life's work.

In 1935 Hayek edited a book called *Collectivist Economic Planning*. This contained critiques by him and others of the idea that a centrally planned, socialist economy could operate 'rationally' in economic terms. Hayek's particular emphasis was to argue that such a centrally planned regime would be confounded by the problem of knowledge that it would encounter. This problem would be not just the volume of information that any centralized planning of a complex economy would require, but the nature of that knowledge. Economically relevant knowledge, Hayek argued, is always particular, contextual and subjective, and therefore could not be accumulated and deployed by a central agency, whatever its computational capacity.

This essentially epistemological point was a key building-block in Hayek's approach to society. He stressed the *limits* of human knowledge, and used this to defend a liberal regime, with minimum government. For him the key error of socialism (which he equated with any extensive government intervention) was its claim to be able to plan and organize society on the basis of a rational understanding of how society works. For him, human knowledge was highly imperfect, and attempts to reconstruct society according to a rational plan grounded on such knowledge suffered from a 'fatal conceit' (the title of one of his last essays).

Hayek thus brought to bear a new emphasis within a pre-existing debate which was essentially about the scope and role of government. In *The Road to Serfdom*, Hayek's most directly political work, his basic position was spelt out, though much of the theoretical elaboration came later. The *Road* argued that, as governments attempted more and more to plan their economies, they would find that they had to attempt the impossible task of centralizing economic knowledge. Once set on this path, they would willy-nilly have to acquire increasingly authoritarian powers, and this would lead to the suppression of liberty, as had happened in Soviet Russia and Nazi Germany. Government intervention and planning, however well intentioned, must lead to serfdom.

The Road to Serfdom attracted wide publicity in the 1940s, including the accolade of a Reader's Digest condensation in the USA. But it appeared to have little effect, especially in the phase of post-war reconstruction in most of western Europe. Increasingly, Hayek saw the tide running against his ideas, and set himself the task of restating the 'ideal of freedom which inspired modern Western civilisation', a restatement required by the fact that 'for almost a century the basic principles on which this civilisation was built have been falling into increasing disregard and oblivion'. The quotes are from the opening pages of *The Constitution of Liberty* (1960), which is Hayek's central work. If the message of its 400-odd pages can be summarized in one sentence, it is that there has been an *intellectual* failure to understand the conditions of liberty, and that these conditions need to be restated and reworked. The *Constitution* is thus the centrepiece of an attempt to rebuild the foundations of traditional liberalism, where that term means essentially minimum government and the maximum freedom of individual action.

The starting point of the case for that liberalism is a negative concept of liberty, liberty as minimizing constraints on individuals' thought and behaviour. The grounds for this are essentially epistemological: 'The case for individual freedom rests chiefly on the recognition of the inevitable ignorance of us all concerning a great many of the factors on which the achievement of our ends and welfare depends' (Hayek, 1960: 29).

The hostility to government derives above all from the fear that it will undermine the conditions for such liberty, especially government based on representative institutions and majority rule. Democracy, for Hayek, is not a great, positive virtue of modern society; rather, it is a condition which is on balance desirable, but which poses substantial dangers if not held in check:

> Not only peace, justice and liberty but also democracy is basically a negative value, a procedural rule which serves as a protection against despotism and tyranny, and certainly no more but not much less important than the first Three Great Negatives – or, to put it differently, a convention which mainly serves to prevent harm. (Hayek, 1979: 133)

This minimal democracy requires constitutional limits on the powers of the majority, and Hayek polemicizes vigorously against the idea of parliamentary sovereignty, which has led to the untrammelled rule of the majority and the suppression of liberty.

This view of the centrality of liberty and the threat posed to it by democracy is traditional liberal doctrine. Hayek's particular twist is to argue for a constitution which will embody *traditional* values against the claims of majorities to remake the world in the name of *reason*. Hence one of Hayek's heroes is Edmund Burke, whose attack on the French Revolution was, of course, based on the claim that the revolutionaries were destroying society in the name of reason, undermining the true foundations of society, which are to be found in custom and tradition (Burke, 1790/1968).

Here perhaps we are closest to Hayek's central propositions about society. For him, the Burkeian tradition of political thought has unfortunately lost out to the (French) rationalist tradition. The West has come fatally to ignore the fact that 'a successful free society will always in large measure be a tradition-based society' (Hayek, 1960: 61). This is not an argument against the use of reason, indeed reason is a 'man's most precious possession' (1960: 69), but it is an argument against the arrogance of reason. His argument is an 'appeal to men to see that we must use our reason intelligently and that, in order to do so, we must preserve that indispensable matrix of the uncontrolled and non-rational which is the only environment wherein reason can grow and operate effectively' (1960: 69).

This approach to the limits of human reason is applied most explicitly to law. For Hayek, the law is not a promulgation of legislative bodies, but a body of rules which have evolved. Hayek is opposed to arguments about natural rights, but he suggests that certain legal principles have emerged from this evolutionary process: 'stability of possession, of transference by consent and of the performance of promises' (1960: 158). These, of course, are the legal foundations of a system of private property and market relationships.

Law, like other human institutions, should not be radically remade in the name of excessive rationalism. This is what Hayek perceives that Bentham and the utilitarians of the early nineteenth century proposed – a remaking of law on rational principles. Hayek rejects this approach, and celebrates instead the British common-law tradition of a slow accretion of marginal emendation of laws, which permits their slow adaptation to changing circumstances, but in accordance with the broad thrust of the overall pattern of rules.

The purpose of law, in Hayek's schema, is not to achieve any specific end, but to provide a stable framework within which human purposes can be pursued. Logically, it follows that justice is abiding by the rules of conduct laid down by law. Justice is not about the achievement of any particular ends, but about proper adjudication of the rules of conduct within which individuals may pursue their own objectives. Justice is a *procedural* concept:

> Since the consequences of applying rules of just conduct will always depend on factual circumstances which are not determined by their rules, we cannot measure the justice of the application of rule by the result it will produce in a particular case ... That it is possible for one through a single just transaction to gain much and for another through an equally just transaction to lose all, in no way disproves the justice of these transactions. (Hayek, 1976: 38)

This view has radical implications for any concept of social justice, an issue returned to in the next section of this chapter.

It should be evident from the above brief account of Hayek's overall social philosophy that he combines traditional liberal doctrines with some important twists of his own. The most important of his specific contributions to liberal argument is the epistemological: the limits of human reason are used to attack rationalistic, reformist actions by government. Against this, Hayek asserts the importance of tradition, as grounded on the evolutionary development of human understanding, an understanding always partial and fragile and in need of constant sustenance and reinforcement.

This position raises two obvious issues. The first is one of definition – is Hayek a (theoretical) liberal or a (theoretical) conservative? His liberal credentials are evident in the primacy accorded to liberty in his scale of political goals, the emphasis on individuals as the best judges of their own interests, and the desire for tight constitutional limits on distrusted parliamentary democracies. On the other hand, the veneration of tradition, the belief in evolutionary progress, and the distrust of reason as the basis for government action appear much more typical of conservative thought. This, I would suggest, is not just a problem of nomenclature, but relates to a fundamental tension in Hayek's work.

Hayek's work is caught between a transparent desire to deploy reason to improve the human condition – by providing a better understanding of the conditions of liberty – and an emphasis on tradition and custom as the foundations of the good society. This tension is most apparent in his specific reform proposals. For example, he proposed major changes to the constitution, giving very strong powers to an upper house elected exclusively from 45-year-olds, and advocated the 'de-nationalization of money': that is, the end of central bank monopoly of money issue, and allowing any private bank to issue its own.

The point here is not the merits of these individual proposals, but their compatibility with an evolutionary approach. They are both radical reforms of existing arrangements, seemingly based on the 'constructivist rationalism' that Hayek so abhors. This suggests perhaps that the tradition/reason dichotomy that Hayek works with is ultimately untenable. We may all agree that society should never be seen as a blank sheet of paper on which anything may be written, unless we want disastrous results (Pol Pot). But once we accept both that customs and traditions are integral to what we mean by society, and that calculated (rational) reform is possible and desirable, we are left with no guidance from Hayek as to where to go. Why are his particular proposed reforms compatible with evolution-ary development and respect for custom, but those of others to be condemned as constructivist rationalism leading down the road to serfdom? This would seem to be a key tension in Hayek's overall project.

Hayek and social welfare theory

Hayek's main interests were not directly linked to social welfare or social policy, but his broad theoretical positions do have implications for many ideas about such welfare. Certainly he now figures prominently in texts on the New Right, including those which focus on social policy (Plant *et al.*, 1980): esp. 58–63, 176–88; Bosanquet, 1983: ch. 2; George and Wilding, 1985: ch. 2; Glennerster and Midgley, 1991: 3–4, 13). In addition, *The Constitution of Liberty*, though primarily a work of theory, does include some 'applied' chapters, parts of which relate to social welfare. This section will look at both the general implication of Hayek's position for social welfare and his more specific arguments in that area.

Hayek's concept of a 'spontaneous order', in which both law and government essentially aim to provide only a framework within which individuals can pursue their own goals, leaves no scope for activist government, aiming to try and change the results of that spontaneous process. In other words, Hayek is staunchly anti-egalitarian because he believes that the unequal rewards generated by the market are the necessary conditions for a dynamic, growing society. But beyond that he argues that governmental attempts to apply any measure of merit or justice to economic rewards is unworkable because there is no such agreed measure, and its pursuits can only lead to greater and greater tyranny (Hayek, 1976: 80–4). This is a development of the position described in the previous section; the attempt to apply a 'rational' ordering of economic rewards will inevitably lead down the road to serfdom. To try and impose equality on society is therefore not only economically damaging, but also politically fatal for believers in liberty.

It is important to note here that Hayek does *not* argue that the reward pattern generated by a market economy is just. He is consistent in not applying that word to *any* set of outcomes: justice is a purely procedural term. Thus the case for market-based rewards is not one of substantive merit; in a market economy, rewards are generated by meeting others' needs evaluated in the marketplace: 'these values which services will have to their fellows will often have no relation to their individual merits or needs' (1976: 72). The case for the market economy rests only on these incentive effects, in rewarding those who meet others' needs.

Such a position must lead not only to a hostility to equality as a political goal, but also to a hostility to any notion of social justice. Indeed, Hayek reserves particular venom for this phrase, writing that 'I have come to feel strongly that the greatest service I can still render to my fellow men would be that I make the speakers and writers among them thoroughly ashamed ever again to employ the term social justice' (1976: 97). The grounds for such depths of hostility are spelt out elsewhere:

> First, it tends pervertedly to insinuate a notion ... that what has been brought about by the impersonal and spontaneous processes of the extended order is actually the result of deliberate human creation. Second, following from this, it appeals to men to *re*design what they never could have designed at all. And third, it also has acquired the power to empty the norms it qualifies of their meaning. (Hayek, 1988: 116).

Hayek was therefore hostile to much of the postwar development of the welfare state because he saw as lying behind it the drive towards social justice and equality that he so vigorously denounced: 'It seems to be the fate of all unitary, politically directed schemes for the provision of such services to be turned rapidly into instruments for determining the relative incomes of the great majority and thus for controlling economic activity generally' (Hayek, 1960: 303).

Hayek was not opposed to all provision of income or services by the state. He was happy to accept state (preferably local) provision of public amenities, such as parks; the provision of some minimum income security via both social insurance and charity; and the provision of goods where there are substantial 'externalities' involved – that is, where relying on the market will lead to underprovision – as consumption levels will reflect any individual benefits that accrue to all from generally high standards of education, or the prevention of infectious diseases.

But even within this minimal programme, Hayek had clear objections to many forms of provision – above all, where they lead to unitary, exclusive forms of provision by the state. An example was his attitude to provision for the indigent. The old communities which used to provide support for the old, sick and unemployed, he argued, have broken down in modern, urbanized societies. Public provision is now necessary, 'be it only in the interest of those who require protection against acts of desperation on the part of the needy' (1960: 285). In wealthy societies, such relief is likely to be above a bare minimum, which will attract those who could otherwise have supported themselves. This justifies a compulsory insurance scheme, so that such people will be forced to contribute to their upkeep. For Hayek, therefore, compulsory insurance is not *per se* objectionable, unlike for some extreme libertarians. But what is objectionable is for this compulsion to be applied to a unitary, monopoly scheme controlled by the state. This would lead not only to a lack of evolution in forms of insurance, but more importantly to a movement away from insurance proper to the pursuit of other ends: 'An apparatus originally meant to relieve poverty is generally being turned into a tool of egalitarian redistribution' (1960: 289).

The superior alternative to such unitary systems, he argued, would be a two-tier approach. There would be a 'proper' insurance scheme, whereby contributions generated unconditional rights to benefit when insured contingencies arose, and with no more redistribution than would be involved in, say, fire insurance. Alongside this would be provision for indigence, with support only on the basis of proven need.

For Hayek, two of the most dangerous parts of welfare as they had developed by the end of the 1950s were provision for old age and for health care. In the case of old age, Hayek saw the provision of pensions for all, paid for out of current tax revenues, and hence from the income of those currently in work, as inevitably leading to exaggerated claims for pension levels. This abandonment of the strict insurance principle in providing benefits was bound to lead to the pensions issue being a 'play ball for vote-catching demagogues' (1960: 296) who would buy the votes of the old with offers of excessive pensions. This process would, in turn, provoke such a response from the young who paid for the pensions that 'concentration camps for the aged unable to maintain themselves are likely to be the fate of an old generation whose income is entirely dependent on coercing the young' (1960: 297).

As far as health was concerned, Hayek reserved most of his ire for the National Health Service (NHS). This system was, in his view, highly objectionable because it was based on the notion that there is an objective standard of health care that could and should be met, and that such a system will pay for itself because of its impact on restoring the health of the workers. The actual result of the NHS, he argued, would be a situation of infinite demand because of the zero price at the point of use. This would lead to a 'misdirection' of resources away from the temporarily incapacitated worker towards the chronic sick and aged. As a result, the NHS would lead to a low average standard of health care for all. In addition, with doctors as the paid servants of the state, the way would be open to the political abuse of medicine, as in the Soviet Union (1960: 298–300).

Similar lines of argument may be found in Hayek's discussion of the education system (1960: ch. 24). He favours compulsory education, with public funding for the poor, but is against general public provision. He tentatively endorses the voucher system as the best way of obtaining these objectives.

As can be seen from above, in many of his specific arguments about social policy Hayek had little to say that was significantly different from what has been said by many other conservative writers before and since. What is perhaps more distinctive is his continual linking of discussion of specific institutional arrangements to the need to avoid any egalitarian objective being pursued. For Hayek, the most objectionable feature of state welfare is in providing an opening to the pursuit of such objectives, and hence the pursuit of the anathemized 'social justice'.

The limits of social policy are contentious, but in my view should certainly embrace employment policy, given the key role of access to employment in determining individuals' welfare, and the crucial underpinning for public welfare provision given by the buoyant tax revenues of a fully employed economy. In this context, Hayek is of some importance because he was a strong polemecist against the emphasis on full employment as a policy goal, especially in the postwar UK.

Hayek's hostility to full employment as a policy goal is the counterpart to his virulent antipathy to inflation. For him, inflation distorts market prices as the basic signals of the capitalist economy, ultimately causing fluctuations in activity far greater than a tighter anti-inflationary policy would cause. The rise in inflation was for Hayek one of the great disasters of the postwar period, and one he traced back to Keynes and the Keynesians: 'The responsibility for current world-wide inflation, I am sorry to say, rests wholly and squarely with the economists, or at least with that great majority of economists who have embraced the teaching of Lord Keynes' (1978: 192).

For Hayek, Keynes' error arose fundamentally from his scientific, rationalist approach to the economic system. This approach legitimized the ending of the balanced-budget rule for governments, which Hayek regarded as one of those evolved conventions which safeguarded the public good against inflation arising from the vote-catching activities of politicians. Hence the need to reinstate monetary discipline by the 'denationalization' of money. Although Hayek's solution to the problem was not used, these polemics against inflation achieved considerable prominence once inflation did start to rise sharply in the 1970s. The other side of this line of argument was to debunk governments' capacity actively to achieve full employment. All governments could and should do was provide a non-inflationary environment, and let the market provide full employment.

Hayek and the policy debate

In February 1981, Margaret Thatcher offered a paean of praise to Hayek in the House of Commons: 'I am a great admirer of Professor Hayek. Some of his books are absolutely supreme – *The Constitution of Liberty* and the three volumes of *Law, Legislation and Liberty* – and would well be read by almost every honourable member.' These comments registered the place that Hayek had come to occupy in the pantheon of New Right thinkers, whose impact seemed so evident in the revival of neo-liberalism especially in the UK and the USA in the 1970s and 1980s.

Undoubtedly, Hayek deserves his place in this set of thinkers because, of all the recent New Right theorists, he can claim to have contributed most to that intellectual revival. How far he can be said to have been influential in policy debates and especially policies, however, is much more problematic, especially if we focus specifically on social policy.

First, of course, there are general problems in understanding the relationship between political action and intellectual thought. Political action is plainly often highly opportunist in its deployment of theory, taking up what is deemed politically congenial and often distorting theory to support short-term political goals. On the other hand, however difficult it is to pin down, there is an 'intellectual climate' which helps shape how politicians, among others, view the world and approach practical policy problems. In the 1970s and 1980s, Hayek did play a considerable role in shaping that climate in the UK and the USA.

Partly this was because Hayek was always a highly political animal. Although most of his writings are abstract and theoretical, almost all have a polemical intent. Also Hayek has often been engaged in what may be called 'intellectual politics' – for example, he played a leading role in founding the Mont Pelerin society, a grouping of like-minded liberal intellectuals founded in Switzerland in 1947 (Hayek, 1967: ch. 10). He also played a part in founding the Institute of Economic Affairs in 1957, which later became a significant instrument for the dissemination of his and other New Right theorists' arguments to a wider audience.

However, it was the battering given to the postwar 'consensus' by the stagflation of the 1970s that provided the opportunity for the emergence of what might otherwise have remained a quite marginal intellectual movement. But once that opportunity opened up, Hayek was prominent in pushing his arguments into the space provided. Equally, politicians were pleased to be able to draw on such a figure to give intellectual weight to arguments which generally were strikingly lacking in novelty.

Hayek produced more political and policy-oriented work in the 1970s and 1980s than in any previous period of his long life. Much of this was published by the Institute of Economic Affairs, and focused on inflation, unemployment and trade unions. Little of what was said was new – indeed Hayek made a point of emphasizing the continuity of his anti-Keynesian polemics from the 1930s –

but it did achieve a wider audience than had ever read the *Constitution of Liberty* or his other earlier works.

Hayek's influence has been said to have been quite direct in inspiring two kinds of legislation under the Thatcher government – the anti-union measures (Wedderburn, 1989) and the poll tax (Leathers, 1989). Certainly Hayek contributed some powerful polemics against the trade unions (e.g. Hayek, 1980), although his distinct contribution on this theme is difficult to identify, anti-trade unionism having a long pedigree on the New Right, and indeed well beyond it into most of at least Anglo-Saxon conservatism. Equally, while the flat-rate, non-redistributive aspect of the poll tax conformed well with some Hayekian themes, it was based on a visceral hatred of autonomous local government which fits uneasily with Hayek's enthusiasm for decentralized provision of some inescapable minimum of public provision.

A similarly ambiguous relationship between Hayek's thought and recent policy debate and action on social welfare may be seen in such areas as reforms of education and health provision. In the UK at least, these reforms seem to have been dominated by two trends – an opening up to market forces, and a rapid growth in managerial strata geared to ideas of close management control as the route to efficiency (Cutler and Waine, 1993). Hayekian influence may be found in the former aspect, but hardly in the latter, whose intellectual provenance remains highly obscure.

Overall, Hayek's influence on debate in the specific area of welfare should not be exaggerated. His contribution has been most important in the broader areas of debate about the dangers of expansion in the scope of government, the need for constitutional constraints on that scope, and the linkage between such political changes and economic policy. Even in these issues he has clearly been part of a broader school, with his particular contribution difficult to disentangle. However, it is in the explicit and extended attack upon equality and social justice that Hayek has been both most individual in his arguments and most closely linked to issues of social welfare. In so far as British social welfare policy has traditionally been grounded on arguments for equality and social justice, Hayek may be said to have had most impact in this area, by trying to focus attention on the fundamental nature and problems of definition of such goals, and away from issues simply of how to achieve them.

However, in assessing the importance of this attack on the recent development of the welfare state in the UK, a number of qualifications have to be entered. First, as emphasized, for example, by Hindess (1987: 93) and Klein (1983: ch. 1), equality and egalitarianism played quite a small part in the set of ideas upon which the welfare state was founded. 'Social justice' more commonly meant *minimum* standards for all, rather than equality, in the eyes of many supporters of enlarged social provision.

Second, while there is a literature on equality, this seems by and large curiously disconnected from the debate about social welfare. A book like Joseph and Sumption's attack on equality (1979) is interesting, partly because Joseph later became a minister in Thatcher's government, but more because it stands out among recent New Right polemics for its almost unique willingness *explicitly* to attack equality. As they themselves note, against the arguments for equality by Rawls and Tawney there is only the 'formidable but solitary figure' of Hayek (Joseph and Sumption, 1979: 2).

The point is not to deny that much New Right writing is profoundly anti-egalitarian, and that Hayek is the major intellectual source of much of this position. But when it comes to policy making, little of the argument against welfare provision has deployed explicitly anti-egalitarian arguments. Rather, attacks on social policy have come under other slogans – about efficiency, incentives, 'dependency', etc.

On a more empirical issue, it is worth noting that the recent striking growth of inequality in the UK has *not* primarily been the result of changes in social policy registered in the income maintenance system. The main cause has been changes in 'original' incomes from property ownership and labour market participation, plus changes in taxation. The welfare state has mitigated the inequality generated by these changes (Glennerster and Midgley, 1991: 60–1).

Overall, the impact of Hayek's thought on the *specifics* of the debate on British social policy has been rather limited. He has been used to give an aura of profundity and originality to arguments which in many cases seem strikingly unoriginal, and in many cases are regurgitations of arguments put forward and refuted before the First World War. Arguments that welfare provision reduced savings, undermined work incentives, created state dependency and undercut the family were the staple diet of those who argued against the early beginnings of welfare provision by the state, just as they are at the centre of New Right arguments today (Johnson, 1986).

It is an understandable tendency of academics to exaggerate the role of 'ideas' in policy formation, and this may have happened in recent discussions of the impact of the New Right on welfare provision in Britain. Critics of the New Right have often seemed to feed the conceit of that group in their estimation of the impact of New Right ideas. This point is perhaps especially true for Hayek, whose impact until the 1970s and 1980s was minimal. What changed in those decades was the economic and political environment, and it was only in that environment that his ideas could hope to flourish. So we need to be sure that any analysis of his ideas is coupled to discussion of that environment if we are not to exaggerate his role.

Key texts

Some of Hayek's economics work is almost impenetrable (e.g. Hayek, 1931, 1941), but fortunately this is not true of those works most important for his general philosophy or approach to issues relevant to social welfare.

The Road to Serfdom was aimed at affecting postwar opinion in the UK and the USA, which Hayek foresaw drawing the wrong conclusions from wartime experience. The danger was that the perceived success of wartime government control of the economy would blind public opinion to the dangers of central economic planning. Dedicated to 'The Socialists of all Parties', it predicted the emergence of an interventionist consensus that would threaten the growth of government, which in its mistaken search for economic control and a just social order would open the path to totalitarianism.

Hayek's arguments in this text were based on a negative notion of freedom, in which every extension of the government's role is a further step on the road to serfdom. This style of argument was effectively countered by Wootton (1945), who suggested that freedom and liberty are best seen as consisting of a plurality of freedoms and liberties, that there is no good reason to suppose that these different freedoms and liberties would strengthen or erode simultaneously, and that their compatibility with different states of social organization was an *empirical* matter, not to be decided on the basis of first principles. Her position seems retrospectively justified by the failure of Hayek's polemic to halt the growth of government, without bringing as a result the erosion of freedom he envisaged.

The Constitution of Liberty is a much more serious work, mainly composed of theoretical argument, but also with some 'applied' chapters. Much of the theoretical section is taken up with a detailed elaboration of the relationship between the Burkeian-style emphasis on tradition and custom, and the evolution of the institutions of a liberal (capitalist, free-market) society, contrasted with the development of the hostile rationalist tradition. The two traditions create the fundamental divide in our understanding of society, 'the first based on an interpretation of traditions and institutions which had spontaneously grown up and were but imperfectly understood, the second aiming at a construction of a utopia, which has often been tried, but never successfully' (1960: 54).

The dichotomous formulation, it has already been suggested, creates a fundamental problem in Hayek's work. On the one hand, the arguments about the significance of custom and tradition certainly undercut any enthusiasm for the politics of year zero; but on the other hand, taken to its logical conclusion, *any* reform proposal has a rationalistic aspect, so unless we have a politics of total inactivity, a line must be drawn. Hayek's work, however, seems to offer little to differentiate legitimate 'piecemeal social engineering' from illegitimate attempts at radical reform. Hayek alerts us to the dangers of certain kinds of social reform, but helps us little in deciding which are likely to open up the dangers he so fears.

The three volumes of *Law, Legislation and Liberty*, as their title suggests, are concerned mainly with the legal foundations of a liberal society. It is here especially that Hayek presses the argument about the political dangers of a politics founded on the search for equality and social justice. For him, the attempt to achieve these ends must lead to an attempt at a moral categorization of all individuals, in order to allocate just rewards. He conjures up the awful prospect of a kind of universal Charity Organization Society, in which we are all subject to some finely graded measurement of our deserving or undeserving nature.

But must the pursuit of equality and social justice lead to this result? The answer is surely no. Governments in most capitalist countries do intervene in the distribution of income via the tax and benefit system, and provision of services in kind, without this kind of invasion of private domains. Of course, these interventions are 'rough and ready'; they do not and cannot embody a wholly consistent criterion of merit. But such systems can reduce inequality without addressing questions of individual merit. It is the disparities in the overall income distribution which some systems can be aimed at correcting, not the place of particular individuals in that distribution.

References

Barry, N. (1979) *Hayek's Social and Economic Philosophy*, London: Macmillan.

Bosanquet, N. (1983) *After the New Right*, London: Heinemann.

Burke, E. (1790/1968) *Reflections on the Revolution in France* (ed. by Conor Cruise O'Brien), Harmondsworth: Penguin.

Cutler, T. and Waine, B. (1993) *Managing the Welfare State: The politics of public sector management*, Oxford: Berg.

George, V. and Wilding, P. (1985) *Ideology and Social Welfare*, London: Routledge & Kegan Paul.

Gissurarson, H. (1987) *Hayek's Conservative Liberalism*, New York: Garland.

Glennerster, H. and Midgley, J. (1991) *The Radical Right and the Welfare State: An international assessment*, Hemel Hempstead: Harvester Wheatsheaf.

Gray, J. (1986) *Hayek on Liberty* (2nd edn), Oxford: Blackwell.

Hayek, F.A. (1931) *Prices and Production*, London: Routledge & Kegan Paul.

Hayek, F.A. (1935 edn) *Collectivist Economic Planning*, London: Routledge & Kegan Paul.

Hayek, F.A. (1941) *The Pure Theory of Capital*, London: Routledge & Kegan Paul.

Hayek, F.A. (1944) *The Road to Serfdom*, London: Routledge & Kegan Paul.

Hayek, F.A. (1960) *The Constitution of Liberty*, London: Routledge & Kegan Paul.

Hayek, F.A. (1967) *Studies in Philosophy, Politics and Economics*, London: Routledge and Kegan Paul.

Hayek, F.A. (1973) *Law, Legislation and Liberty*, Vol. I, London: Routledge & Kegan Paul.

Hayek, F.A. (1976) *Law, Legislation and Liberty*, Vol. II, London: Routledge & Kegan Paul.

Hayek, F.A. (1978a) *A Tiger by the Tail: The Keynesian legacy of inflation*, London: Institute of Economic Affairs.

Hayek, F.A. (1978b) *New Studies in Philosophy, Politics, Economics and the History of Ideas*, London: Routledge & Kegan Paul.

Hayek, F.A. (1979) *Law, Legislation and Liberty*, Vol. III, London: Routledge & Kegan Paul.

Hayek, F.A. (1980) *1980s Unemployment and the Unions*, London: Institute of Economic Affairs.

Hayek, F.A. (1988) *The Fatal Conceit: The errors of socialism – The collected works of F.A. Hayek*, Vol. I, London: Routledge.

Hindness, B. (1987) *Freedom, Equality, and the Market*, London: Tavistock.

Johnson, P. (1986) 'Some historical dimensions of the welfare state "crisis"', *Journal of Social Policy*, **15**, 4, pp. 443–65.

Joseph, K. and Sumption, J. (1979) *Equality*, London: John Murray.

Klein, R. (1983) *The Politics of the NHS*, London: Longman.

Kukathas, C. (1989) *Hayek and Modern Liberalism*, Oxford: Oxford University Pess.

Leathers, C. (1989) 'Scotland's new poll taxes as Hayekian policy', *Scottish Journal of Political Economy*, **36**, 2, pp. 194–201.

Plant, R., Lesser, H. and Taylor-Gooby, P. (1980) *Political Philosophy and Social Welfare*, London: Routledge and Kegan Paul.

Tomlinson, J. (1990) *Hayek and the Market*, London: Pluto.

Wedderburn, W. (1989) 'Freedom of association and philosophies of labour law', *Industrial Law Journal*, **18**, 1, pp. 1–38.

Wootton, B. (1945) *Freedom Under Planning*, London: Allen and Unwin.

2 Friedman

Norman Barry

Brief biography

Milton Friedman was born in New York in 1912, the son of poor Jewish immigrants. In less than propitious circumstances, he managed to graduate from Rutgers University in 1932. Although his early interests were mathematics rather than economics, Friedman went to the University of Chicago where he was greatly influenced by a number of prominent free-market economists, including Frank Knight (to whom he always refers as 'my revered teacher'), Aaron Director (whose sister Rose he later married) and Henry Simons (see Butler, 1985: ch. 1).

Although financial circumstances forced him to leave Chicago, Friedman was able to pursue his doctoral studies at Columbia. His experience there provides an intriguing anticipation of his later disputes with the 'establishment' in political economy. His research was into the professional career structures of lawyers, doctors and accountants. He showed that the restrictive practices operated by them, especially doctors, enabled significant 'economic rent' to be obtained. The supply of trained personnel was artificially reduced and this forced up the costs to consumers. The work was later published as *Income from Independent Professional Practice* (Friedman and Kuznets, 1945) and aroused considerable hostility from the professions, especially medicine, which, it is said, delayed the award of his doctorate. This incident is a good example of a feature of Friedman's intellectual life: that despite his association with 'right-wing' economics and politics, this has never been a party-political commitment, but has always involved the ruthless application of market principles to all aspects of economic and social life. Middle-class and professional interests that benefited from extra-market privileges are as likely to be the targets of such analyses as are labour and working-class organizations.

After some government service and work in various universities, Friedman returned to the Economics Department of the University of Chicago to a permanent professorship in 1948. He had a distinguished career there as a formal, technical economist, specializing in monetary theory and policy, and as an indefatigable polemicist. He was awarded the Nobel prize for economic science in 1976, primarily for his work in monetary theory. He retired from Chicago in 1977. Since then he has been a research fellow at the Hoover Institution on War, Revolution and Peace, Stanford, where he has continued his work in economics and public policy.

Throughout his life, Friedman has exhibited a rare genius for presenting quite complex ideas in economic theory and policy in ways that can be easily understood by the intelligent layperson; yet he has never compromised the integrity of the principles on which his popular expositions rest. It is perhaps his flair for controversy and talent for lucid description that has prevented his *social* ideas from being treated as seriously as they should be. The most accessible of his general works are *Free to Choose* (1980) and *The Tyranny of the Status Quo* (1985), both co-authored with Rose Friedman. However, an earlier and more sophisticated exposition of his social philosophy, *Capitalism and Freedom* (1962), remains the best guide to his thought.

Friedman's life's work lies in all the major areas of economics and social science, but it involves primarily an attack on two major orthodoxies: the Keynesian consensus on macroeconomic theory and policy that ruled western economies from the early post-war years until about the mid-1970s, and the 'agreement' on the welfare state that united the major political parties in western democracies for about the same length of time. At its simplest, Friedman's doctrine holds that there is very little in the way of government correction and control that a modern private enterprise market economy, subject to well-defined property rights and strict and *predictable* rules of law, requires if it is to maximize welfare. In the demonstration of this, he has been remarkably consistent. Detectable changes in policy consist mainly of nuance rather than substance. Indeed, in later writings Friedman has been concerned as much with showing *how* it is that governments have successively repudiated the message of free market economics (and in this endeavour he has become increasingly influenced by public choice theory) as with making innovations to the fundamentals of the doctrine.

Economics

In economics, Friedman has been known as an inveterate fighter against inflation and a staunch critic of governments' prewar and postwar monetary policy. They have, he argues, been responsible for both deflation (the Great Depression was caused, he claims, by a catastrophic collapse in the money supply engineered by the American Federal Reserve System) and inflation (postwar inflations were natural consequences of the mistaken attempts to 'fine-tune' the economy by monetary and fiscal methods, on the assumption that markets were not self-correcting but would produce periodic bouts of instability). In this, of course, he was a firm opponent of Keynesianism. In Friedman's theory, the demand for money is over the long period fundamentally stable, so that there is little governments can do to regulate economic activity by playing on the monetary levers. There is no 'trade-off' between unemployment and inflation, and any attempt to get unemployment below its 'natural rate' (which is determined by microeconomic factors, such as trade union power and government-inspired impediments to market-correcting processes) will not result in increased output, but will merely produce a rise in the general price level. Governments should be deprived of any discretion in monetary matters, and limited by a fixed rule that should govern permissible increases in the supply of money and credit. Friedman explored these themes in his monumental *Monetary History of the United States* (co-authored with Anna Schwarz, 1963). The scientific background to this empirical account of mismanagement of the currency by central authorities can be found in a series of articles (Friedman, 1969) dating back to the 1950s. Friedman's famous presidential address to the American Economics Association in 1967, in which he defended a revised version of the traditional quantity theory of money, is a landmark.

Methodology

Friedman's battles with his opponents over inflation and the conduct of macroeconomic policy have been conducted within a particular methodological framework – *positivism* (Friedman, 1953). He has always shown a distrust of a priori theorizing, and believes that most of the disputes in the social sciences can be settled by the empirical method: by tracing out the policy implications of theories and subjecting them to rigorous statistical (and econometric) tests. This applies just as much to his many writings on welfare as it does to his critiques of Keynesian macroeconomics. Most of the claims of welfare theorists, he argues, are refuted by the evidence. Examples he frequently cites are rent control (Friedman and Stigler, 1946), which causes homelessness by reducing the supply of rented property, and minimum wage laws, which, by fixing the price of labour above marginal productivity, render low-productivity workers (needlessly) unemployed (Friedman and Friedman, 1980: 237–9).

It might be thought that Friedman's ultimate position is a simple utilitarian one, that comparisons between rival welfare policies are possible only by reference to their potentially measurable consequences. Indeed, true to another aspect of his positivism, he does seem to believe that values cannot be given a rational foundation. In an important essay, Friedman once wrote that, when it comes to values, men 'can ultimately only fight' (Friedman, 1953: 5). However, on a number of occasions he has implied that there is much less disagreement about values than is often supposed, and that the real disputes among economists are about analytical methods and empirical evidence. On these issues, reason can apparently adjudicate.

Friedman's assumption that there is a consensus about values is no doubt optimistic, as are his convictions about the benign workings of an unhampered market system. There is room for considerable disagreement about the values that underlie it (especially in relation to the perennial disputes between liberty and equality) and about the empirical tests of its efficacy.[1] The remorseless allocative processes of the market undoubtedly leave victims, and it is well worth asking whether it is legitimate for Friedman to assert, as he sometimes does, that *in aggregate* the market performs better than any alternative system of which we have experience, without considering its effects on those disadvantaged by it. One doubts that the empirical method is either as value-free or as conflict-resolving as he supposes.

However, regardless of these complex issues, a careful reading of Friedman's works reveals that the fundamental basis of his social philosophy is not utilitarian but ethical. In *Capitalism and Freedom* (1962: 132) he wrote that 'I am led to the view that capitalism cannot in and of itself be regarded as an ethical principle; that it must be regarded as instrumental, or a corollary of some other principles, such as freedom'. Thus, even if it could be shown that some other system generated more (measurable) utility than could capitalism, Friedman would still prefer the latter precisely because it embodies liberty. Similarly, he argues that payment by 'merit' (in the sense of the market's determination of wages) is not merely efficient in that it attracts labour to its most productive uses, but also a recognition of an 'ethical absolute' (1962: 32). There is, then, a curious and uneasy combination of (ultimately unjustifiable) ethical values and empirically based utilitarianism in Friedman's social philosophy.

Again, although much of his critique of the policies and institutions of the welfare state turns on their alleged inefficiencies (in the sense that they often produce perverse effects), Friedman's fire is also directed towards the *paternalism* that he detects in most of them. For example, social insurance schemes that compel people to save for their old age is a simple example of the state dictating people's time preferences (the rates at which they discount the future): it is for him a fundamental affront to personal liberty. Germane to his welfare philosophy is a perhaps optimistic faith in the ability of individuals to use effectively that liberty which a market society grants them.

Friedman's account of liberty (1962: ch. 1) is perhaps not too sophisticated. It consists of a somewhat crude version of 'negative' liberty: that is, the idea that a person is free to the extent that his or her actions are not restrained by coercive law. He shows little interest in enquiring into the social and economic conditions that may make one person's freedom more valuable than another's, or into sources of constraint or human action other than law and politics; and least of all in considering the possibility that collectively supplied welfare might increase people's autonomy or their sense of citizenship. Still, Friedman (1962: ch. 1) undoubtedly has important things to say about the connections between economic liberty and political liberty, and the contributions that the institutions of traditional market society make to individual well-being.

Despite what he sometimes says, Friedman does argue about values, especially in the context of social welfare policy. Here his main target is egalitarianism. For Friedman, there is a fundamental conflict between equality and liberty. It is not one that can be conclusively settled by empirical methods. In his concept of the person, *choices*, in effect, constitute agency, and egalitarian policies, apart from their inefficiency, are destructive of Friedman's concept of individuality. For him, even inherited differential property rights are logically no different from diversity in natural talents and should not be altered by the state. What depresses Friedman most about state intervention is its tendency to generate uniformity (1962: ch. 2). He does not consider the obvious fact that the market system, with its array of *legally protected* property rights, effectively reduces some people's choices. His only concern is with politically inspired impediments to liberty.

Friedman's conception of welfare

There are two crucially important features of Friedman's philosophy of welfare: first, it is almost exclusively individualistic; and second, it derives almost entirely from his work as an economist. With regard to the first, his argument rejects any notion of 'social' welfare, any idea that we can speak meaningfully of satisfactions or well-being that are detached from individual experiences. Thus he would dismiss as vacuous those communitarian accounts of welfare that attribute value to collectively delivered social policies, policies that in some way might integrate citizens into the wider society, and which might soften the divisiveness that is said to accompany market society. Thus, even if Friedman were to believe in redistribution, which he does not, it would have to be in a form which permitted individuals to purchase *privately* whatever health, pensions and unemployment insurance arrangements they wished. This is not to say that Friedman decries communal values completely – indeed, he is a great upholder of *traditional* American social ideals – it is just that he believes that they emerge, and are sustained, spontaneously without the interference of the state.

The second, and related, general feature of Friedman's welfare theory is really an elaboration of the economist's understanding of personal satisfaction or well-being as a result of a voluntary exchange in the market (see Barry, 1990: ch. 4). This derives from Paretian[2] welfare economics: a welfare improvement can be said (scientifically) to take place only if, from one or more exchanges, at least one person is made better off and *no one is made worse off*. It is an attempt to interpret welfare in purely maximizing terms, and rejects any redistributive ideas of welfare precisely because these involve highly contestable, and unscientific, notions of equality and social justice. The theory specifically excludes interpersonal comparisons of utility: that is, no outside observer can objectively compare the utilities of persons engaged in any interaction. Thus progressive income tax (no matter how *ethically* desirable) cannot be consistent with this notion of welfare, since even the minor losses of the rich cannot be compared with the possible great gains to the poor so as to produce an increase in overall social utility.

This approach can be contrasted with traditional utilitarianism (or Benthamism): a doctrine which does permit interpersonal comparisons of utility and the construction of social welfare functions which are not ultimately reducible to private choices. The Pareto theory has serious implications for social theory, since it implies that everyone must gain, or at least no one be made worse off, from the implementation of particular policies. The only ground for government intervention would seem to be the orthodox public good argument:[3] that is, in circumstances of market failure, it is legitimate for state to intervene so as to generate Pareto improvements (those that make everybody better off). As we shall see below, Friedman tries to justify some state welfare on precisely this ground: welfare without redistribution.

An austere interpretation of this approach would forbid any change from the status quo if it worsened at least one person's position. This could, theoretically, permit the survival of many unjust and undesirable social practices. Most welfare theorists would make a moral judgement in such circumstances, but this is difficult for Friedman because of his doubts about the effectiveness of values in economic arguments. This methodology has the awkward implication for a free marketeer that movements away from a status quo characterized by a myriad of statist interventions would not be a welfare improvement if they harmed some people, as they clearly would. Even the nineteenth-century movement to free trade in food would not strictly be a Pareto improvement, since the repeal of the Corn Laws harmed the interests of the landowners.

Some welfare economists desperately attempt to preserve their 'scientific' integrity by devising all sorts of arcane compensation devices for 'losers' from what they would regard as technically necessary economic and social change. In *The Tyranny of the Status Quo* (Friedman and Friedman, 1985), it is openly admitted that the re-establishment of a market society in a statist world would involve some losers, but Friedman claims that 'if government were required to compensate every vested interest in society ... the cost would be impossible to bear' (1985: 49). In fact, most of the time Friedman adopts a kind of rough-and-ready utilitarianism, that society in aggregate would benefit from the free-market measures, even though this manoeuvre is not strictly consistent with his methodology. However, even though he is opposed to most existing welfare *state* arrangements, Friedman would not leave people uncompensated if these policies were to be replaced by more market-based forms of welfare provision. This is largely because he regards individuals in a collectivist status quo as victims of government intervention, especially in social security, where people have been forced to save in government schemes.

It is important to stress the foundational aspect of Friedman's welfare theory because it underlies the limited amount of state welfare that his doctrine permits. What he wants to show is that a non-redistributive form of compulsory welfare provision can be justified within the tenets of market theory. Some state welfare in his view is a kind of public good, the supply of which makes everyone better off (the donors as well as the beneficiaries), and is therefore consistent with both liberty and the market. The fact that his system of state welfare is very different from those that we are familiar with in western democracies should not distract the critic from the fact that Friedman does have a compulsory welfare theory, unlike the more extreme libertarians (e.g. Nozick, 1974;[4] Rothbard, 1980) who argue that state welfare policies violate fundamental rights. Friedman's theory is not a rights theory (despite his ethical belief in liberty), but a *maximizing* theory, and in all such theories, the possibility that the state may make welfare improvements on a pure market system does exist.

Welfare as a public good

Friedman's welfare theory is perhaps encapsulated in one crucially important passage in *Capitalism and Freedom* (1962: 191). He writes:

> I am distressed by the sight of poverty; I am benefited by its alleviation; but I am benefited equally whether I or somone else pays for its alleviation; the benefits of other people's charity therefore partly accrue to me. To put it differently, we might all of us be willing to contribute to the relief of poverty, *provided* everyone else did. We might not be willing to contribute the same amount without such assurance. (italics in original)

What he is trying to show here is that the relief of a poverty is a public good (like clean air, or national defence) and is not therefore strictly speaking redistributive, since everyone (including the rich who do not have to endure the sight of social deprivation) gains from such action. The assumption here is that people have altruistic preferences (although Friedman never actually uses that word), which cannot be expressed in the market because of the 'public good trap': that is, the contribution that one person's generosity makes to the alleviation of the problem is so infinitestimally small that it is not worth his or her while making it. It is worth noting, with some irony, that Friedman's fundamental position is not unlike that of Richard Titmuss (1970): both claim that public welfare is a function of the caring attitudes towards each other that people are said to have. To put it slightly more technically, Friedman assumes the existence of interdependent utility functions, that a person's well-being depends partly on other people's welfare, as well as on his or her own private satisfactions. However, quite unlike Titmuss, Friedman believes strongly that compulsory welfare should take the form of simple cash aid because to deliver it 'in kind' (particular services such as health care and pensions) would be paternalistic and hence destructive of personal liberty.

It might well be asked: if people care about each other, why do they not express this through voluntary charitable activity? Indeed, Friedman (1962: 190) comments favourably on the significant amount of eleemosynary activity that has historically been a feature of western capitalist societies. Furthermore, what kind of altruism is it which has to be supplied compulsorily? How can coercive taxaton be made consistent with Friedman's fundamental belief in liberty?

All these questions could be satisfactorily answered if, and only if, compulsory welfare were a genuine public good. But one can doubt that it is. After all, one person's contribution to the alleviation of poverty does make some, often discernible, difference. This is not the case with pollution problems (or the supply of national defence), in which co-operation is absolutely essential. If the relief of deprivation were a *genuine* public good, no eleemosynary activity would ever take place, yet clearly it does. The implication of it must surely be that people regard such action as a fulfilment of a moral *duty* rather than the production of a public good. If private welfare provision is thought to be a moral duty, then its extent will not be determined by the motivations that are highly relevant to the production of conventional public goods.

In a penetrating critique of Friedman's theory, Robert Sugden (1984) argues that it produces an extremely odd prediction. Since the important point of the theory is that it does not matter *who* contributes to the alleviation of poverty (the important thing is that poverty is relieved), it would imply that, if people *knew* that the income from a charity were going to fall, they would in fact contribute more as their income rose, subject only to the constraint that their own original consumption of private goods remained the same. It is only the 'assurance problem' (i.e. the uncertainty about other people's behaviour) that apparently prevents them from doing this. Yet it is difficult to imagine that it is that alone which prevents charitable donations. It is much more plausible to suppose that it is the altruistic impulse itself that is weak. People would not give all of their extra income if that were needed to supplement the charity's income. Of course, it would follow from Friedman's theory that the converse should hold, that people would give less to charity if they knew that others were giving more. But again, it is unlikely that a person's altruistic motivations are directly influenced by what other people are doing.

It is true that people's benevolence may be influenced by some extraneous forces – for example, voluntary donations do tend to be greater the lower the tax rate (Obler, 1981) and people probably do give a *little* more to charity as their incomes rise – but it is difficult to imagine that there are sufficient altruistic motives to generate even the limited level of welfare that Friedman would be prepared to tolerate. The point here is surely that, with regard to public policy, the demands of welfare conflict with liberty (in this case, the freedom to retain as much as possible of one's own income), and there would appear to be no overriding principle that can adjudicate between these competing moral imperatives. Indeed, it is a further example of a conflict between fundamental values which Friedman thinks can be resolved by the empirical method. Friedman's attempt to show that the alleviation of poverty is a public good, the supply of which benefits everyone, is a bold attempt at such a reconciliation, but it would appear to be conceptually flawed.

The negative income tax

Although Friedman undeniably favours some public welfare, he has long been a fierce critic of the form in which it is customarily delivered in western democracies – the welfare state. This acts through compulsion in the delivery of education, pensions, health care, unemployment benefit and so on, and is financed by obligatory social insurance and redistributive taxation. It invariably acts paternalistically and reduces free choice. Although he recognizes the need for some paternalism, especially with regard to education (he would here qualify the freedom of parents by permitting the state to act in the best interests of children), and also is prepared to admit public good arguments to justify some compulsion (again, education might be an example, as some public financing, if not direct provision, is required to inculcate appropriate social values in children), Friedman's attitude is generally hostile to the delivery of services in kind. His preferred solution to welfare problems is the negative income tax (NIT), which was first described in *Capitalism and Freedom* (1962).

The NIT is, superficially, a neat system. In principle, it implies that all the in-kind services should be abolished and money allocated to the poor, on a cash basis, so that they are then free to spend it on whatever welfare goods (which would actually be supplied by the market) they desire (Friedman, 1962: ch. XII; Friedman and Friedman, 1980: 120–3). He thinks that this would not only have the virtue of maximizing free choice, but also make efficiency improvements on the present system, since it would eliminate the need for a large bureaucracy administering particular programmes. If a person's income fell below a certain level, he or she would simply receive a specified amount (subject to certain adjustments to take account of such things as the size of family) as a straight income supplement. Oddly enough, in theory it has certain advantages which could appeal to left-wing welfare thinkers: there is clearly no problem of stigma or of the phenomenon of less than maximum take-up, both of which are features of highly bureaucratized schemes.

Yet the scheme's very simplicity has drawn critical fire from both the left and the right. Many people regard it as a spectacular version of the 'Speenhamland system' (the pre-1834 Poor Law arrangement which supplemented wages by 'outdoor relief' and was much criticized by David Ricardo), and claim that it would therefore be similarly subject to escalating costs. It also suffers from the very serious defect that poverty is not simply calculated by easily assessable low income, but is often a product of particular circumstances, such as chronic illness, highly disadvantageous family circumstances, the seasonal and often unpredictable nature of some employment, and a host of other special needs. Yet if the NIT were adjusted to take account of all these, it would gradually slip into the original welfare arrangement. It also places a tremendous burden of choice on people who perhaps cannot be relied upon to act rationally; also, their possible short-sightedness might have adverse effects on other people, especially in the context of the family. For these and other reasons, the left value the common consumption of some services.

Of course, a major criticism has been its supposed disincentive effect: it is said that the guaranteed receipt of income support, with no concomitant social obligation on the part of the beneficiary, will reduce the willingness to work. In fact, Friedman has always conceded this and has said that the demand for welfare is like the demand for any other good: if it is offered at anything approaching zero price, demand will, in theory, be infinite. He offers no suggestion as to how his own scheme would counter this universal tendency. In a similar way, it is obviously the case that, as people earned more money from employment, they would necessarily lose some (or all) of their NIT, so that they would in effect be facing very high marginal tax rates (the familiar poverty trap).

There is considerable disagreement among commentators (see Goodin, 1988: ch. 12) as to what exactly the disincentive effects of various income supplement schemes are, and they merit more attention than Friedman gives them. Of course, the lower the NIT were fixed, the less disincentive effect there would be. But how low would it have to go? If it were very low, it would make life incomparably harder for those with special disabilities that might not be catered for in the simple cash version of the NIT. They would be the victims of the necessary attempt to discipline the indolent. It is very difficult to avoid the necessity of having some test of objective 'need', to be made by an administrator. It is just this which Friedman tries to avoid.

Friedman is well aware of the fact that the level of the NIT will not be set by fully informed administrators, but that it will emerge from the democratic process. He is worried about the possibility that electoral competition may bid up the value of the cash aid, so that the natural altruistic desire of the majority to help the minority may be perverted into a system whereby the majority taxes, for its own benefit, an unwilling minority. In *Capitalism and Freedom* (1962: 194), he wrote that 'I see no solution to this problem except to rely on the self-restraint and goodwill of the electorate'. In his later work, he has come to doubt that this is an adequate constraint and, under the influence of public choice theory, has sought more rigorous constitutional limits on the growth of federal income support expenditure (Friedman and Friedman 1985: ch. 9). Although these particular measures do not correspond to his own NIT, it is likely that, if the latter were implemented, it would show the same tendency to grow.

It is noticeable that some conservatives of a similar 'small government' persuasion to Friedman have perhaps been his severest critics on the NIT. The argument has been that it is wrong to suppose that the problem of poverty is merely that some people lack cash resources: the real issue is partially a *moral* one of personal responsibility for action. The problem is not merely lack of money, but the absence of independence on the part of the poor. For some conservatives, an NIT would exacerbate the welfare crisis by producing a 'dependency' culture. In Friedman's view, it is not people's moral condition that requires alleviation, but their financial distress. However, Charles Murray, in his influential study *Losing Ground* (1986: ch. 11), argued that where the NIT was tried in two cities[5] (Seattle and Denver) it produced alarming results in terms of increased defection from work and a rise in marital breakdown. In a more conservative study, *Beyond Entitlement* (1986), Lawrence Mead maintained that the very worst welfare methods were those that created cash 'entitlements' without corresponding social obligations.

Apart from some critical comments he might want to make about the cost of cash provisions, Friedman's foundational welfare philosophy precludes him from making the familiar conservative criticism. If welfare is a public good then its supply benefits the donor as well as the recipient. Furthermore, an argument to the effect that the donor might demand a say in how it is distributed (a Pareto-type solution might plausibly require that welfare should be distributed in the form of *particular* services in order to satisfy the desires of the donors: see Hochman and Rogers, 1969) is ruled out by Friedman's libertarian political philosophy.

Overall, Friedman's view rests upon an optimistic belief in the capacity of individuals to organize their own lives successfully if the right market environment exists. The NIT might work for those in employment (despite its disincentive effects) because it would be an income supplement to those who already had the appropriate work ethic. However, the conservative critics of welfare are concerned about its deleterious effects on those who have never worked and who live entirely on various forms of income support (see Mead, 1991). On this Friedman really has nothing to say.

The critique of the welfare state

A large part of Friedman's welfare theory is concerned with his critical analysis of existing forms of welfare intervention in the free market. There is hardly an aspect of the modern welfare state that has escaped his attention, and indeed some of his best work is of this negative kind. His searching critique of almost all welfare institutions centres on a small number of claims: the almost uncontrollable rise in their costs, the denial of free choice in their consumption, the tendency of some of them to produce perverse redistributions towards middle-income groups, and the production of a variety of unintended consequences. A selection of just a small number of typical welfare state programmes will illustrate these themes.

Compulsory old-age pensions are perhaps the best example of welfare policy that Friedman opposes most eloquently. In America, in his view, retirement pensions combine inefficiency, inequality, paternalism and horrendous future cost, to make a potentially deadly social cocktail. What they do is to confuse the insurance principle with the welfare principle (see Barry, 1985). Americans do not regard old-age pensions as welfare at all because they think that they have paid for them through a lifetime's contribution to an insurance-based scheme; yet this is not so actuarially. Under the 1935 Social Security Act, payroll taxes (paid by both employer and employee) were introduced with the aim of providing for retirement pensions out of accumulated savings. Since then, the range of coverage has been extended so that it now encompasses close to 100 per cent of all Americans; the scheme is indexed to wages, extends beyond the workforce to include families and 'survivors', and consists basically of tax transfers from the young to the old, since an actuarially sound 'fund' has never been built up (despite the original intentions of its founders) out of which pensions could be paid. Some econometricians have estimated the scheme's unfunded liability at eight trillion dollars. It takes no account of demographic changes (notably the relative decline in the American birth rate) or of the fact of increased longevity through improvements in health care. Its existence poses a special problem for Friedman's methodology, since a serious reform of it would undoubtedly harm people: 'entitlements' have been built up (even though they have not been properly earned) which it might very well be thought immoral to repudiate. Furthermore, since these entitlements are linked to earnings, inequalities in wages are reproduced in old-age pensions: a perverse form of redistribution.

Friedman, like other rigorous free-market economists opposes compulsory old-age pensions (1962: ch. XI). In his doctrine it is fundamentally illiberal for the state to determine people's time preferences. Pensions are simply deferred wages, and the decision as to how an individual spends and saves his or her income over a lifetime should be entirely a personal one. He argues that, even if it were legitimate for the state to compel people to save for their old age, it goes about it in precisely the wrong way. If it were concerned that people had too high time preferences, all it would have to do would be to compel individuals to save a certain amount (by analogy with third-party motor insurance) but permit them to invest it in the competitive market. Instead, they are compelled to purchase annuities from the state.

This is really an efficiency argument. In a market system, old-age savings would be invested in stocks and bonds, which would lead to a deepening of the capital structure and go some way towards coping with the problem caused by a decline in the workforce. Indeed, there is good evidence (Feldstein, 1974) that investments in this form would lead to higher pensions than those earned through the tax investment system (costly though this already is). Instead, America has a complex system of intergenerational (and inequitable) transfers: the young 'agree' to support the old on the condition that a future generation will support them when they reach retirement. It has led to an inexorable increase in the payroll tax since 1935. The system is in fact much less liberal than the British state earnings-related pension scheme, since that does permit 'contracting out' (although Americans do save privately for their old age in addition to the compulsory scheme). In fact, most young Americans think that the social security system will 'bust' by the time they reach retirement.

Friedman does concede that there might be a problem of 'moral hazard' in the absence of compulsion. People in distress in old age would be assisted by the state anyway, and this very fact might encourage even more individuals not to take care of their futures. However, he denies that people are so short-sighted (1962: 188–9). In fact, it is government that is myopic in allowing vast debt to be built up. This is once again an example of Friedman's optimism about individual behaviour. The most he will admit is that in certain peculiar times, like the Great Depression, there may be a case for government relief for the aged, but even this should be treated as a general welfare provision. There was, of course, at one time a close connection between old age and poverty, but in modern, prosperous western economies, in his view, this is no longer the case.

Friedman has been a pioneer in the movement to extend choice in education. While not denying the need for some compulsion here, he has been active in opposition to the public sector's quasi-monopoly in schooling. He would, in fact, claim that his arguments are made on behalf of the poor: the rich can opt out of the state system, but the underprivileged have no alternative but to send their children to publicly controlled schools. Again, competition is the key concept because, in his opinion, its absence has caused a steady decline in educational standards in America (Friedman and Friedman, 1980, ch. 6), despite a quite significant increase in state expenditure in real terms over the past forty years. The main reason for this decline, he claims, is that teachers determine what is taught, and how it is taught, irrespective of the wishes of consumers (parents).

The recommended solution to this problem is the famous 'voucher' system, which Friedman pioneered (1962: ch. vi) and has continued to support enthusiastically (Friedman and Friedman, 1980: ch. 6). Under it, any parent would be issued with vouchers (in theory, the voucher could vary in value according to income) which they could spend at any school of their choice, public or private. Under competitive pressure, schools would be forced to raise standards or face closure through lack of demand. The obvious technical problems here may be excess demand for particular schools and relative inelasticity of supply. The poor might end up going to the worst schools anyway (largely because they live in deprived areas). However, Friedman argues that increased competition would mean that higher standards throughout the whole system would be achieved. He hopes that state schools might gradually become privatized. It has been tried, with limited success, in a small number of education districts in America. Friedman claims that the main obstacle to its widespread acceptance is the entrenched power of the teachers' unions; an example of what he calls the 'tyranny of the status quo' (Friedman and Friedman, 1985).

Friedman is particularly severe on government aid to university education (especially vocational), since graduates tend to earn high incomes because of this investment in human capital, but it is paid for by poorer members of the community. This is a classic example of the perverse redistributions of the welfare state.

The final area of the welfare state worth considering is health care. Here, the arguments of Friedman's opponents look compelling, both morally and economically. There may very well be a consensus over the claim that objective need rather than ability to pay should determine entitlements to medical treatment. Furthermore, there is surely asymmetric information in health care between doctor and patient, so that the former may be able to exploit the ignorance of the latter (Arrow, 1963). Of course, in an insurance-based system, there may actually be a silent conspiracy between doctor and patient to exploit the insurance company. Once a person has paid his or her insurance premium, the marginal cost to the patient of treatment is zero, and therefore the temptation to demand possibly unnecessary health care is irresistible. This, of course, leads to higher insurance premiums later, but no one individual has any incentive to refrain from action that is ultimately costly all round. This is perhaps why 37 million Americans find themselves priced out of health insurance (though, despite what is said, they are treated), while the nation as a whole spends a staggering 14 per cent of GDP on health care.

All these phenomena are examples of market failure which would justify state intervention, if not a fully fledged national health service (this possibly leads to underspending as the decisions on medical care are ultimately made by politicians). However, Friedman will have none of this. In his opinion, the inefficiencies in health care are entirely a result of state intervention (Friedman, 1991: 8).

Contrary to popular opinion, the major rise in cost to the American health system has occurred in its public sector. Medicare (zero-priced treatment for the old) and Medicaid (the same for the poor), both enacted in 1965, now absorb 41 per cent of America's health costs, and in Friedman's opinion are heavily bureaucratized systems in which output, measured in terms of hospital bed occupancy and other types of treatment, has declined relative to input: that is, the cost of care and administration. He claims that the reason why the cost of private insurance has risen (though by less than the state system) is that tax deductibility for insurance premiums is, under federal law, claimed by employers not individuals. In Friedman's view, greater competition would occur if individuals could shop around for the best deal. This would lower costs through increased competition.

Friedman's only concession to paternalism now would be to make some form of minimum health insurance obligatory for everyone. And, in a modification to his original NIT, he would authorize federal aid to the poor who could not afford to pay the premiums. But perhaps his most controversial claim is that Medicare and Medicaid should be abolished (Friedman, 1991: 8). He argues that the excessive bureaucratization that they encourage is mainly responsible for the rise in costs (though he does not consider a number of studies that claim to show that nationalized health services are cheaper administratively than private schemes). As a libertarian, he cannot object to rising *private* expenditure on health, although from his earliest days he has blamed some of this on the rent-seeking and anti-competitive activity of the medical profession.

Conclusion

Of all free-market thinkers, Friedman has been adept at combining theoretical rigour with intimate knowledge of the various welfare institutions that have come to dominate western social democracies. What is perhaps most noticeable is his anti-conservatism. His individualistic methodology is a threat to all established institutional arrangements whether they are inspired by left or right ideologies. Even writers who find his policy proposals offensive cannot deny that they are motivated by a sincere belief in personal liberty and a desire to use the market mechanism to improve the welfare of everybody. Perhaps the really controversial aspect of Friedman's social theory is his refusal to admit the claims of equality (apart from the equal rights guaranteed by liberal democracies) in his projected welfare calculus. A redistribution of initial resources (such as through inheritance taxes) would be anathema to him even if subsequent market-determined differentials in income and wealth were permitted. Furthermore, most critics would be unhappy to allow market forces to determine the welfare of all citizens, even if their incomes were supplemented by an NIT. He also seems uninterested in the possible efficiency gains that could be made by the state in welfare (Barr, 1987). For Friedman, market failure is very rare indeed.

The NIT is itself controversial, since Friedman makes no recommendations as to how its likely high costs could be controlled. Furthermore, such an open-ended method of welfare provision makes tremendous demands on individual rationality. As we have seen, Friedman would now make some modifications to it by insisting that the purchase of some welfare goods, such as health, be obligatory. The absence of correlative social obligations has disturbed some conservatives, and the freedom to purchase welfare goods privately alarms socialists. The latter would complain that this free market would undermine the 'integrative' functions that collectivized delivery has. But Friedman does not have much of a notion of individuals as *citizens*; rather they are maximizers whose self-interested actions are ultimately harmonized through the price system. Any alternative approach for him would mean the triumph of politics over economics, with all the inefficiencies which that entails.

However unsatisfactory the ultimate foundations of Friedman's welfare theory may be, few could deny the intellectual significance of his negative attacks on the current structure of welfare states in western democracies. In the partial breakdown of the consensus about welfare that has occurred, Friedman's has been the dominant voice. It is likely to remain so as these countries approach some of the welfare crises that Friedman predicted from his earliest days as a social critic.

Key texts

Capitalism and Freedom (1962) is a comprehensive guide to a free-market philosophy of society. In it Friedman argues for personal liberty against the state, and maintains that there can be no political freedom without guaranteed property rights and the right to exchange labour and capital. While accepting the basic tenets of liberal democracy, he claims that the market is a superior method for registering individual preferences to voting, a choice procedure that produces uniformity. In his view, the self-correcting mechanism of the market shows a tendency towards full employment equilibrium. Distortions at the macro level are produced by Keynesian demand management, and at the micro level by government intervention to fix prices, subsidize industry and privilege trade unions. Welfare measures, apart from the negative income tax for the very poor, are both counterproductive and paternalistic. Almost all of Friedman's welfare policy proposals are contained in this book.

Free to Choose (1980) originated as a TV programme designed to bring the merits of the market to a wide audience. The book contains statistical refinements to, and an updating of, the material in *Capitalism and Freedom*. There is a particularly informative chapter on education. The arguments in favour of the voucher scheme are refined and the author's comments on private university education are instructive. Here the Friedmans show how a free society can generate endowments and private foundations without the formal price mechanism.

The Tyranny of the Status Quo (1985) is self-explanatory. The authors argue that progress towards a free society is hindered by the dominance of entrenched groups in society. They are particularly critical of the political class and the bureacracy, all the members of which profit from the maintenance of the freedom-reducing and inefficient policies and institutions of semi-collectivized societies. The book is notable for its discussion of various constitutional reforms that should be introduced to protect the public permanently from the rent seeking of those interest groups that predominate in simple-majority-rule democracies.

Essays in Positive Economics (1953) is an earlier and more philosophical work. In it, Friedman explains his positivist methodology. This is his belief that economic and social theories are useless unless they can be subjected to rigorous tests. He challenges the view that 'assumptions' are important in economic theory. His positivism extends to ethics, where he maintains that moral disputes are irresolvable, but insists that there is much more agreement about ends than is usually supposed. He illustrates his argument from what he believes to be mistaken welfare policies.

Notes

1. An important survey of the opinions of British economists by Ricketts and Shoesmith (1992) reveals important disagreements within the profession about values and methods.
2. Vilfredo Pareto (1848–1923), the Italian economist, is the source of modern welfare economics.
3. Public goods cannot be supplied by the market, largely because those who do not pay for them cannot be excluded from their consumption.

4. Nozick (1989) has since departed from his previous radical libertarian views.
5. No state could unilaterally implement a genuine NIT because some welfare is a responsibility of the *federal* government.

References

Arrow, K. (1963) 'Uncertainty and the welfare economics of medical care', *American Economic Review*, 53, pp. 941–73.

Barr, N. (1987) *The Economics of the Welfare State*, London: Allen and Unwin.

Barry, N. (1985) 'The state, pensions and the philosophy of welfare', *British Journal of Social Policy*, 14, pp. 468–90.

Barry, N. (1990) *Welfare*, Milton Keynes: Open University Press.

Butler, E. (1985) *Milton Friedman: A guide to his economic thought*, London: Gower.

Feldstein, M. (1974) 'Social security, induced retirement and aggregate capital formation', *Journal of Political Economy*, 82, pp. 905–26.

Friedman, M. (1953) *Essays in Positive Economics*, Chicago, Ill.: University of Chicago Press.

Friedman, M. (1962) *Capitalism and Freedom*, Chicago, Ill.: University of Chicago Press.

Friedman, M. (1969) *The Optimum Quantity of Money and Other Essays*, Chicago, Ill.: Aldine.

Friedman, M. (1991) 'A cure for America's health-care ills', *The Wall Street Journal Europe*, 18 November.

Friedman, M. and Friedman, R. (1980) *Free to Choose*, London: Secker and Warburg.

Friedman, M. and Friedman, R. (1985) *The Tyranny of the Status Quo*, Harmondsworth: Penguin. First published 1984.

Friedman, M. and Kuznets, S. (1945) *Income from Independent Professional Practice*, New York: National Bureau of Economic Research.

Friedman, M. and Schwarz, A. (1963) *A Monetary History of the United States, 1867–1960*, Princeton, NJ: Princeton University Press.

Friedman, M. and Stigler, G. (1946) *Roofs or Ceilings?*, New York, Foundation for Economic Education.

Goodin, R. (1988) *Reasons for Welfare*, Princeton, NJ: Princeton University Press.

Hochman, H. and Rogers, J. (1969) 'Pareto optimal redistribution', *American Economic Review*, 59, pp. 542–57.

Murray, C. (1984) *Losing Ground: American social policy, 1950–80*, New York: Basic Books.

Mead, L. (1985) *Beyond Entitlement*, New York: Basic Books.

Mead, L. (1991) 'The new politics of the new poverty', *The Public Interest*, 102, pp. 3–20.

Nozick, R. (1974) *Anarchy, State and Utopia*, Oxford: Blackwell.

Nozick, R. (1989) *The Examined Life*, New York: Basic Books.

Obler, R. (1981) 'Private giving and the welfare state', *British Journal of Political Science*, 11, pp. 17–48.

Ricketts, M. and Shoesmith, E. (1990) *British Economic Opinion*, London: Institute of Economic Affairs.

Rothbard, M. (1982) *The Ethics of Liberty*, Atlantic Highlands: Humanities Press.

Sugden, R. (1984) *Who Cares?*, London: Institute of Economic Affairs.

Titmuss, R.M. (1970) *The Gift Relationship*, London: Allen and Unwin.

Part II

The Middle Way

Introduction

The term 'middle way' has been used in two rather different ways over the years. Macmillan's book with that title in 1938 epitomized the first meaning of the term: managed capitalism with a modicum of social service provision. The market is the best mechanism for allocating resources, encouraging economic growth and preserving individual freedom, but it has to be controlled and regulated. During the 1960's however, the term came to be used in a rather different way. Several American and British social scientists referred to Sweden as a country representing the 'middle way' between, on one hand, the Soviet Union with its authoritarian central planning and total state ownership of the means of production and distribution and, on the other, the USA and several of the European countries. The distinction made here was between the advanced Swedish welfare state and the residual or modest welfare states of the West. However, it is with the first meaning of the term that this section is concerned.

The writers we have included in this section differ on many important issues, but they agree on the fundamental premise that capitalism is a superior system to all other systems devised so far, but that it needs to be reformed if it is to prosper and survive. *Laissez-faire* capitalism is not a realistic option any more. It creates far too many economic and social problems that threaten its very existence. It leads to high rates of unemployment, poverty, homelessness and the like that need to be tackled if it is to retain the allegiance of the general public. It is these giant 'evils' that Beveridge wanted to slay through his programme of reform in the 1940s in order to create a better society.

Welfare reforms are desirable and necessary, however, not only because they reinforce capitalism, but for other reasons too. Some reforms, like education, are investments in human capital that increase productivity in the economy. Others, like a comprehensive social security system, are desirable for largely humanitarian reasons because they help to abolish poverty, which is considered an affront to civilized values in affluent societies. Most social services directly or indirectly provide living evidence to the ordinary citizen that welfare capitalism is a far superior system to either *laissez-faire* capitalism or socialism. Social services are neither a threat to individual freedom as the New Right claim nor stepping stones towards socialism as the left argues, but realistic and useful ways of providing goods and services in areas where the market cannot function well enough.

The extent and nature of these measures, however, must be such that they do not undermine individual initiative and family responsibility. People have duties first and social rights second, and the fulfilment of one presupposes the fulfilment of the other. Welfare measures should, therefore, encourage rather than discourage private and voluntary provision; they should be concerned with achieving minimum standards rather than with reducing inequalities in society. Subsistence poverty is a social cancer that must be abolished; inequality is both necessary and inevitable, for without it economic incentives will vanish.

There is a clear tension in the desire of this group for welfare measures that on one hand humanize capitalism and abolish 'giant evils', and on the other do not undermine the core values and practices of capitalism. The dividing line between these two objectives is not always clear and, as the New Right are only too eager to point out, they can be mutually exclusive. To achieve its objectives, welfare provision will inevitably grow, with obvious implications for taxation rates, work incentives and individual freedom. Reluctant collectivism ultimately leads to the same encompassing welfare state as socialist collectivism.

Writers of the 'middle way' will dismiss this grand theorizing. For them, the issue is obvious: there are problems in society which the state, for a variety of reasons, cannot ignore or leave to the market, it has a duty to tackle them as best it can. Pragmatism rather than grand theorizing is the driving force behind their policy proposals. If state expenditure becomes too heavy for the economy, it has, of course, to be curtailed. But this is a pragmatic and not an ideological or theoretical decision. Economic and social policy are of equal worth to society, and neither should be allowed to dominate the other.

The five writers that we have included in this part of the book – Macmillan, Beveridge, Keynes, Marshall and Galbraith – constitute a formidable group in terms of both government experience and theoretical sophistication. In everyday politics, they may well belong to different political parties, but they share a substantially common approach to the welfare state. Their opposition to both *laissez-faire* capitalism and centrally planned and provided socialism may vary in degrees, but their support of welfare capitalism as a superior, enduring and lasting system is undoubted. Galbraith's aphorism that the co-existence of private affluence and public squalor is a disgrace and a danger to civilized society will be unreservedly supported by all in this group. The differences between them will emerge in the policy application of this principle, as the various chapters in this part will show.

3 Macmillan

Daniel Ritschel

Early career

Although Harold Macmillan is best remembered as a Conservative Prime Minister between 1957 and 1963, his place in the pantheon of modern thinkers on welfare was secured largely by his intellectual and political activities between the wars. It was in the midst of the prolonged interwar slump that Macmillan established his reputation as a persistent critic of economic orthodoxy and an outspoken proponent of radical reform, who nearly single-handedly kept alive the flame of Disraeli's 'one nation' Toryism within the Conservative Party. His dissident activities stretch back to the mid-1920s, but he is identified most closely with *The Middle Way*, a comprehensive programme of social and economic reconstruction that he published in 1938.

Considered one of the defining Conservative texts of this century, *The Middle Way* sought to reinterpret Conservative ideology in a more progressive light, advocating a pragmatic compromise between the principles of individual and economic freedom, and the collectivist tendencies of modern society and economy. Macmillan's 'middle way' anticipated many of the key features of the postwar welfare state, including the 'mixed' economy of public and private ownership, Keynesian demand management to ensure full employment, and extensive social reforms designed to guarantee a universal 'social minimum'.

Although his ideas were spurned by the Conservative Party establishment in the 1930s, Macmillan came into his own in the postwar period, when changing popular attitudes brought about by the experience of the war and the party's devastating electoral defeat in 1945 forced Conservatives to re-examine their entire social and economic philosophy. After 1945, *The Middle Way* furnished the Tories with an appropriately progressive language and pedigree which allowed them to accommodate themselves to the changed political mood of the nation. Indeed, its author has come to be regarded as the intellectual godfather of postwar 'progressive' Conservatism, who had helped the Conservative Party not only to adjust to the new political climate after the war, but eventually to claim it for its own under his leadership in the 1950s.

Sources of Macmillan's radicalism

The above, at any rate, is the shorthand narrative of Macmillan's early career as a Tory radical. The full story of the genesis of the 'middle way' is considerably more complex, tracing a rather more complicated political and intellectual journey than the above account suggests. Macmillan's radicalism sprang from three broad sources, whose conflicting influences help greatly to explain the evolution of his thought. As is well known, his formative political experience as MP for the depressed Durham constituency of Stockton-on-Tees, where he was first elected in 1924, provided him with first-hand evidence of the effects of the interwar slump and mass unemployment on the lives of his working-class constituents. The 'lessons of Stockton' have become a clichéd explanation of Macmillan's interwar radicalism, but there is no doubt that the conditions he found in Stockton produced within him a passionate commitment to reform which was to dominate his entire career. Nor is there any question that the semi-collectivist approach to social and economic policy that he would eventually embrace in *The Middle Way* owed much to this backdrop.

Yet, at the same time, it must be remembered that Macmillan was also a businessman, both as an executive in his family's publishing firm and as a director of the Great Western Railway, who initially identified most closely with the neglected interests of the hard-pressed business community. Indeed, his initial remedies for the slump were distinguished by the unorthodox combination of his insistent demand for fundamental economic reconstruction with his equally strong concern to protect private enterprise from the threat posed by the interventionist or collectivist solutions favoured by those to the left of the Conservative Party. This was the dual purpose behind his early espousal of the peculiar prescription of 'planned capitalism': a quasi-corporatist scheme of economic control under the auspices of organized private industry. As such, Macmillan was until the mid-1930s associated most closely not with the collectivist stance he would eventually adopt in *The Middle Way*, but with the considerably less progressive image of a right-wing proponent of 'monopoly capitalism' and, for some, the 'corporate state'. Macmillan's evolution from the sponsor of 'planned capitalism' to the champion of the 'middle way' is in fact one of the more intriguing developments of modern British politics.

The explanation for this evolution is to be found in the last important source for his radical dissent. Macmillan came from a long line of Tory radicals whose commitment to reform sprang from their concern about the potential political consequences of inaction in the face of pressing social or economic problems. In Macmillan's case, the pressing problem was the interwar slump and his concern was that the unimaginative neo-liberal orthodoxy of the Conservative Party and governments not only failed to offer an adequate answer to this economic calamity, but also undermined confidence in the traditional values and institutions of British society. In the 1920s, he attacked his party's unthinking adherence to *laissez-faire* as a 'gospel of despair', which offered little constructive alternative to the alluring promises of the Labour Party. 'If we dismiss Socialism,' he challenged Baldwin after the party's defeat in 1929, 'what have we to offer in its place?' (Macmillan, 1929). His fears were only heightened by the impact of the world economic crisis after 1929. The formation of the Tory-dominated National Government in August 1931 may have stabilized the political situation, but trade and industry continued to stagnate and mass unemployment remained an intractable feature of the national economy throughout the 1930s.

Like many at the time, Macmillan interpreted the depression as a symptom product of the rapid disintegration of the nineteenth-century free-market economy. He also continued to worry that the government's complacent response to this crisis did little either to reassure the people or to avoid the utimate crash. Increasingly, he became convinced that, unless existing society proved its ability to heal its economic wounds and replaced the free market with a more stable economic system, the disaffected masses could easily succumb to the false promises of demagogues from either the left or the extreme right. As he warned dramatically in 1933:

> the present will be seen in retrospect as a period in which the helpless futility of moderate men prepared the ground for catastrophe, and their lethargy or incompetence created the situation in which the violent and ruthless could appeal successfully to the passions of a disillusioned and despairing people. (Macmillan, 1933a: 1)

It was this acute fear of the potentially disastrous consequences of inaction, together with his orthodox conservative desire to protect private enterprise from the rising challenge of state collectivism, that first led Macmillan to champion the cause of 'planned capitalism' early in the 1930s. However, his party's repeated failure either to heed his warnings or to endorse his proposed economic solution gradually prompted him to look for allies outside of traditional Conservative circles. This search involved him with several of the more prominent opposition groupings of the 1930s, from the early stages of Sir Oswald Mosley's New Party in 1931, through the cross-party Next Five Years group in the mid-1930s, to a leading role in the agitation for a Popular Front towards the end of the decade. While Macmillan remained throughout a convinced Conservative, his work with such opposition bodies led him progressively to dilute his original stance with ever-greater doses of state interventionism until, in *The Middle Way*, he came to espouse many of the social and economic policies which he had originally set out to pre-empt with his scheme of 'planned capitalism'. The great irony is that in the end Macmillan embraced moderate state collectivism as the best possible defence of both private enterprise and traditional society.

Development of 'planned capitalism'

In order to explain the genesis and meaning of Macmillan's ideas, it is necessary
to review their evolution in their proper historical context. Having first entered
Parliament in 1924 at the relatively young age of thirty, Macmillan did not waste
much time in establishing his credentials as a backbench rebel. His early discontent
with Stanley Baldwin's uninspiring leadership first manifested itself in his
involvement with the 'YMCA', a group of young Tories who published in 1927
Industry and the State, a tract which challenged their party's attachment to the
'Liberal' tenets of *laissez-faire* and sought to reopen the debate on the principles
of Conservative economic policy (Boothby *et al.*, 1927). By the end of the decade,
Macmillan was involved in plots to replace Baldwin and the 'old men' at the
helm of the party with a younger and more enterprising leadership (Taylor, 1972:
268). After the Conservative loss in 1929 and his own defeat at Stockton,
Macmillan was for a time drawn to Sir Oswald Mosley's ill-fated attempt to
form a 'centre party' in national politics. Although he wisely avoided Mosley's
siren call and regained his seat as a Tory in the general election of 1931, his
radicalism continued unabated. By the early 1930s, his demand for a more
constructive Conservative approach crystallized in his embrace of the idea of
economic planning. 'There is no alternative except a planned economy', he told
the House in one typical speech in 1932 (Macmillan, 1932: c. 2203). In the same
year he had made the obligatory pilgrimage to the Soviet Union. By the middle
of the decade, several pamphlets, numerous articles and speeches, and a book,
Reconstruction: A plea for a national policy (1933a), attested to his crusading
devotion to the new cause.

In the light of Macmillan's subsequent career and reputation as the author of
The Middle Way, his early ideas on economic planning are usually interpreted
in terms of a progressive philosophy of pragmatic state interventionism, patterned
on the Disraelian tradition of Tory paternalism and the newer economic theories
of Keynes (Addison, 1977; Greenleaf, 1983; Horne, 1988; Marquand, 1988).
Yet if in later years Macmillan did indeed push Conservative thought towards
the collectivist middle ground of modern poltics, his position in the first
half of the 1930s represented an entirely different strand of radical economic
thought.

First, it is important to establish that Macmillan cannot at this stage be classified
as a 'Keynesian'. To be sure, he came closer to Keynes than most of his Tory
colleagues. In his frequent attacks on the National Government's complacent
approach to unemployment, he firmly aligned himself with the expansionist
approach, urging capital expenditure programmes to revive trade and induce
recovery, particularly in the distressed areas. At the same time, however,
Macmillan was clearly highly sceptical about the long-term efficacy of this
approach. In fact, he tempered his advocacy of Keynesian reflation with repeated
warnings that such 'inflationary methods' could never be a 'permanent cure',
but were merely temporary palliatives which, unless accompanied by deeper

reforms, would only lead to a 'fresh disequilibrium' and a 'relapse into further depression'. 'I do not believe', he wrote in this vein, 'that by the manipulation of currency or financial policy *alone* we can find an adequate solution to our problems.' Only physical planning of industry could establish and maintain the proper 'balance of production' necessary for permanent stability (Macmillan, 1933b: cs. 1293–4; 1933c: cs. 350–5; 1934a; 1935: cs. 444–6).

Yet neither can we at this point categorize Macmillan as an advocate of collectivist planning by means of state intervention or public regulation of the economy. Indeed, the central theme of his position at the time was his rejection of any association of planning with the state. 'Too often,' he complained in *Reconstruction*, 'planning is made to look like a system of bureaucratic regulation.' Instead, drawing on the experience of delegated industrial controls during the war, precedents established by the movements towards trade association and rationalization of industry in the 1920s, and corporatist ideas long current within Conservative thought itself, Macmillan proposed a model of planning as a system of 'industrial self-government' by representative Industrial Councils. Elected by employers within each major industrial sector, and invested with regulative powers amounting to monopoly, the Councils were to develop and implement central production and marketing plans for their industries as a whole. On the national level, they were to be joined in a Central Economic Council or 'Industrial Parliament', through which organized industry would assume collective respon- sibility for the nation's economic affairs. State intervention, on the other hand, was to be limited purely to assistance – financial and legislative – to private industry's attempts to create its own self-governing institutions. Macmillan acknowledged the danger of restrictive practices and monopoly exploitation implicit in the scheme, but felt certain that consumer vigilance and the 'public spirit' of industrialists themselves would be more than adequate safeguards. Nor was he prepared to accept workers' participation in management or representation on the sectoral Councils: 'Even in Russia they've had to give up trying to do that.' At most, trade unions were to be granted a consultative status and the Trades Union Congress was to have a voice on the National Economic Council. The goal of his 'planning' was to erect a self-governing structure for industry as a permanent bulwark against any sort of interference with private enterprise. 'The whole intention of the policy here advanced', Macmillan emphasized, 'is to achieve planning through self-government as an alternative to bureaucracy' (Macmillan, 1933a: 25–63; 1934c).

Macmillan represented his proposals as a 'reasonable compromise between the rival claims of individualist and collectivist conceptions of society', and thus 'in the true tradition of English development' (Macmillan 1933a: 127–8). However, contemporary observers detected strong parallels with rather more alien doctrines, and Macmillan's ideas were frequently linked with continental corporatist ideology. More accurately perhaps, they should be described as a philosophy of business corporatism or, as a reviewer in *The Times* put it, 'Guild Capitalism' (*The Times*, 1 December 1993). It was essentially a socially conservative vision of a business commonwealth, nominally subservient to parliamentary authority, but in practice free to determine the course of national economic development. Macmillan himself depicted his scheme as the tactical answer of 'organized' or 'planned capitalism', meant to safeguard private enterprise from both the breakdown of the market economy and the dangers of either fascist or socialist state control. As he explained in a speech in the Commons early in 1935, 'this is an idea for making the world safe for capitalism' (Macmillan, 1935a: c. 447)

It was with this goal in mind that Macmillan founded in 1933 the Industrial Reorganization League. Composed of prominent industrialists and Tory back-benchers, the League lobbied the National Government on behalf of an Industrial Reorganization Enabling Bill, designed to give industrial trade associations statutory powers to enforce their schemes of corporate self-government. The League mobilized substantial support within business and Conservative circles, including the active backing of a group of twenty-odd 'Tory planners' and a vote in favour of the bill at the 1934 party conference. However, its efforts also met with fierce resistance. Although the most vocal criticism came from within Labour and Liberal quarters, even more damaging was the opposition to the bill from within the business community itself, particularly the smaller firms and businesses which feared that statutory self-government would spell their permanent subjection to their larger rivals. Faced with such opposition from within the ranks of its own business constituency, the National Government rejected the League's proposals. Its position was determined less by doctrinal considerations than by a purely political reluctance to assume responsibility for so dramatic a reconstitution of the economy. Nevertheless, the bitterly disappointed Macmillan attributed the government's stance to ideological intransigence. He ascribed his defeat to the 'old *laissez-faire* of the Manchester school', which, he maintained, had taken root in 'some of the darker recesses of that part of the Tory party which has suffered from a continuous infusion of Whigs' (Macmillan, 1935: c. 442; Ritschel, 1991).

Evolution of the 'middle way'

It was at this point that Macmillan began the process of ideological transformation which would eventually establish his reputation as a 'progressive Tory'. Up to the mid-1930s, his ideas of 'planned capitalism' may have constituted a radical alternative to the economic strategy pursued by the National Government, but they also represented a type of right-wing radicalism which was the antithesis of the state collectivism which would later figure so prominently in *The Middle Way*. Nor is there in his writings or speeches in the first half of the 1930s much evidence of a serious interest in social policy issues. Indeed, despite Macmillan's strong rhetorical appeal to the tradition of paternalistic Toryism, and his vociferous assaults on the government for its failure to deal with the impact of unemployment and regional distress, critics frequently complained that his own counter-strategy of 'capitalist planning' would have had a negative impact on living standards, since it involved the abdication by the state of its responsibility for social and economic policy in favour of private business monopolies. While Macmillan saw this as the essential first step towards the stabilization of market conditions and an eventual recovery, others feared that his strategy would give free rein to the restrictionist impulses of the business community, and lead to both increased unemployment and diminished public capacity to deal with its consequences.

Not surprisingly, Macmillan earned himself a reputation in opposition circles as the most dangerous of right-wingers, a man who had garbed his ideas on monopoly capitalism in the deceptively progressive language of planning. 'Socialists should be on their guard against such vicious proposals', warned the Labour economist, Douglas Jay, 'when advanced by well-meaning "planners", such as Mr Harold Macmillan under the guise of "self-government for industry" and so forth' (Jay, 1937: 328n). Other critics portrayed him as an advocate of the 'corporate state' and 'industrial fascism', whose scheme would undermine not only working-class living standards but parliamentary democracy itself (Conze and Wilkinson, 1934: 225–6, 234–5; Murphy, 1934: 8–9; Alexander, in *Manchester Guardian*, 17 September 1936). This was a politically inspired exaggeration, but it does suggest that we should reconsider our image of the early Macmillan as a left-of-centre progressive.

However, in the second half of the decade, Macmillan's frustration with the government's rejection of his plans was to propel him into an increasingly maverick political trajectory which would fundamentally revise his entire social and economic philosophy. His disenchantment was a matter partly of thwarted personal ambition, but mainly of his continued anxiety that the depressed state of the economy and the widespread disappointment of the hopes originally invested in the National Government were laying the grounds for a more violent reaction during the next economic crisis. As he prophesied glumly in 1935: 'a collapse now would spell revolution' (Crossley *et al.*, 1935: 6). Dismayed by the complacent attitude of ministers and his party's somnolent acquiescence to their unimaginative style of government, Macmillan set out to mobilize the proponents of a more radical economic course outside Conservative ranks.

Initially, Macmillan worked within the confines of the 'National' camp, but he soon began to cast about in an ever-widening search for allies and combinations on the opposition benches. In the process, his ideas followed a parallel course of incremental radicalization. They would always remain those of a Tory radical, anxious to press ahead with judicious reforms lest the pent-up pressure for change break out in uncontrolled directions. But Macmillan had a quintessentially Peelite willingness to compromise on peripheral issues in order to strengthen his defence of more central principles. In the interests of constructive economic reform, he was prepared both to seek support outside traditional Conservative circles and to accept ever more radical ideas, declaring himself concerned more that a positive policy was adopted 'than with the particular "label" which may be attached to the practical proposals' (Macmillan, 1934b: 348).

This search led him first to the Next Five Years group, which he launched in 1934 together with Clifford Allen, Sir Arthur Salter and several other disenchanted former supporters of the National Government, drawn mainly from the ranks of the 'National' Labour and Liberal factions. Their purpose was to rally national opinion behind a non-party programme of economic reform, hoping either to induce the government to adopt a more positive strategy or, if necessary, to push for the formation of an alternative coalition of a more progressive hue. To this end, the group drafted *The Next Five Years: An essay in agreement*, which was published in 1935 with the signatures of over 150 prominent national figures and personalities. The book's premise was that economic reform was being thwarted by the sterile conflict between the ideological opposites of individualism and socialism, which had deeply polarized political opinion since the war and effectively blocked the consideration of more moderate policy alternatives between the two extremes. To break this deadlock, the book put forward a compromise programme of moderate social and economic reconstruction meant to secure the approval of all but the most intransigent ideologues. The compromise rested on the central theme of a 'mixed economy' of private and public enterprise. Its strategic purpose was spelled out in the introduction, which declared that the historic controversy between individualism and socialism could be effectively side-stepped in favour of 'co-operation in a practical programme', if only the advocates of economic reform would drop their ideological fundamentalism and accept the compromise solution of a 'mixed system' composed of the best features of both (*The Next Five Years*, 1935: 1–8).

The book has long been upheld as an early example of the sort of progressive agreement that prepared the way for the economic consensus which emerged in the UK during and after the war (Marwick, 1964). Yet it is perhaps far more revealing of the ideological difficulties of consensus-building in the 1930s, as well as of Macmillan's own highly qualified adherence to the progressive agenda. Indeed, after early controversy within the group over its definition of the 'mixed economy', the group had secured Macmillan's continued participation in the effort only by allowing him a free hand in the drafting of the industrial section of the programme. As a result, the 'mixed economy' outlined in the book bore only a faint resemblance to the system established in the UK after the war. It defined the envisioned 'mix' as a combination of three distinct sectors. The first covered the major utilities, including the banks, electricity supply and transport, which were to be transformed into state-regulated public corporations. The second sector, consisting of small and newer trades, was to retain essentially free-market conditions. However, for the rest of large-scale industry, Macmillan again proposed the corporatist framework of private self-government. He thus mixed competitive small enterprise with a measure of public control, but still managed to reserve the largest portion of the economy for his scheme of 'planned capitalism'.

However, in return for Allen's concession on industrial self-government, Macmillan did endorse the book's call for a social strategy of a 'National Minimum'. This strategy, designed mainly by Allen, fell somewhat short of the promise of its grandiose title. But it did recommend substantive measures of social reform, most notably the 48-hour week, revision of the Unemployment Insurance Fund to allow a higher level of benefits, a less harsh application of the Family Means Test, the payment of higher old-age pensions to the needy, and the raising of the school-leaving age to sixteen, intended both to relieve the congested juvenile labour market and to improve educational standards. The book also highlighted a limited programme of public works under the auspices of a National Development Board. The additional revenue to finance such measures was to be raised by a more progressive system of graduated taxation, aimed primarily at 'unearned' income.

None of this was particularly novel or revolutionary: nearly all of the book's social policies were drawn from a common stock of ideas current in left-wing and progressive circles since the war. What was far more significant was the support now lent to these ideas by a Conservative like Macmillan. Macmillan clearly saw this support as a tactical concession necessary to secure reciprocal approval of his ideas on capitalist planning. 'My Conservative colleagues and I', he later wrote in his memoirs, 'naturally yielded on some of these questions, in order to meet the many concessions made towards our views on industrial organisation' (Macmillan, 1966: 374–5). But he also began to portray his new position as a reaffirmation of the long-neglected strain of 'one nation' Toryism and an antidote to the socially divisive economic liberalism which had captured his party. As he told an interviewer at the time: 'Toryism has always been a form of paternal Socialism, and the great mass of people suspect Conservatism to-day because it has become too Liberal in the laissez-faire sense of Liberalism' (*Star*, 25 June 1936). In restrospect, his work with the Next Five Years group reveals Macmillan's willingness to contemplate an ideological compromise in the interests of political agreement with his new progressive allies.

Unfortunately, this elaborate attempt to re-establish a centrist position in national politics failed to overcome the profound polarization of contemporary political culture. Although the Next Five Years programme attracted the support of a host of old-style Liberal progressives and disenchanted National Labourites, its unorthodox ideological blend alienated most of Macmillan's Tory and business colleagues, who complained that the radical extension of public ownership implied by the mixed economy represented a dangerous surrender to socialist ideas. At the same time, it failed to win support from within the Labour Party, whose spokesmen complained that the mixed economy was little more than a crude attempt to dress up capitalist planning in 'progressive' clothes. In addition, the book's impact was overshadowed by the nearly simultaneous publication in the summer of 1935 of Lloyd George's similar 'New Deal' programme. This initiative effectively upstaged the Next Five Years group and led to a damaging internal row about its relationship with the elder statesman. Significantly, while many viewed Lloyd George as a spent and disruptive force, Macmillan saw him as a potential leader of a new 'progressive block' in national politics. These differences led to a series of increasingly bitter disputes within the Next Five Years group, which effectively wrecked the group's hopes of making any sort of impact on the course of the 1935 general election. Macmillan, however, remained undaunted. He fought the election on an openly independent platform, explicitly qualifying his promised support for the government with a pledge to pursue the policies of the Next Five Years programme (Macmillan, 1966: 376–8; Kennedy, 1974).

Although Macmillan was safely re-elected at Stockton, his days in the Conservative Party were clearly numbered. The rapidly deteriorating international situation after 1935 provided the final push behind his apostasy. The growing anxiety over the rise of fascism on the continent, which came gradually to overshadow British politics after Hitler's accession to power in 1933, was suddenly transformed early in 1936 into an outright fear of fascist aggression and war. Mussolini's invasion of Abyssinia, Hitler's march into the Rhineland, and the outbreak of civil war in Spain in July, all brought the spectre of a military conflict in Europe to the forefront. In the UK, such fears were only heightened by the government's seemingly equivocal attitude to the League of Nations and the idea of collective security, its apparent willingness to accommodate the dictators, demonstrated most vividly in the abortive Hoare–Laval pact, and its neutrality over Spain in the face of open assistance to Franco by the fascist powers. This lent support to the widespread suspicion that the National Government was at best indifferent to the fascist menace or, worse yet, secretly sympathetic and willing to stand by while reaction destroyed democracy on the continent. By the middle of 1936, critics of appeasement were beginning to float the idea of a 'Popular' or 'Progressive Front', meant to unite the previously fragmented opposition in a temporary coalition designed either to generate enough pressure to force a turnaround on appeasement or to displace the government altogether.

For Macmillan, too, appeasement became the final straw that broke his already tenuous sense of loyalty to the National Government and the Conservative Party. In April 1936 he voted against the government's Unemployment Insurance Bill. In June, when the government formally dropped sanctions against Italy, he supported Labour's motion of censure. A week later he resigned the party whip, charging that the government's disastrous complacency at home had now been compounded by an even more dangerous complacency abroad. By then he was deeply involved in work on behalf of the Popular Front. His main contribution was the launch of the *New Outlook*, a journal meant originally to propagate the ideas of the Next Five Years group, which Macmillan now redeployed in support of the Popular Front. Its first issue came out in June 1936, and its pages were soon filled by a heterogeneous body of opinion from all sides of the political spectrum, firmly united in condemnation of appeasement and belief in the urgent need for some type of broad alignment of anti-appeasers of all faiths. The campaign attracted socialists like John Strachey and G.D.H. Cole, independent Liberals such as Walter Layton and Sir Richard Acland, and a handful of dissident Tories, including Robert Boothby, Lord Robert Cecil and Winston Churchill himself. Macmillan began once again to speculate about the possibility of a 'Left Centre progressive party' (Macmillan, 1936b, 1936c).

The difficulty, of course, was that, while the diverse proponents of the Popular Front may have been as one in their opposition to the government's policy abroad, they had precious little in common in domestic policy. Yet they required an agreed domestic programme, both to overcome their own previous differences and to have an attractive platform to appeal to an electorate which by no means shared their determination to confront the dictators. This problem was tackled by the People's Front Propaganda Committee, launched in the summer of 1936 by Macmillan and Cole to formulate a positive domestic programme, which could be sponsored collectively by the various groups and individuals attracted to the idea of a Popular Front. It was an unlikely partnership which well reflected the remarkable extent of their determination to bury their past differences in the interests of immediate unity. Although for much of the decade Macmillan and Cole had figured prominently on the opposite sides of the political barricades, they were now willing to extend a conciliatory hand to one another and to meet at least half-way in matters of domestic policy. As Macmillan argued in the *New Outlook*, beyond agreement on an 'immediate programme' for the Popular Front, there was 'no need for an investigation into the precise character of political faith' (Cole, 1936a, 1936b, 1937; Macmillan, 1936b: 19, 1937a, 1937b).

They found the ingredients for such an 'immediate programme' in the economics of Keynes. Macmillan's embrace of Keynes can be traced to the publication in February 1936 of *The General Theory*, which finally furnished Keynes' long-standing policy advice with a convincing theoretical backing, and thus helped to launch the 'Keynesian Revolution' in economic theory. Macmillan clearly had his own earlier doubts dispelled by its authoritative statement of the case for expansion, and turned almost overnight from a cautious sceptic into an enthusiastic convert, treating the Commons to a lengthy exposition of the new theory within weeks of the book's publication (Macmillan, 1936a). Yet the political circumstances of his search for a compromise programme for the Popular Front were no less important a factor in his conversion. Macmillan was certainly among the first to grasp the political opportunities offered by Keynes' 'new economics', and the first to apply it in his negotiations with Cole over the Front's programme.

What Keynes offered to the Popular Front was a basis for an electorally attractive domestic platform, which made possible a short-term alliance between anti-appeasers of different political faiths. Macmillan and Cole agreed on an immediate programme of loan-financed national investment in industrial renovation and development, meant to revive employment and induce general recovery. At the same time, this reflationary strategy was to be backed by a parallel offensive of 'increasing consumption' through public expenditure on work-creation projects and welfare services, including house building, road improvement, higher pensions and the replacement of the Family Means Test by a 'more humane' system of maintenance. Following the advice of Sir John Boyd Orr and Eleanor Rathbone, both strong supporters of the Front, they also endorsed family allowances and the adoption of policies for the betterment of the health and nutrition of the people, most notably the distribution of free milk and meals to schoolchildren. Crucially, public expenditure on welfare was justified as an integral part of the overall strategy of Keynesian demand management, meant to revive consumer demand in the depression (Cole and Macmillan, 1936; Cole, 1936a, 1937; Macmillan, 1936b).

The programme thus promised to break the stranglehold of the slump, to ensure full employment and social welfare, and at the same time to gather electoral support behind the Popular Front. But perhaps even more important was the fact that Keynes' economics offered all this without involving the Front's supporters in any deep ideological debate about the future shape of British society. His new policy-paradigm constituted a compromise congenial to both sides: it promised to satisfy immediate socialist and progressive priorities by generating full employment; yet it also met Macmillan's Conservative preconditions by achieving recovery by the indirect tools of fiscal and monetary demand management, and without direct state controls of private enterprise. In other words, Keynes made political agreement possible by demonstrating that prosperity could be had with only minor modifications of the status quo. 'The important thing', Macmillan explained to Cole, 'is ... not so much now to argue about the outward forms of control and ownership but to find out what we ought to do about monetary policy under capitalism or planned, controlled capitalism' (Cole and Macmillan, 1936: 42). Thus while the fear of appeasement may have led Macmillan to expand his search for allies to the left wing of the contemporary political spectrum, it was Keynes who provided the grounds for his embrace of the kind of progressive social and economic reforms which made this political alliance possible.

Despite this breakthrough, the Popular Front campaign never coalesced into a viable opposition movement, much less a serious threat to the National Government. Its failure was due mainly to the adamant refusal of the opposition parties to co-operate either with one another or with the proponents of the fledgling Front. Faced with such intransigence, this early stage of the Popular Front movement rapidly fell apart as its supporters drifted back to their respective parties. Macmillan himself returned to the Conservative whip early in 1937. However, he continued to be active in opposition against appeasement, and to play a prominent role in the sporadic negotiations between the Tory group of anti-appeasers and the Labour Party. More importantly, his own thought also continued to be preoccupied by his earlier work on the Popular Front programme. Its ideas certainly dominated his last and most notable contribution to the interwar policy debate: *The Middle Way* of 1938.

Its rationale for reform echoed the basic themes of its author's position since the mid-1930s. In Macmillan's view, the UK was threatened by the spectre of dictatorship both at home and abroad. At home, the threat was chronic economic decay and the possibility that unrelieved distress would drive the masses into the arms of extremists; abroad, the threat was the menacing posture of the fascist regimes, which had themselves been born of the economic crisis and disillusionment with democracy on the continent. Unfortunately, British political leaders were too preoccupied with the stale ideological controversy between the opposites of *laissez-faire* and state socialism to notice the real dangers confronting the nation, much less to unite behind a constructive response. Yet, unless the forces of democracy came together to deal with the pressing economic and international challenges, the cause of freedom could easily succumb to either the enticing appeal of extremist ideologies or the military might of the dictators. *The Middle Way* thus represented Macmillan's attempt to articulate the Conservative terms for such a *rapprochement*: a 'middle way' which would allow for a broad alignment of democrats of all political faiths in the interests of unity against both the domestic and external evils (Macmillan, 1938: 1–18).

Macmillan's outline of such a compromise position also rested on policies familiar from the Popular Front campaign, including the mixed economy and Keynesian planning for full employment. Where *The Middle Way* broke new ground was in Macmillan's exposition of an extensive programme of social reform. This programme built upon earlier Next Five Years and Popular Front social policy themes, but this time Macmillan outlined a far more comprehensive blueprint for a welfare strategy designed to guarantee every citizen 'an irreducible minimum standard of life'. To achieve this aim, Macmillan called for minimum wage legislation, children's allowances and a 'national nutrition policy' based on the production and distribution of essential foodstuffs by state-owned public utilities. Even more ambitious was his suggestion for state provision of housing, electricity and fuel supply to the needy. The whole project was presented as the first step towards a welfare system which would ensure a minimum supply of necessities for everyone. As before, Macmillan defended public spending on welfare as not only a 'humanitarian thing', but also a vital tool of Keynesian economic management. By providing the poor with a guaranteed minimum level of income and conditions, such policies would put a 'bottom' to consumer demand, stabilize purchasing power and thus help iron out the trade cycle (1938: 38–104, 301–70).

This was all quite radical stuff, conveyed in a language far closer to the collectivist left than any of Macmillan's previous writings. Yet we should not forget that Macmillan was outlining a 'middle way', and that he therefore balanced his collectivist proposals with more Conservative priorities. Indeed, side by side with its bold collectivist message, the book mounted a spirited defence of private enterprise, arguing that, once the state took sufficient powers over the economy to guarantee full employment and minimum social standards, there was no reason why society could not continue to rely on private enterprise to provide the drive and initiative necessary for further social and economic progress. In fact, though he now favoured public ownership of the major utilities, the Bank of England and the various trades involved in the provision of the essential foodstuffs included in the social minimum, Macmillan also insisted that his strategy would make unnecessary any further extension of control or ownership by the state. The combination of Keynesian fiscal and monetary policies would provide the state with more than adequate tools for effective management of the national economy:

'For, although it will not control the enterprises engaged upon production, it will control the conditions to which these enterprises respond' (1938: 300). Macmillan's 'middle way' thus rested on a characteristic compromise, which endorsed a dilution of capitalism by a large dose of strategic state management, including a broadening field for public enterprise to secure minimum human needs, but which was also meant to justify the continued existence of private enterprise outside the areas conceded to the state. Indeed, in keeping with his established views on industrial organization, Macmillan again envisioned that the private sector would be granted the powers of statutory self-government (1938: 194–239).

The contested legacy

The Middle Way has since become something of a legend in the history of modern politics, as an influential statement of a revised Conservatism which first spelled out the terms for the Tory side of the postwar consensus. It was certainly treated in this light by his colleagues in the Popular Front movement, including G.D.H. Cole, whose 1938 review declared the book to have a 'great deal in common' with Labour policy, and suggested that it could easily serve as the basis for co-operation with the more enlightened Tories (Cole, 1938). During the war, its centrist approach and many of its ideas were also embraced by reforming Tories like R.A. Butler, Robert Boothby and the Tory Reform Group in their efforts to push the Conservative Party in a more progressive direction (Boothby, 1943; Tory Reform Committee, 1943). Yet they were at the time resolutely ignored by mainstream Conservative opinion. It was only the shock of electoral defeat in 1945 that finally induced the Conservatives to rethink both their own position and their attitude to Macmillan's message.

Macmillan, who had risen to prominence on Churchill's coat-tails during the war, became directly involved in the refashioning of the Tory programme after 1945 and played a leading role on the policy committee which produced *The Industrial Charter* of 1947. The *Charter*, which signalled the party's belated accommodation to the new Keynesian consensus, has been described by another of its authors as a 'second edition' of *The Middle Way* (Lord Butler, 1971: 144; see also Hoffman, 1964; Ramsden, 1980). Crucially, it adhered closely to Macmillan's original recipe for a Conservative 'middle way', endorsing central demand management for full employment, while at the same time extolling the virtues of private enterprise and rejecting any more direct interference with industry (Conservative and Unionist Central Office, 1947). But no less important was the political symbolism of Macmillan's prewar thought. Although the 'mixed economy' and the welfare state established by the postwar Labour governments went considerably beyond Macmillan's original vision in *The Middle Way*, the very existence of his earlier proposals served to validate the Tories' adhesion to the new social democratic consensus. The great irony is that Macmillan's rebellious attempt in the 1930s to revive the long-lost tradition of 'one nation' Toryism, so roundly rejected by the party at the time, now came to be employed to legitimize its hurried reclamation of this very same tradition. As Quintin Hogg insisted in 1947: 'Conservatives have always sought progress along *The Middle Way*' (Hogg, 1959: 137; Greenleaf, 1983; Schwarz, 1991).

Macmillan himself climbed quickly up the political ladder after 1945, greatly assisted by his own dramatic transformation from his prewar persona of a dissident intellectual into the polished Edwardian grandee of the 1950s. But he also reaffirmed his reputation as a social reformer when, as the Minister of Housing in 1951–4, he managed to meet and surpass the government's improbable election promise to build 300,000 houses a year. Both his career and brand of progressive Toryism reached their pinnacle when he succeeded Anthony Eden as Prime Minister in 1957, and rallied his party to an unexpected victory in the general election of 1959. In power, Macmillan sought to steer the middle course of the welfare state and Keynesian full employment in between the extremes of the socialism of the opposition Labour Party and the Conservatives' own discredited *laissez-faire* past. His notorious boast during the 1959 election that Britain had 'never had it so good' may have been a crude journalistic paraphrase of his actual words, but it was not an inaccurate assessment of the projected image of Macmillan's Conservatism.

Yet, despite this astonishing personal vindication, Macmillan's impact on Conservative thought and policy has been remarkably short-lived. Certainly, while *The Middle Way* may have served to validate the Conservative ideological turnabout after 1945, and Macmillan's leadership helped even more directly to revive the long-neglected strain of paternalistic Toryism, neither can be said to have brought about a permanent shift in the ideological balance of power within the party. Although the party endorsed the welfare state in opposition and maintained its institutions once in power, Conservative social policy in the 1950s was at best a grudging inheritance from their Labour predecessors, maintained with increasing reluctance only because of the party's unwillingness to risk a repeat of the débâcle of 1945 (Raison, 1990; Jones, 1991). Conservative economic discourse in the 1950s also suggests that, despite the formal commitment in the *Industrial Charter*, the party did not embrace the new economics with unreserved enthusiasm (Howard, 1987: ch. 11; Rollings, 1988).

Moreover, by the time Macmillan himself came to power at the end of the decade, the Keynesian foundations of the welfare state were already beginning to crumble. The hopes of managed growth had been replaced by the reality of the debilitating 'stop–go' cycle of alternating rounds of reflation and deflation, while the benefits of full employment appeared increasingly overshadowed by the growing menace of inflation and recurrent balance of payments crises. Macmillan's belated attempts in 1961–2 to impose a measure of planning on to the Keynesian market economy, in the shape of a national incomes policy and the tripartite National Economic Development Council, failed to halt the decay. All this fuelled the rise of a new generation of party dissidents, although this time they harked back to the neo-liberal economics of the prewar days. The resignation in 1958 of Macmillan's entire team of Treasury ministers over their opposition to the rising levels of public spending, and Macmillan's own firing in 1962 of another Chancellor of the Exchequer, Selwyn Lloyd, over his similarly deflationary policy preferences were only the most notable incidents which signalled the rapid erosion of Conservative allegiance both to the Keynesian paradigm and Macmillan's related brand of progressive Toryism. Indeed, Edward Heath's next Conservative government began in 1970 by repudiating Macmillan's Keynesian legacy, although economic adversity soon forced it into a humiliating retreat. However, Margaret Thatcher's election to the Conservative leadership in 1975 finally confirmed the party's triumphant return to neo-liberal Conservatism, brought suitably up to date in the scholarly guise of monetarist economic theory. Although monetarism itself did not survive for long, Thatcher's governments after 1979 formally renounced the commitment to full employment and moved aggressively to dismantle the edifice of the welfare state.

Macmillan has since become one of the contested symbols in the bitter internal struggle for the soul of the Conservative Party. For the defeated Tory 'wets', he serves as an important ideological icon in their rearguard struggle for the preservation of 'progressive Toryism' within the party. Although their confidence in the Keynesian approach has been greatly undermined by intervening experience, and their support for state welfare is lukewarm at best, the wets continue to stress active social policy and pragmatic government intervention in the economy as vital preconditions of both balanced economic development and the historic Tory priorities of social cohesion and harmony. From this perspective, they contrast Macmillan's ideological flexibility to the rigid *laissez-faire* beliefs of the dominant Thatcherite tendency, often suggesting that the dogmatism of the latter places its adherents outside the Tory tradition of sensible adaptation (Gilmour, 1977, 1983; Pym, 1985; Raison, 1990). Michael Helestine, who came perhaps the closest to reviving Macmillan's rebellious spirit in the 1980s, and who has put forward an industrial strategy of closer government–industry co-operation which strongly echoes many of the initiatives undertaken by Macmillan's government early in the 1960s, continues to hail Macmillan's legacy as 'proof of the Party's commitment to an undivided society' (Heseltine, 1987: 96–129). Shortly before his death, Macmillan himself joined the Tory critics of the Thatcher governments with his own occasional forays in defence of the 'middle way', including the devastating 'family silver' speech of November 1985.

Yet the influence of such ideas within the party has been effectively marginalized with the ascendancy of the neo-liberal Thatcherites, who regard the postwar politics of the 'middle way' as a corrupt and debilitating compromise with socialism which diverted the party from the true Conservative path. They hold Macmillan particularly to blame for this aberration, and revile him as an irresponsible opportunist who sold out his party's ideological heritage, and the country's long-term economic future, for the fleeting electoral success of inflationary Keynesianism (Joseph, 1976). Indeed, for many in the party today,

Macmillan scarcely qualifies as a Conservative. According to the historian Norman Gash, Macmillan's economic and social thought was 'despite the promotional label of *The Middle Way*, closer to contemporary socialist policy than any recognizable Tory tradition' (*The Times*, 31 December 1986). Whatever the merits of such arguments, pragmatic flexibility has clearly not fallen entirely out of fashion within the Conservative Party, as renewed fears of electoral calamity recently induced the party to turn out Margaret Thatcher herself. Whether this most recent turnabout also represents a return to the substance of Macmillan's Toryism remains to be seen.

References

Addison, C. (1977) *The Road to 1945*, London: Quarto.

Boothby, R. (1943) *The New Economy*, London: Secker and Warburg.

Boothby, R., de V. Loder, J., Macmillan, H. and Stanley, O. (1927) *Industry and the State: A Conservative view*, London: Macmillan.

Lord Butler (1971) *The Art of the Possible*, London: Cape.

Cole, G.D.H. (1936a) 'Planning and socialism', *New Statesman*, 9 May.

Cole, G.D.H. (1936b) 'A British People's Front: why and how?', *Political Quarterly*, Oct–Dec.

Cole, G.D.H. (1937) *The People's Front*, London: Gollancz.

Cole, G.D.H. (1938) 'Half-way house', *New Statesman*, 18 June.

Cole, G.D.H. and Macmillan, H. (1936) 'After dinner dialogues: can we abolish unemployment?', *Service*, V, 2, pp. 37–51.

Conservative and Unionist Central Office (1947) *The Industrial Charter*, London: CUCO.

Conze, E. and Wilkinson E. (1934) *Why Fascism?*, London: Selwyn and Blount.

Crossley, A., Ellis, G., Glossop, C.W.H., Heilgers, F., Kerr, H., Lindsay, K., Lindsay, N., Macmillan, H., Martin, T.B., Molson, H., Peat, C., Percy, E., Tree, R. and Watt, H. (1935) *Planning for Employment*, London: Macmillan.

Gilmour, Sir I. (1977) *Inside the Right*, London: Hutchinson.

Gilmour, Sir I. (1983) *Britain Can Work*, Oxford: Martin Robertson.

Greenleaf, W.H. (1983) *The British Political Tradition*, Vol. 2, *The Ideological Heritage*, London: Methuen.

Heseltine, M. (1987) *Where There Is a Will*, London: Hutchinson.

Hoffman, J.D. (1964) *The Conservative Party in Opposition*, London: MacGibbon.

Hogg, Q. (1959) *The Case for Conservatism* (revised edn), Harmondsworth: Penguin. First published 1947.

Horne, A. (1988) *Macmillan, 1894–1956*, London: Macmillan.

Howard, A. (1987) *The Life of R.A. Butler*, London: Jonathan Cape.

Jay, D. (1937) *The Socialist Case*, London: Faber.

Jones, H. (1991) 'New tricks for an old dog?: The Conservatives and social policy, 1951–5', in Gorst, A., Johnman, L. and Lucas, W. Scott (eds) *Contemporary British History 1931–1961*, London: Pinter.

Joseph, Sir K. (1976) *Stranded on the Middle Ground?*, London: Centre for Policy Studies.

Kennedy, T.C. (1974) 'The Next Five Years group and the failure of the politics of agreement in Britain', *Canadian Journal of History*, IX, 1, pp. 45–68.

Macmillan, H. (1929) 'Where is Conservatism going?', *Saturday Review*, 2 November 1929.
Macmillan, H. (1932) 269 HC Deb. 5s., 4 November
Macmillan, H. (1933a) *Reconstruction: A plea for a national policy*, London: Macmillan.
Macmillan, H. (1933b) 275 HC Deb. 5s., 8 March.
Macmillan, H. (1933c) 275 HC Deb. 5s., 22 March.
Macmillan, H. (1934a) 'A plea for an "above party" policy', *New Britain*, 17 January.
Macmillan, H. (1934b) 'My reply to Eimar O'Duffy', *New Britain*, 7 February.
Macmillan, H. (1934c) 'Trade unionism in the society of the future', *Listener*, 4 July.
Macmillan, H. (1935) 300 HC Deb. 5s., 3 April.
Macmillan, H. (1936a) 312 HC Deb. 5s., 20 May.
Macmillan, H. (1936b) 'Outline for an economic policy', *New Outlook*, June.
Macmillan, H. (1936c) 'In defence of liberty', *New Outlook*, October.
Macmillan, H. (1937a) 'Prospect and retrospect', *New Outlook*, February.
Macmillan, H. (1937b) 'Looking forward', *New Outlook*, May.
Macmillan, H. (1938) *The Middle Way*, London: Macmillan.
Macmillan, H. (1966) *Winds of Change*, London: Macmillan.
Marquand, D. (1988) *The Unprincipled Society*, London: Fontana.
Marwick, A. (1964) 'Middle opinion in the thirties: planning, progress and political "agreement"', *English Historical Review*, LXXIX, pp. 285–98.
Murphy, J.T. (1934) *Fascism! The socialist answer*, London: Socialist League.
Pym, F. (1985) *The Politics of Consent*, London: Sphere.
Raison, T. (1990) *Tories and the Welfare State*, London: St Martin's.
Ramsden, J. (1980) *The Making of Conservative Party Policy since 1929*, London: Longman.
Ritschel, D. (1991) 'A corporatist economy in Britain? Capitalist planning for industrial self-government in the 1930s', *English Historical Review*, CVI, pp. 41–65.
Rollings, N. (1988) 'British budgetary policy 1945–54: A "Keynesian revolution"?', *Economic History Review*, 41, 4, pp. 283–98.
Schwarz, B. (1991) 'The tide of history: the reconstruction of Conservatism, 1945–51', in Tiratsoo, N. (ed.), *The Attlee Years*, London: Pinter.
Taylor, A.J.P. (1972) *Beaverbrook*, New York: Simon and Schuster.
The Next Five Years: An essay in agreement (1935) London: Macmillan.
Tory Reform Committee (1943) *Forward – by the right!*, London: TRC.

4 Keynes

Karel Williams and John Williams

Brief biography

John Maynard Keynes was born on 5 July 1883 in Cambridge and never really left there. He did a brief stint at the India Office (1906–8) and served in the Treasury in both world wars. After 1918 this took him to France for (part of) the Versailles peace talks; in the 1940s he went frequently to the United States, attempting with his charm and intelligence to modify the logic of the essentially suppliant British position. But for most of his life he was associated with Cambridge, shuttling between there and London, college and club, King's and Bloomsbury. After a local prep school, followed by Eton, he went to King's College as a scholar in 1902, became a fellow in 1909 and first bursar in 1924. Like his father, John Neville Keynes, before him (and after him, since his father lived on till 1949), his life was anchored in a Cambridge college. Keynes was exceptional not only for the range, but also for the depth of his interests: economics, public affairs, the arts, journalism, philosophy, rare books. His earlier homosexuality faded with his marriage in 1925 to the Diaghilev ballerina, Lydia Lopokova.

He was joint editor of the *Economic Journal* from 1911 to 1944; served on Royal Commissions (Indian Finance and Currency, 1913; Industry and Trade, 1929–31); and became chairman of the Liberal journal *The Nation* in 1923, continuing when it merged with the *New Statesman* in 1931. Keynes largely financed the establishment of the Arts Theatre, Cambridge, in 1935, was a Trustee of the National Gallery, and became Chairman of the Council for the Encouragement of Music and the Arts. He was created baron in 1942 and died on 21 April 1946.

Main ideas

Perhaps the most striking initial impression conveyed by a list of the main books written by Keynes is of the disparate nature of the subjects covered. It is not easy to see a single thread uniting *Indian Currency and Finance* (1913); *The Economic Consequences of the Peace* (1919); *A Tract on Monetary Reform* (1923); *A Short View of Russia* (1925); *The Economic Consequences of Mr Churchill* (1925); *The End of Laissez-Faire* (1926); *Can Lloyd George Do It?* (1929); *A Treatise on Money* (1930); *Essays in Persuasion* (1931); *Essays in Biography* (1933); *The General Theory of Employment, Interest and Money* (1936); *How to Pay for the War* (1940). None the less, after acknowledging the range of his thinking and without doing too much violence to the texts themselves, it is possible to see an element of unity and continuity. To do so needs only the acceptance of the overall judgement that Keynes' overarching intellectual achievement was in the subject of economics, where he made a major shift in economic thought. If this is an assumption, it is one which is much weaker than those generally needed in economic theory itself: there would not be much dissent from the view that it is Keynes the economist whose ideas still command attention.

A very rough justice is done when the ideas of so fecund an intellect are reduced to a small compass. It will be done, or attempted, by bundling a large number of topics into a very few broad themes, and by further stripping these of their technical expression. Four wide headings are used to approach, and to indicate the flavour and significance of, his thinking for twentieth-century economics. These are Keynes' recurring concern with the establishment of a workable international economic order; the level of employment within national economies and the relation of this to the levels of saving and investment; the importance of uncertainty in determining behaviour and the significance of this for economic theories; and his perceptions of the limitations of *laissez-faire* and the need for government intervention.

The 1914–18 war acted as a catalyst for Keynes' concern over the nature of the international economy. This was a major theme of *The Economic Consequences of the Peace* (1919). If Keynes perhaps attributed too much to its function as the 'foundations on which we all lived and built', he was more clear-sighted than most about the precariousness of 'the delicate, complicated organisation' (1919: 1–2) He understood that the Versailles settlement would exacerbate the war damage already wrought on an essentially fragile international trading mechanism. Both 1925 and 1931, the UK's return to and abandonment of the gold standard, led him to question the excessive rigidity of that financial system. None the less as a life-long believer in free trade as a first-best system, Keynes was dismayed at the breakdown of the multilateral trading system in the 1930s. Much of his time at the Treasury during the Second World War was thus given to thinking about how a stable multilateral international economy could be restored.

There were three central ingredients to his solution. First, there needed to be some flexibility in exchange rates, the so-called moveable peg. Countries were to fix their exchange rates, but where a country was in 'fundamental disequilibrium' over its foreign trade balance, the level could be adjusted. Devaluation was seen as an alternative to deflation as a method of correction for deficit countries. Second, creditor as well as debtor countries should be required to take positive steps – revaluation and/or inflation – to correct international imbalances. One of the major deficiencies of the gold standard was that, in practice though not in theory, all the pressure for correction fell on deficit countries: Keynes wished to redress this balance. Third, Keynes felt that short-run disequilibria could and should be prevented from forcing countries into downward escalating deflation, by providing sources of international finance which could (at a cost) be automatically drawn upon. There should be an international 'bank of last resort', akin to the service provided for domestic commercial banks by the national central banks.

How far these ideas were incorporated into the post-1945 settlement is still a matter for discussion and debate. But there can be little doubt that Keynes' attempt to reconstruct an international financial system which would allow a robust and feasible mutilateral international economy to flourish was central to his life-long commitment to liberal values. Equally, his position as the UK's central negotiator at all the major wartime discussions enabled him to ensure that some influence attached to his ideas. For a man whose economic thoughts and theories nearly always had some direct connection with policies, this was a culmination of sorts.

The post-1945 international settlement had been preceded in the 1930s by an almost universal preoccupation of countries with their domestic economic affairs. In the UK, the issue which dominated the interwar years was the level of unemployment. The emergence of the new phenomenon of persistent mass unemployment seemed to fit uneasily with the implicit assumption, which saturated orthodox economics, that there could be no involuntary unemployment except of the most temporary kind. Attempts at reconciliation (Pigou, 1927; Beveridge, 1930) asserted that the application of the theoretical conclusions had been impeded by the disruptions of war and the obstruction of trade unions, which slowed structural change and prevented wages being brought back into line with prices. If the plausibility of this diminished as the war receded and after the defeat of the unions in the General Strike of 1926, the existing theory still prevailed. It was partly on this rock that the pragmatic proposals for reducing unemployment made by Keynes at this time foundered. To overcome these theoretical objections, Keynes brought to fruition his long-pondered alternative analysis of the determination of the level of employment in a capitalist society. In his *General Theory* (1936), probably the most influential work in economics in the twentieth century, Keynes sought to demonstrate – among other things – that under an unregulated capitalist economy the existence of a stable (equilibrium) position of underemployment was both possible and likely.

A central thread in this fundamental reappraisal was that there could be a more or less permanent deficiency in aggregate demand. The key to this was the possible failure of investment to fill all the gap left in the economy by the savings which were taken out. Savings were not fully and automatically transformed into investment simply by adjusting the rate of interest: investment was instead determined by the confidence and expectations of businesspeople. And if the level of investment fell short of what was needed to create a full employment level of activity within the economy, there was no automatic self-correcting mechanism which would necessarily prevent an underemployment equilibrium. One way of restoring demand to a full employment level was, Keynes suggested, through the government running a budgetary deficit by raising its expenditure and/or reducing taxation.

Keynes' analysis of the determinants of investment and his proposals for influencing the level of demand lead on to the other two aspects of his thinking singled out here: his emphasis on uncertainty and the need for positive intervention. Each of these had long been maturing in his agile mind. *A Tract on Monetary Reform* (1923) had been characterized by its stress on the role of uncertainty in shaping economic decisions. In the *Treatise on Money* (1930) this had been extended to a general examination of economic fluctuations, while many of the basic concepts of the *General Theory* (1936) were based on human behaviour driven by uncertainty, expectation and 'animal spirits'. These conclusions were based on a methodology which is highly relevant to social issues generally. In his *Treatise on Probability*, Keynes had already taken the view that the prediction of human behaviour and events could not be addressed successfully through the principles of statistical probability (1921: 334–9); an additional ingredient of 'Intuition or some further *a priori* principle' was needed (*Collected Writings*, hereafter *CW*: vol. viii, 94). The reservations of Keynes over the usefulness of statistical probability to 'explain economic outcomes that come into being under uncertainty' (Rima, 1988: 12–22) serve as a pertinent cautionary comment on the post-1950 conquest of economic methodology by econometrics. But Keynes was far from opposed to empirical research and the use of statistics – indeed, he was at the centre of most such initiatives at the time – and he took the view that, while natural science could treat its material as constant and homogeneous, it was dangerous to do so in economics, which 'deals with motives, expectations, psychological uncertainties' (*CW*: vol. xiv, 300, letter to R.F. Harrod, 16 July 1938). He would have had no hesitation about extending this verdict to the social sciences generally.

Perhaps the most pervasive theme unifying Keynes' intellectual development was the increasing emergence of the notion of the justification and necessity for positive intervention in the economy and society. This was especially significant for one who had been nurtured in nineteenth-century liberalism and steeped in its most rigorous expression, English classical economics. From his initial civil service career at the India Office in 1906 to his First World War stint at the Treasury and his repugnance at the 1919 peace settlement (Skidelsky, 1983: esp. 175–9, 297–300, 376–7), Keynes became increasingly eager to intervene in public affairs. This was the theme which unified the *Essays in Persuasion* (1931) – those 'croakings of a Cassandra who could never influence the course of events in time' (1931: v.). In particular, Keynes was seeking to break the *laissez-faire* mould into which economics had long settled. Hence the importance of his conclusion in *The End of Laissez-Faire* that:

> The world is *not* so governed from above that private and social interest always coincide. It is *not* so managed here below that in practice they coincide. It is *not* a correct deduction from the principles of economics that enlightened self-interest always operates in the public interest . . . Experience does not show that individuals, when they make up a social unit, are less clear-sighted than when they act separately. (*CW*: vol. ix, 287).

Keynes actively practised what he preached. The high points were perhaps his attack in *The Economic Consequences of Mr Churchill* (1925) on the decision to return to the gold standard at the pre-1914 parity; his active furtherance of the Liberal case for a large programme of public expenditure in the 1929 election; the ingenious anti-inflationary scheme for turning high taxes into postwar credits in *How to Pay for the War* (1940); and his role as architect of the post-1945 international economy. But he was more or less constantly seeking to shift economic policies through journalism, radio broadcasts and the use of his contacts in high places. None of this should be interpreted as a rejection of capitalism *per se*. On the contrary, as will be argued below, he saw capitalism as the most reliable basis for his transcending values of liberty.

Keynes' ideas and social welfare

Keynes' economics always reflected a tension between the attractions of theory and the necessities, as he perceived them, of public policy. It could be said that it was this tension which led him to rethink theory and contributed to the slow evolution of the *General Theory*. Between Keynes' ideas and social welfare there was not so much a tension as a paradox. The basis of this paradox is that, while Keynes rarely said anything directly about social welfare, his ideas were central to its acceptance – and the forms taken by that acceptance – in the UK after 1945. The first task is thus to establish the broad validity, or otherwise, of this paradox.

The first proposition – the absences – might at one level seem inherently implausible given Keynes' desire to shape public policy. But in fact his interventions all centre on such questions as returning (and leaving) the gold standard, public works, the level of investment, the desirability – in particular circumstances – of tariffs, and the proper structure for an international economy. Among these high issues of finance and macroeconomics it is difficult to find traces of interest in industrial and regional policies, much less social issues. The substantial research and literature during the 1930s on urban poverty and the human effects of unemployment seem not to have touched him, or at least not to have elicited anything in the way of recorded comment.

The last point draws attention to the fact that, at another level, Keynes' relative lack of concern about issues of social welfare can be decisively and dramatically demonstrated. A reasonably attentive trawl through the thirty volumes of the collected works of Keynes nets only a very few, and small, social welfare fish. They would certainly be outweighed by his learned reflections on ancient coinages. There are occasional references to the working class, but mostly as a concept: it seems doubtful if Keynes' direct experience reached even as far as that of Lytton Strachey, which seems to have been confined to the close proximity necessitated by a First World War Conscientious Board medical, where he marvelled at the whiteness of their skin. Certainly not for Keynes a postgraduate stint in an East End settlement like Beveridge: at that stage he was captured by G.E. Moore's philosophy, which made a 'religion' of love, beauty and hedonism. Nor was there much contact with working-class leaders, unless they happened to be prime ministers or cabinet ministers. He took Bevin to his London clubs for lunch – but largely to bend the ear of a fellow member of the Royal Commission on Industry and Trade. As early as 1904 Pigou had described Keynes as clear-headed rather than human, and it is perhaps a not unjust description of the range, though not the depth, of his sympathies (Skidelsky, 1983: 125). It is indicative that the term 'social welfare' (or any reasonable proxy) does not force its way into the index of either of the first two Skidelsky volumes on Keynes, or into the indices of two volumes specifically directed to looking at Keynes' links with public policy (Hamouda and Smithin, 1988a, 1988b).

All this reflected Keynes' lifestyle (from 1926 he added minor county squirehood to the other 'grandee' aspects when he leased Tilton in Sussex); his philosophy; his politics; and his intellectual interests. He was always aloof from working-class concerns and not particularly sensitive to them. Even when, at the time of the General Strike in 1926, he declared that 'my feelings as distinct from my judgement are with the workers' (*CW*: vol. xix, 530–2) this somewhat equivocal support mostly rested on their role as the abrupt and hapless victims of the 1925 return to the gold standard: indeed, it is difficult to suppress the thought that Keynes (the polemicist) almost welcomed the way their plight so rapidly vindicated his view of the economics of Mr Churchill.

The demonstration of the second proposition – the centrality of Keynes' ideas to the postwar social settlement – is more complex. It can perhaps be suppressed into a simple analogy: what Keynes did was to provide the legs for the three-legged stool on which the post-1945 social welfare structure was, for a time, solidly settled; and when, over time, this stool became increasingly rickety, the cause could largely be traced to the dangerous erosion of one of these legs. One substantial leg is derived from the extent to which Keynes provided both the instruments and the justification for their use, which are essential to social welfare. Another derived from the role of Keynes as assistant midwife to the 1942 report: from the support and encouragement he gave to Beveridge during the drafting of the White Paper on *Social Insurance and Allied Services*, and even more from the assistance he gave towards, if not removing, then circumventing Treasury opposition. But above all, if Keynes had not seemingly provided a solution to mass unemployment, the nature and scope of the postwar social welfare experiment would certainly have been different.

Almost any meaningful provision of social services requires some intervention against the free operation of the market. And any such intervention requires instruments for leverage. Those proposed by Keynes were confined almost entirely to monetary and fiscal policy. Once accepted, the purposes for which these instruments could be used were capable of substantial expansion, but for Keynes himself they were deliberately limited and for a limited end. Keynes did not intend them for such things as income redistribution, or regional and industrial policy: they were essentially to influence and control the level of investment in order to sustain a high level of activity.

The restriction of method and purpose was a direct consequence of Keynes' overall political and philosophical objective. He wished to maintain capitalism, but his experience and analysis suggested that unrestricted capitalism was inherently unstable, which endangered its continuance in a broadly democratic society. The fiercest opposition to his schemes came, as he expected, from the main beneficiaries: 'the capitalist leaders in the City and Parliament are incapable of distinguishing novel measures for safeguarding capitalism from what they call Bolshevism' (*CW*: vol. ix, 297). Keynes saw *laissez-faire* as no longer adequate: intelligent intervention was required. Intelligent, but also – and perhaps especially – minimal intervention. 'I seek to improve the machinery of society, not overturn it' (*CW*: vol. ix, 250, letter to Sir Charles Addis, 28 July 1924). Keynes wished to see investment sustained to keep up the level of income and activity, but beyond such occasional and limited action, the market could then be left to operate. His stance on liberal collectivism carried an implication of as much liberalism – and as little collectivism – as possible. And capitalism was the most desirable – or, at least, the best available – social organization for 'respecting and promoting the individual – his freedom of choice, his faith, his mind and its expression, his enterprise and his property' (quoted by Cranston, in Thirlwall 1978: 112).

The impact of Keynes on welfare policies and debates

The leverage which Keynes provided for social welfare policies was greater than that provided by his specific policy instruments. His work was more influential through the general case that he made, in both his theoretical work and his policy pronouncements, for government action. He constantly reiterated his early conviction that the conditions had disappeared which had made nineteenth-century *laissez-faire* feasible:

> I abandon *laissez-faire* – not enthusiastically, not from contempt of that good, old doctrine, but because whether we like it or not, the conditions for its success have

disappeared. It was a double doctrine – it entrusted the public weal to private enterprise *unchecked* and *unaided*. Private enterprise is no longer unchecked . . . and if . . . not unchecked we cannot leave it unaided. (*CW*: vol. ix, 248, 7 June 1924).

From this negative, it was a short march for Keynes to assert the positive:

> I believe that some considerable act of intelligent judgement is required as to the scale on which it is desirable that the community as a whole should save . . . I do not believe that these matters should be left entirely to the chances of private judgement and private profits, as they are at present. (*CW*: vol. ix, 292, *The End of Laissez-Faire*).

It may be that the influence of Keynes' ideas in shaping attitudes and conjuring atmospheres makes this his major contribution to promoting social welfare, but such influences evade measurement or certainty. Nor is it possible to quantify his contribution to Beveridge's wartime White Paper, but the latter is at least more directly observable. Treasury opinion was mostly opposed to the Beveridge proposals; disturbed at the way Beveridge had converted the June 1941 intention of a review of existing social service arrangements into a new comprehensive scheme; and alarmed at the potential costs. Beveridge asked for, and Keynes gave, advice and assistance. From the *Collected Writings* (vol. xxvii) it is abundantly clear that Keynes, despite his quite different Treasury responsibilities, spent much time in the crucial period between March and October 1942 helping to make more acceptable these proposals for 'a vast constructive reform of real importance' (*CW*: vol. xxvii, 204, Keynes to Beveridge, 17 March 1942). He urged on Beveridge modifications (especially on child allowances and pensions, and especially during a transitional period) which would make large savings in cost, enabling Keynes then to urge on his Treasury colleagues the modesty of Beveridge's demands upon the Exchequer once the contributions from employers and employees were allowed for (see, especially, *CW*: vol. xxvii, 246-53, Keynes to Sir Richard Hopkins, 13 Oct. 1942). Keynes was, indeed, still commenting on the final version of the report on its way to the printers. He had wished to make support of Beveridge the occasion of his maiden speech in the Lords (but refrained because his Treasury colleagues would have been offended); and he expressed dismayed surprise when the wartime coalition government – which initially had been frightened by the cost – proposed a more lavish and expensive immediate scheme for pensions, the extra cost of which arguably largely undermined a major contributory plank of the Beveridge scheme (*CW*: vol. xxvii, 253–5, 256, 261–3).

However one assesses the effects of Keynes' mediating efforts between Beveridge and the Treasury in 1942, there can still be little doubt that Keynes' main contribution to social welfare came indirectly through his attention to unemployment. The concern with unemployment was central to his theoretical and political thinking for much of the interwar years; the level of unemployment was (and is) equally central to the building and maintenance of a social welfare system. It could plausibly be said that Keynes seemed little concerned with the unemployed, who receive almost no mention in his writings, but concentrated on the concept of unemployment, which he saw as 'wasteful' and 'inefficient', and as an indicator of the need to adjust the existing capitalist order. But there was no doubt that it dominated his thinking: 'heavens,' he wrote in reply to one critic of the *General Theory*, 'my doctrine of full employment is what the whole book is about' (*CW*: vol. xiv, 22–7, letter to D.H. Robertson, 1936). In *Social Insurance and Allied Services*, Beveridge similarly emphasizes the strategic role of employment in the assertion that 'a satisfactory scheme of social insurance assumes the maintenance of employment and the prevention of mass unemployment' (Beveridge, 1942: 163).

But are the two connected and does it matter? Beveridge's economics had always been of the most orthodox. The conclusion of his 1909 book on unemployment had been about the need to make 'reality correspond with the assumptions of economic theory' (Beveridge, 1909: 231); even in 1930 this was repeated unchanged in the second edition; and soon afterwards Beveridge had offered Hayek a chair at the London School of Economics (LSE) in part specifically to counter Keynes' Cambridge heresies, since Beveridge 'heartily dislikes Keynes and regards him as a quack in economics' (Skidelsky, 1992: 400, quoting Beatrice Webb, 22 Sept. 1931). Beveridge's hostile, but uncomprehending, response to the *General Theory* provoked the short, sharp riposte 'that I have really had a total failure in my attempt to convey to you what I am driving at' (*CW*: vol. xiv, 56, letter to W.H. Beveridge, 28 July 1936). Beveridge felt so strongly that he 'publicly denounced [*The General Theory*] in his farewell oration to LSE' (Harris, 1977: 331).

This backlog of antagonism lends plausibility to José Harris' assertion that the theories of Keynes had little influence on Beveridge in the construction of the 1942 report (Harris, 1977: 492). It could be said, however, that this ignores the supporting effect given to Keynes' view by rearmament, the war and his pamphlet on *How to Pay for the War*, to say nothing of the possibility (to put it mildly) that Keynes would have exercised his considerable powers of persuasion at their various discussions at clubland tables between the spring and autumn of 1942. Be that as it may, Keynes himself immediately made the connection between his policies for full employment and those of Beveridge for a comprehensive social welfare system. In the critical debate within the Treasury on the macroeconomic prospects for the UK after the end of the Second World War, the essential difference between the pessimists (led by Henderson) and the optimists (led by Keynes) turned on assumptions about the level of unemployment. Henderson's memo, fearful of inflation and chained to expectations of an action replay of post-1919, seemed to be 'scared to death lest there might be some date at which the figure of unemployment fell below three million' (*CW*: vol. xxvii, 271, comment on Treasury memo, 8 April 1942). Keynes not only plumped for much lower unemployment (an average of 5 per cent), but stressed the interconnections:

high employment would increase incomes (and taxes), allowing the setting aside of 'say, £50 millions a year for the next twenty years' to be spent adding amenities to 'the civic life of every great centre of population' (characteristically, Keynes saw these amenities mostly in the form of new universities, theatres, concert halls and galleries, but also cafés and dance halls); but the provision of these facilities would at the same time help to ensure a high level of employment. 'We shall, in fact, have built our New Jerusalem out of the labour which in our former vain folly we were keeping unused and unhappy in enforced idleness' (*CW*: vol. xxvii, 269-71, postwar employment policy, 1942).

Whatever may have been the situation in 1942, there were no doubts in 1944 when Beveridge produced *Full Employment in a Free Society*, where the inspiration was explicitly Keynesian. Full employment was to be the instrument through which Beveridge's evil giants (Want, Disease, Squalor and Ignorance) were to be, if not killed, then kept in chains. Beveridge's notion of full employment was, moreover, full-blooded: an average of 3 per cent (which even Keynes thought unattainable), and 'having always more vacant jobs than unemployed men' (Beveridge, 1944: 121). For almost a generation it seemed to work: with unemployment *always* below even Beveridge's 'wildly optimistic' *average* figure, it proved possible to sustain benefits without raising too much opposition to the regressive poll tax basis of contributions. But from about 1970 the whole social settlement came to be called more into question as governments – especially after 1980 – burst through the supposed political road block preventing unemployment straying over one million.

By the early 1990s there were, and had been, a variety of factors, ideological and otherwise, threatening the level and range of social welfare provision; but there had also emerged a powerful and, more or less, objective factor. With three million plus unemployed (and their families) to add to the increasing armies of the aged and single parents, the number of people dependent on income support was reaching towards one-third of the total population. It was simply becoming politically infeasible that the remaining two-thirds would contribute on the scale required to maintain earlier relative levels. Whatever the causes and possibilities, the removal of full employment does demonstrate how closely tied to its existence was the system of social welfare. In this respect, Keynes despite having little to say directly on the subject, was crucially important to the post-1945 provision of social welfare in the UK.

Key texts

Most of the writings of Keynes can be seen as leading towards, or contributing to, the mature expression on his economic ideas in the *Treatise on Money* (1930) and *The General Theory of Employment, Interest and Money* (1936). This can be seen as early as 1919. Keynes left the peace conference in 1919 because of his objection to the harsh economic terms it was intending to impose on Germany,

an action doubtless reflecting those Bloomsbury values which had led him in
1916 – despite his Treasury exemption – to apply for military exemption on
conscientious grounds (Skidelsky, 1983: xxiv). But *The Economic Consequences of
the Peace* (1919), the hugely influential book he wrote, expressed more than his
indignation at what he saw as a dangerous injustice; it also stressed his new
realization that the conflict had revealed the fragility of the pre-1914 economic
settlement, both nationally and internationally. Internally, it had depended on
the willingness of the industrial entrepreneurs not simply to not-spend but to
invest:

> Europe was so organised socially and economically as to secure the maximum
> accumulation of capital ... If the rich had spent their new wealth on their own
> enjoyments, the world would long ago have found such a regime intolerable. But
> like bees they saved and accumulated, not less to the advantage of the whole
> community because they themselves held narrower ends in prospect ... I seek only
> to point out that the principle of accumulation based on inequality was a vital part
> of the pre-war order of Society and of progress as we then understood it ... The
> war has disclosed the possibility of consumption to all and the vanity of abstinence
> to many. (1919: 16, 19)

Externally, Keynes showed that the delicate multilateralism of the international
trade mechanism could not accommodate such destructive sentiments as retri-
bution against a major trading partner:

> Round Germany as a central support the rest of the European economic system
> grouped itself, and on the prosperity and enterprise of Germany the prosperity of
> the rest of the Continent mainly depended ... In our own case we sent more
> exports to Germany than to any other country in the world except India ... If we
> aim deliberately at the impoverishment of Central Europe, vengeance, I dare predict,
> will not limp. (1919: 14, 15)

The essential notion that free trade, the gold standard and stable internal markets
were somehow 'natural' was thus being implicitly questioned. Keynes was already
giving muted expression to a consistent vein of his thought: that a free capitalist
system did not run automatically but required the application of human
intelligence to the management of economic affairs. 'The economic motives and
ideals of that generation no longer satisfy us: we must find a new way' (1919: 238).

The significance of Keynes' active participation in the Liberal campaign for
the general election of 1929 is that he used the occasion to put into the form of
practical policy proposals some of the conclusions which he had earlier embodied
in his pamphlet attacking Britain's return to the gold standard in 1925. In
particular that earlier work had proclaimed that 'Deflation does not reduce wages
"automatically". It reduces them by causing unemployment' (1925b: 19). Keynes
had then concluded that what was needed to restore prosperity was an easy credit
policy. 'We want to encourage businessmen to enter on new enterprises'

(1925b: 19). These ideas were echoed and elaborated in *Can Lloyd George Do It?* (1929). This brief book was written with Hubert Henderson to explain, defend and justify the Liberal programme, at the 1929 general election, of a strong use of government expansionary activity to reduce unemployment. The programme was essentially a scheme for large-scale public investment (in roads, telephones, housing, electricity): thus the reason for such intervention was central to any justification. For this Keynes drew upon, and made accessible, his parallel reworking of fundamental theory that was to be developed in the two volumes of the *Treatise of Money* (1930). In particular, popular expression was given to the rejection of the notion that savings were, through the mechanism of the rate of interest, 'automatically' invested:

> So far from the total of investment ... being necessarily equal to the total of saving, disequilibrium between the two is at the root of many of our troubles ... When investment runs ahead of saving we have a boom, intense employment, and a tendency to inflation. When investment lags behind, we have a slump and abnormal unemployment, as at present. (1930: 35–6)

And it was this last point which was stressed to refute another common objection – again based on the orthodox assumption that the 'normal' situation was one of full employment – namely, that any additional capital expenditure by the government would lead directly to inflation:

> A large amount of deflationary slack has first to be taken up before there can be the smallest danger of a development policy leading to inflation. To bring up the bogy of inflation as an objection to capital expenditure at the present time is like warning a patient who is wasting away of the dangers of excessive corpulence. (1930: 36).

The *Essays in Biography* (1933) represent Keynes at his most wide-ranging and lucidly readable. In its original edition, it included a section of 'Sketches of politicians' and another on 'Lives of economists'; in a later (1951) edition issued after his death, his brother, Geoffrey, added three further essays, including a sparkling piece on a major scientist and 'Cambridge's greatest son', Isaac Newton. The sketches of politicians were mostly 'based on direct acquaintance' (1933: v) and included, beyond the Big Four at Versailles in 1919 (President Wilson, Clemenceau, Lloyd George and Orlando), Bonar Law, Asquith and Churchill. These varied in length and style and offered insights into himself as well as his subjects. The most well known is the piece on Lloyd George, laced with a malicious wit: 'this syren, this goat-footed bard, this half-human visitor to our age from the hag-ridden magic and enchanted woods of Celtic antiquity'. But, curiously, for one who admiringly described Newton as a 'magician' and who himself placed high value on 'intuition', Lloyd George stirred little empathy – perhaps because for Keynes, the quintessential Englishman, in Lloyd George these qualities had a Celtic 'existence outside or away from our Saxon good and evil' (1933: 35).

The more substantial lives of the economists represent both the homage of Keynes to his deep roots in the Cambridge school and also – especially in his essay on the Revd Thomas Malthus ('the first of the Cambridge economists') – some of the origins of his own alternative theories. It would probably be true that a better statement of Keynes' attempt directly to mix his economic and political philosophies can be found in the short book on The *End of Laissez-Faire* (1926), but the biographical essays are important in demonstrating his mastery of a different genre and the breadth of his intellect.

But it was only with the publication of the *General Theory* in 1936 that Keynes brought together his long struggle to rethink economics. Part of the towering significance of this text derives from the fact that the nature and import of his theoretical innovations are still a source of rumbling debate. In the half century since his death, as well as in the decade which preceded it, books and articles on all aspects of Keynes the economist have gushed forth, not least – an expressive irony – from those who deny that he made any theoretical contribution of significance. In part the sceptics draw plausibility, if not strength, from the driving force behind Keynes' development as a theorist: it arose directly from a desire to influence policy. As, from the 1960s, economics increasingly retreated into honing techniques, many of the high theorists tended, in their sniffy way, to dismiss his work as 'merely' economic policy – but it should be added that what drove some of those who took this line was antipathy towards the directions in which Keynesian policy-making pointed. Keynes had always recognized the need, though his impatience sometimes eclipsed the necessary tact, to convince other economists. This was an explicit aim of, especially, the *General Theory*, and partly explains the high abstraction and uncharacteristically clumsy arrangement of that work: 'when it appears, it will be on extremely academic lines, since I feel, rather definitely, that my object must first of all be to try and convince my economic colleagues' (*CW*: vol. xxi, 344, letter to R.H. Brand, 19 Nov. 1934).

Keynes, with characteristic confidence, had no doubt that what he had done was both different and significant: 'I believe myself to be writing a book on economic theory, which will largely revolutionise – not, I suppose, at once but in the course of the next ten years – the way the world thinks about economic problems' (*CW*: vol. viii, 42, letter to G.B. Shaw, 1 Jan. 1935). Simply expressed, the *General Theory* cut through the basic orthodox presumption of a natural tendency towards equilibrium at a high (full employment) level of activity. It did so by shifting the main object to explaining the level of employment. Although orthodox economists like Pigou and Henderson could in 1930 join Keynes in calling for *ad hoc* policies (like public works), it was still the widely accepted view of professional economists that unemployment resulted only from short-lived 'frictions, temporary disequilibrium or the monopoly power of trade unions' (*CW*: vol. viii, 42). Keynes aimed to undermine this proposition by providing a theory (the *General Theory*) of the determination of the level of employment. It was the provision of the theory, as an explicit alternative to orthodox theory, that provided the justification for the counter-cyclical policies that many were ineffectively urging on pragmatic grounds.

From this perspective, a central idea of the *General Theory* was that a stable equilibrium was possible below a full employment level. The theoretical explanations need not here concern us: it is enough to notice that ripples – and more – continue to eddy forth from the pebbles which Keynes dropped into the economic pond in 1936.

References

Beveridge, W. (1909) *Unemployment: A problem of industry*, London: Longmans, Green and Co.

Beveridge, W. (1930) *Unemployment: A problem of industry* (2nd edn), London: Longmans, Green and Co.

Beveridge, W. (1942) *Social Insurance and the Allied Services*, London: HMSO.

Beveridge, W. (1944) *Full Employment in a Free Society*, London: Allen and Unwin.

Collected Writings of J.M. Keynes.

Cutler, T., Williams, K., and Williams, J. (1986) *Keynes, Beveridge and Beyond*, London: Routledge and Kegan Paul.

Hamouda, O. and Smithin, J. (eds) (1988a) *Keynes and Public Policy after Fifty Years.* Vol. I: *Economics and Policy*, Aldershot: Edward Elgar.

Hamouda, O. and Smithin, J. (eds) (1988b) *Keynes and Public Policy after Fifty Years.* Vol. 2. *Theories and Method*, Aldershot: Edward Elgar.

Harris, J. (1977) *William Beveridge: A biography*, Oxford: Clarendon Press.

Keynes, J.M. (1913) *Indian Currency and Finance*, London: Macmillan.

Keynes, J.M. (1919) *The Economic Consequences of the Peace*, London: Macmillan.

Keynes, J.M. (1921) *A Treatise on Probability*, London: Macmillan.

Keynes, J.M. (1923) *A Tract on Monetary Reform*, London: Macmillan.

Keynes, J.M. (1925a) *A Short View of Russia*, reprinted in *Essays in Persuasion* (1931), London: Macmillan.

Keynes, J.M. (1925b) *The Economic Consequences of Mr Churchill*, London: Hogarth Press.

Keynes, J.M. (1926) *The End of Laissez-Faire*, reprinted in *Essays in Persuasion* (1931), London: Macmillan.

Keynes, J.M. (1929) *Can Lloyd George Do It?*, reprinted in *Essays in Persuasion* (1931), London: Macmillan.

Keynes, J.M. (1930) *A Treatise on Money*, 2 vols., London: Macmillan.

Keynes, J.M. (1931) *Essays in Persuasion*, London: Macmillan.

Keynes, J.M. (1933) *Essays in Biography*, London: Macmillan.

Keynes, J.M. (1936) *The General Theory of Employment, Interest and Money*, London: Macmillan.

Keynes, J.M. (1940) *How to Pay for the War*, London: Macmillan.

Keynes, J.M. (1971–81) *The Collected Writings of John Maynard Keynes*, vols. I–XXIX, London: Macmillan, for The Royal Economic Society.

Pigou, A. (1927) 'Wage policy and unemployment', *Economic Journal*, September, 355–88.

Rima, I. (1988) 'Keynes' vision and econometric analysis', in O. Hamouda and J. Smithin (eds), *Keynes and Public Policy after Fifty Years*. Vol. 2. *Theories and Method*, Aldershot: Edward Elgar, pp. 12–22.

Skidelsky, R. (1983) *John Maynard Keynes*. Vol. 1, *Hopes Betrayed, 1883–1920*, London: Macmillan.

Skidelsky, R. (1992) *John Maynard Keynes*, Vol. 2, *The Economist as Saviour, 1920–37*, London: Macmillan.

Thirlwall, A. (ed.) (1978) *Keynes and Laissez-Faire*, London: Macmillan.

Thirlwall, A. (ed.) (1982) *Keynes as a Policy Adviser*, London: Macmillan.

5 Beveridge

Richard Silburn

Brief biography

William Beveridge was born in 1879, and educated at Charterhouse and Oxford. After graduating in 1901, he quickly abandoned plans for a career at the Bar in favour of social research, when he accepted the post of sub-warden at Toynbee Hall, specializing in the study of unemployment and the London labour market. In 1903 he became a leader-writer for the *Morning Post*, until in 1908 he joined the Board of Trade to plan the introduction first of Labour Exchanges and then of National Insurance. He remained a civil servant throughout the Great War, among other things devising the system of food rationing that was introduced in 1917. In 1919 he was invited to become the Director of the London School of Economics (LSE), a post he held for eighteen years before becoming Master of University College, Oxford. Throughout this period he maintained close links with the public service, serving on the Royal Commission on Coal in 1925–6, and as Chairman of the Unemployment Insurance Statutory Committee in the 1930s. Hopes of a return to high public office at the outbreak of the Second World War were frustrated, and he was reluctantly 'pushed sideways' into accepting the commission to chair an interdepartmental committee on Social Insurance and Allied Services. He turned what promised to be a humdrum task into a personal triumph; the Beveridge Report of 1942 far exceeded his original brief and was seen as a blueprint for comprehensive postwar social reconstruction. He followed up this report with two further (unofficial) inquiries, into Full Employment in 1944 and Voluntary Action in 1948. In 1944 he became, for a few months only, the Liberal member for Berwick on Tweed, a parliamentary seat he lost to a Conservative a few months later in what was nationally a landslide victory for the Labour Party. He took a seat in the House of Lords in 1946, and was Chairman of the Newton Aycliffe Development Corporation for five years after the war. He died in 1963.

Beveridge and the social sciences

Beveridge's social thought was never rooted in a single philosophical or ideological position. Intellectually, he had little interest in or facility for social, economic or political theory. He prided himself upon being a practical man, his ideas fuelled by common sense and reliable factual evidence rather than theoretical speculation. At school and later at Oxford, Beveridge's education centred on the classics, although 'my free bent, in serious reading, had been towards natural science . . . Before I ended school I had got on to *Man's Place in Nature* by T.H. Huxley, and at Oxford . . . I became one of Huxley's devotees; four volumes of his lectures and essays . . . stand on my shelves today' (Beveridge, 1960: 93). Huxley's views on the scope for a science of Society, as spelled out in an 1854 address on 'The Educational Value of the Natural History Sciences', remained a life-long inspiration and aspiration for Beveridge. The same scientific methods of investigation that had been so conspicuously successful in the development of the natural sciences, methods based first on 'observation, experiment, induction to general propositions, and verifications of observations' (Beveridge, 1953: 247) could be applied as fruitfully to human life and social institutions. The social scientist who had grasped the essential scientific laws that governed human behaviour and social organization would have the expertise and authority to propose and carry through effective social reforms and enhance human well-being.

It was science rather than philanthropy that attracted Beveridge to social reform. Defending his decision to work at Toynbee Hall to his unhappy parents, he carefully distanced himself from the social work or welfare motivation of most settlers: 'If anyone ever thought that colossal evils could be remedied by small doses of culture and charity and amiability I for one do not think so now. The real use I wish to make of Toynbee and kindred institutions is as centres for authoritative opinion on the problems of city life' (Beveridge, 1953: 17). He was also clear as to how these authoritative opinions were to be formed: 'I wish to go there because I view these problems in a scientific way . . . I utterly distrust the saving power of culture and isolated good feelings as a surgeon distrusts Christian Science . . . my motive is . . . to study certain branches of the state as a scientist studies his subject matter . . . please do try to think of me in the light of that parallel to the scientist. It is absolutely true' (Harris, 1977: 43). The specific parallel he drew with the work of the surgeon is an interesting one. Surgeons develop their knowledge, understanding and skills not for their own sake, but so that they can contribute to the mending of a sick body. In the same way for Beveridge, the social scientist develops specific knowledge and skills first to understand and then to address the ills of society. Society is perceived as a machine or organism which, like the human body, grows, develops and changes. Social science provides the knowledge base that will enable social developments and change to be planned purposefully, to achieve desirable social goals, to reduce social tension and conflict, and to increase individual opportunity.

Throughout his life, Beveridge retained this narrowly empirical vision of the social sciences. Most of his own research and writing is underpinned by a fastidious concern to assemble 'the facts', to gather statistical evidence and to report in detail on practical experience, as a necessary preamble to arriving at a rational recommendation for policy and action. Moreover, Beveridge did not regard his particular choice of method as a matter either of personal preference or even one of selecting the method most appropriate to the solution of the particular problem being confronted from a range of methodological possibilities; rather, he saw it as the only valid social scientific method. This conviction encouraged in Beveridge a life-long distrust of theoretical speculation, and deductive reasoning and argument. This gave rise to some serious professional and academic conflicts during the eighteen years that he was Director of the London School of Economics. Beveridge was convinced that it was the intention of the founders of the School, Sidney and Beatrice Webb, 'to base economics, politics and all the other social sciences on collection and examination of facts rather than the analysis of concepts; they wanted in effect, to see applied to the study of human society the methods by which natural scientists had won their many triumphs in discovering the secrets of nature' (Beveridge, 1960: 83). In his autobiography, he reproduced with delight and approval Beatrice Webb's diary entry for 20 February 1900, when she wrote:

> We have always claimed that the study of the structure and function of society was as much a science as the study of any other form of life and ought to be pursued by the scientific methods used in other organic sciences. Hypothesis ought to be used, not as the unquestioned premise from which to deduce an unquestioned conclusion, but as the 'order of thought' to be verified by observation and experiment. (Beveridge, 1953: 395)

The links between the social and the natural sciences extended beyond a shared method. There was a substantial grey area of important overlap, where biology met eugenics or psychology. Indeed, Beveridge drew that very parallel when he argued that he 'wished to see economics, with the other social sciences, established as an inductive science of observation, nearer to biology than to mathematics or philosophy' (1953: 247). Perhaps the greatest academic disappointment he was to suffer while Director at the LSE was the failure to consolidate the teaching of Social Biology (for example, 'genetics, population, vital statistics, heredity, eugenics and dysgenics' (Harris, 1977: 287)). This would have been to fulfil another of the Webbs' dreams. 'They [the Webbs] had hoped to "break up Economics", replacing analysis of concepts by collection and examination of facts, and ... they did not want theoretical politics either. They had hoped for contact between natural science and social science, with biology and mathematics as introductions to an economics degree' (Beveridge, 1960: 109).

This restrictive view of social science brought Beveridge into serious conflict with academic colleagues, particularly those who took an active part in the great ideological battles of the period. Among the professors at the London School in the 1930s were such powerful intellects as Hayek and Robbins, ideologically of the right, and Harold Laski and Hugh Dalton, prominent political activists of the left. Robbins suggests that Beveridge

> had a positive antipathy to economics as it was developing in this period. His ideas of scientific method were primitive in the extreme. He thought that even astronomy proceeded simply by the 'unbiased collection of facts'. No disciple of Schmoller or the extreme American institutionalists could have exceeded in emphasis his denunciations of abstract theory ... the bias of his preconceptions made nearly all departmental developments on the theoretical side something of a struggle. (Robbins, 1971: 136–7)

Meanwhile 'Laski was deeply sceptical about "scientific" approaches to politics, and indulged in the kind of abstract speculation that Beveridge criticized. As Laski grew more interested in Marxist political theory, the gulf between them widened' (Newman, 1993: 169).

Beveridge's inability to come to terms, perhaps even to understand, the increasingly influential views of Keynes, stem from this intellectual myopia. In 1931, Beatrice Webb commented that Beveridge 'heartily dislikes Keynes and regards him as a quack in economics' (Webb, 1985: 260). The publication of the *General Theory* in 1936 'intensified Beveridge's sense of estrangement from current economic and political thought. Politically he sympathized with the Keynesian liberals, but he found their economic policies not merely objectionable, but virtually incomprehensible. "I have tried to understand Mr Keynes," he recorded sadly, "I have probably failed".' (Harris, 1977: 331).

The following year Beveridge left the LSE and took the opportunity in his valedictory address to restate his continuing belief in Huxley's vision of science, and then 'with all the professoriate lined up on the platform exposed to public view, he delivered a passionate attack, first on the economists – this indirectly in the guise of a critique of Keynes and his methods – and secondly – much more nearly directly – on the unfortunate Laski ... in the guise of those who took advantage of academic privilege to pursue political aims' (Robbins, 1971: 141). In later life Beveridge chose to write of this occasion in at least two places.

> Keynes had challenged existing economic theory in its foundations, as Einstein had challenged Newtonian physics and Euclidean geometry. The parallel with Einstein was drawn by Keynes himself. But the parallel did not apply to methods. Einstein had started from observation ... he had gone back to observation ... for testing of his theory. Keynes had started not from any fact but from definition of a concept. He had announced his conclusions as certainties without verification of any kind. And Keynes' procedure had been accepted as adequate by practically all professional economists. (Beveridge, 1953: 253)

He concluded that 'the distinguishing mark of economic science . . . is that it is a science in which verification of generalizations by reference to facts is neglected as irrelevant'. Instead a large part of economic writing was 'argument from the positions of philosophers – of Ricardo, or Karl Marx or Marshall, or the Austrian School or the Stockholm School' (Beveridge, 1960: 95). Robbins comments that 'the effect was shattering and saddening . . . I walked away with one of the most senior and reserved members of the staff, a staunch conservative on whose lips I had never heard any, even the least, improper sentiment. "I always suspected", he said, "that he was not quite a gentleman. *And now I know it.*" ' (Robbins, 1971: 141–2).

Beatrice Webb knew both Beveridge and Keynes well, and in her diary entry of 23 September 1931 she includes a characteristically shrewd if cruel assessment of their different characters and temperaments:

> These two men are equally aloof from the common man, but they have little appreciation of each other; Keynes, the imaginative forecaster of events and speculator in ideas, his mind flashing into the future; Beveridge bound down to the past, a bureaucratic statistician . . . the contrast is carried out in the women of their choice – the perfect artist Lopokova, with her delightfully sympathetic ways, and the hard-faced administrator and intriguer Mrs Mair – the Russian prima donna dancer and the Scottish business woman and social arriviste. (Webb, 1985: 260–1).

Beveridge's mistrust of the place of social theory in the academic armoury was matched by an impatience with political ideology. He was for a few months a Liberal MP in 1944–5, and he later sat as a Liberal peer in the House of Lords. But for most of his life he had only fleeting contacts with the Liberal Party; he was not a member of any of the key Liberal policy groups or 'think-tanks'. Jose Harris describes Beveridge as an 'intellectual hybrid' (1972: 11) and suggests that he 'was in fact highly eclectic and frequently self-contradictory . . . he veered between an almost total commitment to the free market and an equally strong commitment to an authoritarian administrative state' (Harris, 1977: 2). In a letter to his mother written when he was twenty-four, he described himself as 'slow of invention and in getting convictions'. But during his twenties he slowly elaborated and consolidated not so much a coherent theory as a set of views and attitudes about society, the economy, and the changing role of the state. His ideas are an amalgam of individualistic and collectivist characteristics, and combine a recognition of the need for social reform and planned change together with an appreciation of the continuing importance of essential personal and constitutional freedoms. He makes the case for wider state intervention, if need be using compulsion and regulation, while insisting on the need to maintain individual economic incentives and a due sense of personal and social responsibility. Very few of his ideas were in any sense original; on the contrary, Beveridge borrowed his ideas freely from many diverse and disparate contemporary sources, although they can be seen as broadly within the framework of Edwardian Liberal thought (Freeden, 1978; Cutler *et al.*, 1986; Williams and Williams,1987).

In summary, Beveridge held the following views:

1. The social and economic systems may be seen as a complex organism, which, like all organisms in nature, is constantly evolving and changing, and (arguably) becoming a higher-order, more sophisticated organism in the process.

2. Evolutionary and unplanned social change produces or exacerbates social conflict and tensions of a potentially disruptive and destructive kind, which undermine social cohesion and weaken social solidarity.

3. Industrial society is manifestly capable of creating hitherto unparalleled wealth; to maintain productive and wealth-creating power, entrepreneurial enterprise, material rewards and incentives for effort are required. These are best safeguarded within a free-market system.

4. Social conflict and tension, and social problems such as poverty, arise not because the economy is incapable of generating sufficient wealth, but because it is unable to distribute it efficiently. The institutions of the free market appear to be unable or unwilling to resolve these distributional problems unaided.

5. Empirical social science has the capacity to advance knowledge and understanding of the machinery of society, and of the social laws which underpin the processes of social change. A proper understanding of these laws and processes, applied to the problem of maldistribution, gives the social scientist the expertise to propose appropriate institutional change. These changes will improve efficiency and increase productive power, and at the same time will reduce social conflict, enhance social cohesion, and secure individual welfare.

6. Such institutional change requires 'the extension of deliberate social action – in a word, organization – over fields hitherto left to the blind play of conflicting interests' (Harris, 1977: 87). The state has a positive role to play in regulating and controlling the lives of its citizens, but must do so in ways that do not undermine the economy's capacity to increase wealth, or the individual's sense of responsibility for and control over his or her own destiny.

7. Mechanisms are required for these reforms to be introduced and implemented. Existing organizations such as employers' associations or trade unions represent important sectional and vested interests, and cannot be trusted to transcend the interests of the lobbies they represent. Political parties are increasingly identified with one group or class within the community, rather than with the nation as a whole, while more direct forms of democracy give individuals an irresistible opportunity to further their own personal interests, probably at the expense of the greater good. In order to ensure that progress is not impeded by powerful self-interest, 'social organization' should be entrusted to impartial, expert, public servants and bureaucrats, who can be relied upon to rise above class and sectional interest to recognize and strive for the superior national interest; 'it replaces the rule of natural law by the rule of the expert' (Harris, 1977: 87). The state is the only impartial and benevolent institution able to represent the interest of the nation in its entirety.

8. The task of the benevolent state is essentially an organizational one. It intervenes in situations where there is evidence that the free market is not working effectively, but it is not intended to substitute for the market. Rather, it facilitates a social partnership, involving the individual, both employer and worker, the civil society of voluntary associations and organizations, and the state. Social organization should therefore have strictly defined and limited aims, to reduce inefficiencies and remove intolerable obstacles to social progress. The state is not to become a major provider of goods or services; nor should it introduce procedures which require persistent or detailed intrusion into those considerable areas of life where individual freedom and responsibility should, as a matter of principle, continue to prevail.

Unemployment and the labour market

Beveridge's thinking about 'social organization' crystallized between 1903 and 1908; his major preoccupation during this period was the problem of unemployment. Beveridge studied the many different attempts to deal with the unemployed, including the Poor Law, private philanthropy, public works schemes and experimental measures such as labour colonies. He came to the view that they had all failed because they were addressed at symptoms rather than causes; they focused on the unemployed individual rather than the root of the problem, which was one of industrial disorganization.

> Unemployment is a question not of the scale of industry but of its organization ... the solution of the problem of unemployment must consist, therefore, partly in smoothing industrial transitions, partly in diminishing the extent of the reserves required for fluctuation or their intervals of idleness, partly, when the plan can go no further, in seeing that the men of the reserve are properly maintained both in action and out of it. The problem is essentially one of business organization ...
> (Beveridge, 1930: 193)

Labour Exchanges would be the organizing agency. Their role was to be an administrative one, acting as a clearing-house to facilitate the bringing together of employer and employee. Because they would be organized as a nation-wide network, unfilled vacancies in any one office that could not be filled from the local population could be advertised more widely, enabling employers and workpeople separated by long distances to be put in touch with one another. By monitoring their own work, they could help to assemble detailed and accurate information about the labour market, local, regional and national, and they could pinpoint skills shortages and surpluses. In these and similar ways, they could avert wasteful loss of production and wealth creation, and reduce the personal stress, material loss and social degradation of the unemployed person, without serious restriction on essential freedoms or responsibilities. They would act as a lubricant to the economic engine, not to replace or supersede it, but to help it run more smoothly and effectively.

But Labour Exchanges do not address the problems of employment caused by cyclical fluctuation in industrial activity, or the immediate material distress of the unemployed person. Beveridge's principal recommendation here is insurance:

> Insurance against unemployment, therefore, stands in the closest relation to the organization of the labour market, and forms the second line of attack on the problem of unemployment ... The Labour Exchange is required to reduce to a minimum the intervals between successive jobs. Insurance is required to tide over the intervals that will still remain.

Insurance 'is for the individual workman an averaging of earnings between good and bad times, and for the body of workmen a sharing of the risk to which they are all exposed ... it does this without injury to self-respect and at a cost which in comparison to the effect produced is extremely small' (Beveridge, 1930: 223–30). The payment of an insurance contribution establishes a contractual relationship, in which a payment would be made in respect of an insurable risk without stigma or dependency, without loss of self-respect or social esteem, without further tests of needs, means or character. As with Labour Exchanges, the role of the state is an administrative one: to establish a system for the collection and recording of contributions, and an office for the receipt of claims and the making of payments. In this way, material distress is reduced with minimum impact on the normal operations of the labour market, and without creating dependency and stigma.

Here, in a rather large nutshell, is the essence of Beveridge's views on the proper role of the state. The state has the capacity and the responsibility to help enhance national efficiency, avoid waste, reduce social discontent and advance individual welfare. This is to be done by way of administrative and organizational interventions that enable people to function more effectively as free members of a free society. The scale of intervention is determined pragmatically by the degree of disorganization to be corrected. Timely action will help to ensure that enterprise can thrive, incentives be maintained, and the fundamental strengths of the market-system be reinforced. The aim is to make the free-market system work more effectively than it otherwise would.

The reforming task of the state is to determine what, at the least, needs to be done, and by what mechanisms that minimum can best be accomplished, and then to ensure that the necessary legal and administrative framework is in place to ensure that this is satisfactorily achieved. This is an enabling view of state activity, concerned to preserve and reinforce existing key values rather than to replace them. At the administrative level, the aim is to increase the efficiency and effectiveness of the economic and social systems without undermining essential freedoms; at the personal level, it is to provide a degree of social security and welfare without destroying self-respect or weakening a sense of personal responsibility.

Social security and insurance

Beveridge's lasting reputation as a founding father of the welfare state is based upon his mature work, towards the end of his active life. Best known is the 1942 Beveridge Report, on *Social Insurance and Allied Services* (HMSO, 1942), but this needs to be read in conjunction with the two other (unofficial) reports, *Full Employment in a Free Society* (1944) and *Voluntary Action* (1948). The first two reports reveal Beveridge at his most interventionist, whereas by 1948 he was beginning to draw back from that position.

The Beveridge Report (HMSO, 1942) is an ingenious mixture of radicalism, proposing a scheme of universal and comprehensive social insurance, and caution, identifying a number of familiar core-values that should on no account be threatened. Social security was to be one part of a comprehensive assault on 'the five giants on the road to reconstruction' (para. 8), yet was to be based on the tripartite partnership of individual, employer and state familiar since at least 1911. 'The State should offer security for service and contribution', but at the same time 'the State in organizing security should not stifle incentive, opportunity, responsibility' (para. 9). The report outlines a scheme of universal contributory social insurance the purpose of which is nothing less than the abolition of want. For Beveridge, a person is in want when they 'lack the means of healthy subsistence' (para. 11). Beveridge's scheme would ensure that basic subsistence needs would be met through state-administered contributory social insurance. Benefits should be adequate to meet all subsistence needs, and to continue to meet them for as long as was necessary. Want would be overcome, without the need for administratively complex and personally offensive tests of means.

Social insurance was to be comprehensive, compulsory, contributory and uniform. It was to be comprehensive in two senses. First, it should address all needs which were universal, or so general and widespread that they could reasonably be included in a compulsory scheme, and where it would be hazardous to rely upon people taking out voluntary insurances. Second, it would be comprehensive in that everyone would be included as contributors, and be entitled to receive benefit. This was not to be a scheme directed only at the poorest sections of the community, but would involve everyone.

To be comprehensive, it had to be compulsory: people could not be free to choose whether or not they wished to join the scheme. Indeed, Beveridge argued that 'each individual should stand in on the same terms; none should claim to pay less because he is healthier or has more regular employment ... the term "social insurance" ... implies both that it is compulsory and that men stand together with their fellows' (para. 26).

Social insurance should be contributory. For Beveridge this was a cardinal principle, from which he was not to be deterred or distracted. Beveridge advanced a number of reasons for this approach. First he asserted that 'benefits in return for contributions, rather than free allowances from the State is what the people of Britain desire' (para. 21). 'The insured persons themselves can pay and like to pay, and would rather pay than not do so' (para. 274). Second, the contributory principle is 'the firm basis of a claim to benefit irrespective of means' (para. 21). The means test is unpopular with claimants, it is administratively complex and costly, and it involves the state in intrusive investigations of individual and family circumstances. Means-testing to establish need arouses 'resentment at a provision which appears to penalize what people have come to regard as the duty and pleasure of thrift' (para. 21). This is a very important objection: if people are to be encouraged to take responsibility for their own well-being, by saving some of their money, or by contracting for additional voluntary insurance, then they must be allowed to enjoy the benefits this will attract without losing their state entitlements. Third, the requirement to pay contributions also encourages people to see the clear link between what they pay and what they receive; they 'should realize that they cannot get more than certain benefits for certain contributions, should have a motive to support measures for economic administration, should not be taught to regard the State as the dispenser of gifts for which no-one needs to pay' (para. 274), and it will remind them that they 'should not feel that income for idleness, however caused, can come from a bottomless purse' (para. 22).

Contributions and benefits were to be paid at a uniform flat-rate level for two major reasons. First, benefits are intended to meet subsistence needs and these are broadly similar for everyone. Second, to recommend flat-rate contributions and benefits 'follows from the recognition of the place and importance of voluntary insurance in social security' (para. 304). Social insurance benefit should, as a matter of principle, be confined to meeting basic subsistence needs. Those who hope to live at a higher standard of material comfort would be encouraged to think of additional voluntary insurance, savings plans and so on.

The influence of Beveridge: an assessment

How are we to assess Beveridge's long-term influence on social thought and welfare policy? At one level it is incalculable: Beveridge and his report have developed a standing and authority that is mythic. Beveridge himself is reverentially referred to as a founding father of the welfare state (a term, incidentally, that he disliked), and the Beveridge Principles (however they are understood) have come to have a scriptural authority, a symbolic resonance that is separate from, and often indifferent to, their specific content. Widely contrasting, indeed conflicting, proposals for social policy reforms recommend themselves as a welcome return to the Beveridge Principles, as though this in itself was a sufficient legitimation.

In part, this extraordinary reputation may be explained by the very particular political and social circumstances of the mid-1940s; published during a prolonged and destructive war, but at the very time when ultimate victory first seemed possible, the Beveridge Plan articulated widespread, if vague, aspirations for a better postwar world. Support for the Beveridge Plan became an earnest of political good intentions, in a way that went far beyond endorsing a particular set of prescriptions for social security. The rhetoric of the Five Giants captured the public imagination, and fuelled the legislative programme that between 1944 and 1948 established the postwar social welfare framework. The principle of universality (the insistence that social policy should apply to everyone because we all confront the same essential human needs) expressed an implicit and attractive democratic and socially unifying spirit. Within a very few years, these important bureaucratic and political changes were transmuted into a world-historical phenomenon in the writings of T.H. Marshall:

> Marshall's grand teleology of a historical progression through a trinity of modes of citizenship, from civil to political and finally to social rights, portrayed the Beveridge/Labour reforms as the culmination of a centuries long progress and imbued them with a transcendent importance that carried them, in terms of their role in history, far beyond what a framework of social policy legislation would otherwise have aspired to. (Baldwin, 1992: 24)

From this perspective, Beveridge's ideas go far beyond technical questions of social reform to proclaim a radically enhanced view of social citizenship, which reverberates to the present day.

Looking at the broad sweep of postwar welfare reconstruction, the influence of Beveridge is clear. In outline, at least, his scheme was adopted and implemented. A single scheme of contributory social security was introduced, supported by family allowances, and a comprehensive National Health Service. Meanwhile, the maintenance of full employment as a prime goal of economic policy was acknowledged. The central inspirational importance of Beveridge's ideas was publicly acknowledged by the key players in the postwar Labour government, despite a number of significant departures from Beveridge's specific recommendations.

Perhaps the phrase the 'Beveridge Principles' is unhelpful and misleadingly overprescriptive. The word 'principles' suggests an underlying force of argument and moral authority that would defy compromise and trimming. But Beveridge's own approach was always robustly pragmatic. He certainly had strong views and he could be stubborn; he advanced and defended his ideas vigorously. But if a concession was necessary to advance the whole project then he made it. Indeed the Beveridge Report is itself the outcome of prolonged negotiation and significant compromise. Some important adjustments were made directly by Beveridge himself, while still in Committee: for example, difficulties over the treatment of rent led to a compromise solution which undermined at the margins the principle of adequacy in favour of administrative simplicity and a rejection of means-testing. Further substantial modifications were made during the months before publication when Beveridge was engaged in detailed discussion with the Treasury about the financing of his scheme. In order to reduce costs to a level that the Treasury would accept, Beveridge agreed to recommend the gradual phasing in of contributory pensions over a twenty-year period, and to drop the idea of paying a family allowance for all children, including the first born. Both of these changes weakened the notion of adequacy, and transitional pensions would have retained means-testing of many elderly people for at least the duration of the transition. Further changes were made by the 1945 Labour government as it prepared legislation. For example, Family Allowances were to be paid at a lower weekly rate than Beveridge had calculated as necessary to meet subsistence costs. On the other hand, it was decided that pensions were to be paid out straight away, without the long period of transition, but at a substantially lower level than Beveridge had recommended. This change was one that Beveridge deplored: not only did it fail the adequacy test, but as a consequence it inevitably forced many old people to apply for indefinitely long means-tested assistance. This was a price too great.

Other key features of the Beveridge Plan were initially incorporated in the postwar social security legislation, but have since been amended or modified. For example, the flat-rate principle was replaced by graduated contributions and benefits from 1959 onwards, while means-tested supplementary pensions became firmly institutionalized from 1966 onwards. These two changes are major departures from Beveridge's ideas, and indicate a significant redirection of social security policy.

Meanwhile other, sometimes fundamental, elements of Beveridge's thought are now severely criticized. We shall examine just one of these criticisms, which is that Beveridge's analysis of the causes and consequences of poverty is simply inadequate; even in 1942 it was at best a partial explanation, and it has become increasingly inappropriate during the intervening years.

Beveridge convinced himself that the root cause of Want is the interruption of earnings, in which case it is amenable to remedy through an insurance scheme for those in paid work. He justified his analysis by referring to the evidence of a number of poverty surveys carried out between the wars.

But did the evidence justify this conclusion at the time, and has it remained the case since? Is poverty simply a consequence of interrupted earnings? Even during the 1940s, there were many people, particularly women, who for a variety of reasons were effectively excluded from full entry into the paid-labour market, and whose capacity to become paid-up members of the contributing classes in their own right was therefore limited. By far the largest group were the seven out of eight married women who (using figures from 1931) did not have paid work outside the home, but were housewives. Then there were chronically sick and disabled people, many widows, separated, divorced or otherwise unsupported mothers, and those who we might now call 'carers', characteristically women who are unable to take paid work because of other caring responsibilities (in the 1940s there was a large group of so-called 'domestic spinsters' looking after their elderly parents without payment). None of these groups fitted comfortably within Beveridge's framework, and for many different reasons would not be able to build up the long-term contributory record needed to make them fully eligible for benefit in their own right.

Beveridge was, of course, aware of these problems, and he exercised great ingenuity in developing a classification system that would squeeze as many as possible into the social insurance framework. The largest single group were housewives, amounting to 9.5 million women or 20 per cent of the total population. The Beveridge Report writes at some length about housewives as a group of women who, as mothers, are engaged in (unpaid) work of national importance, and, as wives, are players in a domestic team or partnership. This complex role carried with it insurable risks (including widowhood and separation) that would be met by the components of the Housewives Policy for all Class 3 contributors (e.g. housewives), entitlement to be derived from the contribution record of their working husband's Class 1 or 2 contributions. In the report, the Housewives Policy was to include a marriage grant, maternity grants, a separation allowance based upon provision for widowhood, and the provision of paid domestic help as part of treatment in times of illness. Much of this is, of course, deeply uncongenial to contemporary ideological taste, but it is at least a consistent, if Procrustean, attempt to incorporate housewives into a social insurance scheme.

This is more than can be said for the situation of the 2.5 million other people who form Class 4, 'Others of Working Age'. This group included 'unmarried women engaged in domestic duties not for pay' (para. 317) and 'cripples, chronic bronchitics and other classes of permanent invalids' (para. 352). Beveridge proposed that they should pay or have someone pay a contribution on a Security Card, otherwise they would have to seek means-tested social assistance, a major breach in the principle of comprehensiveness. In practice, most people in this group have always been dependent not on insurance-based benefit, but on means-tested assistance, precisely the kind of intrusive and discriminatory system that Beveridge hoped to abandon.

Very little is said directly about lone parenthood in the Beveridge Report. Widowed mothers would be able to claim a subsistence-level guardian's benefit. So would many separated or divorced mothers, the clearly innocent victims of a husband's defection. But Beveridge was very uncertain how to deal with the many messy cases where it would be very difficult to attribute blame, or even to establish precisely what the situation was, let alone how it had arisen. This is a case which 'in practice calls for further examination' (para. 347), but with the broad hint that this is another group for whom assistance rather than insurance is the appropriate route. The unmarried mother is not mentioned at all, except to note that she can seek an affiliation order against the father, and that the authorities may be able to recover any benefit paid to her by proceeding against the father. But it is hard to see what insurance rights an unmarried mother could possibly have. We must, of course, remember that at this time marriage breakdown and, even more so, illegitimacy were the subject of considerable social stigma, and were certainly not topics where social policy interventions were thought appropriate beyond marriage guidance in the first case, and moral guidance in the second. Since then there has been a major shift in social values and practices, the financial support of lone mothers and their children has become a major item in the social security budget, and the best strategy for the long-term needs of both mothers and children is now a topic of anguished public discussion. But it is certainly no longer credible to present the needs of this group as arising simply from 'interruption of earnings'; rather more plausibly it might be called the practical 'impossibility of earnings'.

A second major criticism of Beveridge's concept of poverty concerns the notions of subsistence and adequacy. Beveridge argued for a basic subsistence rate of benefit as a matter of principle. It was an expression of the idea of the national minimum as a goal of policy, and was consistent with the limited role that social policy and the state were meant to play in underwriting individual welfare. But in the last resort, the definition of subsistence is as much a matter of judgement as science. Seebohm Rowntree in his interwar survey of York had adjusted his original measures of subsistence needs to include a wider range of goods and services, recognizing some socially defined patterns of consumption in addition to the needs of brute survival. Beveridge himself wrote in the report that 'what is required for reasonable human subsistence is to some extent a matter of judgement: estimates on this point change with time, and generally, in a progressive community, change upwards' (para. 27). But the discussion of want has in recent years moved a long way from any imaginable principle of subsistence. It is idle to speculate how Beveridge would have responded to the relative definitions of poverty which have become prevalent in recent years, but clearly the tone of modern discussion is not about physical survival, but about acceptable living standards.

Poverty is about social exclusion, about a person's capacity to take part in everyday social activities; it is about the restricted share of goods and opportunities that an individual, a family or a social group can command. Poverty (or whatever more neutral term may be preferred) tends now to be discussed by reference more to average wages and rewards than to budget standards. This focuses attention on how income is generated and distributed, rather than on establishing thresholds of survival adequacy. But it does raise in an acute form the issue of adequacy. For Beveridge, subsistence was both the minimum and the maximum, the threshold and the ceiling. Certainly, to argue that the social security system should meet subsistence needs in full was a radical suggestion at the time. But how should we define adequacy today, starting from an appreciation of want as a relative concept? This is a grave question which, in Beveridge's phrase, 'calls for further examination'. What we can say is that even if benefits today meet subsistence standards (which can be judged empirically), then they certainly do not meet any contemporary standard of adequacy, in the sense that they safeguard living standards, or approximate to an acceptable proportion of average earnings.

Finally, Beveridge's model of the labour market now appears very dated. He made the avoidance of mass unemployment a prerequisite for any viable social security system, and his recommendations about contribution and benefit rates imply stable life-long employment at rates of pay at least sufficient to meet the subsistence needs of a couple with one child. For a full generation after the war, this seemed to have been achieved. Employment opportunities were plentiful, and wage levels seemed to be able to support steadily rising living standards for most working people. But since the late 1960s or early 1970s, we have experienced sluggish rates of economic growth and steadily rising unemployment. Full employment as an achievable goal, or even as a matter of public discussion, seems to have been abandoned since the middle of the 1970s. More recently still, profound changes in the international structure of the labour market have led to even higher rates of unemployment, lasting for much longer periods of time; part-time contracts and the casualization of employment have become widespread, and there has been a downward pressure on the rates of pay among many of those lucky enough to have jobs. All of these trends have undermined Beveridge's analysis, and enfeebled the scope for social insurance as a solution. In this respect, some of the characteristics of the Edwardian labour market, analyzed by Beveridge in 1908, have reappeared, and the difficulties of sustaining an insurance-based social security system in a context of deep-seated chronic underemployment have become daily more transparent.

What then is left of the Beveridge Principles? Is Beveridge now to be regarded as the last in a progression of Liberal reformers, important perhaps in their generation, but of no contemporary relevance, or do his views still command respect and attention? Clearly at the level of practical day-to-day social policy making, Beveridge's ideas have been overtaken by events. The world of the 1990s is a very different one from Beveridge's, and social and economic aspirations have changed profoundly. Yet the myth remains, and like all good myths it retains a very powerful and charismatic appeal.

At its simplest, this might be because the challenge that faced Beveridge, the abolition of want, remains. The Five Giants have not been overcome, and the implicit call to action still moves people. There may be, at this particular moment, a twinge of bad conscience about the materialist excesses of the 1980s, and the incontrovertible evidence that poverty has become more widespread and visible than at any other period in living memory. But more deeply, some of Beveridge's ideas have an enduring ideological force and power which arises from the intuitive way in which he tried to reconcile the tension between personal and social identities, between the public and the private, between the desire for autonomy and the recognition of dependency. Beveridge achieved this reconciliation not by stressing one set of values at the expense of another, but by striving for a synthesis between individualism and collectivism, retaining the strengths and merits of both, while each curbed the excesses of the other. The radical principle of universality recognizes that we all face common life-hazards, and that, if we stand together as a collective, they can be confronted and overcome. Standing together as a collective simultaneously defines and reinforces social solidarity, and the organic unity of society. Meanwhile, the balancing principle of subsistence ensures that collective action will not be allowed to weaken individual responsibility, or encourage debilitating dependency. Personal responsibility will both encourage and be encouraged by an individual sense of self-respect, dignity and worth.

Beveridge tried to achieve an elegant balance between the apparently opposed principles of solidarity and autonomy, each of which has its attractions as well as its dangers. Clearly he was not entirely successful, and we have seen some of the ways in which his model was inadequate. But the goal was and is an admirable one, the contemporary welfare debate is mesmerized by the same oppositions, the tensions remain unresolved, and the legacy of Beveridge, and his mantle, remain prizes worth pursuing.

Key texts

We conclude with a brief review of some of Beveridge's major writings, starting with the 1930 edition of *Unemployment: A problem of industry*, then *Full Employment in a Free Society*, published in 1944 as an unofficial sequel to the report on social insurance. Together these works cover Beveridge's most important writings on unemployment. The Beveridge Report itself has already been discussed at some length, so we shall conclude with *Voluntary Action*, which was published in 1948, and intended as the third and final volume in the trilogy that started with the report on social insurance.

The 1930 edition of *Unemployment: A problem of industry* is really two books bound into one cover. The first half is a reprint of the first edition published in 1909; the second half consists of seven chapters which trace the development of policy over the intervening period, and in which Beveridge tries to find explanations and remedies for the mass unemployment of the late 1920s. The 1909 book is a confident review of the evidence about, and explanations of, unemployment. As we have already seen, Beveridge is emphatic that unemployment is a problem that can be remedied by better labour market organization, and the potential of both labour exchanges and unemployment insurance is discussed in some detail in the book.

In 1930 Beveridge reiterates that some part of the current unemployment arises through continuing inadequacy of labour market organization. The promising start made prewar by unemployment insurance and Labour Exchanges had been undermined during the 1920s as insurance was transformed into open-ended unemployment relief, and the Labour Exchanges abandoned their first duty to decasualize employment. But Beveridge now identified an additional cause for increased unemployment: the substantial increases in real wages achieved through the spread of successful collective bargaining, without matching increases in productivity. Equilibrium between wage levels and productivity would have to be re-established (probably by the lowering of wages) if the consequent unemployment was to be avoided. In essence, Beveridge was accepting an orthodox economic view, that market forces must be allowed to reassert themselves in this area.

Full Employment in a Free Society (1944) was written in very different circumstances as the Second World War was drawing to an end, and it is inspired by an optimistic assessment of the possibility of simultaneously maintaining both full employment and liberal freedoms after the war was won. The essential new ingredient was Beveridge's acceptance of, even conversion to, some essential Keynesian views: in particular, the idea that unemployment arose through deficiencies of demand for goods and services, and that this demand could be successfully manipulated by budgeting for full employment. The task of the Chancellor would be to prepare an annual Budget in which, 'after estimating how much . . . private citizens may be expected to lay out that year on consumption and private investment, he must propose for that year public outlay sufficient, with this estimated private outlay, to employ the whole manpower of the country' (Beveridge, 1944: 136). This could be achieved in a number of different ways, singly or more likely in combination. These include 'communal outlay on non-marketable goods and services . . . public business investment in industries now under public control . . . private business investment . . . private consumption outlay', all of which can be reduced, increased or steadied 'by State action in redistributing income, by measures of social security, and by progressive taxation' (Beveridge, 1944: 30). In these ways, production would be adjusted to the supply of labour, ensuring the fullest levels of employment.

At this time, Beveridge had become persuaded, perhaps by wartime experiences of public administration, perhaps by the arguments of his advisory group of economists (in general, more left-wing than himself), that this programme could be put into effect without the loss of the essential personal freedoms and responsibilities he had guarded so jealously in his programme for social security. Four years later he published *Voluntary Action* (1948). This is a curious report, which lacks the precision and the focus of the earlier reports. The modern reader is baffled by the considerable space given to the importance of the Friendly Societies. Their history is an interesting one, and their nineteenth-century importance is beyond dispute. But they had been in serious decline for a very long time, and Beveridge's attempt to redefine the role they might play in the new 'social service state' seems entirely unconvincing. At the same time, he has very little indeed to say about the role of the trade unions, although they are an example of voluntary organizations with a long pedigree and (in 1948) with an evidently important and growing part to play in national life. There is an interesting section of brief biographical profiles of some of the great philanthropic figures, mostly of the nineteenth century, finishing with Sidney and Beatrice Webb; what is not clear is why it is there in the first place, and what we are supposed to learn from the example of these admirable people. There is a section which describes some of the kinds of tasks that might be addressed through voluntary action, especially by the redeployed Friendly Societies, but little discussion of how these tasks should be organized, administered or paid for. The conclusion restates a number of obviously heart-felt sentiments about fraternity: that happiness 'depends upon ourselves as citizens, not on the instrument of political power which we call the State' (1948: 320); that the need for 'private enterprise, not in business but in the service of mankind, not for gain but under the driving power of social conscience ... is beyond debate' (1948: 322); that 'mankind in brotherhood shall bring back the day' (1948: 324). They read plaintively, as though Beveridge at the last had become profoundly ambivalent about some of the social processes and changes that he had played so important a part in bringing about.

References

Baldwin, P. (1992) 'Beveridge in the longue durée', in *Social Security 50 years after Beveridge*, papers from an international conference at the University of York. Vol. A.

Beveridge, W.H. (1930) *Unemployment: A problem of industry* (revised edn), London: Longmans Green and Co. First published 1909.

Beveridge, W.H. (1944) *Full Employment in a Free Society*, London: George Allen and Unwin.

Beveridge, W.H. (1948) *Voluntary Action*, London: George Allen and Unwin.

Beveridge, W.H. (1953) *Power and Influence*, London: Hodder and Stoughton.

Beveridge, W.H. (1960) *The London School of Economics and its Problems 1919-1937*, London: George Allen and Unwin.

Cutler, T., Williams, K. and Williams, J. (1986) *Keynes, Beveridge and Beyond*, London: Routledge and Kegan Paul.

Freeden, M. (1978) *The New Liberalism*, Oxford: Clarendon Press.

Harris, J. (1972) *Unemployment and Politics*, Oxford: Clarendon Press.

Harris, J. (1977) *William Beveridge*, Oxford: Clarendon Press.

HMSO (1942) *Social Insurance and Allied Services* (The Beveridge Report), London: HMSO.

Newman, M. (1993) *Harold Laski*, London: Macmillan.

Robbins, L. (1971) *Autobiography of an Economist*, London: Macmillan.

Webb, B. (1985) *The Diary of Beatrice Webb*, Vol. 4. London: Virago/LSE.

Williams, K. and Williams, J. (1987) *A Beveridge Reader*, London: Allen and Unwin.

6 T.H. Marshall

Robert Pinker

Brief biography

T.H. Marshall was born in London, just over a hundred years ago in 1893. He was educated at Rugby School and Trinity College, Cambridge, and graduated with first-class honours in the History Tripos in 1914. Having spent the First World War as a civilian prisoner in Germany, where he had gone for a short period of study, he returned to England, and was elected to a Cambridge history fellowship in 1919. In 1925 he went to the London School of Economics (LSE) as a tutor in social work – a subject of which he later said he 'knew nothing'. He also remembered that when he joined Morris Ginsberg's department in 1929 he was almost equally ignorant of sociology 'in the professional sense'. Until then his academic reputation had rested on his work as an economic historian.

In 1930 Marshall was made a reader in sociology, in which capacity he played an important part in launching the *British Journal of Sociology*, and he edited a number of major publications on stratification and population. During the Second World War he was posted to the Foreign Office, returning to the LSE in 1944 as Professor of Social Institutions in what is now the Social Policy Department. He went back to Germany in 1949 as an educational adviser to the British High Commission and, after working at the LSE from 1951 to 1956 as head of the Sociology Department, he was finally appointed director of Unesco's Department of Social Sciences. His formal retirement took place in 1960.

Marshall's academic career developed in two stages. Most of his sociological work was completed between 1945 and 1960, but most of his writings on social policy were published after his retirement. He died at home in Cambridge in 1981. Marshall was a man of broad and diverse cultural interests. An accomplished violinist, he shared with his second wife Nadine a profound feeling for music, and his writing was graced by felicitous qualities of clarity and form (Blake and Nicholls, 1990: 266–7).

Main ideas

Marshall became a sociologist while he taught at the LSE, 'very naturally, almost totally under the influence of Hobhouse, as interpreted by Ginsberg' (Marshall, 1973: 95). He referred to his use of 'Hobhouse's threefold categorization of kinship, authority and citizenship as the basic principles of social order' and to his study of the works of Max Weber, Emile Durkheim and Karl Mannheim as forming the basis of his sociological education as well as his own distinctive and original contribution to the subject.

His first collection of sociological essays, *Citizenship and Social Class*, appeared in 1950, and was republished in 1963 as part of a larger collection *Sociology at the Crossroads*, of which the title essay was presented as an inaugural lecture in 1946 (Marshall, 1950, 1963). In this essay Marshall stressed the importance of sociology as a synthesizing influence in relation to other disciplines such as economics, psychology, education and social administration.

As Marshall saw it in the 1940s, sociology stood at a crossroads, faced with a choice of directions. One path would lead to a search for 'universal laws and ultimate values'. 'We might call it', he suggested, 'the way to the stars and, although few at any one time can profitably follow it, it should never be barred' (Marshall, 1963: 13). The other path, he thought, might be called 'the way into the sands'. 'It leads to the expenditure of great energy on the collection of a multitude of facts with sometimes an inadequate sense of the purpose for which they are being collected' (1963: 15).

Rejecting both of these paths, Marshall chose 'a middle way which runs over firm ground', leading 'into a country whose features are neither Gargantuan nor Lilliputian, where sociology can choose units of study of a manageable size – not society, progress, morals, and civilization, but specific social structures in which the basic processes and functions have determined meanings' (1963: 16).

This approach is further developed in another of the *Crossroads* essays, 'Sociology: the road ahead', in which Marshall defined as 'the central concern of sociology ... the analytical and explanatory study of social systems', a term which he took to cover not only general social phenomena such as nations and states and different kinds of polity but more specialized phenomena at an institutional level. He acknowledged that there are many features of social life which do not wear a systematic appearance but he observed that

> If society were not systematic there could be no social science ... if the fundamental elements of which social systems are made were not essentially the same in all societies (though differently combined), and if the possible ways of using these fundamental elements were not limited in number, the social sciences, so called, would be devoid of all general theory. (1963: 27)

Marshall did not equate the idea of a social system with total functional interdependence. He pointed out that in all societies we can observe 'non-system' elements, activities which are not relevant to 'the system as such' and which constitute areas of free choice, and that there are also 'pro-system' areas of relatively free choice in the forms of social activity, which are 'not strictly repetitive but nevertheless have room made for them within the system, and in fact help to make it work'. He also drew attention to 'anti-system' elements of conflict or deviance which are not compatible with the orderly operation of the social system (1963: 28–9).

Marshall's model of society does not therefore preclude the occurrence of conflict or of unsystematic aspects of social life. As Marshall put it, the task of sociology is 'to explore the interplay of these elements and to find the clue to their relationships. And it undertakes this task by studying both social institutions and individual behaviour' (1963: 31).

Marshall was almost the only major contributor to social policy studies to express the view that a modified form of capitalist enterprise is not incompatible with civilized forms of collectivist social policy. Indeed, it appears to be central to his thesis that the creation and enhancement of welfare depend on the existence of a free economic market. His major essays, *Citizenship and Social Class* (1963), contain the earliest systematic exposition of this thesis, whose development is as much historical as it is sociological.

Marshall took as his starting point the question posed by the economist Alfred Marshall: will it eventually prove possible through the amelioration of economic and social progress to make every man 'by occupation at least' a gentleman? (Marshall and Bottomore, 1992: 5). Alfred Marshall put forward the view that, by reducing the incidence of soul-destroying manual labour and extending educational and cultural opportunities, the divisive effect of class would give way to new forms of social consensus and co-operation within a society still characterized by a free-market economy. In his response, T.H. Marshall replaced the term 'gentleman' with the term 'civilized', observing that Alfred Marshall 'was taking as the standard of civilized life the conditions regarded by his generation as appropriate to a gentleman' (Marshall and Bottomore, 1992: 6).

He then reinterpreted the question in order to explore the relationship between the evident inequalities of class and the prospective equality of citizenship. He identified three elements in the concept of citizenship. The civil element concerns the 'rights necessary for individual freedom – liberty of the person, freedom of speech, thought and faith, the right to own property and to conclude valid contracts, and the right to justice' (Marshall and Bottomore, 1992: 8). Marshall located the origin of these rights in the eighteenth century, but noted also their embodiment in seventeenth-century statutes such as the Habeas Corpus Act and the Toleration Act, as well as 'Catholic Emancipation, the repeal of the Combination Acts, and the successful end of the battle for the freedom of the press ... It could then be more accurately, but less briefly, described as the period between the Revolution and the first Reform Act' (Marshall and Bottomore, 1992: 10). The political element of citizenship is 'the right to participate in the exercise of power' either as a representative or as a voter, and the social element comprises 'the whole range from the right to a modicum of economic welfare and security to the right to share to the full in the social heritage and to live the life of a civilised being according to the standards prevailing in the society' (Marshall and Bottomore, 1992: 8).

Marshall observed that the most significant extension of political rights occurred in the nineteenth century, although not for women, and that it was an extension of rights already enjoyed by a minority to the majority of the adult male population. The more universal enjoyment of social rights he saw as a feature of the twentieth century, pointing out that the relationship between social rights and their exercise was not always direct and positive because the processes of institutional differentiation gradually separated the societal bases of their legitimacy. He also drew to our attention the significance of the change in emphasis from local rights and obligations based on small communities to those based on the rise of national institutions. With these changes a national dimension was added to the idea of citizenship, so that, 'When freedom became universal, citizenship grew from a local into a national institution' (Marshall and Bottomore, 1992: 12).

In order to set this central point of his argument in historical context, Marshall went back to feudal society, in which the three elements of citizenship 'were wound into a single thread. The rights were blended because the institutions were amalgamated.' The rights which people enjoyed then were not, however, comparable with those of modern citizenship because in feudal society

> status was the hallmark of class and the measure of inequality. There was no uniform collection of rights and duties with which all men ... were endowed by virtue of their membership of society. There was, in this sense, no principle of the equality of citizens to set against the principle of the inequality of classes.

Only in the towns were a few examples 'of genuine and equal citizenship' to be found, but these were local phenomena (Marshall and Bottomore, 1992: 8–9).

It was the growth of national institutions in government and law which broke up this unity and set each element of citizenship on 'its separate way, travelling at its own speed under the direction of its own peculiar principles' (Marshall and Bottomore, 1992: 9). The example of the New Poor Law can be taken to illustrate the conflicts of interests and rights which attended these changes. The New Poor Law required that the enjoyment of a social 'right' to poor relief should be contingent on the surrender of political rights (Marshall and Bottomore, 1992: 15).

Similarly, the special claims of women and children to protection under the Factory Acts came to be recognized because neither women nor children enjoyed political rights. They were fit subjects for protection because they were dependent. Thus, Marshall reminded us, after 1834 'The tentative move towards the concept of social security was reversed. But more than that, the minimal social rights that remained were detached from the status of citizenship' (Marshall and Bottomore, 1992: 15). None the less, while it was 'appropriate that nineteenth-century capitalist society should treat political rights as a secondary product of civil rights', it was 'equally appropriate that the twentieth century should abandon this position and attach political rights directly and independently to citizenship as such' (Marshall and Bottomore, 1992: 13).

Marshall defined citizenship as 'a status bestowed on those who are full members of a community. All who possess the status are equal with respect to the rights and duties with which the status is endowed' (Marshall and Bottomore, 1992: 18). Within his analytical framework citizenship becomes a basis for social solidarity and a measure of consensus; civil and political rights become a precondition of the extension of social rights and, once universalized, ensure that such extension will take place. But Marshall included within his model of equality and fraternity on the basis of citizenship the seeming paradox that the egalitarian extension of rights coincided with the development of capitalism precisely because capitalism is a system based on economic inequality. In Marshall's opinion these trends are complementary, not incompatible: 'Differential status, associated with class, function and family, was replaced by the single, uniform status of citizenship, which provided the foundation of equality on which the structure of inequality could be built' (Marshall and Bottomore 1992: 21).

Marshall maintained that the enjoyment of social rights in the form of social and educational services contributed more to the equalization of statuses than to the equalization of incomes, but that the proper and necessary purpose of social services is the abolition of poverty, not the abolition of inequality. Finally he discussed

> the combined effects of three factors. First, the compression, at both ends, of the scale of income distribution. Second, the great extension of the area of common culture and common experience. And third, the enrichment of the universal status of citizenship, combined with the recognition and stabilization of certain status differences chiefly through the linked systems of education and occupation. The first two have made the third possible. (Marshall and Bottomore, 1992: 44)

The rights of citizenship inhibit the inegalitarian tendencies of the free economic market, but the market and some degree of economic inequality remain functionally necessary to the production of wealth and the preservation of political rights.

Marshall recognized that a 'conflict of principles' springs from the very roots of our type of society but he concluded that these 'apparent inconsistencies are in fact a source of stability, achieved through a compromise which is not dictated by logic', although he suggested that 'This phase will not continue indefinitely' (Marshall and Bottomore, 1992: 49).

In discussing the ends of social policy in his essay 'Value problems of welfare–capitalism', Marshall separated the abolition of poverty from the abolition of inequality, commenting that 'Poverty is a tumour which should be cut out, and theoretically could be; inequality is a vital organ which is functioning badly' (Marshall, 1981: 119), and he stated unequivocally that 'The task of banishing poverty from our "ideal type" society must be undertaken jointly by welfare and capitalism; there is no other way' (1981: 117). The alternative is 'something more totalitarian and bureaucratic, and that is not at all what the more novel and significant elements in the movement of protest are seeking' (1981: 121). Marshall's central theme is that collectivist social services contribute to the maintenance and enhancement of social welfare so long as such interventions do not subvert the system of competitive markets.

If we accept the basic premises of the argument set out in 'Value problems of welfare-capitalism', the chief commitment in welfare will be to resolve the persisting incompatibility of the three separate sets of values and aims represented in the social market, in the economic market and in democratic political processes. Marshall pointed out that we had so far failed to devise a formula for social justice which would enable us to equate 'a man's value in the market (capitalist value), his value as a citizen (democratic value) and his value for himself (welfare value)', and that we would also have to contend with the continuing conflict between the welfare ethic, which stresses 'the equality of persons', and the democratic ethic, 'which *also* stresses equality of opportunity' (1981: 119).

In Marshall's view, these issues constituted 'a structural problem' to which 'there is no purely structural solution', and his conclusion was that 'It is futile to imagine that differentials can be made acceptable simply by scaling them down, however necessary this may be. It can be done only by changing the attitude towards them' (1981: 119).

These are the issues to which Marshall returned in his 'after-thoughts' on 'Value problems of welfare-capitalism'. He looked again at this 'hyphenated' phenomenon, reminding us that 'The hyphen links two (or it can be three) different and contrasting elements together to create a new entity whose character is a product of the combination, but not the fusion of the components, whose separate identities are preserved intact and are of equal and contributory status' (1981: 124). It is this juxtaposition of competition and equality that distinguishes Marshall's approach from the Titmussian tradition, with its implication that in a better-ordered society the values of the social market would, as it were, take over and dominate those of the economic market. Titmuss' ideal of social welfare was based on a normatively unitary model of society, but in Marshall's view the differing institutional elements in society 'strengthen the structure because they are complementary rather than divisive' (1981: 124–5).

Marshall explained that the quality of 'hyphenation' in his term 'democratic welfare-capitalism' exists because all of its component institutional parts 'enjoy a measure of autonomy derived from the power inherent in their axial principles' (1981: 125). To illustrate this separateness, he pointed out that 'The welfare principle cannot be derived from any principle of majority rule; its duty is not to provide what majorities want but what minorities need – which once led to the question: should welfare recipients have votes?' (1981: 126). Similarly, Marshall drew attention to the problem of reconciling the claims of democracy, socialism and welfare in a free society, and reminded us that, in practice, policy boundaries had come to be drawn around the seemingly unitary and universalist idea of a welfare state:

> The part did duty for the whole and claimed for itself the authority, and the autonomy to which the whole would have been entitled. And that is where the hyphen came in. For authority inherent in, not bestowed upon, a part provides a basis for the hyphenated relationship of autonomic interdependence. With the emergence, not of a socialist, but of a mixed economy, the tripartite pattern was complete. The golden calf of democratic socialism had been translated into a troika of sacred cows. (1981: 129)

Marshall returned on several occasions to the changing relationship between universalist and selectivist policies and the problem of poverty. In *Social Policy in the Twentieth Century*, apart from the lucid historical exposition, he focused on three things – what he termed 'the dilemma of the gap' between the levels of benefit granted under social insurance and those granted selectively as supplementary benefits, the anomaly of the 'poverty trap', and the 'discrepancies between economic and welfare values' manifested in the 'wage stop'. He concluded that 'Perhaps we are getting the worst of both worlds' – an inefficient and anomaly-creating network of selectivist policies and universalist services which are inadequate if they are economical, but could only become adequate if they were also extravagant. His search for remedies was pragmatic: 'how to devise a scheme of general application which operates selectively, and how to unify the systems of income taxation and income maintenance' (Marshall, 1970: 195). Marshall concluded that the variability and idiosyncratic nature of human needs is such that there will always be an essential role for discretion and selectivity. What matters is that they should be exercised within a Titmussian type of universalist infrastructure (1970: 198) and that the necessary discrimination should not entail humiliation.

In his essay 'The Right to Welfare', Marshall returned to the linked issues of rights and discretion, arguing that 'There can be no legal right in the fullest sense to benefit the award of which is subject to discretion' (Marshall, 1981: 86), but he asked why discretionary assistance should be accorded lower status than benefits given as a right. He pointed out that means tests can be administered in the spirit of a needs test, and that 'It would be nearer the truth to say that this notion of discretion as positive, personal and beneficent can only be realized in a "welfare society" ... that recognizes its collective responsibility to seek to achieve welfare, and not only to relieve destitution or eradicate penury.' (1981: 88). In Marshall's view, the exercise of discretion can be taken as evidence of a felt obligation on the part of society to meet need irrespective of legal rights. It is the status of citizenship which makes this kind of 'right' an authentic one. What the courts cannot do, he added as an 'afterthought', is to 'convert discretion into rights in cases where the law has left an area free for discretionary judgements' (1981: 98).

The links between the exercise of discretion and the idiosyncrasies of human need are further explored in 'Welfare in the context of social development' where Marshall drew our attention to what he called two dimensions, or axes, 'along which welfare moves', one being defined in terms of welfare and happiness – which 'mark the boundaries of the territory in which welfare dwells' – the other moving between individualist and collectivist dimensions, which must both be encompassed in welfare policies if they are to have regard for the whole person (1981: 55). This essay is complemented by 'Welfare in the context of social policy', in which Marshall demonstrated how civilized social policies become expressions of 'mutual aid on the basis of common citizenship', when they bring together the formal provisions of statutory services and informal family and neighbourhood services – a process of enlargement offering the best protection against the intrusion of services which might isolate and humiliate the needful.

Where then, asked Marshall, should we 'put the emphasis in all human situations which are *psycho-social*?'. His answer was 'bang in the middle, on the hyphen' because 'At that point of perfect balance the social worker can exercise an expertise which is not that of the psychiatrist, a systematized procedure which is not that of the bureaucrat, and a personal influence which is not that of a moral censor' (1981: 81).

The relevance of Marshall's thought to social policy studies

That Marshall's work is highly relevant to the study of social policy is perhaps more widely recognized now than it was in his lifetime. Marshall's enduring commitment to sociology as a synthesizing discipline provided the intellectual grounding for his model of social welfare, which made allowance for the structural and cultural determinants of needs and for the way in which policies might also take account of these factors. His model encompassed both the formal and the informal dimensions of welfare and its multidimensional institutional aspects, including the connections between wealth and poverty and the exercise of freedom and power. The Marshallian approach is uniquely well suited to showing how specific issues of policy such as the exercise of discretion are related to the broader institutional issues of citizenship, class and welfare typologies. Marshall's guidance over the 'stepping-stones of the middle distance' prepares the ambitious student for bolder excursions into the wider ranges of national and comparative analysis.

Marshall argued that the essence of a sociological approach to the study of social policy resides in 'a disciplined command of a body of knowledge and concepts, a style of thought and an accumulation of experience in their use [which] is, like the diagnostic skill of the physician and the forensic skill of the lawyer, both individual and, at the same time, collegial' (Marshall, 1973: 98). Marshall was always ready to protect the integrity of his own subject, having no wish to launch out on enterprises of academic imperialism or to establish a coterie of like-minded scholars during his lifetime.

His writings exemplify a rare form of academic achievement. They stand as an original and authoritative contribution in two fields of social science, and they can be read both as social policy and as sociology. Marshall played a vital part in establishing the academic identity of a field of knowledge previously categorized almost exclusively by common 'social ideals and political purpose'. Many students are drawn to a subject like social policy in the hope of being confirmed in their beliefs or of finding a basic theory or model capable of providing answers to the dilemmas of social welfare. Reading Marshall reminds us that the first task of students is to get rid of their prejudices. Far from offering unitary explanations, the logic of Marshall's analysis shows that the dynamics of social policy stems from a set of institutional dilemmas which are by their very nature unresolvable.

Marshall is seen by George and Wilding as a 'Fabian socialist', and by Dennis and Halsey as one of their six exemplars of English ethical socialism (George and Wilding, 1976: 62–84; Dennis and Halsey, 1988: 122–48). While it is true that Marshall's views on welfare are socialist rather than collectivist, they are none the less part of a broader political analysis which readily accepts competitive market capitalism as the best available guarantee of economic prosperity and social welfare. Even in today's sceptical context, Marshall's dictum that 'The task of banishing poverty ... must be undertaken jointly by welfare and capitalism' would not pass for a socialist sentiment (Marshall, 1981: 117).

Marshall's conceptualization of citizenship and his account of its evolution in modern times are perpetuated in current debates about social change and the nature of social rights, responsibilities and needs. Baker and Giddens have criticized Marshall for expounding an evolutionary, even a Whiggishly optimistic, theory of the growth of citizenship (Baker, 1979; Giddens, 1982). More recently, Hirschman has called for 'a corrective of Marshall's optimism', and a greater awareness of the 'dilemmas and conflicts' which he overlooked would be worth cultivating – if Marshall had indeed overlooked them in the first place (Hirschman, 1991: 86).

Other commentators like Turner and myself are more interested in the importance given to institutional conflicts and value contradictions in his analysis. Citizenship may play a balancing role between the moral claims of the economic and social markets, but the balance is never more than precarious. Marshall was as alive to the possibility of regress as to that of progress in social change, and he did not claim that the rights of citizenship developed in immutable order. As Turner observes, Marshall's account of citizenship 'does not *necessarily* entail some commitment to an immanent logic in capital; on the contrary, his view of citizenship appears to rest on a contingent view of historical development' (Turner, 1986: 45; see also Pinker, 1981: 1-28). The development of social welfare is determined by fortuitous changes of circumstance rather than by forces of historical necessity.

Marshall's sense of historical contingency was complemented by his understanding of normative relativism and ethical relativity. It may be, as Jayasuriya observes, that Marshall's approach to citizenship was 'framed primarily within a liberal, individualist tradition' of philosophical thought (Jayasuriya, 1992: 22–3). Nevertheless, in his analysis only a pluralist model of welfare was capable of encompassing the variety of principles and aspirations that demand expression in complex industrial societies. With regard to the problem of choosing between equally desirable but potentially conflicting ends in policy making, Marshall's approach inclined towards the relativities of compromise rather than the absolutes of economic freedom or state-regulated security. As Marshall himself remarked, 'This kind of ethical relativity has been a feature of very nearly every society since civilization began' (Marshall, 1981: 129).

At the present time, when the whole institutional basis and rationale of the British welfare state is the subject of radical reappraisal from all points of the political compass, students will find Marshall's position in the middle ground a useful starting point for their own reading and reflection. The value issues addressed by Marshall are still at the heart of the debate about the nature of welfare rights and obligations that has been gathering momentum since the early 1980s. Plant, Lesser and Taylor-Gooby's *Political Philosophy and Social Welfare* links this debate to the seminal works of Rawls and Nozick, and Barry on justice brings it up to date (Rawls, 1971; Barry, 1973, 19; Nozick, 1974; Plant *et al.*, 1980).

Rieger comments on the historically specific and individualist nature of Marshall's conceptualization of the rights of citizenship, which is far removed, in his opinion, from what he describes as 'the modern view' of these rights, which accords them the status of 'natural rights' (Rieger, 1992: 28-33). Like other collectivists, Rieger draws attention to the undeveloped communitarian possibilities contained in Marshall's approach. Like Jayasuriya and Turner, he argues that only by encouraging more active forms of political participation can citizenship become an authentic framework for social solidarity and integration (Rieger, 1992). Turner goes further, in arguing that Marshall's approach to citizenship 'can be used as the basic definition of modernization' and as a 'universalist criterion of social development which is not ethnocentric, teleological or idealist' (Turner, 1986: 59).

Other writers, like Walzer, have interpreted and broadened the concept of citizenship to include multiple 'spheres of justice' encompassing a variety of social goals (Walzer, 1983). Among Marshall's critics, Barbelet has linked his concepts to a wide range of social movements committed to advancing the civic claims of women, ethnic groups and environmental issues (Barbalet, 1988).

Marshall wrote little on women's issues, and the main focus of his writings was on citizenship as a feature of sovereign independent states. Williams, however, is wide of the mark in claiming that Marshall does not face the 'fundamental contradiction that although women developed their political rights as individuals, a woman's eligibility to many social rights through welfare policies is as a dependant of her husband or the man with whom she lives' (Williams, 1989: 129).

Marshall did in fact address this issue in *Citizenship and Social Class* in order to emphasize a different but closely related point – that protection (under the early Factory Acts) was confined to women because they were not considered to be full citizens and, as he remarked, the 'champions of women's rights were quick to detect the implied insult' (Marshall and Bottomore, 1992: 15).

Marshall attached as much importance to fulfilling obligations as to the assertion of rights, recognizing the symbiotic nature of their relationship in free societies. Here his approach has much in common with that of Janowitz, Glendon and Mead (Janowitz, 1976; Mead, 1986; Glendon, 1991). When the debate loses contact with legal, economic and other institutional realities, it degenerates into the 'rights-babble' of political activism.

On the question of citizenship defined within the terms of nationality, it has been pointed out by Bottomore and others that since Marshall's death two divergent trends have emerged in the relationship between citizenship and national identity. The first is the dramatic growth in the number and variety of separatist movements throughout the world, a phenomenon apparent in places as different and as far apart as Canada, Spain, Northern Ireland, Italy and the former Soviet Union and Yugoslavia. These movements are largely driven by powerful cultural ideologies in which issues concerning civil rights are given enormous importance. Where autonomy is achieved, we see the formation of smaller nation-states with a strong sense of their own distinctive and exclusive rights and obligations.

The second trend embraces powerful political movements driven by ideological, economic and technological imperatives, and committed to unifying existing states within new international entities. Islam is one such force, the European Community another. Throughout Europe we can observe both centrifugal and centripetal forces at work. Massive postwar migrations have also diversified the cultural and ethnic characteristics of many western nation-states. In the case of the European Community, the trend is towards creating a shared framework of legally sanctioned civil, economic and social rights. Rieger, however, points out that, while the Social Chapter may be seen as an incipient form of European citizenship, it reflects in reality 'a community of quite limited liability' with regard to the status of migrant workers and the largely symbolic nature of its general provisions (Rieger, 1992: 29–30).

The continuing friction between the UK and other member states over the principle of subsidiarity suggests that these provisions will remain largely symbolic for some time to come. In a recent essay, Spicker utilizes the universalist elements in Marshall's concept of citizenship to support the idea of an authentically European framework, noting that 'The challenge to universalist social policy goes beyond a simple clash of values', but adding that 'As the community develops, services will become progressively more comprehensive in their scope.' He acknowledges that 'The kind of model this is consistent with is the argument for "citizenship" put, for example, by T.H. Marshall or more recently by Ruth Lister' (Spicker, 1993: 221; Lister, 1990).

The principle of citizenship underlies the concept of 'democratic welfare-capitalism' as a distinctive form of mixed economy and a specific, historical social system in its own right. Marshall stands out as the intellectual precursor of our current analysts of mixed economies of welfare and welfare pluralism, his ideas forming a recurring point of reference for advocates and critics alike. He saw the competitive market as a central element in a mixed economy, in which the pursuit of private interests was to be encouraged, and a measure of inequality in income and wealth accepted – although not beyond the point at which they might undermine the equal rights of citizenship on which the general enhancement of welfare ultimately depends. At times he could be taken to be advocating a more positive relationship, not so much between welfare and capitalism, but between welfare markets and competitive markets.

This distinction has exposed him to justifiable criticism from different quarters. Some Marxists have argued that, so long as a competitive market operates to the extent proposed by Marshall, the society in question will remain quintessentially capitalist. On the New Right, the theory is that when a competitive market is restricted to the extent proposed by Marshall it ceases to be truly competitive and becomes a subordinate feature of a collectivist command economy.

There is a third interpretation to be found, however, in Marshall's own analysis, in his 'afterthought' on 'Value problems of welfare-capitalism'. Here he observed that

> The substitution of the mixed economy for capitalism marks the passage from arguments about values to attempts to analyse a specific historical social system – the one which evolved in Britain and most of Western Europe in the first twenty years or so after the war, and still survives in a recognizable though, at least in Britain, a rather battered condition.

However, he allowed that 'It is perfectly legitimate to assign this system to the broad category of capitalism (some call it neo-capitalism), but it is a type of capitalism of which a distinguishing feature is the presence of a mixed economy' (Marshall, 1981: 123). Marshall did not live to see the full extent of the battering that was still to fall on the British welfare state – or the extent to which the concept of a mixed economy could be stretched to accommodate divergent models of pluralism (Pinker, 1991).

He believed that the best balance was one permitting marginal shifts and adjustments to take place over time, but stopping well short of changes which would be likely to lead to a serious diminution of political freedom – without which welfare in its fullest sense cannot be said to exist at all. His idea of welfare rested on this balance between the claims of different kinds of right and the satisfaction of different kinds of need. He considered that economic, political and social rights all expressed different dimensions of welfare, and that it was not possible to go on extending any one of these rights at the expense of the others without crossing the critical threshold at which the relationship between freedom and security becomes one of diminishing marginal utility.

The impact of Marshall's thought on social policy

I take the term 'classical sociologist' to refer to someone whose work displays a deep understanding of the structure of major social institutions, of the processes which cause these institutions to survive and change, and of the ways in which they affect the lives of ordinary people. Marshall chose social policy as the institutional context for his explorations, but it is the clarity and originality of his sociological understanding that give his work enduring relevance. His sociological influence can be seen in Turner's *Citizenship and Capitalism*, Harris's *Justifying State Welfare* and Miller's *Market, State and Community*, books concerned with the development of new institutional frameworks for the analysis of social policy issues. In them the normative balances are made to shift between different versions of 'democratic welfare-capitalism' and 'democratic-market socialism', and this adds to our understanding, as old ideological stereotypes are broken down (Reisman, 1984; Turner, 1986; Harris, 1987; Miller, 1989).

In his comparative study of the politics of social solidarity, Peter Baldwin states the premise that solidaristic policies 'have become accepted, legitimate and uncontroversial only to the extent that they are regarded as a right rather than as charity or altruism', adding that this was 'the point of Marshall's trinity of rights and the concept of social citizenship' (Baldwin, 1990: 29). Pierson, in an equally informative reappraisal of welfare states, links Marshall's work to theories of modernization and the extension of political rights (Pierson, 1991: 22–5). Describing Marshall as a 'new liberal' – which strikes me as more accurate than labelling him a socialist – Pierson draws parallels between Marshall and Rawls relating to their social democratic values, and in his conclusion he suggests that Marshall, like his 'new liberal forerunners', failed to show 'how citizens are to exercise effective control over a state from which their capacities as citizens derive' (1991: 202). Failure in this respect, however, may be seen as characteristic of all the other social and political theorists who go beyond the idea of a minimalist state. They in turn have to ask how the rights of the poorest citizens are to be protected without a measure of statutory intervention and provision.

It is revealing to compare Marshall's essays in *The Right to Welfare* with Esping-Andersen's *Three Worlds of Welfare Capitalism*. Esping-Andersen makes much of the concept of 'de-commodification' in delineating and justifying the processes by which citizens are emancipated from dependence on market forces for the meeting of certain basic needs through the extension of statutory social services. What he does not show is why dependency on the state is any more liberating than dependency on the market. He agrees with Marshall's proposition 'that social citizenship constitutes the core idea of a welfare state', but insists that the concept must be 'fleshed out' (Esping-Andersen, 1990: 21) by taking fuller account of the status of individuals *vis-à-vis* the market and commodification, the system of stratification and the family's role in social provision.

Marshall, however, was acutely sensitive to the effect of market forces on the status of individuals. He did not use the term 'de-commodification', but he was well aware of the process which it describes and, with characteristic succinctness, he gave an interpretation of the liberating and disabling propensities of market capitalism that was rather different to Esping-Andersen's. He observed that 'Socialists have maintained that capitalism treats labour as a *commodity*. Of course it does, and that is its contribution to freedom, for the alternative was to go on treating the *labourer* as a commodity, and that meant slavery and serfdom' (Marshall, 1981: 163).

To turn to a very important part of the subject-matter of social policy, relating to more substantive and specific issues such as the links between needs, rights and discretion, and the causal connection between poverty and inequality – if, as seems likely, the government dismantles what is left of the universalist framework of the British welfare state, there can be no guarantee that a future Labour government would have the will, the resources or the political mandate to put it together again. Unlike Beveridge, Marshall did not place unequivocal emphasis on the superiority of benefits based on insurance rights, rather than those deriving from the exercise of discretion as the expression of a felt obligation on the part of society to meet need irrespective of legal rights. In his view, it was the status of citizenship which made this kind of 'right' an authentic one. Troubled in his last years by the policy trends and rising incidence of unemployment which were beginning to drive more and more people into states of welfare dependency, Marshall deplored the economy's increasing inability to meet its social obligations, and he feared that the end result would be 'the gradual degradation of the welfare principle' (1981: 135).

The combination of recession, high levels of unemployment, welfare retrenchment and demographic pressures is testing the conceptual and institutional credentials not only of democratic welfare-capitalism, but of other hybrids like 'democratic-market socialism'. This state of crisis across the western world is partly due to intermittent failures of capitalist markets as a system of wealth creation, and partly due to the more comprehensive failure of the various forms of socialism, both democratic and *dirigiste*, to meet welfare expectations. If, as a result of these problems, statutory social service provision becomes residual, and universal welfare gives way to selective welfare, the Marshallian concept of social citizenship will be able to survive only if the rights which it embodies are given some form of constitutional status. Without such reinforcement, the institutional links between the concept of universal citizenship and the right to welfare – at however modest a level – will be broken.

Finally, there is Marshall's contribution to the textual legacy of social policy and administration. In 1976 the Joint University Council for Public and Social Administration surveyed the popularity of standard texts on the subject. Marshall's *Social Policy in the Twentieth Century* (1970) and two of Titmuss' books were among those most frequently recommended. Since then this work has been cogently revised and updated by Tony Rees, and it continues as one of the leading introductory texts (Rees, 1985), even though Marshall retired from the world of undergraduate and graduate teaching in 1956.

In the face of ever-lengthening reading lists, students will find one special cause for gratitude to Marshall. He always used his remarkable talent for conceptualization and synthesis in the interests of clarity and brevity. Perhaps the most impressive tribute paid to his scholarship over the years is to be found in Michael Oakeshott's review of *Citizenship and Social Class* in 1951, shortly after its publication: 'Professor Marshall', he remarked, 'is not a voluminous writer, but when he gives us something of this quality we can resign ourselves to his long periods of silence' (Oakeshott, 1951: 629–30). Oakeshott thought that Marshall's treatment of social rights was too narrow, neglecting as it did some of their legal and religious dimensions. Nevertheless he acknowledged Marshall's 'subtlety and reflectiveness' and the non-partisan quality of his writing, and he observed that 'Nobody can read him without enlightenment and the pleasure that comes from a sincere and cogent argument' (1951: 629–30). At a superficial political level, Marshall and Oakeshott had little in common, but they had the same distaste for zealotry and the same devotion to the pursuit of knowledge for its own sake.

Key texts

Marshall's seminal essays on *Citizenship and Social Class* (1950, reprinted 1992) set out the historical and institutional framework on which he subsequently built his pluralist model of 'democratic welfare-capitalism'. His essay on 'Value problems of welfare-capitalism' first appeared in the *Journal of Social Policy* (1972), and was subsequently republished in *The Right to Welfare* (1981), along with an 'afterthought' on 'The "hyphenated society"' and other essays on poverty, power, the relationship between rights and discretion, and freedom and welfare in the context of social development. In 1985 A.M. Rees published a revised and updated edition of *T.H. Marshall's Social Policy* (1985).

References

Baker, J. (1979) 'Social conscience and social policy', *Journal of Social Policy*, 8, 2, pp. 117–206.
Baldwin, P. (1990) *The Politics of Social Solidarity: Class bases of the European welfare state, 1875–1975*, Cambridge: Cambridge University Press.
Barbalet, J.M. (1988) *Citizenship*, Milton Keynes: Open University Press.
Barry, B. (1973) *The Liberal Theory of Justice: A critical examination of the principle doctrine in A Theory of Justice by John Rawls*, Oxford: Clarendon Press.
Barry, B. (1989) *A Treatise on Social Justice*, Vol. 1, *Theories of Justice*, Hemel Hempstead: Harvester Wheatsheaf.
Blake, Lord, and Nicholls, C.S. (eds) (1990) *The Dictionary of National Biography: 1981–1985*, Oxford: Oxford University Press, entry on 'Marshall, Thomas Humphrey', pp. 266–7.

Dennis, N. and Halsey, A.H. (1988) *English Ethical Socialism: Thomas More to R.H. Tawney*, Oxford: Clarendon Press.

Esping-Andersen, G. (1990) *The Three Worlds of Welfare Capitalism*, Oxford: Polity.

George, V. and Wilding, P. (1976) *Ideology and Social Welfare*, London: Routledge and Kegan Paul.

Giddens, A. (1982) *Profiles and Critiques in Social Theory*, London: Macmillan.

Glendon, M.A. (1991) *Rights Talk: The impoverishment of political discourse*, New York: The Free Press.

Harris, D. (1987) *Justifying State Welfare*, Oxford: Oxford University Press.

Hirschman, A.O. (1991) *The Rhetoric of Reaction*, Cambridge, Mass., and London: Belknap Press of Harvard University Press.

Janowitz, M. (1976) *Social Control of the Welfare State*, New York: Elsevier.

Jayasuriya, L. (1992) 'Citizenship and welfare: rediscovering Marshall', paper presented at the Conference on Beyond Economic Rationalism: Alternative Futures for Social Policy, University of Western Australia, Perth, pp. 22–3.

Lister, R. (1990) *The Exclusive Society*, London: Child Poverty Action Group.

Marshall, T.H. (1950) *Citizenship and Social Class and Other Essays*, Cambridge: Cambridge University Press.

Marshall, T.H. (1963) *Sociology at the Crossroads and Other Essays*, London: Heinemann.

Marshall, T.H. (1970) *Social Policy in the Twentieth Century*, London: Hutchinson.

Marshall, T.H. (1973) 'A British sociological career', *International Social Science Journal*, **xxv**, 1/2, p. 95.

Marshall, T.H. (1981) *The Right to Welfare and Other Essays*, London: Heinemann Educational Books, p. 119.

Marshall, T.H. and Bottomore, T. (1992) *Citizenship and Social Class*, London and Concord, Mass: Pluto (including a long commentary by Tom Bottomore).

Mead, M. (1986) *Beyond Entitlement: The social obligations of citizenship*, New York: The Free Press.

Miller, D. (1989) *Market, State and Community*, Oxford: Clarendon Press.

Nozick, R. (1974) *Anarchy, State and Utopia*, Oxford: Blackwell.

Oakeshott, M. (1951) *The Cambridge Journal*, **iv**, 10, pp. 629–30.

Pierson, C. (1991) *Beyond the Welfare State*, Oxford: Polity.

Pinker, R. (1981) 'Introduction', in T.H. Marshall, *The Right to Welfare and Other Essays*, London: Heinemann.

Pinker, R. (1991) 'On rediscovering the middle way in social welfare', in Wilson, T. and Wilson, D. (eds), *The State and Social Welfare: The objectives of policy*, London and New York: Longman.

Plant, R., Lesser, H. and Taylor-Gooby, P. (1980) *Political Philosophy and Social Welfare*, London: Routledge and Kegan Paul.

Rawls J. (1971) *A Theory of Justice*, Cambridge, Mass.: Belknap Press of Harvard University Press.

Rees, A.M. (1985) *T.H. Marshall's Social Policy in the Twentieth Century*, London: Hutchinson.

Reisman, D. (1984) 'T.H. Marshall and the middle ground', in Boulding, K.E. (ed.), *The Economics of Human Betterment*, London: Macmillan.

Rieger, E. (1992) 'T.H. Marshall's theory of citizenship rights revisited: social rights in the nation state and in the European Community', paper presented to the Conference on Comparative Studies of Welfare State Development, University of Bremen, September, pp. 28–33.

Spicker, P. (1993) 'Can European social policy be universalist?', in Page, R. and Baldock, J. (eds), *Social Policy Review 5*, Social Policy Association, University of Kent.

Turner, B.S. (1986) *Citizenship and Capitalism: The debate over reformism*, London: Allen and Unwin.

Walzer, M. (1983) *Spheres of Justice: A defense of pluralism and equality*, New York: Basic Books.

Williams, F. (1989) *Social Policy: A critical introduction*, Oxford: Polity.

7 Galbraith

David Reisman

Brief biography

Galbraith is a political economist in the multidisciplinary mould of Smith and Mill. He is a social democrat like Tawney and a persuader like Crosland. Few contemporary thinkers have attracted so great a popular readership, or stimulated so much debate on the big issues of affluence and poverty, market and state, business and society.

John Kenneth Galbraith was born in Canada in 1908. Initially a student at the Ontario Agricultural College, he travelled across the continent in the era of the Great Depression, *The Grapes of Wrath* and the 'Hoovervilles' of the homeless, to do a Ph.D. in agricultural economics at Berkeley. In 1933 he was appointed to an instructorship at Harvard (where he read the *General Theory* and was convinced of the market failure that Hitler's public works and Roosevelt's New Deal were already involved in correcting). After that came wartime service in charge of price control, where he came to the conclusion that full employment without inflation is possible only if the government enforces its guidelines; then Harvard again, where he retired in 1975 from the prestigious post of Paul M. Warburg Professor of Economics. Active in the Democratic Party, American Ambassador to India, and a high-profile media commentator, Galbraith has written works of fiction and a book on Indian art as well as the social science classics with which this chapter will principally be concerned.

The economic framework

Galbraith is a non-Marxian determinist and an evolutionary thinker. Convinced that institutions develop in a broadly similar manner – 'Given the decision to have modern industry, much of what happens is inevitable and the same'

(Galbraith, 1974: 388) – he has long predicted the convergence of economic systems and the end of the Cold War. Ideas can speed up the unavoidable and channel events at the margin. Their autonomous power is for all that extremely limited. It makes no sense to argue for competitive markets in a world of economies of scale in which 'large tasks require large organizations' (Galbraith, 1977: 277). It makes no sense to champion consumer sovereignty where corporate success is dependent upon effective manipulation. World-views have their place and even Canute was able to emancipate belief. All things considered, however, thought is afterthought and ideology arrives *post festum*: 'Given a little time, circumstances will prove you either right or wrong' (Galbraith, 1973: 21).

Like the Joseph Schumpeter of *Capitalism, Socialism and Democracy*, Galbraith argues that big business is in the vanguard of technological progress. Giant corporations are innovative and adventurous. They are also exposed and vulnerable. Large amounts of sector-specific capital must be sunk many years in advance of the product being marketed, first in research and development and later in specialized plant. The corporations would simply not be able to take the risk if they did not have a high degree of confidence that the demand would ultimately be forthcoming for the output they supply. Thence their dependence on what Galbraith calls 'planning'. Planning is predicting the future, but it also means the exercise of an active influence such that the future fits in and does not disrupt. Thus the corporation will use advertising and selling skills to sell a target quantity at a target price. It will make tacit non-aggression pacts with its rivals and abstain from expanding into their market share. It will press the state to forgo *laissez-faire* in favour of guaranteed markets, progress payments, tariffs, quotas, subsidies, tax concessions and relevant infrastructure. It will make long-term contracts with suppliers and outlets, integrate backwards into raw materials or forwards into retailing, and go multinational in order to minimize its uncertainty. It will give the unions generous pay rises to prevent disruption through strikes. It will finance new investment from internally generated resources in order not to become exposed to the scrutiny of outside lenders. All of this is a world away from the demand-led flexibility of the idealized economic market. The old-style sequence is still to be found in the small-firm part of the developed private sector. On the other hand, the corner newsagent or local café can hardly be said to be forcing the pace of change.

Economic dynamism, Galbraith asserts, is closely correlated with business power: to reject the lobbying and the sales techniques is in that sense to reject the jet aircraft and the pharmaceutical breakthroughs that are the by no means unattractive consequences of size. Frightening or beneficent, corporate power is nowadays a fact of life – and so is the concentration of authority within the giant organization. The power to decide is no longer the prerogative of the capitalist owner: dispersed, amorphous, anonymous, the shareholders' freedom to instruct has fallen victim to a process of euthanasia that has left the managers and the technocrats *de facto* accountable to no one but themselves. Out go the old-style goals of profit maximization that once motivated the business to please the shopper. In come the new-style goals of job satisfaction, security and growth that are more in keeping with the personal objectives of highly educated experts working in teams than would be the pursuit of dividends that the executive on a salary is unlikely ever to pocket.

The message of Galbraith's non-Marxian determinism might appear to be the gloomy inference that the shareholder and the community alike are doomed for ever to be bullied by committees of specialists in command of scarce knowledge. Determinism, fortunately, also generates the requisite countervailing power in the form of the intellectual community and the politically radical. These constituencies may be expected successfully to catalyze a public opinion that is itself increasingly sceptical of the squirrel-wheel dominion of the technocrat. The university teachers and the responsible politicians, the Galbraiths and the Kennedys, may be expected to guide their community in the direction of the middle path, neither free market nor stifling command. The result will be balanced and mixed, environmental and aesthetic – and the social services will come into their own.

The idea of welfare

Galbraith's approach to the social services state is an integral part of his more general vision of the balanced society. It is, more specifically, an integral part of his theory of 'private opulence and public squalor' (Galbraith, 1973: 212).

The private sector, Galbraith says, is percentagewise too large. Consumer credit and aggressive marketing stimulate demand almost exclusively for commercial output: governments are stigmatized for debt and criticized when they manufacture expectations that they would not otherwise have been asked to satisfy. Also, income tax having a progressive bias, the marginal service simultaneously means a marginal burden that, not neutral, reopens old antagonisms between the rich and the poor: the spending being wedded to the redistribution, the compromise is that 'the money is frequently not appropriated and the service not performed' (1973: 216). The private sector and not the state has benefited most from the conventional definition of national wealth as saleable commodities: such a standard makes school-desks and cars productive, teachers and police officers a drain on other people's value-added. The private sector and not the state has stood to gain most from the individualism of economists and libertarians who assume *laissez-faire* and deduce free enterprise: while no one can have any real warmth for autocrats who build palaces when the masses have to eat cake, it is Galbraith's contention that it is an error and an exaggeration to tar the Health Service with the brush that was meant for the Gulag. The private sector and not the state has, in short, enjoyed the lion's share of prestige and expansion. The resulting imbalance is as graphic as too many cars, not enough roads; as deplorable as too much rubbish, not enough collectors.

The private sector is percentagewise too large. The public sector is percentagewise too small. Galbraith regards the current mix as morally objectionable, as an 'obscene contrast' (Galbraith, 1966a: 30). More importantly, he also believes that the underfunding of the state is increasingly out of step with the structural imperatives of modern conditions. A convinced determinist, Galbraith insists that his interventionism is 'not ideological', but 'compelled by circumstance' (Galbraith, 1975: 295).

Some of the public services which Galbraith encourages the community more generously to provide have the character of the economist's 'public good'. It is in the nature of such a commodity that, exclusion being technically impossible or prohibitively expensive, free access must be granted to all if supply is to be forthcoming at all to any. Such is the case, for example, with law and order and the fire services, the spillovers from mass literacy and the containment of infectious disease. As national income rises, so people demand more and more of these public goods – and the state alone can meet the felt wishes of the sovereign citizens.

Some public services have the character of public goods. Others are undemanded but deserving, goods that individuals ought to demand but sometimes do not. Capable of being a paternalist and an élitist, Galbraith not only is dismissive of the popular demand for the gold-plated mousetrap, but is also of the opinion that the community has a duty to guide its members down the road of unrevealed preferences that leads to museums and not to cigarettes, to subsidized television and not to violent soaps. The demand for beautiful architecture and classical music will follow the supply that primes the pump. Like Keynes, Galbraith has real confidence in wise politicians who, like wise dentists, know best what is in the innocent individual's long-term best interest.

It often happens, of course, that people know precisely what they want, but still are not in an economic position to put their money where their mouth is. A third group of public services picks up the satisfaction of those wants which the community regards as high priority, but which the market refuses to meet in the absence of payment. Low-income housing is a case in point: 'In no economically advanced country . . . does the market system build houses the poor can afford' (Galbraith, 1993: 44). It is not the only example: health care, drug addiction centres, occupational training and retraining – where the poor cannot pay, the nation that wants these services to be provided must provide them itself.

Looking at the three classes of public services that may be identified in Galbraith's political economy, what is striking is the redistributive bias that he imputes to each. In the first case, the public playgrounds and the public parks are likely to be of disproportionate benefit to those who cannot join golf clubs or cultivate luxurious gardens in their villas. In the second case, the need that precedes the demand is more likely to be the latent desire of the less educated than it is of the well pianoed and the precociously balleted. In the third case, the slum schools and the public pools are likely to be the only game in town for those too deprived to pay pipers and call tunes. The phrase 'private affluence, public poverty' evidently has a double meaning: referring explicitly to the commercial/state mix, it relates at one and the same time to the 'great deprivation amidst the great wealth' (Galbraith, 1973: 21) that Galbraith detects in rich countries such as the United States, and which he believes can be corrected only through a significant expansion in public spending. It should surprise no one that Galbraith originally intended to call *The Affluent Society* by the mirror-image name of *Why People Are Poor*. Poor people figure prominently in Galbraith's work – and the government is the answer to their distress.

The integration of the disadvantaged into the mainstream of productive life is seed-corn that produces a rich harvest for all: 'Good health services increase the number of people who are physically and mentally able to take part in the economy ... Mostly this is what a good educational system accomplishes ... We should help people to participate in the economy; we should help them to help themselves' (Galbraith, 1966b: 21). Such welfare is clearly not the dependency culture so much as the assisted take-off into self-sustaining assiduity. To that extent the call to welfare is also an appeal to the enlightened self-interest of the growth-conscious community. Growth by itself will not raise up the sickly or put the illiterate on the escalator to affluence: growth by itself 'only helps those who have a foothold in the system and ... helps most those who have the most' (Galbraith, 1971a: 101). Reversing the argument, however, the sickly and the illiterate can in the long run make a valuable contribution to living standards – provided that self-liquidating public expenditure first enables them to make a good start. No growth-conscious community will fail to see the attraction of such a public investment.

Some go up. Some stay down. In the case of the downs as well as the ups, the appeal to interest is persuasive: 'Perhaps the disadvantaged are now too few to make a revolution. But they could make life uncomfortable for all' (Galbraith, 1980: 5). The angry inner city in flames is a powerful reminder to the haves of what can happen when the have-nots lose faith in the escape valve of intergenerational upward mobility: 'As this process comes to an end – as membership in the underclass becomes stable and enduring – greater resentment and social unrest should be expected' (Galbraith, 1993: 40). Never explaining precisely why it is that he feels increasingly pessimistic about the progressive *embourgeoisement* of the urban black or the immigrant Hispanic, what Galbraith does say in his later work is that the prosperous can no longer assume that the no-hopers will remain politely out of sight. In an earlier historical epoch, the affluent responded to the call of interest when the threat was from the proletariat: 'Capitalism wouldn't have survived if it hadn't had the rough, harsh edges taken off by the welfare state' (Galbraith, 1988: 81). Determinism now makes the same appeal to interest when unemployment compensation and the negative income tax are promised to a disaffected sub-class dwelling beyond the pale of the American Dream.

Interest, certainly, but compassion as well. Galbraith writes considerably less about the social ethic and the gift relationship than do British theorists of citizenship and community such as Tawney and Titmuss. Even so, he has no difficulty in situating the humanitarian sentiments in his evolutionary schema: 'I am persuaded, as was Marx . . . that economic development is itself an education in social cohesiveness and cooperation' (Galbraith, 1979: 95). Again and again in his work, Galbraith advances proposals that cannot appeal to interest and must be anchored in altruism. He supports benefits for the disabled and the elderly. He is prepared to countenance welfare instead of work where the job in question is, like shining shoes, demeaning and marginal. He is unsympathetic to the means test because it is 'an affront to human dignity' (Galbraith, 1966a: 30). He is accepting and non-judgemental of controversial claimants such as alcoholics and addicts. Examples such as these remind the reader that social values alongside structure and function play a prominent part in Galbraith's legitimation of the welfare state.

Galbraith looks to public spending to meet the needs of the disadvantaged. Thus it is that he is an advocate of selective discrimination in favour of the most deprived. State schooling is a case in point: there, he says, opportunities should be equalized through disproportionate expansion, through the concentration of resources 'in the congested urban areas and in the poor rural districts . . . instead of spreading them over the whole educational system' (Galbraith, 1965: 658). What he would do about the dispersed – the schizophrenic, the paraplegic, the retarded – is less clear. Selective discrimination to the benefit of the financially at-risk would appear in such circumstances to be impossible without a personal means test capable of distinguishing the rich pensioner from the poor pensioner, the single parent with savings from the single parent without support. Galbraith in his later work has expressed guarded support for the negative income tax. It may be that he has come to regard the automaticity and the invisibility of the tax code as a useful halfway house between the perennial form filling on the one hand, and the universalistic free-on-demand on the other. If he has, the compromise would serve coincidentally to make his theory of redistributive discrimination properly symmetrical. The affluent, after all, have long been singled out for special treatment by means of the progressive tax bands that Galbraith has described as 'a powerful force for equality and the stability of our economic institutions' (Galbraith, 1964: 24).

Galbraith sees a direct relationship between public spending and social balance: 'There are few problems in New York City which would not be solved by doubling the city budget' (Galbraith, 1971b: 33). Importantly, he has also sought to make state regulation as well as state support a useful part of the welfare whole. A quota requirement would compel private enterprise to improve minority access to executive positions. A minimum wage would be a source of countervailing power for the scattered, the ununionized and the inarticulate. An incomes policy would both twist differentials in favour of the lower-paid and combat inflationary pressures without a loss of jobs. A commitment to higher taxes rather than to higher interest rates would protect borrowers (normally less affluent than lenders) from regressive burdens consequent upon macroeconomic restraint. In these and other ways, the government regulation of the market economy becomes an instrument of social welfare fully on a par with the social services that are provided by the state.

So, for that matter, does the market economy itself. Increasing affluence means across-the-board upgrading and the common culture of mass consumption. Rising living standards defuse relative resentments and act as a 'solvent of the tensions once associated with inequality' (Galbraith, 1973: 123). The sub-division of labour throws up parallel ladders and forces the rich to compete for prestige with intellectuals and technocrats, politicians and artists. Unlike Tawney and Titmuss, in short, Galbraith is able to welcome the private sector as an ally in the struggle for social integration without radical redistribution. To some extent the absolute upgrading may be regarded as a cosmetic concealment and not as a philosophical resolution: 'Increased real income provides us with an admirable detour around the rancour anciently associated with efforts to redistribute wealth' (Galbraith, 1961: 195). On the other hand, to those who accuse him of prettifying advanced capitalism by papering over the cracks in the stratified society, Galbraith is able to make the entirely reasonable reply that the issue of equal incomes has ceased to arouse any real passion in the more prosperous societies: 'The fact that a tacit truce exists on the issue of inequality is proof of its comparative lack of social urgency' (Galbraith, 1973: 251). And for that Tawney-like equilibrium, the market economy must justly take the lion's share of the credit.

Questions and adaptations

Galbraith's multidisciplinary model of social balance was at its most influential in the age of uncertainty that extended from the Soviet Sputnik in 1957 to the fall of Saigon in 1975. As social debate gave way to entrepreneurship and technocracy, it was bound to be not so much eclipsed by new theories as brushed aside in the rush for *how tos*. Galbraith's political economy of the welfare society remains a valuable synthesis and a useful guide. That does not mean, however, that the reader has no right to question or adapt the specific hypotheses that make up the model.

Private consumption is a case in point. Galbraith asserts that marginal utility *ex* manipulation tends in an affluent society rapidly to approach the zero of satiety. A typical consumable would then seem to be a frivolous toy such as 'a lawn mower that can be guided by transcendental meditation' (Galbraith, 1978: 50), the economic problem the glut and not the scarcity: 'Obesity is now rather more a problem than malnutrition, and far more ingenuity now goes into the packaging of food than the producing of it' (Galbraith, 1963: 22). Higher pensions and support to the arts are purchased in such a perspective at the opportunity cost of goods that are not worth consuming and that would not have been demanded at all in the absence of trickery. An alternative perspective would, however, suggest different inferences merely by rejecting the intolerant leaderliness of the Keynesians and the ascetic humourlessness of the Webbs. Such a perspective would stress that individuals' preferences must always be treated with respect. It would fail to make the puritan's distinction between clothing that protects and clothing that decorates. It would insist that the marginal taste is more likely to be for the microwave oven or the package holiday than it is for the exaggerated improbability of the gold-plated mousetrap. It would play down the ability of the advertisers to create demands in their desired image, while playing up the diffusion of information that is the free gift of competitive publicity. Such a perspective, it is clear, would reach the conclusion that private consumption is a thing worth having – and that public spending is purchased at the cost of a genuine sacrifice. Galbraith's welfarism is an easier option. Denying that the private sector delivers significant well-being-added beyond a moderate cut-off point, Galbraith is able to defend the redistribution towards the state with the argument that the resources transferred would elsewhere have all but gone to waste.

Were the confrontation to be a more equal one, the private/public trade-off would involve a tougher contest. Even then, however, the game would not have to be zero-sum so long as economic growth continued to generate new wealth. It is the great attraction of economic growth that it provides expanding tax revenues even as it raises households' living standards. Both sectors expanding at the same time, voters will almost certainly be better prepared to pay for public services than they would where stagnation made them defensive of their accustomed status quo. Besides that, growth itself is a source of indisputably social benefits. Like Keynesian deficits, it is a corrective of involuntary unemployment. Like affirmative action, it creates opportunities for the worker on the margin. Like comprehensive schooling, it upgrades and it integrates. Like political radicalism, it substitutes the kaleidoscopic for the conservative. Growth, it is clear, can be not only the most acceptable means of public finance, but the functional equivalent of the public sector as well. Yet supply presupposes demand – and Galbraith on private consumption is hardly enthusiastic about marginal tastes and preferences. Adopting the alternative perspective that is non-judgemental about demand-led growth, at least the unintended outcome might be more public spending and less social deprivation. The ends are Galbraithian. The means are not.

The funding of public services and the relief of social deprivation are closely connected in the Galbraithian model. The convergence is not complete. Public goods like roads are used by chauffeur-driven limousines as well as by crowded public buses. Paternalist services like libraries are patronized by the graduate entry at least as much as by the shop floor. Poverty programmes like clinics deliver factory fodder healthy enough to make a productive day's contribution. The non-deprived can gain and not just the less advantaged; but still Galbraith is insistent that the poor reap a benefit from the public sector that they would otherwise not be in a position to reap at all. In Galbraith's own words: 'Far more than is realized, the present problem of poverty stems from the past neglect of the public sector of the economy and the special service this sector renders to the poor' (Galbraith, 1966a: 30). Since Galbraith is convinced that 'it is the poor who need parks and whose children need swimming pools' – 'The well-to-do family can escape to the country' (Galbraith, 1964: 23) – one would have expected him to have made it his highest priority to target and to select. In the event, his proposals are stronger on the expansion of public services than they are on the skewing of those budgets to the benefit of the most at-risk. The areas inhabited by the poor are to be accorded special resourcing. The poor themselves are not, however, to be offered housing vouchers, means-tested to keep out the rich. The defence contracts, farm supports and corporate bail-outs of the privileged classes are to be subjected to critical scrutiny. The privileged classes themselves are not, however, to be exposed to user charges for their schooling and a graduate tax on their university. Galbraith's accusation is of a bias towards the powerful and a neglect of the silent: 'However intervention by the state may be condemned in the age of contentment, it has been relatively comprehensive when the interests of the contented are involved and relatively limited when the problems are those of the poor' (Galbraith, 1993: 162). Capitalism for the poor, socialism for the rich – Galbraith's assessment of the modern mixed economy is so much a cause for concern that the reader must wonder if Galbraith's proposals are genuinely adequate to bend back the bent rod.

Fine-tuning ought to appeal to Galbraith's supporters, convinced as they will be that the needy must be ranked above the comfortable in the allocation of public expenditure. Fine-tuning, coincidentally, will appeal as well to the welfare sceptics who, sharing Galbraith's sympathy with the out-of-work and the out-of-luck, believe none the less that the state sector is *in toto* not too small but rather too large.

One objection will involve the non-judgemental nature of Galbraith's welfarism. Car-owners are to be given roads and music-lovers a new hall. The unemployed are to receive benefits at or near the average weekly wage and the period of eligibility is to be lengthy. The dependent family is to receive accommodation and income without any suggestion that the right to welfare carries with it a duty to avoid contributory negligence. As the claims mount up, so the sceptic will wonder if the escalation will ever come to an end. Road congestion could be relieved by levies as well as services. The unemployed could be asked to document their search for work. The chronically alcoholic could be required to collect their benefits at rehabilitation centres. Galbraith does not explore these judgemental alternatives to tolerant acceptance. His humanitarianism is infinitely preferable to the Darwinian alternative of encouraging starving parents to eat their starving children. On the other hand, his willingness to concede claims and his reluctance to impose conditions must inevitably mean that some observers at some stage will complain that the state is taking away more satisfaction than it is actually putting back.

A related objection has to do with the poverty line. Some theorists identify the poor with the absolute deprivation of the hungry and the cold, the inadequately clothed and the primitively housed. Galbraith goes further by making deprivation a relative as well as an absolute standard: 'People are poverty-stricken when their income, even if adequate for survival, falls markedly behind that of the community. Then they cannot have what the larger community regards as the minimum necessary for decency' (Galbraith, 1973: 259). The focus is the organism and not just the cell. The hurdle is comparative and not merely individual. The orientation is generous – and the outcome is cost. Galbraith's critics will suggest that his 'markedly' and his 'decency' are synonyms for luxury and indulgence. They will add that so high a poverty line tends to make the public sector not too small but rather too large.

Then there is the status of value for money. Galbraith treats cost-effectiveness and internal efficiency as if they were shopkeeper fossils left behind from the pre-affluent society. A less extreme view would be to say that audits and accounts are not substitutes for welfare, but rather complements to it. In squeezing out waste, in curbing organizational slack, calculation and appraisal ensure that the social services sector can expand without exposing it to the criticism that it has grown too large on over-ordering and confused duplication.

Finally, there is public finance. Galbraith brushes aside the likelihood that high income tax will be a serious disincentive to effort: 'To be an executive would still be far better than fitting bolts on the shop floor' (Galbraith, 1975: 283). He is equally dismissive about the danger that intolerable inflation would result from the macroeconomic cocktail of low interest rates, high public spending and deficit finance through the mobilization of savings. Even if inflation were to become a threat to fixed incomes and to economic stability, Galbraith would say, an incomes policy still provides an effective solution. Galbraith's critics will by no means share his optimism and his confidence. Burdensome taxes discourage. Excessive inflation distorts. Incomes policies fail. To neglect important considerations such as these, Galbraith's critics will contend, is ill-advisedly to expand the state beyond the limit that the economy can afford – not, that is, without a deceleration in the rate of growth such as Galbraith would regard as no bad thing in the overdeveloped nations of the affluent West.

Key texts

Galbraith is a prolific author. Some of his books are tracts for the times (*How to Get Out of Vietnam*), some are novels (*The Triumph*), some are historical (*The Great Crash, 1929*), some are autobiographical (*A Life in our Times*). Four are of special relevance to the topic of welfare. Each is built around a key duality.

The Affluent Society (1958) examines the nature of social balance. Beginning with a history of economic thought, Galbraith argues that economics as a dismal science of allocation and scarcity is now out of date in the affluent conditions of the prosperous societies. What has taken the place of private poverty is public poverty. That being the case, the eighteenth-century invisible hand must be returned to the museum of obsolete ideas, and the state sector must be given the encouragement it needs to expand.

The New Industrial State (1967) is concerned with the organizational dynamics of corporate capitalism. Technocrats in committees (the 'technostructure') pursue objectives of their own that have little or nothing to do with the national interest. Intellectuals and teachers (the 'educational and scientific estate') champion less myopic causes and enlist the support of enlightened politicians. Given time and debate, Galbraith is convinced, the tail will cease to wag the dog, and moderation and mix will come to prevail.

Economics and the Public Purpose (1973) is a study of the dual economy. On the one hand, there are the corporate giants (the 'planning system'), innovative, powerful and oligopolistic. On the other hand, there are the small businesses (the 'market system'), backward, weak and competitive. Not neglecting the misery of the unemployed and the destitute, Galbraith says, it would still be a mistake for the state to fail to meet the very real needs of small entrepreneurs and their defenceless employees ground down by the sheer inequity of the unequal contest.

The Culture of Contentment (1992) contrasts the contented in their golden ghettoes with the underclass in the inner city. Arguing that government policy is abnormally responsive to the interests of the articulate, Galbraith makes himself the spokesman for an alienated sub-proletariat that does not know how to demand services in its own right. Galbraith is a determinist, but he is also a persuader. The sophistication of this mix combined with the coverage of his synthesis make his political economy of social welfare a whole that is greater than the sum of its parts.

References

Galbraith, J.K. (1961) *The Great Crash 1929*, Harmondsworth: Penguin. First published 1954.

Galbraith, J.K. (1963) *The Liberal Hour*, Harmondsworth: Penguin. First published 1960.

Galbraith, J.K. (1964) 'Let us begin: an invitation to action on poverty', *Harper's Magazine*, March.

Galbraith, J.K. (1965) 'Critic of affluence', *The Listener*, 6 May.

Galbraith, J.K. (1966a) 'An agenda for American liberals', *Commentary*, June.

Galbraith, J.K. (1966b) 'The starvation of the cities'; reprinted in Galbraith, J.K., *A View from the Stands*, London: Hamish Hamilton, 1987.

Galbraith, J.K. (1971a) 'Galbraith answers Crosland', *New Statesman*, 22 January.

Galbraith, J.K. (1971b) *The American Left and Some British Comparisons*, Fabian Tract 405, London: Fabian Society. This pamphlet reprints the substance of *Who Needs the Democrats*, Garden City: Doubleday and Co., 1970.

Galbraith, J.K. (1973) *The Affluent Society*, Harmondsworth: Penguin. First published 1958.

Galbraith, J.K. (1974) *The New Industrial State*, Harmondsworth: Penguin. First published 1967.

Galbraith, J.K. (1975) *Economics and the Public Purpose*, Harmondsworth: Penguin. First published 1973.

Galbraith, J.K. (1977) *The Age of Uncertainty*, London: BBC and André Deutsch.

Galbraith, J.K. (1978) *Almost Everyone's Guide to Economics* (with Nicole Salinger), Boston, Mass.: Houghton Mifflin Co.

Galbraith, J.K. (1979) 'Barbara Ward'; reprinted in Galbraith, J.K., *A View from the Stands*, London: Hamish Hamilton, 1987.

Galbraith, J.K. (1980) 'Two pleas for our age'; reprinted in Galbraith, J.K., *A View from the Stands*, London: Hamish Hamilton, 1987.

Galbraith, J.K. (1988) *Capitalism, Communism and Coexistence* (with Stanislav Menshikov), Boston, Mass.: Houghton Mifflin Co.

Galbraith, J.K. (1993) *The Culture of Contentment*, Harmondsworth: Penguin. First published 1992.

Part III

Democratic Socialists

Introduction

At the beginning of the twentieth century, socialism seemed poised to overtake and replace capitalism in Europe. At the end of the century, it is in general retreat despite the fact that capitalism itself is suffering from one of its periodic deep economic crises. The decline of socialism is due not simply to the collapse of the authoritarian regimes of Eastern Europe but, more importantly, to the inability of democratic socialist governments in Europe to meet their socialist, as distinct from their welfare, objectives. Of the four writers included in this part of the book, only Plant is alive to witness this change of fortunes for socialism, although Harrington was aware of it before his untimely death.

Democratic socialists have been the most fervent supporters of the welfare state, but they have always seen it as a staging post on the long march towards socialism. They have always advocated universalist social services partly because they believe that the very nature of such services creates a more altruistic social climate, which is an indispensable ingredient of a socialist society. Like the writers of the 'middle way', they consider the functions of welfare provision in positive terms. Where the two groups differ is that, while the middle way sees social services as reinforcing capitalism, democratic socialism sees them as eroding the ethical credentials of capitalism. So far, history is on the side of the middle way. Without the social services, capitalism in many European countries might have been overthrown or transformed by now.

This public rejection of traditional socialism has inevitably led to a re-examination of both the nature of socialism and the nature of socialist social services. It is, of course, true that socialism comes in many varieties, and for this reason it is more accurate to speak of socialisms rather than to pretend that there is a generally agreed socialist model. This is not the place to discuss this in detail. Suffice it to say that since the end of the last war, three main versions of socialism have dominated political debates. First, there was the socialism of Crosland, which was not very different from welfare capitalism. In this version of socialism, private ownership of the means of production would be the rule and public ownership the special exception. The abolition of poverty would be vigorously pursued, but inroads into income and wealth inequalities would be minor and incidental rather than major and planned. The second brand of socialism, as an economic system where the means of production and distribution are owned largely by the state and where the reduction of income and wealth inequalities is a primary goal for socialist governments, was the generally accepted view during the 1960s and 1970s. This view, however, finds fewer supporters nowadays among socialists. Instead, market socialism commands wide support: a mixture of co-operative, state and private forms of ownership all run with a substantial involvement by the workforce. Some adherents of market socialism insist that the co-operative and the public sectors jointly will dominate the private sphere, while others take a more pragmatic view of the relative significance of each of the three sectors.

In recent years, there has also been a move away from the traditional view that the running of universalist social services can be entrusted to professionals and bureaucrats. The belief that changing the structures of the social services from residual to universal would inevitably encourage the creation of public-spirited professionals has not happened. The mood among socialists today is towards a client and citizen participatory model of the social services. While Titmuss saw properly trained professionals as working for the common good of the users of the services, there is now a suspicion that professionalism can also be a form of occupational imperialism that has to be met with people power. Very little thought, however, has yet been given to how this can exactly be accomplished and what problems it might create. Superficially, it also seems to be not all that different from the ideas of social charters advocated by many of the New Right and others. In essence, however, it is substantially different, for it is based on the assumption that state universal social services are a necessary prerequisite to a participatory model of social welfare.

Democratic socialists have always been confused and divided on the role of the private sector in social welfare. Most have always accepted the predominant role of the private sector in housing, and that a minor role in social security and social care was compatible with socialism; but most either rejected totally, or accepted only a very secondary role for, private provision in education and health. Today, the role of the private sector in both these areas is widely, if reluctantly, accepted as part of the more general acceptance of the regulated market under socialism. There is no doubt that in this as well as in other areas, socialist thinking has recently become more amenable to the role of capitalist practices within a socialist society. As the chapters in this part will show, Plant, the youngest of our four thinkers, raises objections to capitalism that are less fundamental than those raised by the other three writers. This is a reflection of the now prevailing socialist view that the old enemies are not totally irreconcilable; rather, they can somehow complement each other to create a new system with more socialist than capitalist features. Logically this may well be doubtful, but politically it is the only way forward for democratic socialism.

8 Tawney

Nicholas Deakin and Anthony Wright

Brief biography

There is an initial paradox about Tawney. Although he was a resolutely unconventional figure in his personal style and attitudes, most of his specific deviations from conventionality followed fairly well-trodden paths. Born in India in 1880, into the imperial middle class (his father was Principal of Presidency College, Calcutta) and brought up in the comfort of the home counties, he had the customary education of his time and class. At Oxford, Balliol College imprinted upon him the ethic of social service which clever scholars with a social conscience had acquired there for two generations past. In the East End of London, at the Toynbee Hall settlement, he rapidly discovered (as others had done before him) the limits of Victorian philanthropy and cast around for different ways of addressing the social problems of Edwardian England. Like several fellow-travellers on the same road, he toyed with leader-writing for daily newspapers as a means of securing some influence over events, but settled upon adult education as his distinctive contribution to the achievement of the fundamental changes which, like most young radicals, he believed to be necessary.

Tawney's views found political expression through the Independent Labour Party (ILP), which he joined in 1909. He was married in the same year to the sister of his Balliol contemporary William Beveridge; and found a focus for his academic concerns at the London School of Economics (the future Prime Minister Clement Attlee took a similar route). To outward appearances he was settling down to become one of the useful young men that the Webbs would customarily call upon to help them pursue one or more of their current concerns, like 'the boy Beveridge'.

But behind this façade there were distinctive features not perceived by his contemporaries. The publication years after his death of Tawney's commonplace book (diary), covering the period between 1912 and 1914, reveals someone not merely deeply concerned about the social issues of the day (the public record makes that sufficiently clear), but struggling to place them in the framework of a consistent morality (Tawney, 1972). In essence, that framework derived from a deeply pessimistic view of human nature balanced by a strong personal faith in Christianity. Believing, as he did, that 'what goodness we have reached is a house built upon piles driven into black slime and always slipping down into it unless we are building night and day', Tawney set himself the task of creating a consistent social philosophy, which could be expressed in the complete overhaul of the inadequate institutions of the day and a fundamental change in the values of society. Tawney rejected the notion that an increase in material wealth would resolve the problems that he (and others) identified, because 'you cannot achieve a good society *merely* by adding one to one until you reach your million'. Equality was, then and afterwards, the cornerstone of Tawney's moral system; but 'in order to believe in human equality it is necessary to believe in God. It is only when one contemplates the infinitely great that human differences appear so infinitely small as to be negligible ...'

These concerns were for the moment private ones – although they helped to shape most of Tawney's subsequent career; but for the time being they were overshadowed by a public event: the First World War. It is impossible to overstate the influence of that episode on those who survived it. Tawney very nearly did not; he enlisted in 1914 in the ranks of the Manchester Regiment, took part in the battle of the Somme, and amid the prodigious slaughter of the first day was left for dead for twenty-four hours in no man's land. His autobiographical account of that episode (*The Attack*, 1953) is a classic; the resolution Tawney formed in its aftermath was that 'this is a war after which there will be no Restoration' – no return, that is, to the values whose inadequacy the war had so vividly exposed.

After the Great War, the distinctive pattern of Tawney's life was set. He stood four times – although without success – for Parliament as a Labour candidate, refused the offer of a peerage (enquiring ironically 'what harm have I ever done the Labour Party?'), and helped draft successive party policy statements. In addition, there was his involvement in education policy in all its forms and his work as an economic historian, based from 1919 at the London School of Economics (LSE). Then there was his close connection with the Church of England and with initiatives designed to strengthen its social mission. Finally, linking all of these apparently diverse activities are the two angry, passionate texts that sum up his contribution to social philosophy: *The Acquisitive Society* (1921) and *Equality* (1931). In some senses these are better described as tracts. One grew from a Fabian pamphlet; the other was originally delivered as lectures, like the 'lay sermons' of his Balliol youth. In them can be found in summary form all the concerns that had preoccupied him throughout his adult life. Their contents – together with some passages from essays published separately – form the basis for the next section.

Main ideas

Tawney's basic approach rests essentially on his concept of morality, which is in turn derived from his belief in an organic society imbued with common social values. These values are derived from a Christian inheritance, in which the equal worth of all human beings is a central feature. This notion of a society with a strong sense of social purpose held in common looks back to Victorian social philosophers: John Ruskin, in particular. Tawney was also strongly influenced by William Morris in his views about the usefulness of certain forms of labour which use the skills and personal commitment of workers, and the contrasting purposelessness of much mechanical toil.

This approach leads directly to Tawney's use of the concept of function. In employing this, he shows the influence not only of Ruskin and Morris, the development of their ideas by Guild Socialists (with whom he was briefly associated) and their promotion of self-government in industry, but also of the work of a little-known Spanish expatriate theorist, Ramiro de Maeztu (Greenleaf, 1983). Tawney defines a function as 'an activity which embodies and expresses the idea of social purpose. The essence of it is that the agent does not perform it for personal gain or to gratify himself, but recognizes that he is responsible for its discharge to some higher authority' (Tawney, 1921: 15). A functional society is one in which all social purposes are met by the collective discharge of mutual obligations, on the basis of freely entered exchanges.

Much of what passes for economic activity is in fact functionless, according to Tawney's view, because it serves no morally defensible purpose: as he says, 'it may be harmless, amusing, or even exhilarating to those who carry it on; but it possesses no more social significance than the orderly business of ants and bees, the strutting of peacocks, or the struggle of carnivorous animals over carrion' (1921: 15). It also follows that the possession of much of the property owned by individuals cannot be seen as a right, where that property is functionless – that is, if it serves only to gratify the acquisitive instincts of those who own it, rather than common social purposes. Hence, it should be seen merely as a privilege, Tawney's definition of a privilege being 'a right to which no corresponding function is attached' (1921: 28). This does not necessarily imply that private property as such should be done away with:

> for it is not private ownership as such but private ownership divorced from work that is corrupting to the principle of industry; and the idea of some Socialists that private property in land and capital is necessarily mischievous is a piece of scholastic pedantry as absurd as that of those Conservatives who would invest all property with some kind of mysterious sanctity. (1921: 82)

The better regulation of economic activity and the benefits deriving from it is, however, a means, not an end in itself. There are a series of major objectives that a political and social system restored to proper health should meet; and the first of these is the promotion of freedom.

One of the main problems generated by the growth of functionless economic activity, in Tawney's view, has been that, in conferring disproportionate and unearned rewards on the minority, it has deprived the majority of freedom of choice and opportunity. The question of power and its misuse is not therefore merely a matter of the way in which the political system functions; it also encompasses events across the whole spectrum of activity within society.

In general, Tawney had some confidence in the responsiveness of political institutions as a means of achieving change, provided that the principle of democracy was preserved. Writing in the 1930s, he observed that

> It is not certain, though it is probable, that socialism can in England be achieved by the methods proper to democracy. It is certain that it cannot be achieved by any other; nor, even if it could, should the supreme goods of civil and political liberty, in whose absence no socialism worthy of the name can breathe, be part of the price. (Tawney, 1953: 165–6)

But to secure and retain freedom would require some practical safeguards. Democracy by itself is insufficient if viewed merely in political terms. As Tawney writes in the preface to *Equality*, 'democracy is unstable as a political system, as long as it remains a political system and nothing more, instead of being, as it should be, not only a form of government, but a type of society and a manner of life that is in harmony with that type' (Tawney, 1931: 30). Practical benefits of the extension of democratic freedoms would include banishing the emotion that is 'the most degrading and least compatible with freedom': fear. For

> the brutal fact is that, as far as the mass of mankind are concerned, it was by fear, rather than by hope, that the economic system was in the past kept running – fear of unemployment, fear of losing a house, fear of losing savings, fear of being compelled to take children from school, fear of what one's wife would say when these agreeable events all happened together ... Whatever might be the merits of such arrangements, they were certainly incompatible with the freedom of all but the minority who profited from them, and on any but the shortest view, with political, as well as with economic freedom. (Tawney 1953: 90–1)

Therefore, the extension of liberty from the political to the economic sphere was among the most urgent tasks of any industrial society; and checks on the arbitrary exercise of economic power, as well as proper accountability for the exercise of political power.

How was this redistribution of power across society as a whole to be achieved? First, by a shift in the balance in favour of working people and their families. One way in which Tawney expressed this was as a constant struggle by (and on behalf of) a symbolic working man, Henry Dubb, as against 'Superior Persons, & Co.' In part, Dubb's interests could be served through revised constitutional arrangements for the organization of economic activity. Tawney expressed interest in nationalization as a means to this end, but not complete conviction about its merits. His main concern was that, if functionless private ownership of industry is replaced by public ownership, that will not necessarily bring about the change in values that can come only from active participation. For

> if industrial reorganization is to be a living reality and not merely a plan upon paper, its aim must be to secure not only that industry is carried on for the service of the public, but that it shall be carried on with the active cooperation of the organizations of producers. (Tawney, 1921: 149)

The device that Tawney proposed for securing this involvement was that industry should in future be treated as a profession. In making this proposal he was not suggesting that the narrow, excluding values of the early twentieth-century middle-class professions should be taken as a model. Rather, he was arguing for the adoption of a combination of self-government and the values of public service – 'the association', as he puts it 'in the service of the public of ... professional pride, solidarity and organization' (1921: 129). Part of this is Tawney's own, part of it inherited from the Guild Socialists, with whom he shared a strong concern about the diffusion of power and about relations between the central state and other bodies. He argues strongly for the merits of decentralization, commenting that

> the objection to public ownership, insofar as it is intelligent, is in reality largely an objection to over-centralization. But the remedy for over-centralization is not the maintenance of functionless property in private hands, but the decentralized ownership of public property. When Birmingham and Manchester and Leeds are the little republics that they should be, there is no reason to anticipate that they will tremble at a whisper from Whitehall. (1921: 155)

The second form in which power can be restributed is by the setting up of new collective institutions, unrestricted access to which will help to empower those who have previously been excluded. As Tawney puts it, 'because men are men. social institutions – property rights, and the organization of industry, and the system of public health and education – should be planned, as far as is possible, to emphasize and strengthen, not the class differences which divide, but the common humanity which unites them' (Tawney, 1931: 49). But, here again, the idea is not merely to achieve an increase in the practical freedoms available to the vast majority of the population; it is to help meet the next major objective on Tawney's list – the securing of equality.

Equality, in Tawney's formulation of that notoriously difficult concept, is probably best conceived of as the principle of equal worth of all human beings, deriving ultimately from Tawney's religious beliefs. In common with his approach to the concept of freedom, Tawney's main concern was to try to identify the practical consequences that would flow from the acceptance of this principle. In the first place, he argues, there can be no acceptance of unequal access to the necessities of life. As Tawney puts it in his response to Burke's notion that men can have equal rights but not to equal things:

> unfortunately, nature, with her lamentable indifference to the maxims of philosophers, has arranged that certain things, such as light, fresh air, warmth, rest and food shall be equally necessary to all her children, with the result that, unless they have equal access to them, they can hardly be said to have equal rights. (1931: 36)

Nor could there be any question of unequal access to education, for Tawney always the most important of all public services. As he argues, 'the English educational system will never be one worthy of a civilized society until the children of all classes in the nation attend the same schools. Indeed, while it continues to be muddied by our absurd social vanities, it will never even be efficient as an educational system' (1931: 144).

The same sharply critical attitude is shown towards the idea that an acceptable surrogate form of equality can be achieved by providing equality of opportunity. 'Nothing could be more remote from socialist ideals', he declares, 'than the competitive scramble of a society that pays lip-service to equality but too often means by it merely equal opportunities of becoming unequal' (Tawney, 1964: 187). In an image that was to become famous, Tawney calls this a 'tadpole' philosophy, which justifies inequality of outcome by the specious argument that every tadpole has had its chance of becoming a frog.

At the same time, by arguing for the paramount importance of making equal provision and maintaining equal access, Tawney is clearly not arguing for strict equality of outcome. As he writes in another famous passage, in *Equality*:

> to criticize inequality and to desire equality is not, as is sometimes suggested, to cherish the romantic illusion that men are equal in character and intelligence. It is to hold that, while their natural endowments differ profoundly, it is the mark of a civilized society to aim at eliminating such inequalities as have their source, not in individual differences but in its own organization, and that individual differences, which are a source of social energy, are more likely to ripen and find expression if social inequalities are, as far as practicable, diminished. (Tawney, 1931: 101)

His 'strategy of equality' therefore offers opportunities but does not impose rigid consequences. It rests on measures that are 'the most familiar of commonplaces', but recognizes that devices like redistribution, which is one of them, must have their limits, if only for practical reasons. And the outcome that he envisages is, again in his own words, 'not a herd of tame, well-nourished animals, with wise keepers in command. It is a community of responsible men and women working without fear in comradeship for common ends' (1931: 101).

Equality, in the sense of recognizing equal worth and working with the grain of the natural human propensity towards co-operation for common ends, leads to Tawney's third principal objective, the promotion of fellowship. This rather stiff, Edwardian term represents what may be the most important of all Tawney's distinctive goals, the creation of a cohesive, solidaristic, fully integrated society based on a common culture with strongly egalitarian social values. Participation in properly functioning democratic institutions (in the economic as well as the political sphere) would be one way of developing this sense of fellowship. Here again, the tradition of Guild Socialism with its stress on the important revitalizing effects of democracy and shared responsibility was influential in shaping Tawney's approach. The achievement of fellowship also requires the execution of another particularly ambitious project: nothing less than the creation of a classless society.

Tawney was well aware of the magnitude and toughness of the task (unlike certain contemporary politicians). Reflecting upon foreign observers' views of the British, he imagined them saying

> here are the people ... who, more than any other nation, need a common culture, for, more than any other, [they] possess, as a result of their history, the materials by which such a common culture might be inspired. Yet so far from desiring it, there is nothing, it seems, that they desire less. They spend their lives making it impossible, in behaving like the public schoolboys of the universe. (1931: 37)

Yet, despite this recognition of the practical obstacles in the way of displacing hierarchy as a basic principle of the British way of life, Tawney continued to hope for – and work towards – a 'classless society, which does not mean a society without undifferentiated groups, but one in which varieties of individual endowment, not contrasts of property, income and access to education are the basis of differentiation' (Tawney, 1953: 60). And such a society would also be one in which common values extended across society without the obstruction of the artificial barriers of class.

Finally, to make significant progress towards the realization of these three crucial objectives – freedom, equality and fellowship – would also be to move towards the overall goal that Tawney first set for himself in his commonplace book near the beginning of his career: the remoralization of British society.

Tawney and welfare

The fact that – as all subsequent observers have remarked – Tawney's is essentially a moral programme does not mean that his thinking is abstract or impractical. On the contrary, in *The Acquisitive Society* and *Equality* and elsewhere he produced a plethora of specific policy proposals. Nor, though much of his analysis there concentrates on the reordering of industry, is his thinking dominated by economic issues. The critique of capitalism is sharp and the case for replacing the acquisitive society with one more responsive to real human needs is central to his thinking. But (like Keynes) Tawney viewed the notion that public policy should be dominated by economic considerations as 'repulsive and disturbing' (Tawney, 1921: 241). Nor did he seek his remedies through action concentrated in the economic sphere. As we have already noted, he was quite explicit in not arguing for redistribution of material resources as an end in itself – merely a means, and an imperfect one at that.

The first lesson that can be drawn for social policy in Tawney's writings lies in the emphasis on co-operation as a means of achieving results and the reshaping of institutions in order to facilitate that process. It is true that Tawney is a trifle dismissive of 'constitutional' action; but none the less he is quite clear on the importance of democratic accountability and the need to diffuse power through decentralization. Unlike some of his contemporaries, he was by no means an unqualified statist: addressing Hayek's warnings about the inevitable conse- quences of state planning, Tawney offers an image of the state as a neutral instrument available for use by whomsoever succeeds in controlling it: what he calls a 'serviceable drudge'. 'We, in England, have repeatedly remade the state and are remaking it now and shall remake it again. Why in heaven's name should we be afraid of it?' (Tawney, 1964: 172). But equally he wants us to be under no illusions about what happens if the state withdraws:

> It is constantly assumed by privileged classes that, when the state refrains from intervening in any department of economic or social affairs, what remains as a result of its inaction is liberty. In reality, as far as the mass of mankind are concerned, what commonly remains is, not liberty, but tyranny. (Tawney, 1953: 87)

A second relevant strand for social policy is Tawney's argument for the introduction of professionalism to areas in which (when he wrote) it was a novel concept. Considered across the gulf in time that now divides us – which has seen the rise of welfare professions and first the growth and then the decline of the white-collar unions, with their large female membership – his argument is liable to be misunderstood. With due allowance for these changes, Tawney was really arguing for what the late twentieth century calls the 'public service ethic'. He emphasizes the notion of duties: the essence of a profession is that 'though men enter it for the sake of livelihood, the measure of their success is the service which they perform, not the gains which they amass' (Tawney, 1921: 108). He goes on to qualify this by pointing to the need for safeguards: for example, professions ought not to have the final voice in charging or in admitting new members. But Tawney also lays especially strong emphasis on standards of service (1921: 111). He underlines the importance of *esprit de corps* as the foundation of efficiency and

> common training, common responsibilities and common dangers. In all cases where difficult and disagreeable work is to be done, the force that elicits it is normally not merely money, but the public opinion and tradition of the little society in which the individual moves, and in the esteem of which he finds that which men value in success. (1921: 186)

Tawney realizes that this would involve fundamental changes in values – the acceptance 'that there were certain things – like advertising, or accepting secret commissions, or taking advantage of a client's ignorance, or rigging the market, or other analogous practices of the present commercial world – which "the service can't do"' (1921: 196). The public service also needs lively critics to prevent it from stagnating; so Tawney envisages the creation of active research groups within government, publishing their conclusions (there is explicitly to be no 'commercial confidentiality'), to which consumer groups could appeal 'as evidence that a change of methods, which the profession might dislike, was justified by the increase in economy or efficiency which it would produce' (1921: 198).

Co-operation also implies a more active role for consumers of services, where possible in collaboration with providers. Tawney envisages a positive role for trade unions, with the 'assumption of the new and often disagreeable obligations of internal discipline and public responsibility' (1921: 200). This approach represents a potentially significant development for management of new public services.

More explicitly, Tawney underlines the bonding effects of the universal use of public services in general, and welfare in particular, in promoting a sense of common identity. Education takes centre stage as the means by which these common values are both asserted and transmitted. Both at the time and subsequently, this is the area in which Tawney's influence on the development of explicit social policies is most evident. But the National Health Service, as it emerged from the 1948 legislation, with its apparent lack of discrimination by ability to pay also won the warm approval of late Tawney (Wright, 1984: 94).

However, the provision of accessible welfare services of good quality, although clearly necessary, was not a sufficient condition for the moral transformation of society that lies at the centre of Tawney's project. His reliance on the ethic of service rather than the principle of rights rests on a debatable assumption: that a new set of values will take hold and become self-perpetuating as the merits of a fellowship embracing both the providers and consumers of public services become self-evident. Late Tawney does consider (but discards) the possibility that the values of a welfare state might turn out to be 'a substitute for equality rather than one of its building blocks' (Wright, 1984: 89). Or, to put it in Tawneyish terms, if Superior Persons & Co. stopped obstructing Henry Dubb and offered him half a loaf instead to keep quiet, might he too readily become content with it and lapse into a state of passive dependency? Does he need the rights that Tawney seems reluctant to extend to him, to protect his position and perhaps even to motivate him to act on his own behalf?

It is difficult not to conclude that Tawney's project – which, after all, predated in all substantial respects the welfare legislation of the 1940s – needs refining and adapting before its insights can be applied to the changed circumstances of the postwar period.

Impact on policy debates

As one of the three 'red professors' whose writings helped to shape the intellectual environment during the period between the two world wars (the others were Harold Laski and G.D.H. Cole) Tawney's general influence on the climate of opinion during that period was pervasive. More than that, his involvement in the preparation of the Labour Party's policy statements, in 1928 (*Labour and the Nation*) and again in 1934 (*For Socialism and Peace*) gave him direct access to policy making. His *post mortem* on the failures of the 1929–31 Labour government ('The choice before the Labour Party' 1932) (Tawney, 1953: 52–70), clear and cool-headed, remains one of the most persuasive analyses of the catastrophe that traumatized the party for a decade, and possible ways out of it. Furthermore, Tawney was recognized, even among political opponents, as someone with a direct contribution to make to policy making in one of his fields of special expertise, education policy. His statement of the case for universal secondary education (1922) (Wright, 1987: 27) formed the basis for Labour Party policy during the interwar period; and the Hadow Report on *The Education of the Adolescent* (1926) was in large measure his work and directly influenced the content of the Coalition Government's 1944 Education Act. Add to that his work on the Sankey Commission on the Coal Industry (1919), on which he represented the trade union side and where Beatrice Webb (perhaps not a wholly impartial witness) commented that 'he raises the whole discussion to the highest planes of moral rectitude and sweet reasonableness' and you have an already formidable schedule of direct involvement in the public policy arena.

Such a list omits the less direct influence he exerted as a teacher of economic history, based from 1919 at the LSE. The focus of his work there was on changes in English society in the century before the Civil War; but his impact extended far beyond the area of his specialism. As the historian W.H.B. Court commented, 'he occupied a position half-way between politics and philosophy [which] made him extremely interesting to young people trying to make up their own minds' (1970: 17). There was also the wider influence of his activities within the Church of England. Here, he was involved in a range of initiatives designed to strengthen the Church's social mission, including the report on Christianity and Industrial Relations (1918) (see Wright, 1987: 24) and the work of the Conference on Christian Politics, Economics and Citizenship (COPEC) in the 1920s. More specifically, on welfare, he was a key figure in the Malvern Conference summoned by Archbishop William Temple at the beginning of the Second World War, and helped draft the programme attached to Temple's resulting Penguin Special, *Christianity and Social Order* (1943), which is widely credited with being one of the formative influences in the establishment of the welfare state.

All that said, however, the precise nature of Tawney's enduring influence remains elusive. He had set out specifically to persuade his party and his country to adopt a social philosophy based on an 'intellectual conversion' involving a restoration of moral values: neither at the time nor since can it be credibly maintained that this objective has been successfully achieved. Tawney's immediate influence in his own lifetime was, arguably, based on an unwillingness to credit that he meant, more or less precisely, what he said. His relationship with the Webbs illustrates the point. Beatrice Webb (who had her own almost equally well-concealed mystical side) recorded in her diary that 'altogether, in his religious opinions, he remains a mystery to his free thinking friends' (diary, 21 Jan. 1939; Wright, 1987: 156). Tawney admired their energy and commitment, commenting of Beatrice after her death, in words that might be applied to himself, that 'she drove, without flagging or losing sight of her goal, several horses abreast and her achievements are too diverse to be easily summarized' (Tawney, 1953: 101). But the best he could find to say when summarizing the Webbs' achievement was that 'they have not done the job for us, but they have given us some of the tools, both intellectual and moral, with which to do it' (1953: 146). The worst was his crushing comment that 'they tidy the room but they open no windows on the soul'. Their preoccupation with state power and the ways in which it should be exercised would lead, he thought, to a 'paralytic paradise' – one in which Beatrice could impose her passion for 'mental and moral hygiene' on her long-suffering fellow countrymen.

In the face of this evidence, assimilating Tawney to a Fabian paradigm (dominant according to subsequent legend, but not in reality during much of Tawney's lifetime) is not easy. It is true, however, that he exerted a very substantial influence on some of the next generation of intellectuals in the Labour Party; and on two in particular, Hugh Gaitskell and Evan Durbin. Gaitskell, who rose to be Leader of the Opposition and was to be Tawney's (uncritical) memorialist, shared his concern that the tools of economic analysis should be used to address a wider range of issues. Durbin, in many ways the more original figure of the two, produced in his influential wartime book *The Politics of Democratic Socialism* (subtitled *An essay on social policy*) (1940) a programme for action after the war that was recognizably in the Tawney tradition, with its arguments about the limits of a strategy based on redistribution through the taxation system and the provision of universal social services.

But the flurry of action in the last year of the wartime Coalition Government and after 1945 by the incoming Labour government bypassed many of these arguments by creating an extensive structure of social welfare programmes – what came to be called the welfare state – and also a programme of selective nationalization alongside it. Tawney's welcome for these developments was a degree or two below the warmth that might have been expected. He saw problems in the overenthusiastic embracing of nationalization as a universally applicable solution, especially if it was at the expense of industrial democracy. He was also concerned about a falling short on the goal of equality, perhaps through distraction by the hobgoblin of equal opportunity. And in particular he feared the consequences of neglect of the real objectives of educational reform, writing that during the last generation, educational progress has been too often envisaged in terms of a more generous selection of exceptional capacity for intensive cultivation. The Labour Government inherited that tradition, and applied it on a scale unknown in the past. The results have been beneficial, but a change of emphasis is overdue. (Tawney, 1964: 187)

Attempts to secure that change came from a variety of directions, during Labour's long period in opposition (1951–64). First and in most developed form it came from the intellectual successors of the 'red professors' – the holy trinity of LSE social administration, Richard Titmuss, Peter Townsend and Brian Abel-Smith. Working with Richard Crossman (who referred to them facetiously as his 'skiffle group'), they provided the first wave of rethinking of the concept of welfare and its policy applications. Titmuss' own contribution falls particularly clearly in line of descent from Tawney, with its concern with the aims, rather than the methods of provision of welfare (which the Gradgrind image of 'social administration' otherwise suggests). His essay on the blood transfusion service, *The Gift Relationship* (Titmuss, 1970), adopts a quintessential Tawney perspective (or, his critics would say, a naive one), with its emphasis on the moral benefits for the donor of the free gift of their blood. It was entirely appropriate that Titmuss should have been invited to reintroduce *Equality* to the British public, in 1964 – and that he should have done so in terms that demonstrated that Tawney's objectives (and his own) were as far as ever from being realized.

Other attempts to restate objectives came from within the Labour party, and in particular as a product of Anthony Crosland's *The Future of Socialism*, (1956), for a generation the most influential attempt to rethink socialism, both celebrated and reviled as the key text of 'revisionism'. Crosland's work is heavily marked by Tawney's influence, both in its identification of equality as the key objective of socialism and in its choice of educational reform as the key instrument for achievement of that objective. Crosland, as Secretary of State for Education, had his opportunity to put those principles into practice – most specifically in his attempt at imposition of universal comprehensive education (circular 1/65). But the general perception is of failure both on the part of the 1964–70 Labour government and of its perceived strategy – socialism achieved without tears by redistribution of the 'dividend of growth'. The discovery that inequality actually increased over this period discredited much of what was being attempted by Tawney's heirs.

So, by the 1970s, Tawney's inheritance was looking 'precarious' (Halsey, 1976) and subsequent attempts at resuscitation have failed. Is there any prospect of rescuing part or all of it for posterity?

Tawney now

At least to outward appearances, it would be difficult to conceive of a period in which the values to which Tawney attached most significance have had less impact than that of the post-1979 Conservative government.

Taking his three basic principles, since the return of the Conservative government to power, equality has been specifically expunged from the list of official policy objectives. Both strategy and tactics point in the opposite direction. Nor is this surprising, given the prominent role played in setting the government's agenda by Keith Joseph, the author of a hostile polemic on the subject of equality (which patronizes Tawney, in passing). Another symbolic act at the beginning of the Conservative term of office was the abolition of the Royal Commission on the Distribution of Incomes and Wealth; and their practical achievement since then has been to secure the greatest degree of inequality in incomes since statistics began to be kept in 1886.

Freedom is, by contrast, an area to which great significance has been attached over the past fifteen years. But what kind of freedom? The form in which this has most often been expressed has been as 'rolling back the frontiers of the state' – but to achieve what? Tawney's answer was very clear: for the powerless, absence of the state implies not liberty but tyranny (or, as he once had it, freedom for the pike is death for the minnows). Nor is there any evidence of an increase in freedom from fear, whose use as an instrument of industrial discipline Tawney (writing in the 1940s when full employment appeared to have been achieved) derided. On the contrary, such fear has been employed very effectively by employers during the 1980s, over the course of two successive recessions.

Such freedom that has been created rests substantially on the increased ownership of material possessions. Tawney's undervaluing of their importance is a key area of weakness in his analysis, and he would certainly have had to concede that the wide diffusion of home ownership has been an important positive development. But it is doubtful whether he would have said the same about the notion of a 'share-owning democracy' – his characterization of investment as 'snatching to hoard' suggests what his likely response to the mass flotations of privatization (with Henry Dubb cast as 'Sid') would have been. The reform of industry was, of course, a major theme of Tawney's; but the form he would have wished to see would have emphasized industrial democracy, with quite different objectives and outcomes.

But it is probably in the area of fellowship that the divergence would be greatest. Tawney would not have cared one bit for a society manifestly being pulled apart into haves and have-nots and the abandonment of the have-nots by the haves as part of the deliberate creation of a 'culture of contentment'. He saw trade unions not just as a defence mechanism for the have-nots but as the focus for development of cohesive values linking workers of all kinds. Given these views, his reaction to the government's trade union legislation is not hard to deduce. Yet this exposes another area of weakness in Tawney's original analysis. Social change has crucially eroded an approach based on a workforce composed of male manual workers – the working class is not just in numerical decline, but changing in composition. The tainted image of 'brotherhood' as the only legitimate basis for action glosses over the feminization of poverty. What union speaks for Henrietta Dubb, the part-time female worker doing screwdriver jobs for Japanese employers?

Despite the government's own attempt at changing values to promote acceptance of enterprise as a proper objective, it is doubtful whether Tawney would willingly have credited the automatic assumption that the better-off would always 'vote with their wallets' (as coarsely stated by one former Conservative minister), even when those wallets had been systematically stuffed through a decade of cuts in direct taxes. But his old sparring partner Beatrice Webb thought that one of the greatest social changes in her lifetime was the disappearance of beggars from the streets. Now they are back, and their presence passes largely without comment.

The means employed to sustain the 'enterprise culture' might also provoke comment, given that functionless economic activity has made such a spectacular comeback. It is not hard to imagine Tawney on foreign exchange dealers – the epitome of meaningless transactions without social significance (one suspects that he might have extended his animal metaphor to include baboons displaying). Wealth creation as an objective in its own right and functionless property for display were both familiar in Edwardian England, too. But despite Tawney's doubts about redistribution, it is doubtful if he would have been prepared for the consequences of the epidemic of conspicuous consumption funded by cuts in direct taxation, especially during the transient episode of the 'British economic miracle' at the end of the 1980s.

More striking still has been collapse of public services and the structure of responsiveness through a sense of professional duty that Tawney proposed to construct. The notion that these things could be better done through the market would be profoundly foreign to him. All the dangers that he foresaw from the transfer of values from the commercial sector to public services can be illustrated in recent practice (as with an NHS Trust Chief Executive telling a radio audience that the size of his salary – though paid from public funds – was no concern of listeners). But this touches again on an area of weakness in Tawney's own analysis. It is difficult to conceive that duty in the narrow sense in which he defined it could ever be strong enough to sustain an efficient and responsive public sector. You do not have to buy the whole case on public choice to see the potential for large bureaucracies to be perverted by the self-interest of their employees.

So Tawney today can easily look like past history (and most of it remote at that). Yet there are signs of continuing vitality in the ideas that Tawney sought to promote, some of them emerging in surprising quarters. As Alan Deacon has recently pointed out, the return of moral issues to the centre of national political debate has resurrected a number of the concerns that were set aside during the period when the welfare state was being established and consolidated. The remoralizing mission was always the aspect of Tawney's thinking that gave his contemporaries most difficulty. But the notion that the rediscovery of moral objectives is part of the political task might last longer. And if the creation of a classless society remains prominent among those objectives, Tawney's messages about community and social solidarity may yet find a new audience.

Key texts

The essence of Tawney's thinking as a social philosopher may be found in two texts. *The Acquisitive Society* (1921) and *Equality* (1931), and supplemented by reference to two collections of essays, published as *The Radical Tradition* (1964) and *The Attack* (1953). The main ideas in the first two are set out in some detail in the second section of this essay. *Equality* provides the keystone for Tawney's system – his concept of equality, which rests on his belief in the equal worth (though not the equal abilities) of all human beings, in God's sight as much as man's, for the morality that underpins this perception is essentially Christian. The failures of the society in which Tawney lived to measure up to these moral standards are excoriated in *The Acquisitive Society*, in which he finds it wanting in almost every respect, in terms of efficiency as well as morality. Both texts promote an alternative approach based on a concept of public service linked to industrial democracy. Tawney's belief in public bureaucracies was never as firm as that of the Webbs (with whom he is sometimes linked); but his judgement that material reward is overrated as a means of motivating their staff has attracted much criticism. *The Radical Tradition* shows Tawney perhaps a little less enthusiastic about the postwar Labour government's reforms than might have been expected; but the title essay of *The Attack*, with its combination of first-hand description of the horrific impact of modern war with meditation on the meaning of the experience that he underwent, still strikes home with undiminished impact.

References

Board of Education Report of the Consultative Committee on the Education of the Adolescent (Hadow Report) (1926), London: HMSO.
Court, W.H.B. (1970) *Scarcity and Choice in History*, London: Edward Arnold.
Crosland, C.A.R. (1956) *The Future of Socialism*, London: Jonathan Cape.
Durbin, E.F.M. (1940) *The Politics of Democratic Socialism*, London: Routledge and Kegan Paul.
Greenleaf, W.H. (1983) *The British Political Tradition: The ideological heritage*, London: Methuen.
Halsey, A.H. (ed.) (1976) *Traditions of Social Policy*, Oxford: Blackwell.
Joseph, K. with Sumption, J. (1979) *Equality*, London: John Murray.
Tawney, R.H. (1921) *The Acquisitive Society*, London: Bell.
Tawney, R.H. (1931) *Equality*, London: George Allen and Unwin.
Tawney, R.H. (1953) *The Attack and Other Papers*, London: George Allen and Unwin.
Tawney, R.H. (1964) *The Radical Tradition* (ed. R. Hinden), London: George Allen and Unwin.

Tawney, R.H. (1972) *Commonplace Book* (ed. J.M. Winter and D.M. Joslin), Cambridge: Cambridge University Press.
Temple, W. (1943) *Christianity and the Social Order*, Harmondsworth: Penguin.
Titmuss, R.M. (1970) *The Gift Relationship*, Harmondsworth: Penguin.
Wright, A.W. (1987) *R.H. Tawney*, Manchester: Manchester University Press.
Wright, A.W. (1984) 'Tawneyism revisited: equality, welfare and socialism', in Pimlott, B. (ed.), *Fabian Essays in Socialist Thought*, London: Heinemann.

9 Titmuss

Paul Wilding

Brief biography

Richard Titmuss was born in 1907. His formal education was extremely limited and ended when he was fourteen; he never sat a formal examination. In 1926 he joined the County Fire Insurance Office, where he stayed until 1942. By the late 1930s, however, Titmuss was beginning to write in a range of journals, and in 1938 he published his first book, *Poverty and Population* (1938). In 1942 he was invited to write the volume in the official war history which covered the work of the Ministry of Health. It was the outcome, *Problems of Social Policy* (1950), which launched Titmuss on his academic career.

Titmuss was Professor of Social Administration at the London School of Economics (LSE) from 1950 until 1973. They were richly productive years. There were best-selling books – *Essays on the Welfare State* (1958), *Income Distribution and Social Change* (1962), *Commitment to Welfare* (1968) and *The Gift Relationship* (1970) – as well as a variety of less well-known but important studies: for example, on the costs of the National Health Service, on population growth in Mauritius, and on health care in what was to become Tanzania (Abel Smith and Titmuss, 1956; Titmuss, 1961, 1964b).

Titmuss was also active on a range of public bodies – the Supplementary Benefits Commission (where he was Deputy Chairman), the National Insurance Advisory Committee, the Community Relations Commission, the Royal Commission on Medical Education, and the Finer Committee on One Parent Families.

More than anyone else, Titmuss established social administration as a subject of academic study and as a worthwhile intellectual activity. He exerted an enormous influence on the subject in its formative academic years, and a more than marginal influence on the development of social policy in the world outside the academy.

Main ideas

In all he wrote, Titmuss was concerned with direct and immediate social policy issues. At the same time, he was also concerned with fundamental questions – the nature of the good society, the nature of social obligation, and the nature of social policy. His concerns and his ideas ranged widely as he moved from the particular to the general and from the general to the particular.

There were certain themes to which he returned time and again: for example, the role of state welfare in industrial society, the need to compensate people for the injustices inherent in market systems, and the potential of social policy as an instrument for promoting the public good.

Distilling Titmuss' main ideas is not an easy task, but it has to be attempted to provide a framework for analysis. I set out his main ideas here as an agenda for the next section, summarizing them under ten propositions.

1. Markets respond to demand not need; their concern is with profit and growth not welfare or need.
2. Industrial societies need systems of state welfare to meet individual and social needs and to express and promote community.
3. Social policy is distinguished from economic policy by its concern with unilateral transfer (as opposed to bilateral transfer) and by its concern for social integration.
4. Social policy is not simply reactive to social problems. It can promote the good society by an 'active social engineering role' (Reisman, 1977: 16).
5. The essence of state welfare is universal provision – to avoid stigma and to promote social integration.
6. Social policy can never be simply about techniques of social engineering. There is no escape from value choices in welfare systems (Titmuss, 1974: 132).
7. Social welfare must be conceptualized in terms of three systems – social or public (the social services), fiscal welfare (tax allowances and reliefs), and occupational welfare (benefits from employers).
8. Private welfare provision is socially divisive, destructive of community and social bonds.
9. Social policies fail to achieve agreed goals because of specific faults and weaknesses in the policies themselves rather than because of any fundamental limitations of social policies as a method or as a mechanism.
10. The development of social policy cannot be understood apart from the particular culture and society in which it takes place. The most helpful approach to understanding is detailed exploration of particular measures rather than attempts at grand theorizing.

The relevance of Titmuss' ideas to welfare

Titmuss' ideas about social policy – as an activity of government and as a subject of academic study – are important in their own right. They gain added importance, however, from the way in which Titmuss dominated his subject. 'Few scholars', Pinker suggests, 'have so dominated the development of an academic subject over so long a period of time' (Pinker, 1977: vii). Hilary Rose claims that 'at its height the Titmuss school reigned unchallenged over the construction of social policy' (Rose, 1981: 484).

Markets and welfare

Underlying Titmuss' whole approach was a hostility towards the market system. There is little acknowledgement in his work of its potential or achievements in wealth creation. The focus is almost wholly critical. Pinker points out that 'throughout the major works of Titmuss economic forces are described in the main as exploitative forces or as the cause of social costs for which society must offer compensation through social policies' (Pinker, 1979: 248). There is much stress on markets as divisive. Markets '"free" men from any sense of obligation to or for other men regardless of the consequences to others who cannot reciprocate' (Titmuss, 1970: 239).

There is little acknowledgement that it is this system which actually generates the wealth on which social policies depend. There is little sense of the centrality of work to welfare – an insight which tends to get obscured at times of full employment. Titmuss does not accept, or acknowledge, the powerful integrative properties of market systems through the way in which they incorporate people as workers.

Titmuss' focus is on social policies. That was his field of study, and in the years of the long boom the virtues of market systems were so plain that an entirely critical stance was perhaps legitimate. What it did, however, was to help to distract the attention of students of social policy from a concern for the successful functioning of markets on which all their hopes depended.

Titmuss set up an oversimplified and artificial choice, between the values of the economic market and the very different values which he saw as expressed in and through social policies. This was the product of two views: his uncompromisingly critical stance towards the market, which seemed to exclude the possibility of taming and regulating for the social good the powerful forces which drove it; and his great faith in the potential and possibilities of social policies.

Titmuss' critical stance towards the market was crucially important to the developing subject of social policy. Pinker blames Titmuss for what he calls 'the tenacity with which the principle of a unitary and institutionally dominant statutory welfare system has been defended within the discipline of social administration in Britain' (Pinker, 1992: 276).

Industrial society and state welfare

Titmuss was convinced that industrial societies need systems of state welfare. Markets were defective; the state could – and should – make good those deficiencies. What essentially propelled the state into a lead role was economic and social change which highlighted market limitations. Titmuss saw state provision as having six main roles and purposes.

First, the social services exist to distribute and redistribute income (in the broadest sense) in a range of ways and directions. Whether or not it aims to be consciously redistributive, no social service or social security programme 'whatever its declared or official objectives, can be utterly neutral in its actual effects on the distribution of incomes' (Titmuss, 1968: 65). Most social service programmes aim to redistribute resources according to some concept of need which is not satisfactorily met by market mechanisms. They can operate to redistribute income in a variety of ways – over the life cycle, between families without dependent children and families with children, between the healthy and the sick, the whole and the handicapped, the employed and the unemployed. Horizontal redistribution is inherent in the very notion of social welfare, and conscious vertical redistribution – from rich to poor – is an option. It is certainly an option that Titmuss favoured. In Miller's view, Titmuss 'regarded the Welfare State as the main engine of greater equality in both a quantitative and qualitative sense' (Miller, 1987: 5).

A second key role of social services, in Titmuss' view, is to promote social integration and socal harmony. Titmuss speaks of this objective of social policy as being 'to further the sense of community and participation; to prevent alienation; and to integrate the members of minority groups, ethnic groups and regional cultures into the total society' (Titmuss, 1968: 65). This integrative function is one of the characteristics which distinguish social policy from economic policy. In *The Gift Relationship*, Titmuss develops the theme of social services as a twentieth-century form of gift exchange operating to bind society together. 'In my judgment', he wrote, 'the National Health Service in Britain has made a greater contribution to integration and ethnic tolerance than brigades of lawyers and platoons of social workers' (Titmuss *et al.* 1968: 9).

Pinker stresses the importance of this emphasis in Titmuss' work on social services as systems for furthering social integration. In his view, Titmuss' true genius probably lay 'in his searching exploration of the role of social policy in the recovery and maintenance of national consensus' (Pinker, 1977: viii).

A third objective, on which Titmuss lays great emphasis, is the role of social services in coping with, and providing compensation for, a range of social costs, in particular with the 'diswelfares' inherent in economic and social change – unemployment, redundancy, the obsolescence of skills, planning blight, pollution, etc. Today, it is quite impossible to identify the agents responsible for many of these diswelfares, and it is this which makes the legal system and private insurance quite unsatisfactory solutions. 'Our growing inability', Titmuss argues, 'to identify and connect cause and effect in the world of social and technological change is thus one reason for the historical emergence of social welfare institutions in the West' (Titmuss, 1967: 352–3). The market allows the costs of such socially generated burdens to lie where they fall. In a sensitive society this is intolerable, and in a society concerned for economic growth it militates against an acceptance of necessary economic and social change.

What Titmuss fails to do in this argument, Reisman suggests, is 'to distinguish between social causation and social responsibility' (Reisman, 1977: 105). Titmuss, in Reisman's view, moves rather too briskly to see individual costs as social costs, and therefore as a social responsibility. The compensatory function of social services is one dear to Titmuss. His concern with the distribution of diswelfares is central to his concern for equity, that sacrifices should be equitably shouldered and the suffering of minorities duly compensated from the social product to which their sufferings make a contribution. He is concerned, too, with the facilitation of social change in the interests of balanced social development. Economic and social growth must, he argues, go hand in hand because 'lagging behind in one has necessarily negative consequences on the other' (Titmuss, 1965: 354). Society can devise the mechanisms necessary to distribute the costs of change with equity and humanity so that the social system survives without undue strain.

A fourth obvious aim and objective of welfare services which is achieved to some degree by most most systems is the promotion of individual and social welfare. Life is enhanced for those with particular needs and handicaps, and for the population in general, through the provision of services free at the point of use. An example of this function is Titmuss' comment that social insurance is 'one of the great social inventions of the twentieth century' because of what it has done 'to relieve misery and to enhance human self respect' (Titmuss, 1968: 59).

A fifth way of looking at social services is to see them as forms of investment. Titmuss was one of the first commentators to argue that it was quite wrong to analyze social service budgets purely in terms of their costs as current expenditure. Expenditure on health or education should be regarded as investing in healthy citizens and healthy, educated workers. Expenditure on industrial training or training for handicapped people should be regarded in the same light. Redundancy payment schemes should be regarded as investment to ease the course of industrial change and the redeployment of labour. Expenditure on social welfare can therefore make a positive contribution to the national income as well as to national social welfare.

The sixth and final function which Titmuss attributes to social welfare systems is the provision of scope for what he styles the biological need to help. Giving, he argues, is a vital element in modern society, and, in fact, is of increasing importance. The good society, as Titmuss sees it, is normatively integrated through a redistributive social policy which facilitates the growth of altruism (Rose, 1981: 482).

Titmuss sees the National Health Service, for example, as having allowed and encouraged sentiments of altruism, reciprocity and social duty to express themselves. Social policy 'can help to actualise the social and moral potentialities of all citizens' (Titmuss, 1970: 238). If, on the other hand, 'the bonds of community giving are broken ... the vacuum is likely to be filled by hostility and social conflict' (1970: 199). So the case for institutions which facilitate and encourage the development of gift relationships is solidly practical.

The range of purposes and objectives which Titmuss analyzes is the basis for his stress on the importance of the state's role in welfare. His analysis places the provision of welfare services at the centre of the duties and responsibilities of the modern state because of the varied and essential nature of the economic and social purposes served by such services.

Economic and social policy

Titmuss' argument that social policy is quite distinct from economic policy is a continuing thread in his work. Partly, it was the product of a desire to define the territory of an emerging subject. Partly, it was the product of Titmuss' own perception of the economic market.

Titmuss' ultimate concern was for community – for fellowship. He saw the market system as making for social division. Social policy, for him, was an integrative mechanism. It could reduce the inequalities which make for division. It could express fundamental unities of interest. It could allow the expression of the potentially bonding force of the biological need to help.

Confidence that the crucial economic problem of the interwar years had been solved, and that the key to continuing growth had been discovered, made this approach rather more reasonable in the 1950s, 1960s and 1970s than in the 1980s and 1990s. Events since Titmuss' death have sharply challenged this approach. Economic welfare cannot be assumed – so leaving a separate sphere for social welfare. The functioning of the economy has emerged as quite crucial for the social integration which Titmuss saw as the specific and particular contribution of social policy. If our concern is 'welfare', then it is plain that economic and social policy must be looked at together. The distinction which Titmuss sought to make is unreal and unsound. It has been a powerful and, to some degree, a fruitful influence on the development and definition of social policy's concerns. But it has contributed to a neglect of the central importance of the economy to welfare.

The possibilities of social policy

Titmuss had enormous faith in the potential of social policy. For him, it was much more than a mechanism for responding to social problems; it was a way of creating the good society.

Titmuss was an idealist. He believed that humankind must be continually reaching out for the politically impossible because 'just as man by his actions creates ill health and misery, so can man by his work create health and happiness' (Titmuss, 1938: xvii). This led Titmuss to enormous optimism about social policy. At the end of his life in 1972 he could still speak of social policy as 'a positive and dynamic agent of change, penetrating economic policies with social welfare objectives and bringing about substantial redistribution' (Abel Smith and Titmuss, 1987: 264).

Titmuss was also immensely optimistic about people. This was what led to his non-judgemental attitudes to would-be service users – Deacon speaks of his total opposition to judgementalism as 'the most striking feature of Titmuss' work' (Deacon, 1992: 6). He was equally optimistic about politicians and those who worked within the welfare system – that they would be sensitive, non-judgemental, diligent and fair.

This optimism came out in his belief that the accountability of the public sector means that it is more likely to be responsive to consumer pressure than the private sector. Sadly, however, that social accountability has too often remained a polite fiction. Those responsible for public welfare have not shown a desire to develop flexible and user-sensitive services.

In other specific ways, Titmuss was an optimist about social policy. One obvious example is in its contribution to social integration. Titmuss stresses the divisive force of the market, but assumes that social policies can combat such a powerful force. That seems prima facie optimistic.

Universalism

Titmuss was a strong defender of universal services – services open to all without any test of means. Reisman describes universalism as '"the key concept" in Titmuss' favoured model of social policy – the institututional redistributive option' (Reisman, 1977: 99). Universalism was needed in 1948, according to Titmuss, 'as a major objective favouring social integration; as a method of breaking down distinctions and discriminative tests between first class and second class citizens' (Titmuss, 1965: 357). It was both to express and to foster the social solidarity and integration which Titmuss saw as at the heart of the good society.

As always, Titmuss was an optimist about the potential of universal services. 'Universal services, available without distinction of class, colour, sex or religion', he wrote in 1972 long after the heyday of universalism, 'can perform functions which foster and promote attitudes and behaviour directed towards the values of social solidarity, altruism, toleration and accountability' (Abel Smith and Titmuss, 1987: 263).

This concern to foster a sense of social unity, of one society, was the key to Titmuss' commitment to universalism. Two other factors were also important. The first is Titmuss' belief in 'unidentifiable causality' (Titmuss, 1968: 134):

that the causes of many modern diswelfares – 'the modern choleras of change' (1968: 133) – cannot be identified. The only sensible response is therefore universal provision irrespective of cause.

The second element in Titmuss' faith in universalism is what he believes to be the implications of the alternative – selectivity. He sees the result of such an approach as stigma, and 'stigma threatens the person stigmatized, the programme, and the society which condones stigmatization' (Miller, 1987: 13). 'If men are treated as a burden to others', Titmuss insisted, 'then, in time they will behave as burdens' (Titmuss, 1968: 26). Furthermore, programmes just for the poor are always more politically vulnerable than universal programmes. To achieve Titmuss' goals for social policy, universalism was necessary, although not sufficient, as we shall see later.

Value choices and social policy

Titmuss saw issues of values as inescapable in any discussion of social policy. Social policy was about alleviating 'problems' and promoting the good society. Both of these tasks involved value judgements. Titmuss' vision of the good society – integrated, egalitarian and with a strong sense of community – grew directly from his fundamental beliefs and values. They are implicit in nearly all he wrote, and they remain remarkably constant and consistent.

Deacon argues that 'the key to Titmuss, is that he was a moralist: concerned to argue what should be rather than to analyse what was' (Deacon, 1993: 236). Interestingly, his last major book, *The Gift Relationship*, was billed by the publishers on the cover as 'Richard M. Titmuss on his social philosophy'. Detailed empirical research is intermixed with philosophical reflection about altruism in complex industrial society. Again, when Brian Abel Smith and K. Titmuss published a selection of Titmuss' writings, they entitled it *The Philosophy of Welfare* (1987).

Titmuss' work put moral and philosophical issues at the heart of debates about the welfare state, and gave them a central place in the academic study of social policy. Social policy could, very easily, have become preoccupied with the study of the nuts and bolts means required to achieve certain ends. Titmuss' legacy ensured that this would not happen.

The social division of welfare

Titmuss' lecture 'The social division of welfare', made generally available in *Essays on the Welfare State* in 1958, was a milestone in the analysis of welfare state policies. In Pinker's words, it gave 'a new analytical dimension to the subject' (Pinker, 1977: vii).

What the paper did was to broaden the field – and so the agenda – of social policy. Traditionally, the focus was concentrated on those institutions known as social services. Titmuss argued that, if the aim and intention was to understand welfare in society, then other systems of welfare must be explored alongside public social services – fiscal welfare and occupational welfare. These were not generally thought of as in any way comparable to conventional social services. Titmuss argued that their aims were similar and pointed out that they were also substantially funded from public services. The most obvious difference was that fiscal and occupational sources were clearly of most benefit to the better-off.

Titmuss' radical reconceptualization of the boundaries of the welfare state ensured, as Kirk Mann puts it, 'that discussions of welfare focus on questions of power, inequality and the division of labour' (Mann, 1992: 24). Students of social policy have, with some notable expections (e.g. Sinfield, 1978), been strangely reluctant to pursue and develop Titmuss' analysis. That must not detract form Titmuss' achievement. His insight opened a new world for exploration and analysis.

Private welfare

Titmuss was a consistent and determined critic of private welfare provision. It challenged many of his fundamental social values and militated against the achievement of what he regarded as the aims and goals of social policy. There were six main points in Titmuss' critique. The first was that private welfare services operate as 'concealed multipliers of occupational success ... simultaneously enlarging and consolidating the area of social inequality' (Titmuss, 1958: 52, 55). Titmuss wished to see a reduction in inequality in society. He believed that social policy could contribute to the purpose. In private welfare systems, he saw an important element in social policy operating to widen and consolidate injustice and inequality.

Second, Titmuss argued that the existence of private welfare systems weakens and damages public services: 'Until we, as a society, can rid ourselves of the dominating influences of the private sector of education,' he declared, 'we shall not have the will to embark on an immensely higher standard of provision for all those children whose education now finishes when it has hardly begun' (Titmuss, 1964a: 23). Private welfare narrows and weakens any sense of general social obligation. In *The Gift Relationship*, Titmuss argued this quite explicitly: 'One of the functions of the atomistic private market system', he wrote, 'is to "free" men from any sense of obligation to and for other men' (Titmuss, 1970: 234).

Third, Titmuss saw private welfare services as socially divisive, not only in their inegalitarian implications, but also in the way they operate in relation to minority groups. Certain social groups are excluded, or harshly treated, by key institutions in the private welfare world: for example, building societies and insurance companies. Such treatment compounds the sense of exclusion and rejection which public social policies struggle to combat.

Fourth, private welfare does not in fact offer the freedom of choice which is supposed to be one of its great advantages. Few employees have a genuine choice as to whether or not they participate in pension schemes. Few, too, can choose the terms on which they participate. Scarcely any schemes give members any role in the organization of the scheme, and in deciding the type and terms of the benefits, or the investment purposes to which contributions are put. Freedom of choice in private welfare is largely illusory.

Fifth, Titmuss criticizes the world of private welfare because of the concentration of power to which it contributes. The great insurance companies and the building societies emerge from any analysis of contemporary society as institutions of enormous size and strength. Writing of the power of the private insurance companies, Titmuss says, 'We do not know how this power is being used in terms of social welfare priorities or how far their massive investment funds are being or will be used to restore the outworn, mid-Victorian social capital of Britain' (Titmuss, 1958: 239). Such power is 'power concentrated in relatively few hands, working at the apex of a handful of giant bureaucracies, technically supported by a group of professional experts, and accountable, in practice, to virtually no one' (1958: 238).

The final element in Titmuss' critique is his argument that so-called private welfare, including of course occupational welfare, is in large measure publicly financed. For this reason, if for no other, a case can be made for greater public regulation and control.

The failure of social policies

Much of Titmuss' work was aimed at documenting the failure of social policies to achieve their stated aims. He cited five major reasons for the failure of social policy to lead to greater equality in the twenty years after 1945. First,

> our conceptual frame of reference was too narrow and too romantic. We have associated 'Welfare' with the 'poor', and it has given us a nice feeling. Secondly, we too readily assumed that social legislation solves social problems. As every social worker knows (or should know) it does not. Thirdly, we failed to develop in the 1950s techniques of social analysis as we have developed techniques of economic analysis. Fourthly, we have tended to 'compartmentalise' welfare; to put it in a separate conceptual box; to see it as a hindrance to economic growth in the long run – as it may be in the short run ... Lastly, we lacked vision and we lacked social inventiveness. We did not see that the task of reaching the poor and minority groups, of redistributing resources in their favour, of getting them to use and benefit from health, education and social services was a far more formidable one than most reformers imagined. (Titmuss, 1965: 362)

The thrust of Titmuss' argument is extremely interesting. Essentially, he locates the failure of social policies to achieve agreed and desired aims in faults and weaknesses in the policies themselves. Those responsible for social policy development too readily assumed that legislation solved problems, they lacked inventiveness, they failed to develop new techniques of social analysis, and so on. At times, Titmuss refers in rather vague and general terms to broader reasons for their failure. 'Perhaps most significant of all', he says at one point, 'we have sought too diligently to find the causes of poverty among the poor and not in ourselves' (Titmuss, 1968: 163). This hints at a broader explanation. In general, however, Titmuss seeks a social policy/social service-centred explanation for the failure. There is little discussion, for example, of the relevance of the distribution of power in society, of the nature of the state, of social class, of the socal groups and institutions with an interest in the failure of social policies, of dominant social values.

The development of social policies

Titmuss' detailed analysis of how and why particular policies developed is always underpinned by a precise and penetrating social analysis. In the end, however, case studies must be 'added up' to distil general theories. This is something which Titmuss avoids . He was prepared to construct a general theory about the potential role of altruism as a force in society on the basis of a study of blood transfusion. But he was not prepared to explore social theory for explanations of the failure of social policies.

Titmuss' contribution to thinking about the development of social policy is ultimately twofold. When serious academic study of social policy was in its infancy, his stress on the variety and complexity of the factors involved, and his insistence that policy development cannot be understood apart from the particular culture and society in which it takes place were extremely important.

Another important contribution which he made was the indirect product of two things: first, of his dislike of the term 'the welfare state', and his insistence that we must look at particular areas of social policy separately; and second, of his deeply rooted humanism. The first of these helped to militate against 'the evolution of the welfare state' approach which sees in the Liberal reforms of 1906–11, for example, the chrysalis which bursts forth as a gorgeous butterfly in 1948. The second, Titmuss' deep-rooted humanism, led him to stress people's freedom to choose. Such a freedom, once recognized, immediately upsets deterministic theories about industrialization, war, etc. To the person who sees people as free to choose, there can only be 'influences' not 'forces' which lead to desirable social developments.

Titmuss' stress on the complexity of the forces and influences at work in the development of social policies was a major advance on the rather simplistic kind of analysis which tended to characterize earlier work on the development of the welfare state. What Titmuss failed – or refused – to do was to attempt to construct any kind of theory of social policy development. His refusal to go down that road had a profound effect on the development of social policy as a subject of academic study.

The impact on policies and debates

Titmuss' impact was on debates rather than directly on policies. He sat on a number of important committees and commissions, and enjoyed a measure of publicity as adviser on pensions to the Labour Party, but his real influence was as teacher and writer.

In these roles, Titmuss had a curiously ambivalent relationship to the welfare state. As Piachaud puts it, 'he became its most perceptive critic and its strongest advocate' (Piachaud, 1973: 521). Kincaid points out the same conflict when he depicts two conflicting themes in Titmuss' work – a sustained questioning of the proclaimed goals of the social services alongside an intense celebration of the British welfare state (Kincaid, 1983: 292). For the whole period of the tenure of his chair at the LSE, Titmuss contributed actively to many of the major debates about the welfare state. There is only space to deal with some of these.

Titmuss was one of those rare people able to anticipate issues and to produce genuinely original insights . His inaugural lecture (Titmuss, 1958: ch. 1) is full of such semi-prophetic insights. For example, he refers there to the issues posed by the emerging power of professional associations, to 'the most difficult question of all: the question of quality', to the problem of measuring needs, to the question of value for money, to the issue of whether services are treating symptoms rather than preventing the causes of need, and to the problems of laypeople understanding professional worlds. Many of these have subsequently become major issues, but there can have been few people at the time who had registered their importance.

Five years later, Titmuss produced his single most original concept, the social division of welfare, which broadened the whole debate about state welfare and set social policy, as an academic subject, a new and much more challenging agenda.

Titmuss' work certainly played a part in rallying and sustaining support for the welfare state in its early days. At a critical time, he and Brian Abel Smith showed that the costs of the National Health Service were *not* out of control – and that the NHS was, in fact, absorbing a smaller percentage of GDP in the early 1950s than in 1948 (Abel Smith and Titmuss, 1956).

At one level, Titmuss worked to rebut criticisms based on an inadequate appreciation of the facts. At another level, it could be argued that Titmuss had an exaggerated confidence in the possibilities of social policy. His confidence in governments' ability to reduce economic and social inequalities through social and taxation policies almost certainly led him to underestimate the importance of reducing inequalities in the original distribution of income and wealth. Titmuss' confidence in state action – the product as with Beveridge of what he had observed in war time – gave him almost unbounded faith in state action in terms of both its potential effectiveness and its benevolence. His approaches helped to trap thinking about social policy in a particular mode – a mode which was valid in the 1940s and 1950s, but which became less valid from the 1960s. However, it was a mode from which social policy found it difficult to escape, partly at least because of the power of the Titmuss legacy.

From the early 1950s, the balance between universal and selective services has been an ongoing matter for debate. In 1967 Titmuss published his classic paper 'Universal and selective social services' (Titmuss, 1968). Titmuss went to the heart of the issue in his insistence that the real challenge was not the choice between universalist and selective services, but rather to work out

> what particular infrastructure of universalist services is needed in order to provide a framework of values and opportunity bases within and around which can be developed acceptable selective services provided, as social rights, on criteria of the *needs* of specific categories, groups and territorial areas and not dependent on *individual test of means?* (Titmuss, 1968: 122)

Another issue on which Titmuss made an important, and possibly a decisive, contribution was the question of private welfare. He was a vigorous opponent of private education and private health care, and a fierce critic of the private pensions industry. This hostility, when coupled with his firm commitment to state welfare, helped to prevent any discussion of what came to be called the mixed economy of welfare. Welfare *is* a mixed economy. That is a simple matter of fact, not opinion. Titmuss' own position helped prevent analysis of the mixed economy and of possibly fruitful relationships between the different elements.

Titmuss' hostility to the market no doubt contributed to his failure to articulate at all clearly a constructive relationship between economic and social policy. In his assumption that social policy has no alternative but to pick up the social costs imposed by the free-market system, he neglects the possibility – and the justice – of the market being compelled to pay directly for some, at least, of the diswelfare it creates.

Again, Titmuss adopts a narrow definition of social welfare which excludes economic welfare. For him, social policy is a separate sphere of activity. When he was writing it was an approach which had more to commend it than it does in the 1990s. It helped, however, to set social policy on a narrow road which ignored key dimensions of welfare.

Titmuss' contribution to thinking about social policy and to the development of social policy as an academic subject was immense. He defined the boundaries of the subject and set an agenda for research and enquiry. Many of the questions which still preoccupy students of the welfare state were questions which he initially asked. His death, however, marks a key dividing line in the postwar years. The long boom was about to end. That meant new problems and new questions. The world was different, but Titmuss provides many of the key signposts.

Key texts

Choosing four of Titmuss' most important publications is obviously difficult because of the range of his writing and because of the mix of major books and short papers. I have chosen two books and two articles to represent his work.

Problems of Social Policy (1950) must be included, although it is probably now the least read of Titmuss' postwar works. To make the history of wartime social policy manageable, Titmuss focused on three topics: evacuation, the hospital services and the problem of homelessness. The finished work shows Titmuss' ability to master an enormous and complex mass of material, to infuse the narrative and analysis with his own deep social concern and draw out the central issues. The work for the book gave him a knowledge and insight which enriched all his subsequent work. T.H. Marshall spoke of it as 'a flawless masterpiece' (Gowing, 1975: 13). Tawney described it, in a long review, as 'this brilliant book' (Tawney, 1950: 456). Pinker's judgement, looking back over all Titmuss' work, was that it was 'still his masterpiece' (Pinker, 1977: xii).

'The social division of welfare' became chapter 2 in *Essays on the Welfare State* (1958). Abel Smith and Kay Titmuss speak of it as 'perhaps the most influential piece he ever wrote' (Abel Smith and Titmuss, 1987: xii). Sinfield says that 'it has probably become the most cited paper in the British literature of social policy and planning, and possibly in the United States as well' (Sinfield, 1978: 129). Deacon speaks of it without qualification as 'the most widely read article in social policy' (Deacon, 1992: 3). What 'The social division of welfare' did was, as Pinker put it, to bring 'a new analytical dimension to the subject' (Pinker, 1977: vii). By redefining the nature of the welfare state to embrace fiscal and occupational welfare, Titmuss redefined the nature and scope of social policy as a subject of academic study.

My third choice is the paper 'Universal and selective social services' which was reprinted as chapter X in *Commitment to Welfare* (1968). The article was originally published in the *New Statesman* on 15 September 1967 – and I can vividly remember reading it on Waterloo Station that evening! The universal/selective debate is an ongoing one in welfare states – though the terms in which it is conducted may vary. Titmuss' paper is certainly less celebrated than 'The social division of welfare', but I would endorse the judgement of Abel Smith and Kay Titmuss that it 'is still regarded by many people as the most penetrating article which has yet been written on this much discussed subject' (Abel Smith and Titmuss, 1987: xiv).

In some senses, *The Gift Relationship* (1970) marked the culmination of Titmuss' work. Piachaud speaks of it as 'his last and, I believe, his greatest book' (Piachaud, 1973). The careful research which it embodied generated conclusions which confirmed two of his fundamental beliefs: that collectivist systems were superior in all respects to market systems, and that altruism was a powerful, if sadly untapped, force for good in society. It shows Titmuss' proven ability to master highly specialized, technical material and draw from it powerful general principles.

Conclusion

Titmuss' work set the study of social policy on a particular course and gave it a vital academic credibility. He emphasized the need for careful empirical study; he stressed the need to relate social policies to economic and social changes; he continually made explicit the unavoidable nature of value judgements in social policy; he sought to draw out the many different purposes and 'functions' of social services; he was an optimist about the possibilities of collective action to promote social welfare; he gave a new dimension to old debates (for example, on universalism and selectivity); he argued, successfully, that public, occupational and fiscal welfare must be explored as differing aspects of so-called welfare states.

This is an impressive list of ideas and emphases which have helped to shape the study and practice of social policy. Predictably, there are issues where Titmuss would now be subjected to criticism – in part because of the wisdom which hindsight brings, in part because of the way the world has changed.

Titmuss was making an emphasis which has turned out to be unfortunate when he stressed the separateness and distinctiveness of economic and social policy. The emphasis in the 1990s is on the inextricable connections between them. Equally, Titmuss can now be seen – and this was true even in his lifetime – to have been over-optimistic about the potential of social policy to reduce inequalities, to promote social integration and to create the good society. It is a less powerful instrument than Titmuss thought – or hoped. Again, few commentators today would be as critical as Titmuss of the market mechanism. There is a greater sense of its potential role in wealth creation and of the way it can offer choice.

For Titmuss, state action was almost always benign. He had little sense of the way the bureaucracies of the welfare state and their professional staff could deny their clients their basic dignity and be, in a significant sense, effectively unaccountable. He was an optimist about people and organizations.

Titmuss believed that the truth about societies and their institutions emerged from painstaking studies at the micro level. He disliked grand theory as almost self-indulgent. Much theory is just that, but it can function as a powerful tin opener, opening up a new reality – for example, on the question of why so many social policies fail to achieve their objectives.

Like most of his contemporaries, Titmuss paid little attention to the functioning of the economy and the centrality of work to welfare. He assumed the continuing success of macroeconomic management in securing full employment. Sadly, he was wrong.

It is unfair to try to weigh against each other the issues on which we recognize Titmuss made – and makes – a contribution, and the issues on which we are more critical. A person's work must be assessed in the context of her or his times rather than evaluated in a different context. By any yardstick, Titmuss made an immense contribution to the study and understanding of social policy. Twenty years after his death, and more than forty years after the publication of some of his work, many of his ideas are still highly relevant to current debates and offer a continuing stimulus to debate and to research.

Acknowledgement

This chapter, draws on a paper 'Richard Titmuss and social welfare', published in *Social and Economic Administration* (now renamed *Social Policy and Adminis- tration*), **10**, 3, 1976. I am grateful to the Editor and to Blackwell, the publishers, for permission to draw on that material.

References

Abel Smith, B. and Titmuss, K. (eds) (1987) *The Philosophy of Welfare*, London: Allen and Unwin.

Abel Smith, B. and Titmuss, R. (1956) *The Cost of the National Health Service*, Cambridge: Cambridge University Press.

Deacon, A. (1992) 'Rereading Titmuss: moralism, work and welfare', inaugural lecture delivered at the University of Leeds, 7 December.

Deacon, A. (1993) 'Richard Titmuss: 20 years on', *Journal of Social Policy*, **22**, 2, pp. 235–42.

Gowing, M. (1975) 'Richard Morris Titmuss 1907–73', from the *Proceedings of the British Academy* LXI, London: Oxford University Press.

Kincaid, J. (1983) 'Titmuss, the committed analyst', *New Society*, 24 February, pp. 292–4.

Maan, K. (1992) *The Making of an English Underclass*, Milton Keynes: Open University Press.

Miller, S.M. (1987) 'Introduction: the legacy of Richard Titmuss', in Abel Smith and Titmuss (1987).

Piachaud, D. (1973) 'Titmuss – teacher and thinker', *New Statesman*, 13 April, pp. 520–1.

Pinker, R.A. (1977) 'Preface', in Reisman, D.A. (ed.), *Richard Titmuss: Welfare and society*. London: Heinemann.

Pinker, R.A. (1979) *The Idea of Welfare*, London: Heinemann.

Pinker, R.A. (1992) 'Making sense of the mixed economy of welfare', *Social Policy and Administration*, **26**, 4, pp. 273–84.

Reisman, D.A. (1977) *Richard Titmuss: Welfare and society*, London: Heinemann.

Rose, H. (1981) 'Rereading Titmuss: the sexual division of welfare', *Journal of Social Policy*, **10**, 4, pp. 477–502.

Sinfield, A. (1978) 'Analyses in the social division of welfare', *Journal of Social Policy*, **7**, 2, pp. 129–56.

Tawney, R.H. (1950) 'The war and the people', *New Statesman and Nation*, 22 April, pp. 454–6 (a review of *Problems of Social Policy*).

Titmuss, R.M. (1938) *Poverty and Population*, London: Macmillan.

Titmuss, R.M. (1950) *Problems of Social Policy*, London: HMSO and Longmans, Green and Co.

Titmuss, R.M. (1958) *Essays on the Welfare State*, London: Allen and Unwin.

Titmuss, R.M. (1962) *Income Distribution and Social Change*, London: Allen and Unwin.

Titmuss, R.M. (1964a) 'Introduction', in Tawney, R.H., *Equality*, London: Allen and Unwin.

Titmuss, R.M. (1964b) *The Health Services of Tanganyika*, London: Pitman.

Titmuss, R.M. (1965) 'Goals of today's welfare state', in Anderson, P. and Blackburn, R. (eds), *Towards Socialism*, London: Fontana.

Titmuss, R.M. (1967) 'Social welfare and the art of giving', in Fromm, E., *Socialist Humanism*, London: Allen Lane.

Titmuss, R.M. (1968) *Commitment to Welfare*, London: Allen and Unwin.

Titmuss, R.M. (1970) *The Gift Relationship*, London: Allen and Unwin.

Titmuss, R.M. (1974) *Social Policy: An introduction*, London: Allen and Unwin.

Titmuss, R.M., Zander, M. and Lynes, T. (1968) *Unequal Rights*, London: Child Poverty Action Group.

10 Plant

Stewart Miller

Brief biography

Born in Grimsby in 1945 and educated there, at King's College, London, and at Hull University, Raymond Plant was Lecturer, then Senior Lecturer in Philosophy at the University of Manchester from 1967 until 1979. In that year he became Professor of Politics at the University of Southampton. In 1992 he was created Baron Plant of Highfield, joining the Labour benches in the House of Lords, and in 1993 he was appointed Master of St Catherine's College, Oxford. In 1991 he assumed the chair of the Labour Party's Working Party on Electoral Systems, which produced reports in 1991, 1992 and 1993. His books include *Hegel* (1973, with a second edition in 1983), *Community and Ideology* (1974), *Political Philosophy and Social Welfare* (with Harry Lesser and Peter Taylor-Gooby, 1981), *Conservative Capitalism in Britain and the United States* (with Kenneth Hoover, 1988), and *Modern Political Thought* (1991a). He has also published several Fabian and other pamphlets and many articles in journals and books.

Main ideas

It would be artificial, and would undermine a central point of importance in Raymond Plant's work, to discuss his ideas and arguments at length outside the context of the state and its responsibility and activity in the field of social welfare. Plant has contributed enormously to taking the debate on the welfare state into the mainstream of political theory, and has brought the discipline of that body of theory to bear on arguments about welfare. The issue of the state and its responsibility for the well-being of citizens is central to his thought, which nevertheless extends far beyond welfare, particularly welfare at the prevailing level of social policy debate. Here, we shall consider his treatment of the nature of political philosophy, his treatment of some key concepts, including community, rights and liberty, and his account of the socialism which he himself espouses.

Raymond Plant's most substantial book, certainly as sole author, is *Modern Political Thought* (1991a). In it he brings together many of the strands of his theoretical discourse. In particular, he deals with the nature of political philosophy; with the debate between communitarian or relativist models of political theory on the one hand, and foundationalist or universalist models on the other, and with the concepts of need, liberty and rights in relation to political theory.

These are themes which appear also, in other contexts and to varying degrees, in other works. Needs, liberty and rights are the currency of Plant's debates with the New Right, conducted over a range of publications to which I shall turn shortly, and of his normative treatment of 'market socialism'. For the time being, let us look briefly at some of the issues Plant tackles under the headings of philosophy itself, and the debate between foundationalist and communitarian philosophers, for his account of these issues can give us some clues to the essence of his own philosophical position. The importance and complexity of philosophy and of meaning within it are touched on in *Community and Ideology*: the question of the descriptive and evaluative meanings of 'community' inevitably leads to the communitarian/universalist debate, which rests on the possibility or otherwise of universal meanings as well as of universal values. It raises the questions of the whole nature of philosophy and of its role in relation to social thought and action.

Community and Ideology (1974) is itself a clear example of Plant's notion, outlined briefly in the book, of the modern philosopher in the service of social science and social debate, clarifying issues and, especially, concepts. This is in contrast with earlier times, when a reader of applied philosophy 'would have expected to find either arguments in favour of certain high level general directives which would guide practitioners ... or would have found merely a catalogue of uplifting ideas' (Plant, 1974: 2). The emphasis has changed to conceptual analysis and exploration:

> [The philosopher] is not concerned with competing with the social scientist in trying to discover data concerning the distribution of community power, for example, but with trying to understand what the sociologist, the politically committed, the social worker and men in the street *mean* when they talk about 'community'. (1974: 2)

'Community' is indeed a good test case for this explanatory role in relation to welfare thought and practice, since it is one of the 'buzzwords' of the field, used in a variety of more or less contested ways which are sometimes argued to have left it bereft of useful meaning. It might seem that the role of the philosopher would be to distinguish between its descriptive and evaluative meanings, and to seek to prescribe one which could be taken as authoritative. In fact, Plant points out that the use of language is incorrigibly more complex than that, and that what is required is rather a deeper understanding of the range of meanings which the word, in the context of its history, can carry and has carried with it. This involves unpicking the descriptive and evaluative aspects of meaning without ignoring the one or the other, and without hoping to find in all uses of the term an utter commonality. Thus Plant seeks to characterize the use of 'community' without prescribing an irreducible essence. He describes its history in radical thought (both conservative and progressive) as producing a conceptual model which emphasizes the degree to which humans interact as whole people rather than in the specialized, distant fashion of modern urban society. The dilemma of progressive thinkers committed to 'community' as a core normative concept is then to reconcile such an ideal with the individual liberty which a more impersonal, rights-oriented model of social relations – as espoused by Dahrendorf, for instance – offers. (I have avoided using the word 'communitarian' here; it appears in a different sense below.)

In all this discussion, both in *Community and Ideology* and in the later *Modern Political Thought*, Plant is seeking to find a philosophical mode of discourse which does not rest on particular sets of culture-bound meanings or moralities. This he sees as a central part of the philosopher's task in an age and society characterized by moral and cultural pluralism. In the latter book and in *Political Philosophy and Social Welfare*, co-authored with Peter Taylor-Gooby and Harry Lesser, Plant makes claims for sheer logicality as a transcendental principle. This, he argues, is at once non-morally based and sufficiently fundamental to avoid the relativism of, among others, the communitarian philosophers who follow through the undermining of would-be universal models of human nature, religion or social life by arguing that all philosophy must start from the accepted values of its social context. One can see why a social critic such as Plant is reluctant to abandon a universal value to which he can appeal as a standard against which to measure current social values and practices; but logical consistency alone seems, first, a rather thin foundation and, second, potentially demonstrable as falling short of supporting social analysis and criticism without the application of value judgements.

The defensibility of the communitarian position is tested in a review article of Plant's dealing with two works by Richard Rorty, as well as one by Richard Bernstein (Plant 1992b). Characteristically, he introduces the crucial dilemma by quoting the psalmist: 'If the foundations be destroyed, what can the righteous do?' (Psalm 11, quoted in Plant, 1992b: 137). The question is, what is to serve as an adequate replacement for the successive theological and moral premises of the classical tradition, from Plato to Marx, whose foundational universalism has been undermined by the critical theory of modern pluralism?

One can see immediately why many political philosophers have assumed that political philosophy would be rather bereft without at least some foundational supports whether these are sought in thin conceptions of the good and human nature or whether they are to be found in rather formalistic conceptions of rationality and rational choice. It is not clear what would be left to political philosophy without some such foundational claims . . . (1992b: 139)

Without this, Plant goes on, it would be difficult to construct philosophical models of, for instance, rights, community or social justice which could be defended on any grounds firmer than pure preference.

The works Plant is reviewing here are entirely inimical to the search for such foundations, belonging to the relativist or communitarian school of political philosophy; and Plant is sceptical of Rorty's success in sustaining the relativist position:

it is not clear that a defence of liberal society which can depend on seeing it as giving us a set of institutions to cope with contingency, as opposed to providing us with positive principles which we believe to be right, is going to be a compelling basis for arguing with those who live within liberal society but reject the contingency which in Rorty's view lies at its heart. (1992b: 144)

But there is an obvious problem here: to adopt the defence of liberal society as a criterion of philosophical effectiveness appears logically impossible without a value judgement on the desirability of that particular kind of society, as against, say, a feudal hierarchy or state-directed communism. This is a judgement which most of us might well make, but it is not the only judgement that is rationally possible concerning the relative desirability of alternative principles of social organization. The task that Plant sets himself, of convincing us that it is indeed the only position open to anyone who acts as a moral agent and attempts to construct a set of universally defensible social principles, is, to say the least, difficult. Some would say that it is inherently impossible and that an evaluative, indeed political, stage of the process, at which a number of quite different judgements and arguments might be adopted, is inescapable. Whether it is impossible to construct *any* kind of theoretical principles from a value-free premise is a different question; but it can be argued that a prescriptive form of political philosophy positing such a model as a liberal society is inherently evaluative and relativist, culturally dependent on something like the kind of social context that the communitarians draw on.

Plant's argument is that the need for political theory is essentially based on humans' nature as moral agents – nothing more specific than this. What is required is a set of principles which guide social organization in such a way as to allow and promote social participation that protects the moral agent status of citizens who act and also that of everyone affected by their actions. So the state ought to act in a way that is moral in these terms, and the only philosophies which allow this are libertarian ones. As we shall see in our discussion of the state and markets below, Plant's version of libertarianism allows for a great deal more intervention and positive action by the state, to maintain the moral agency of citizens in a meaningful way, than do many other liberal views of society. This is because he believes that people's capacity to act in a fully moral and therefore human way, in the market, the community and other social arenas, depends on the meeting of a range of basic needs.

However, it is not entirely self-evident that the best philosophy based on a view of humans as moral agents is one where each is required to give priority to the consideration that others are moral agents. One could argue with at least conscionable force that those with the potential to affect others should act as moral agents so as to meet their obligations to those others, but that this might be in such a way as to pursue some other purpose of priority, such as peaceful co-existence or economic prosperity. And that other purpose might be pursued outside a context of liberty; people might effectively serve the priority purpose without being free to do anything else. In other words, moral agency might imply obligations without necessarily implying rights to strictly reciprocal consideration. So there does seem to be a value judgement behind Plant's drawing of specifically libertarian philosophical implications from the status of humans as moral agents. This conclusion still leaves Plant's libertarianism as a convincing premise for a sustainable political philosophy, albeit of an inescapably relativist kind. And whatever Plant's position may be at this highly abstract level, much of his most effective writing is entirely consistent with such an evaluative, relativist position.

All in all, Plant does not quite resolve the issue of whether philosophy – in particular, political philosophy – needs to be, ought to be, or indeed cannot be based on universal meanings and values; certainly he seems to be more of a relativist than his strictures on Rorty and others might lead us to believe. Moreover, his appeal to such bridge building as that of Rawls's later work suggests that he is not convinced that this question must be authoritatively resolved in favour of one side or the other: 'It is not just that the contrast between foundational and communitarian approaches is a mistaken account of a good deal of the history of political philosophy, it also fails to do justice to recent developments in the subject, particularly relating to the works of John Rawls' (Plant, 1991a: 354). What is clear is that, important as he takes this issue to be, the uncertainties which continue to surround it do little to hinder his critical work at a less abstract level of political thought. And in the sphere of social welfare this is particularly evident, and particularly important – given Plant's crucial role – for the quality of debate.

Raymond Plant is a singularly scrupulous philosopher and teacher, representing to his readers in such a work as *Modern Political Thought* a wide range of social and political thought with utter credibility. But he is also a committed socialist, and has published many pieces in the explicit context of that commitment – though not failing even there to give an almost excessively convincing account of the strength of the case brought by his opponents. In a contribution to Le Grand and Estrin's volume on *Market Socialism*, he identifies himself with that brand of socialist thought: 'I believe that in its most radical form market socialism will go a long way towards accepting the neo-liberal critique of traditional socialism, based as it is upon end states and a conception of the good' (Plant, 1989: 63). This raises the question, why should any socialist or radical system 'go a long way towards accepting the neo-liberal critique'? Essentially, the answer to this, for Plant, involves criteria for legitimacy similar to those he seeks to meet in the philosophical work cited above. It lies in the general liberal project of creating systems which are, so far as possible, not related to specific conceptions of human nature or specific end-states, and which allow for a plurality of moral and customary codes and value-systems.

The rightist criticism of socialism which he feels constrained to respond to concerns the tendency to specify desirable end-states, such as particular patterns of income and wealth distribution. This is not to say that market socialists believe that the accumulating inequalities of the market should be allowed to lie where they fall: 'Genetic endowment and fortunate home background ... are central to the development of personal capacity, including the capacity to act effectively in the market. On the market socialist view these should be compensated for so as to enable people to enter the market on the fairest possible terms.' (1989: 65). Indeed, elsewhere in Plant's work there are a great many apparently disparaging accounts of the market, at least in terms of its operation in contemporary society, which it may be useful to dwell on before going further. In their discussion of the market and the state in *Conservative Capitalism in Britain and the United States*, Plant and his collaborator Kenneth Hoover observe that 'without a redistribution of income and property rights, the market will not be a fair and neutral mechanism' (Hoover and Plant, 1989: 215). Nor do they see equality of opportunity as a satisfactory alternative: 'There is a point beyond which the attempt to secure a fair background for the development of talent cannot go without being intolerably intrusive' (1989: 221). The alternatives are market-based conservatism or:

> to argue for a greater compression of the reward structure and in favour of greater equality of outcome. If the family is to be maintained and personal liberty secured so that measures to secure greater equality of opportunity must be limited, then it is wrong to reward as prodigiously as we do a narrow range of talent for which the individual does not bear full responsibility, and to make the costs of failure so heavy for those whose opportunities have been more modest, and who similarly do not bear full responsibility for their position. (1989: 221)

And in the debate over citizenship and empowerment, Plant responds critically to the rightist suggestion that it is market devices and relations that can best guarantee citizens' rights: 'While accepting the fact that there is an indispensable role for the market in modern society ... there are very clear limits to which the market can empower individuals' (Plant, 1990: 3). And even in his article on market socialism itself, he argues the point, referred to elsewhere in this chapter, that we are obliged to modify the market inasmuch as we can foresee its outcomes, even though they may not be intended (Plant, 1989: 66).

It is a little puzzling, then, to come across the remark: 'None of this in any way lessens the market socialist's commitment to markets' (1989: 66). What he is presenting, he says, is 'an argument in favour of initial redistribution so that people can enter markets on a more equal basis in terms of resources' – 'a starting-gate rather than an end-state principle'. It is a response to 'state failure' as well as 'market failure'. This leads to the recommendation that, so far as possible, services should be provided in forms which enable the citizen to act in the market – cash and vouchers. But he also wishes to ensure that the outcomes of market agency are consistent with socialist values – 'even market socialism needs a theory of distributive justice, equality, and community' (1989: 76) – and it is arguable that the necessity continually to intervene to maintain the guarantee of met need at the starting-gate renders his form of market socialism a reformulation of end-state socialism using a modified market as a distributive device, rather than a radically different concept. But it does greatly advance the discourse on that reformulation, and connects the policy proposals of such as Le Grand and Estrin to the resources of normative philosophy, in a way that is typical of Plant's most effective work.

Relevance for welfare

There are perhaps three aspects of Plant's work in relation to social welfare that can be emphasized as characterizing his contribution to analysis and debate. They are all to do with connections between branches of intellectual endeavour. The first connection is between political theory and social policy analysis and criticism. Social policy academics have frequently drawn on sociology and economics in their work, but to a lesser degree on political science and theory. Plant demonstrates, at a time of uncertainty and conflict over the welfare state, the relevance of the long debate over the role of the state for social policy, as well as the centrality of the welfare effort in that controversy as it applies to the late twentieth century and beyond.

This is perhaps Plant's most important intellectual contribution to the latter. While the enterprise of political theory involves descriptive, etymological and teleological tasks, he evidently sees in it also a moral one. This is no less the case because he perceives the moral task as largely a negative one – a search for neutrality. Both ethically and technically, Plant proposes the necessity for a social and political philosophy which, first, is not based on some particular moral view of the nature of humankind, but rather recognizes the cultural and moral pluralism of the world and its constituent communities, and second, is essentially libertarian. Whether, as he believes, the first automatically leads to the second, or whether, as his critics have suggested, this involves a value judgement, is not absolutely crucial for all purposes in the context of the social welfare debate, in which libertarianism is fairly common ground. We shall see that this does not prevent critical differences arising over the nature and the value of liberty, with enormously important implications for the nature and extent of the state.

The second connection is, within the controversy over the state, between the terms in which the New Right has put its case for a liberal model of the state and the values which are dear to the proponents of a social democratic model. Many social democratic or Fabian thinkers have engaged with the New Right over the legitimate extent of the state, and in particular those redistributive functions concomitant with the welfare role of the state in recent times – specifically, in the post-oil shock period of economic difficulties for capitalism. (Ironically, this has also been a period culminating in the political triumph of liberal capitalism over state socialism in the developed world; and this has added to the impetus of the rightist critique of state activity and extensiveness.) Raymond Plant, however, has been outstanding among the social democrats in dealing with New Right arguments and expressions of value in their own terms, struggling on the ground of those rather broadly shared values, such as liberty, which the New Right have sought to claim as their own.

In addressing the relationship between New Right and social democratic thinking, Plant is working in a post-consensual context. As do many other writers on this theme, he points out that the present debate between the right and its opponents follows a long postwar period in which both rightist and leftist criticism of the social democratic state was effectively swamped by a dominant, neo-consensual ideology. In the terms of that ideology, it was assumed that the welfare state could grow and develop on the proceeds of economic growth, and achieve enough redistribution and reconstruction to ameliorate the problems of a capitalist or 'mixed-economy' society and realize a broad set of social and economic citizenship rights. Conflicts over the practicalities and boundaries of such a state did not cast doubt on the desirability or inevitability of its existence: 'Indeed the degree of consensus over these matters, part of which has been called "the end of ideology", effectively marginalized the writings and warnings of critics' (Plant, 1985: 297). Neo-liberal critics of the redistributive welfare state, such as Hayek and Friedman, 'were often thought of as eccentrics who were attempting to stand in the face of the tide in history'; the development of the welfare state and the entrenching of social and economic rights of citizenship were widely seen as 'a necessary concomitant of the development of a complex urban industrial society' (1985: 297–8).

Plant identifies a number of factors which, he says, have led to disenchantment with the postwar welfare state, and weakened its ideological and political defences. First of these is the difficulty posed by economic recession, which has made all but impossible the trick of financing the welfare state and gradual redistribution out of the margin created by economic growth. Plant cites O'Connor's notion of 'the fiscal crisis of the state': a crisis which stems from the clash, in times of economic difficulty, between the contradictory imperatives of welfare expenditure to secure legitimacy and capital accumulation to secure growth.

High rates of incremental growth might allow both of these imperatives to be pursued at once, a constrained economy on the other hand would make this balancing act difficult to sustain. Faced with contradictory pressures ... the New Right is prepared to cut back welfare provision in order to secure the possibility of capital accumulation. (1985: 299)

The third connection which Plant has striven to make is between the arcane considerations of academic theory and the practical morality of policy, both with direct reference to social welfare and indirectly through his interest in constitutional, particularly electoral, matters. An obvious example of this practice is in his chairing of the Labour Party's Working Party on Electoral Systems. This was set up partly to help the Labour leadership out of a dilemma brought about, on the one hand, by increasing criticism of the parliamentary electoral system and, on the other, by Labour's continuing ambition to form a majority government under precisely that system. It is evident from its reports that this is not the spirit in which Plant conducted the proceedings of the working party, although neither did it distance itself from the hard realities of politics. His analytical approach is evident in the remarks in the 1993 report on fairness:

the idea of fairness is multi-dimensional: and reducing the issue of electoral reform to 'fair votes' does not get us very far. We need to know to whom or to what one is trying to be fair: to individual voters, to parties, to under represented groups, to regions or whatever. These considerations pull in quite different directions; and just applying the idea of fairness to an electoral system is wholly indeterminate. (Labour Party, 1993: 17)

In its interim report, the working party had reviewed the democratic requirements of a variety of representative functions at national and other levels (Labour Party, 1991). In 1993 it recommended a mixture of electoral systems for different purposes, designed to serve different democratic functions through the House of Commons, an elected second chamber and the European Parliament.

All three of these connections will be evident in the discussion below of a number of issues which Plant has tackled, beginning with that of liberty. Given the acceptance of liberty as a positive value in the construction of a theory of politics, it has often been argued that the state is entitled to interfere with the lives of citizens only in such a way as to preserve that liberty; and that the concept of liberty itself can be sustained only as an intrinsically negative notion. Liberals tend to argue that liberty is essentially freedom *from* restriction; what one does with one's freedom is a different issue, and if the state concerns itself with this, it is dealing with capacities and power and is bound to compromise its commitment to liberty. Plant rightly points out that what people can do with their liberty is central to how it is to be valued. Freedom to do what we do not have the capacity to do may have a certain abstract appeal, but its value is not absolute (Plant, 1992a: 25). As we shall see later, this enables him to support, within limits, an interventionist, redistributive state.

Plant is prepared to tackle at once thoughtfully and head-on the argument of the neo-liberal New Right, stemming from the negative view of liberty or freedom, that such social arrangements as the market cannot be coercive or unjust because they do not involve the deliberate action of one social actor on another; their distributive and controlling effects are incidental and unintended. Thus, it is argued, to interfere with the market is to restrict the freedom of its participants without enhancing the freedom of anybody. Plant points out that, while the market in itself may be characterized by a set of non-deliberate (and therefore uncoercive) effects and relations, we can in fact foresee what is likely to happen to particular groups in a market, and are faced with the choice of allowing the effects of market forces to lie where they fall or taking action to modify them:

> *if* as an empirical fact those who enter the market with least will tend to end up with least and *if* this affects the capacity for agency, and *if* this is known to be the case as a foreseeable general outcome, even though it is not intended, and *if* there is an alternative course of action available, namely a market constrained by a redistributive welfare state, then we can argue the market is coercive. (Plant, 1985: 311)

'The market is coercive' might be taken as shorthand for 'the tolerance or promotion of the unconstrained market is coercive' (although this is not quite where Plant takes the argument at this point). Moreover, if we are appealing to principles of justice in the question of intervention,

> it is not clear that injustice is *only* a matter of how a particular outcome came about or arose, but rather is as much a matter of our response to the outcome. Certainly someone who was born with a severe handicap does not suffer an injustice because of the genetic lottery, but where justice and injustice come in is in our response to his position. If we fail to compensate him when we could have done so, at no damaging cost to ourselves, then this is where injustice lies. (1985: 311)

Associated with this, however, is what seems at first sight a less satisfactory argument, at least in the sense of one to which his opponents might feel they had a ready counter. Plant observes that, if liberty is defined in terms of intentional coercion, one society might be thought to be freer than another on a count of intentionally coercive actions permitted:

> This might make a very primitive society with few regulations and forms of interference more free than modern western society. Few would be prepared to accept this and the reason for not accepting it would be that in our sort of society we are in fact able to do far more things. (Plant, 1992a: 25)

This seems rather commonsensically uncritical; many people might well say that the first of these societies was freer than the second, without concluding that it was more desirable. On the other hand, it can be argued, with Plant, that the quality of freedom is related to the quality of choice with which that freedom presents its holders. Freedom and choice are both lauded by the right, and their relationship is taken for granted. But the lack of real choice can surely undermine the value of freedom, such as the freedom to work in an economy shot through with unemployment, or the freedom to exit from a service or institution when there is no realistic alternative. If this is accepted by the right in terms of markets and privatization, it surely suggests that freedom does indeed have a positive aspect, related to choice, ability and capacity.

Raymond Plant has spent a great deal of time and effort struggling with the complex issues surrounding the nature of rights, needs and justice. As is evident from the above discussion, much of his work has been in the context of the debate which he has engaged in with those neo-liberals who have (with some political success) cast doubt on the propriety of much of the modern state's activity in pursuit of these normative concepts as social goals. It is necessary to stress that not all of Plant's work is explicitly directed to this debate, and that his political philosophy is concerned as much with the complexities of these notions as with the proposition of an anti-right, social democratic model of social theory and organization. But as a committed social critic he has devoted much of his output explicitly to the debate with the New Right on the philosophical orientation of practical policy.

As is already evident from the discussion of liberty above, much of the debate centres on the proper relation between the state and the market. It is easy to oversimplify this antithesis, and to appear to suggest that society can be organized almost entirely on the basis of one of these phenomena and without the other. This is nonsense, of course, but the difference of relative emphasis on market and state between the rightist and the social democratic models (or, rather, ranges of models) is sufficiently striking, and the importance of what happens at the margins sufficiently great, for these ideas to attract a kind of attention that implicates rights, needs, justice and a further succession of crucial philosophical issues.

There is a sense in which to organize this discussion largely round arguments for the importance of the market is to concede in advance the terms of reference of those writers whom Plant is concerned to criticize. But, as has already been argued, it is one of the peculiarities and strengths of his work that he does indeed confront the rightist arguments and values which have become so influential in social debate, without bypassing the conceptual frameworks within which they are expressed.

One of the issues which arises around the dichotomy of state and market is, of course, that of the rights which constitute the essence of citizenship. In particular, there is the question of the difference, emphasized by the New Right, between civil rights, which are not seen as improperly inhibiting of freedom and the market, and social rights, which are. The New Right claim that these differences are crucial, leading to the conclusion that social 'rights' are not rights at all. In particular, they argue that social 'rights', such as that to financial welfare, are claims which depend for their realization on resource decisions which are essentially political, rendering the claims unenforceable and therefore not rights. One may feel it consistent with one's rights that an adequate health service be provided, but may be unable to enforce this by the kind of action that characteristically constitutes asserting rights, such as pressing a legal suit. It requires a collective decision to be made in respect of the resources and organization involved. In contrast, civil rights, like the right to personal safety, merely require others to refrain from breaching them and, it is argued, can be enforced.

Plant quite correctly asserts that civil rights, as rights to be realized in practical terms, actually require similar resource decisions and suffer from similar unenforceability in practice (Plant, 1992a: 22–3). Indeed, it can be argued that the substance of civil rights consists as much in the provision of enforcement services such as the police and the courts as in the obligation of other individuals to observe these rights, and 'In the same way as the hospital consultant has the professional discretion to ration scarce resources, so the chief constable has to choose how to allocate resources to protect civil and political rights' (1992a: 25). This is a telling point, which the New Right seem to ignore. Plant does not address the question of whether the *degree* to which a right is based on resource decisions is significant in determining its nature – the entitlement to social benefit consists almost entirely in a claim on resources – but he has convincingly established that, in comparing civil and social rights, it is a continuum we are dealing with and not a qualitative contrast.

What this body of argument amounts to is a defence, grounded in political philosophy and a commitment to liberty conceived as both negative and positive, of the social effort to move towards a society characterized by concerns for justice and the integrity of the citizen, against the intrinsically inegalitarian notion of the state bound by an overriding obligation to observe an entirely negative regime of liberty.

Conclusion

I think we can best summarize Raymond Plant's contribution to the ongoing debate on social welfare under the following three points. First, as a philosophical analyst, he has constructed a libertarian conceptual framework of social and political thought which he is able to bring to bear on a wide range of issues, particularly in relation to the concept of the state. Second, as a scholarly participant in debate, he has introduced the concepts and discipline of political theory into discussion of social welfare, helped to shape the agenda of the debate, and exposed both rightist and leftist arguments on citizenship and welfare to a libertarian theoretical critique which has helped to expose and explicate their strengths and weaknesses. Third, as a proponent of the social democratic left, he has usefully dealt with New Right arguments and valuations on liberty, justice, markets and so on, *on their own terms*, and has constructed a critical, libertarian version of the social democratic argument for social intervention. It is difffcult not to conclude that he remains the most telling and intellectually rigorous of the critics of the New Right, or that his contribution at the other levels previously enumerated remains unique.

Key texts

In suggesting a short-list of Plant's most important texts, one should perhaps have an eye to demonstrating the range of his interests and approaches. Thus one of his early works should be included, and *Community and Ideology* (1974) demonstrates Plant at work in seeking to apply his political theory to a specific area of social practice: community work. *Conservative Capitalism in Britain and the United States* (Hoover and Plant, 1989) demonstrates his engagement with historical development and policy. *Modern Political Thought* (1991a) draws together his theoretical interests within a rigorously academic framework. Finally, a representation is required of Plant the pamphleteer, grappling with the threatened hegemony of the New Right in the philosophical debate over the future of the state. Here it has to be said that there is a great deal of overlap between many of his contributions, as he has brought similar arguments to bear on successive stages of this debate in a fashion which can be seen as admirably consistent or frustratingly repetitious. 'Citizenship and rights', his half of the Institute of Economic Affairs publication *Citizenship and Rights in Thatcher's Britain: Two views* (1990), is an interesting case of entering the lion's den; but perhaps the Fabian pamphlet *Social Justice, Labour and the New Right* (1993), written for submission to the Labour Party's Social Justice Commission, most concisely illustrates his critical commitments to the labour movement, a progressive and defensible conception of justice, and lively political debate.

Raymond Plant has, over what is now a substantial period, provided the social policy debate with a set of bridges between the languages of political theory, moral obligation and practical policy; and his dialogue with the New Right has helped to lend coherence to a debate in which the two sides frequently talk straight past each other, and strength to the social democratic side of the debate which it would otherwise lack.

References

Hoover, K. and Plant, R. (1989) *Conservative Capitalism in Britain and the United States*, London: Routledge.
Labour Party (1991) *Democracy, Representation and Elections*, interim report of the Working Party on Electoral Systems. London: Labour Party.
Labour Party (1993) *Report of the Working Party on Electoral Systems*, London: Labour Party.

Plant, R. (1974) *Community and Ideology: An essay in applied social philosophy*, London: Routledge and Kegan Paul.

Plant, R. (1981) 'Democratic socialism and equality', in Lipsey, D. and Leonard, D. (eds), *The Socialist Agenda: Crosland's legacy*, London: Jonathan Cape.

Plant, R. (1983) *Hegel: An introduction* (2nd edn), Oxford: Blackwell (first published 1973).

Plant, R. (1985) 'Welfare and the value of liberty', *Government and Opposition*, **20**, 297–314.

Plant, R. (1988) 'Socialism, markets, and end states', in Le Grand, J. and Estrin, S. (eds), *Market Socialism*, Oxford: Clarendon Press.

Plant, R. (1990) 'Citizenship and rights', part I of Plant, R. and Barry N., *Citizenship and Rights in Thatcher's Britain: Two views*, Choice in Welfare Series No. 3, London: Institute of Economic Affairs Health and Welfare Unit.

Plant, R. (1991) *Modern Political Thought*, Oxford: Blackwell.

Plant, R. (1992a) 'Citizenship, rights and welfare', in Coote, A. (ed.), *The Welfare of Citizens: Developing new social rights*, London: Rivers Oram.

Plant, R. (1992b) 'Political theory without foundations' (review article), *History of the Human Sciences*, **5**, 137–44.

Plant, R. (1993) *Social Justice, Labour and the New Right*, Fabian pamphlet 556, London: Fabian Society.

Plant, R., Lesser, H. and Taylor-Gooby, P. (1981) *Political Philosophy and Social Welfare*, London: Routledge.

11 Harrington

Robert A. Gorman

Brief biography

Michael Harrington was born in St Louis, Missouri, on 24 February 1928. After graduating from Holy Cross College in 1947, he flirted briefly with conservatism, entered Yale Law School, and within a year enrolled at the University of Chicago to do graduate work in English literature, where in 1949 he earned a master's degree. 'The day I left law school,' Harrington recalled, 'I switched from Taft Republicanism to democratic socialism without even bothering to tarry a while in the liberal camp in between' (Harrington, 1972a: 64).

The belief that socialists needed to organize for the long haul, rather than go it alone as rebels or intellectuals, more than anything else defined Harrington's public life. Socialism to Harrington meant working together for justice, whereas liberal politics meant standing up for narrow interests. So from the outset he was affiliated with organizations that worked co-operatively for the common good.

In the early 1950s, Harrington joined the youth branch of the Socialist Party, where his formidable personal skills – he was intelligent, articulate, hard working, and a sensational orator – fuelled a meteoric rise to power. Harrington became editor of the Socialist Party's official journal, *New America*, and in 1968 was selected as national co-chair. A terminally ill Norman Thomas let it be known that he hoped Michael Harrington would succeed him as leader of America's democratic left.

Political fall-out from US intervention in south-east Asia fractured the Socialist Party in the late 1960s. Harrington resigned in October 1972, and four months later founded the Democratic Socialist Organizing Committee (DSOC). In 1979 Harrington set his sights on those New Leftists who, in 1972, had formed the New American Movement (NAM) to succeed the defunct Students for a Democratic Society (SDS). DSOC and NAM merged in 1983 into the Democratic Socialists of America (DSA). With more than 6,000 members, DSA – still located in lower Manhattan, midway between Wall Street and City Hall – became the largest US democratic socialist organization since the Socialist Party of 1936. Harrington was also active in the Socialist International, a coalition of socialist parties from around the globe, where in 1983 he was chosen Secretary of the Resolutions Committee and Co-ordinator of the Committee on a New Declaration of Principles.

Harrington, in short, dragged socialists from their faded texts into everyday life. But he always kept one foot in politics and one in theory. He was a prodigious writer whose output – seventeen books and hundreds of articles – ferried socialist theory from the gulag on to mainstreet. *The Other America: Poverty in the United States* (1962) was his best-known work, and the philosophical account of Marxism, *Socialism* (1970a), his finest. The most accessible Marxian text ever written by an American, it established Harrington's reputation as a pre-eminent thinker and scholar.

Capitalism and the state

Many intellectuals in the 1950s and 1960s claimed that ideology had become irrelevant because trained technocrats engineered efficient public policies, and politics no longer had to produce winners and losers. What they called 'post-industrialism' was therefore neither capitalist nor socialist. Beginning with *Toward a Democratic Left* (1968), and continuing in articles and books published throughout the next decade, Harrington argued that modern states remained capitalist, public policy always benefited some more than others, and as usual those who controlled the productive apparatus got more than those who did not. Post-industrialism, which Harrington renamed 'socialist capitalism'[1] and which today is usually called 'the welfare state' or 'social democracy', was actually a new way of protecting the old social order.

Welfare states, whose genealogy trailed into Bismarck's Germany, delivered instant relief during the depression without rocking the capitalist boat, and were popular among unemployed European workers who had no other acceptable alternatives. After the war, the Belgian socialist Henri de Man, in his celebrated *Plan du Travail*, called for a common front of all productive strata, including workers *and* capital, against the power of what he called parasitic money. Capitalism, he wrote, should be humanized rather than transformed. Fifteen years later, in the Godesberg Programme of the German Social Democratic Party, the democratic left adopted the entire socialist capitalism platform. Social democrats henceforth helped plan and administer capitalist economic growth. Absorbed by technical concerns, they eventually forgot socialism's original promise to improve everyday living by altering productive relationships.

Socialist capitalism arrived in America in two stages after the depression had already begun. First came scientific, co-ordinated planning, primarily by business, to raise prices and increase consumption. Administered by the business-dominated National Recovery Administration (NRA), this first stage of the New Deal was eagerly backed by the US Chamber of Commerce, for whom economic planning could preserve private enterprise. By the end of Franklin Roosevelt's initial term in office, however, many unions had deserted the NRA, and the Supreme Court had declared it unconstitutional.

The second stage, begun in 1935, shifted power from private to public hands. New Dealers were outwardly hostile to large corporations, and private industry opposed many of Roosevelt's key innovations. But as John Maynard Keynes told FDR, 'You have made yourself the trustee for those in every country who seek to mend the evils of our condition by reasoned experiment within the framework of the existing social system' (quoted in Harrington, 1968: 30; see also 1968: 30–50; 1966: 130–9). Government primed the economic pump with fiscal, monetary and social service programmes, and then let market forces take over. New Deal ideology was actually a mixture of Keynes and Adam Smith, which Harrington called 'Smith-Keynesianism'. Smith-Keynesians defended both the marketplace and government intervention to correct some market inequities. Public money revitalized, humanized and regulated capitalism, but did not transform it. Big business realized by 1939 that welfare statism served its interests.

Harrington considered the New Deal an 'ambiguous event' (Harrington, 1980: 28). It signified the victory of workers, minorities and liberals over reactionary interests. *Laissez-faire* myths were shattered, social security became a national principle, and many newly unionized factory workers became formidable economic and political players. The political landscape, in brief, had shifted to the left.

But the New Deal could not cure mass unemployment. By 1938–9, when Roosevelt lost control of Congress, unemployment remained at an unacceptably high ten million. The Second World War and the smaller wars that followed provided some temporary relief, but unemployment, and poverty as well, remained intractable problems. This was because New Dealers, and socialist capitalists generally, presumed that basic corporate structures were sound, and capital needed to control investment. Employment thus expanded in profitable industries and declined elsewhere. Overproduction in the 1960s and 1970s led to a plague of corporate bankruptcies, buyouts and mergers in the 1980s. Jobs were lost, wages declined and discontent grew. As capitalist economies automated and corporations moved into a global marketplace, good job opportunities became even harder to find. Harrington argued in *The New American Poverty* (1984) that poverty in developed capitalist democracies was now ineradicable because anti-business reforms enraged powerful entrepreneurs, discouraged private investment and intensified the political crisis. Government subsidies to the impoverished, which had frightened corporations in 1929, now helped resolve the contradictions of free-market production by transforming non-productive ex-workers into consumers. 'Once the tumult and social energy of the Great Depression abated,' Harrington observed, 'the system shaped and coopted the very reforms which most of the corporate rich had abominated' (Harrington, 1980: 28; see also Harrington, 1970a: 199–204).

The welfare state, in sum, was a paradox:

> It represents the reluctant concessions of the ruling class, the increments of reform that function to make basic change unnecessary. But it is also the product of conscience and consciousness, that of socialist workers and middle class liberals, of militant blacks and students, and of the aging. As such, it has been the instrument of the oppressed as well as the oppressors, a means of partial liberation as well as partial pacification. (Harrington, 1976: 306)

Harrington was certain, however, that the welfare state was fundamentally capitalist. Its economy was still privately owned and it prioritized corporate profits. European social democrats wisely rejected communism, but did not create feasible alternatives. They may have humanized capitalism and marginally improved social life, but they also sanctioned proletarian misery by reinforcing inherently exploitative relationships. The welfare state, whether or not socialists controlled it, obeyed capitalist rules.

Harrington was a 'democratic socialist', not a social democrat. Whereas social democracy endorsed the welfare state, democratic socialism reversed capitalist priorities by letting labourers make significant public decisions, even in the workplace.[2] In the USA, democratic socialism meant taking the New Deal beyond its first two stages. A 'Third New Deal' (Harrington, 1966: 139; 1968: 30) could empower workers and complete the process begun in 1929, when control of key investments passed from private boardrooms to a capitalist-controlled welfare state.

Why would welfare states permit such fundamental structural changes? Harrington needed to dress the critique with a richer theory of the state, one that probed capitalist politics and mapped the arena where workers could struggle. He decided to strike out on his own by synthesizing the entire spectrum of leftist state theories.

The capitalist state formulated and administered public policy by juggling the interests of significant groups in order to serve the public and maintain power. Liberalism, said Harrington, was partially correct. But the state did not control social production, so its ability to act effectively, its very survival, was in the private sector's hands. By withholding investment or terminating production, capitalists could wreak economic havoc on large segments of the public: 'The state's interest in perpetuating its own rule is thus, in economic fact, identified with the health of the capitalist economy' (Harrington, 1976: 307). The capitalist state also intervened in the economy with countercyclical policies that indirectly subsidized corporations. Communists were thus also correct in spotlighting the political power of capital.

The state was neither a capitalist nor an unthinking tool of capitalists, but it depended on capitalists to survive. It could legislate impartially, but for as long as investment was privately controlled, the public's interest was best served by appeasing capitalists: 'The most honest and incorruptible of public servants wants and works for the maximum happiness of General Motors and Ford' (1976: 310). Public officials 'want' and 'work for' corporate happiness because it warms the economy and fills campaign coffers. They do not just mechanically reproduce capitalism. The state, then, was conditioned by capitalist structures and also had a life of its own. Even when it reinforced capital, it articulated a unified national interest that somehow transcended everyday business transactions and the ability of specific capitalists to control events. Why else could the state occasionally enact pro-worker legislation?

Neither fully autonomous nor determined, the state is what Harrington called 'co-determined' because it acted within a constellation of powerful forces (Harrington, 1970b: 265). The state passively crystallized this environment and also actively sculpted it. It was both determined and determining, depending on what we looked at.

Harrington thus agreed that the welfare state was the 'executive committee' of the bourgeoisie, defending capital's long-range interests even though it occasionally upset specific capitalists.[3] The US state and its wealthy benefactors emerged from the New Deal, for example, stronger than ever despite some short-term sacrifices.

Millions of workers, however, were now more economically secure than ever before. Their political influence was greater than they ever dreamed it could be, and their multiplying opportunities for educational and cultural enrichment made life better. Reformism had transformed the state from a simple instrument of capital into an agent of profound change. By empowering the poor politically, introducing minimal economic security and establishing mass cultural education, reformism had raised proletarian expectations beyond the system's capacities. Reformism, in short, became subversive (Harrington, 1976: 206–7).

The state functioned in a capitalist system and never fully satisfied labour's needs. But the dynamic flow of social events meant that government activity, for example, incrementally transformed the system. Norman Thomas was correct: who governs really does matter, at least as much as what children learn in school, or the economic demands of unionized workers. When the totality changes, so will everything in it, and activism changes the totality. The agitated fusing and splintering of the whole with its parts – the social dialectic – made political activism meaningful even in an undemocratic system.

Harrington thus agreed with both communism and liberalism – and with neither.[4] Capital now ran the state, but popular forces could win valuable practical victories. These eventually strengthened rich people because the state was structurally tilted towards capital. Even in the best short-term scenario, workers could therefore expect to increase absolute living standards, not eliminate systemic inequities. Political struggle, however, also mobilized coalitions of unhappy voters. As reformist victories mounted, and the coalition was empowered, social 'normalcy' drifted leftward. Democratic socialists could push the state to the brink of systemic change, and then let voters abolish profits, transform capital accumulation and alter productive relationships. The state cannot legislate socialism, however, until the rest of society, after years of reformist state policies, becomes socialist.

Harrington's political agenda fitted, in his own words, 'midway between immediate feasibility and ultimate utopia' (Harrington, 1968: 14). While socialism was clearly democratic, in an everyday world where even poor people were anti-socialist he sadly wrote that 'it will never come to pass in its ideal form' (Harrington, 1970a: 344). Socialists had to create new values without shrinking the nation's economic capacity or trashing public culture. They had to be progressive and practical, not dogmatic. The transition to socialism would be slower, more intricate and much less dramatic than the founders of socialism had believed. For Harrington,

> The next step will not be revolution or even a sudden and dramatic lurch to the socialist Left. It will be the emergence of a revived liberalism – taking that term to mean the reform of the system within the system – which will, of necessity, be much more socialistic even though it will not, in all probability, be socialist. (Harrington, 1980: 320–1; see also Harrington, 1975: 102)

Harrington wanted to join unionized blue-collar employees with educated white-collar workers, professionals and special interests (e.g. minorities, feminists, environmentalists, gays and lesbians) – the so-called 'old' and 'new' working classes – into a broad electoral coalition. This could be done, he claimed, within America's two-party system by purging the Democrats of conservatives and the Republicans of liberals, thereby realigning both parties along distinct ideological and class lines, and creating an electoral home for socialists inside the Democratic Party. Harrington argued this case so forcefully and for so many years that tactics were gradually disengaged from theory, and many lost sight of his full agenda. Socialism, remember, was anathema in the USA, but realignment was debated on television and in national journals. Harrington was probably better known as an advocate of Democratic Party reform than of democratically transforming a capitalist party.

Realignment became problematic to Harrington only if and when a mass defection from the Democratic Party took place. A new US party then could attract a significant number of voters. Realignment was thus a means of achieving socialism, not a moral priority. It was the radical edge of a jejune world.

No such exodus occurred in the 1960s and 1970s, although Harrington remarked presciently in 1968 that 'it could happen in the next 20 years' (Harrington, 1968: 274). Almost two decades later the complexion of both parties changed, but Harrington was shocked and saddened by what he saw. A 1970s conservative offensive had succeeded in redefining political discourse in the USA, and large sectors of organized labour, the solid core of the Democratic Party, were disengaged from factory unions during the early 1980s. The 1984 Democratic Presidential ticket included two liberals and one woman, and was endorsed by the influential African-American Jesse Jackson, the technocrat Gary Hart, organized labour and feminists. Convention speeches celebrated working people and minorities, women and immigrants, and the poor. The Mondale campaign united all the forces Harrington deemed essential for realigning the parties, and still lost pitifully. Working voters had chosen image rather than substance. A Democratic platform trumpeting their economic interests fell to the Great Communicator, and to a script that made the nation feel good despite its afflictions. The Democratic Party was cashiered by its own workers, who opted for patriotism and a glassy smile. Nothing was left to realign.

The internal balance of power in the Democratic Party henceforth leaned towards 'moderates' who often repackaged and marketed Reaganism. Lacking a solid institutional home, and uncertain of the future, workers became easy prey for media jackals who now sold politicians instead of soap. America experienced a decline in party loyalty and identification, and the party system became 'dealigned', not, as Harrington once hoped, realigned (Harrington, 1988a: 116; see also Harrington, 1979a: 123–38). This electoral anarchy empowered image-makers and their wealthy clients, who shrewdly manipulated campaigns by selling phoney heros and false issues to vulnerable people. American individualism was trumped. Organizations became less significant than thirty-second TV spots, and commercial polling replaced the wise judgements of candidates and parties.

A chastened Harrington experienced first-hand the real meaning of dialectics. Non-economic cleavages had ripped his New Deal coalition apart. Democrats had simply added new demands on to the party's platform whenever an emergent force coalesced into a significant interest group. The Democratic Party, and the left generally, lacked a broad vision that clarified workers' common economic concerns. Where once Harrington chose realignment, now he realized that democratic socialism, like Reaganism, thrived only by hitting Americans squarely in their everyday experiences. A dealigned weak-party system could not reach that far. Harrington decided to formulate a social ethic that dealt with the putative concerns of old and new workers, minorities, women, gays and other issue groups, and also reattached these to their economic roots.

Cultural and moral factors have always been important in US politics, where class is rarely mentioned. Republicans had already succeeded in the politics of symbolic identification by linking traditional values to a conservative programme, attracting precisely those groups which stood to lose the most. By focusing almost exclusively on politics, Harrington had lost touch with people who took their own cultural and moral heritage at least as seriously as their economic security or their loyalty to the Democratic Party. Harrington's last and in some ways most ambitious venture was to spike traditional values with a dose of radical critique.

The USA needed a new sense of purpose that sanctioned a beloved heritage and also helped people live better. In *Socialism: Past and future* (1989a), Harrington challenged socialists to embrace public culture, once contemptuously called the superstructure, and gently open democracy's floodgates. He wanted a new socialist morality to reach into the US heartland and touch its republican pulse. Harrington's 'New Socialism' resembled those 'little republics' that Thomas Jefferson once said guaranteed liberty. It was part of the nation's ethical conscience: that non-élitist, democratic mentality Harrington called a 'particularly American spirit' (Harrington, 1986a: 190). Socialists needed to reclaim this republican sentiment, which had been kidnapped and abused by Reaganites.

Socialists also needed to empower disenfranchised people, whether or not they were blue-collar labourers or even union members. For one thing, collectively they represented more than half the nation's population. For another, groups based on gender, race, religion, sexual preference or ethnicity often emotionally sustained their members to such an extent that other political organizations could no longer take their place. Harrington always knew that cultural emancipation is almost meaningless if people are poor. Socialist economics was thus in every oppressed group's interest. In his last books he warned socialists to stand up for progressive interests as well as to establish a common denominator of economic need. Democratic socialism, he had learned, actually promoted cultural diversity.

Social policy

Harrington's social policy incubated in his theory of the state and hatched in a historical setting that was lurching to the right. The rise of the New Right coalition during the 1970s and the election of Ronald Reagan as President in 1980 smashed New Dealism and redesigned US politics around the immediate demands of business. It also jolted Harrington into delivering socialism's goods before it was too late.

In the Social Security Act of 1935, the US Congress established a programme called Aid to Dependent Children to provide funds for needy children. Congress added a caretaker grant to provide for needy mothers in 1950, and renamed the programme Aid to Families with Dependent Children (AFDC). 'Welfare', in America, usually means AFDC, and proposals related to AFDC are called welfare policy. Harrington, on the other hand, wanted to end poverty not subsidize the impoverished. His 'welfare policy' included a wide range of short- and long-term social programmes that improved the overall health, well-being and prosperity of everyone. With the nation turning right, and the hapless Democratic Party immobilized, Harrington hoped to convince the vast electoral centre that it would do better with democratic socialism than with conservatism.

AFDC is administered at the state and local levels with grants from the federal government to aid in financing. Different state economies and ideologies have produced discrepancies in funding, and most welfare experts believe that income levels of AFDC families – especially after severe federal cuts in 1982 and again in 1983 – in most states are too low to care properly for children. Harrington wanted the federal government to mandate a national welfare minimum, indexed to median income, that once and for all funded a decent standard of living for the millions of children and their families now receiving AFDC.[5] Recipients, moreover, needed more input into running anti-poverty programmes, and eligibility requirements had to be simplified. Harrington opposed workfare – the federal policy of allowing states to set up mandatory work programmes for AFDC recipients – because jobs that offered medical benefits and day care, and paid significantly more than AFDC and food stamps, were not available.

Harrington also favoured expanding public works and services initiatives, nationalizing health care, making decent low-cost public housing a basic right, raising the minimum wage, guaranteeing free and open access to upgraded public education programmes, and rewarding socially responsible corporate investment with tax incentives (see especially Harrington, 1968: 101–5, 125–7, 142–50; 1970a: 303–6; 1974b: 691–3; 1975: 101; 1980: 171–5, 204–20, 247–53, 280–3; 1982a: 417–19; 1984: 238–51; 1986a: 164ff.; 1988b: 47–54). These proposals maintained or improved living conditions, and were popular with workers, minorities and some professionals in the Democratic Party who had nowhere else to turn.

When Harrington introduced his New Socialism in the 1980s, cultural enrichment became an integral part of his welfare policy. Workers, he realized, were expending the equivalent of an additional month of paid labour each year more than they were two decades ago, but for many the extra hours merely slowed a free-fall into poverty (Harrington, 1989a: 215–16; Schor, 1992). They worked more hours, earned fewer adjusted dollars, and lost valuable leisure time. Harrington emphasized the crisis of time faced by middle-class and poor families. Parents worked so many long hours that they rarely had the time or energy just to be parents, and simple pleasures like shared vacations were rapidly disappearing from family routines. Conservatives aggravated the crisis but none the less used it to their own advantage. Harrington wanted socialists to steal the right's pro-family thunder as it lobbied to help working households.

Leisure time had also become an important cultural issue. In the next century, technology would reduce the orbit of necessary labour to less than one-half of a worker's waking hours. In the past, people identified with the work they did. What would our new identities become? Socialists needed to suggest a range of new possibilities for using leisure hours creatively. Harrington always favoured expanding and improving public education to accommodate every qualified citizen, regardless of wealth. Now he also admitted that 'sending more and more people to college in a society which doesn't create enough jobs requiring the college-educated can be destructive to individuals and wasteful of resources'.[6] People needed better schools and universities, physical investments in theatres, athletic fields, fix-it shops and libraries, as well as increased public support for music, art, poetry, crafts, hobbies, and participatory sports.

Capitalist reforms, like charity, help the needy but do not erase poverty. The centrepiece of Harrington's long-term programme, what he called the 'precondition of all social progress' (Harrington, 1980: 211; see also Harrington, 1979b: 132), was full employment, which would flow through the nation, first creating ripples and later tidal waves of change. Good jobs improved the social standing and motivation of the unemployed, and also reduced crime and violence, which thrive on hopelessness. Full employment raised salaries, resolved racial tensions, pacified cities, motivated students and created compassionate citizens. Even businesses prospered because new consumers increased private production and profits. In short, good economic news for the needy helped everyone. Full employment, said Harrington, was the cure for poverty and the precondition for ending patchwork reforms like AFDC.

In the 1980s, this full employment programme became, in Harrington's own words, 'qualitatively defined full employment' (Harrington, 1988b: 50; see also Harrington, 1986a: 144; 1985b: 139–44; Long, 1988: 103). New jobs had to be meaningful, challenging and wherever possible engaged with labour-saving technology. 'Smart machines', Harrington claimed, worked better if smart people, labouring creatively, ran them. Labourers needed fulfilling work, not just more jobs, so the economy's character as well as its size needed upgrading.

Harrington realized that full employment programmes were unpopular in capitalist democracies because corporations opposed them. His other long-term proposals – democratic planning, socializing some investment and redefining property ownership – were designed gradually to empower workers and to change the pro-business configuration of capitalist politics. They reallocated resources to the job market and altered capitalist structures without destroying everyday values or creating panic on Wall Street.

In most developed democracies since the Second World War, unions have co-operated with government officials and employers in creating policy on a broad range of issues, including investment, collective bargaining, wages, occupational safety and equal opportunity. Unions have also won seats on governing boards of corporations and pension funds. With this in mind, Harrington suggested that a team consisting of elected officials, worker and community activists, and entrepreneurs replace the corporate élite that now controlled US economic planning. Public servants and capitalists in each industry could then sit down together and decide economic priorities, with their relative power based on the nature of production and the expertise and technology each brought to the table. To prevent bureaucratic or corporate abuse, what Harrington called 'command planning', community groups 'counterplanned' (Harrington, 1982a: 423; 1981: 50–3) and were given public funds, computers and expertise. Workers and other interested consumers became watchdogs, scrutinizing major private or public planning decisions and requesting accessible explanations for questionable policies. Perhaps a portion of profits, in the form of equity capital, might be deposited into a fund that financed this kind of worker activity.[7] The President channelled information to local groups by reporting periodically to the nation on basic economic choices and their consequences.[8] Congress then debated the options and selected one as the nation's Democratic Plan. The threat of lost government contracts, tax subsidies and shelters, and guaranteed loans made the financial and symbolic costs of unreasonable corporate haggling exceed the benefits.

This proposal to democratize planning centralized a process that was splintered and haphazard. Centralization, however, was a precondition for decentralizing policy decisions into local communities and factories, where people whose jobs and income were finally secure participated in local decision making. Harrington felt that their small input into the planning process would create a need to control planning entirely. New structures of neighbourhood, metropolitan and regional government, reflecting the actual locations of empowered communities, then replaced traditional state and local units (Harrington, 1968: 121–3; 1971: 694–6; 1974: 68).

Although Democratic Plans carried moral weight, and tax subsidies stimulated responsible corporate investment, Harrington pointed out that the private sector was still free to invest wherever it maximized its return, regardless of social consequences. Developed nations had to democratize corporate investment, initially at least without upsetting the capitalist cart because 'under our present institutional arrangements' Harrington realized, 'it is necessary for the political foes of profit to treat profit more gently than any other sector of the economy'.[9] He suggested that employee and public representatives be placed on the boards of major industrial and financial corporations, including the Federal Reserve Bank, to publicize key investment decisions related to pricing, plant location, technology, wages and personnel (Harrington, 1975: 103–4; 1978: 125–36; 1980: 138–9). When necessary, corporations had to defend these policies publicly.

Pension funds, insurance companies and retained corporate profits now provided most investment capital. If workers could take control of their pensions away from corporate managers and trustees, they would also take control of steadily increasing amounts of investment wealth (Harrington, 1975: 104; 1978: 125–30; 1980: 140). Then their role in corporate investment decisions would expand with their share of the profits. If workers also received company stock from profit-sharing arrangements, democratic investment would grow even more rapidly.

Harrington assumed that workers would rationally defer consumption in favour of increased investment, and balance corporate profitability with the public's welfare. As they earned larger shares of corporate wealth, and became powerful actors, he also assumed they would want even more, and eventually socialist production relationships would be commonplace. In the short term, however, corporate profits remained the major single source of new investment funds. Harrington's investment reform programme placed workers on an activist track, but did not challenge capitalist structures. Most large industries thus remained privately owned for the foreseeable future. But the absolute freedom now enjoyed by business executives was reduced. Some time after Harrington's programme was enacted workers might actually take over corporate decision making. Although the title to private property would have remained undisturbed, its functions would have been socialized without rocking the nation's democratic heritage.

Socialism, then, did not merely redistribute wealth or nationalize factories. It was a lifestyle rather than an economic doctrine, and it let common people decide what the future would be like. Nationalization, moreover, was not necessarily socialist. If it promoted socialism, nationalization was desirable: if it blocked workplace democracy and creativity it was not. Harrington had the courage of his democratic convictions. Enlightened private firms, he conceded, were more progressive than unresponsive, inefficient public ones (Harrington, 1989a: 197–8). Nationalization was an issue for pragmatic discussion and empirical inquiry.

Harrington realized that for the foreseeable future developed democracies would remain mixed economies dominated by private business. Essential production that required large-scale planning and investments, and could not be easily decentralized (e.g. power grids, transportation systems and communications networks), none the less had to be nationalized. Their internal structures, however, and their impact on communities and the nation also needed to be socialized so that workers could make key decisions. In small-scale, high-tech industries, on the other hand, co-operatives and worker-owned enterprises would work best (1989a: 201–2).

Markets played an important role in the transition to socialism, for as long as the demand for resources exceeded supply, because in scarcity socialists *and* capitalists had to promote efficiency (1989a: 239; 1989b: 66). Markets reward innovative producers and penalize lazy ones. In equality, markets are a wonderful device for communicating individual desires. When people are unequal, however, markets exaggerate the desires of the wealthy. Markets therefore could not be sovereign. Harrington felt that socialists had to make markets serve social priorities rather than rich consumers. Socialist efficiency, then, expressed social and global goals, not just private interests. Socialist markets minimized costs, maximized production and allowed producers to share the expanded surplus, all within the broad limits of a democratic plan and alongside the free sector.

Socialized property was a public authority responsible to the nation's elected representatives. Each enterprise had to pay its own way and return a surplus for depreciation, new investment and the social dividend. Unless society decided to subsidize unprofitable but socially useful activities (such as rural postal and rail routes) from the profits of the system as a whole, failing enterprises were terminated. Decisions to subsidize were therefore justifiable only when they were also affordable, and public firms that released workers did so only after consulting with the public and providing job retraining, public works employment, job placement, employer subsidies, moving subsidies and – as a last resort – unemployment compensation. Socialists had to decide what kind of markets were appropriate, not whether markets were necessary. If and when scarcity was replaced by abundance, then socialist markets, like those in capitalism, withered away.

The costs of Harrington's social programme were to be paid from several sources (Harrington, 1985a: 217ff.). Private corporations remained the largest single source of investment revenue, and pension funds also provided an enormous pool of capital for public, private and co-operative sectors. Progressive income and inheritance taxes would increase public revenues and also convince qualified professionals to serve others instead of just getting rich. Savings would dramatically increase with simple innovations such as resurrecting the Post Office savings system, factoring depreciation and new investment costs into the market price of consumer goods, and regulating advertising costs. A peace dividend created by reasonable cuts in the military budget would also raise needed revenue. Finally, profits from public enterprises could create new jobs and programmes. Harrington was certain that 'it would . . . be possible in a socialist transition to plan democratically, to effectuate that plan realistically, and to finance the entire process' (1985a: 219).

The cure for poverty was jobs, not underfunded emergency public services. A combination of national initiatives to co-ordinate and streamline productivity, and local initiatives to democratize the workplace, increased the number of quality jobs, promoted economic growth and fostered republicanism. These moderate structural changes also balanced the public's welfare and business profits. Health care, education, upgraded AFDC programmes and transportation became free goods and services, allocated according to need and publicly financed. The distribution and price of everything else was determined by the market. Public assistance going to the aged and children, and to safety-net social programmes like AIDS research and child care, were adequately fundable, in Harrington's own words, only when full employment resources 'economically and politically permit such decency' (Harrington, 1986b: 617; 1988b: 47–54). If each small reform was part of an integrated long-range socialist plan, Harrington felt that such social decency would be forthcoming. If not, the welfare crisis in developed democracies would only get worse. Harrington's socialism was a humane *and* efficient system of production, not a charity.

Harrington and poverty

Realizing that in his own words, 'the American people are much more receptive to dramatic moments and vignettes than to accounts of macro-economic structures', in 1962 Harrington wanted to shock a complacent nation into action by suggesting poverty's 'look, its smell, its often twisted spirit, with just a few rudimentary references to the underlying trends' (Harrington, 1984: 8). The result was *The Other America*. It mentioned neither Karl Marx nor the word 'socialism', and became an embarrassed Harrington's one and only commercial success. *The Other America* meant well, but did not even come close to depicting Harrington's core values. Most people thus remember Harrington as a charitable and humane reformer, not a democratic socialist.

Poverty had been a statistic, a crossing beyond which an uncertain number of people were in some vague way rendered invisible. Harrington put flesh and feelings on this data, turning an abstraction into a painful experience. He took readers into ghettoes, barrios, dilapidated apartments, empty hamlets, sweatshops and migrant shelters, exposing a nation of 50 million suffering people who lived, largely unnoticed, down the road. He also showed how the descent into poverty was often uncontrollable, and how poverty created inhibiting and demoralizing disadvantages. Poverty, then, was a way of life, a culture, that slowly destroyed its victims, and we were all potential victims.

The Other America was a book for the times. Liberal intellectuals used it to catalyze public aid programmes. Tired of eating goldfish and piling into Volkswagens, but still unable to locate Vietnam on a map, students stumbled on a cause worth fighting for. The book helped inspire President Kennedy to initiate reforms that became the War on Poverty. Martin Luther King, Jr, once laughingly told Harrington, 'You know, we didn't know we were poor until we read your book' (Chernow, 1977: 30). The *Boston Globe* editorialized in 1987 that Medicaid and Medicare, food stamps, and expanded social security benefits were all 'directly traceable' to *The Other America*. Harrington, in short, dramatically impacted US welfare policy, almost by mistake.

Harrington was solicited by Sargent Shriver to help shape the nation's response to *The Other America*. Through the Economic Opportunity Act, passed in 1964 when unemployment was declining and prices were stable, Lyndon Baines Johnson launched the 'official' War on Poverty. This act set in motion community action programmes, VISTA (the domestic Peace Corps), and legal aid programmes for the impoverished.

Politicians believed that prudent fiscal and monetary policies, and ambitious social programmes, would skim some of America's excess wealth to rescue the poor, and also end the business cycle. During the Kennedy and Johnson administrations, Congress created the Occupational Safety and Health Administration, the Equal Employment Opportunity Commission, the Consumer Product Safety Commission, and the Environmental Protection Administration, and also passed the Equal Rights Amendment. Johnson's Great Society programme created more than 200 new social and economic programmes, most with a strong urban emphasis. Between 1962 and 1970, federal aid to the states increased from $7 billion to $24 billion, and the share of federal funds going to urban areas increased from 55 to 70 per cent. Federal programmes were also begun to help the poor and provide added security for others. In 1965 alone Congress passed legislation designed to provide medical care for the elderly, the disabled and the indigent, through Medicare and Medicaid; offer aid to public schools and loans to college students; supplement rents for poor people; establish grants, loans and training programmes for health professionals; and support development efforts in Appalachia. Job Corps and the federal food stamps programme helped sustain many who had fallen on hard times, and the Head Start programme redistributed educational opportunities to children in poor neighbourhoods.

Idealistic students, many after reading *The Other America*, moved from campuses to slum neighbourhoods to help wipe out poverty by struggling for black equality and empowering local communities. They mobilized grassroots support for the Civil Rights Act of 1964, which gave the Attorney General the power to file desegregation lawsuits and prohibited federal aid to school districts that remained segregated. The Voting Rights Act was passed a year later, enabling federal officials to register voters and to suspend literacy tests in areas where less than 50 per cent of the voting-age population was registered for, or had voted in, the 1964 national election. And Community Action programmes actually brought political experience and leadership skills to unprecedented numbers of black and other minority residents of poor and isolated communities.

Poverty, however, stubbornly refused to go away. What was a tactic for Harrington – that is, expanding social welfare reforms – became the *raison d'être* of the War on Poverty, in part at least because of *The Other America*. When economic conditions worsened in the 1970s and 1980s, public revenues diminished and the middle class grew hostile. Taxes, as well as the cost of living, were rising faster than incomes, and the middle class felt that welfare recipients were ungrateful. Conservatives on both sides of the Atlantic rode the raging discontent into power. The conflict between grassroots democracy and capitalist economics, what James O'Connor once called 'the fiscal crisis of the state', eroded the postwar social democratic consensus and the nation's fight against poverty.

Harrington's solution was to end poverty by strengthening reforms and gradually democratizing economic structures. Unfortunately, he lacked a consti- tuency. Leftists were anti-reformist, conservatives were anti-welfare, and the centre simply wanted to help the poor with unaffordable public programmes. Harrington spent the rest of his life explaining that the expanded welfare state that he had helped to create in the 1960s was too capitalist for socialism and too socialist for capitalism. It could not deliver the welfare that it promised, and could not afford what it delivered.

Only time will tell if Harrington's eclectic welfare policy will help industrialized democracies in their hour of need. Capitalism still expands and contracts in cyclic bursts. Now, however, each downturn leaves a permanent residue of misery in poor and middle-class neighbourhoods. The benefits of economic growth are shared by a shrinking number of mostly wealthy people. As social programmes are privatized by conservatives, the gap between rich and poor widens, and economic victims fend, often unsuccessfully, for themselves. In urban areas, among minorities, and in groups of migrant labourers, family farmers and service workers, the prospects for civil disorders on the scale of the 1992 Los Angeles riots increase. The traditional left, centre and right are all motionless in the economic quicksand. Harrington believed in economic justice, reformism and the sanctity of tradition, and cobbled a social policy that might deliver on all three counts. Surely some of his ideas will gradually seep into the crevices that have fissured the post-communist left, and democratic socialists can then finally take part in public debate on welfare policy.

Key texts

Michael Harrington was extraordinarily talented and knowledgeable, and wrote on a wide number of topics ranging from theology and literary criticism to practical politics. I recommend the following books as a casual reader's crash-course on Harrington.

Socialism (1970) uncovers an unknown, democratic Karl Marx who was buried in the debris of twentieth-century communism. Harrington explains why communism is not Marxism, and explores the meaning of Marxian dialectics. This is Harrington's signature work, the required text for anyone interested in democratic socialism.

Socialism: Past and future (1989a) is, in effect, volume two of Harrington's social theory. He paints the history of Marxian socialism as a struggle between materialism and utopian idealism, and suggests that the time is now ripe for synthesizing a 'New Socialism' that combines Marx's humanitarianism with his political savvy. Harrington discusses how markets, economic plans, private property and public ownership peacefully co-exist in authentic socialism.

The New American Poverty (1984) uses anecdotes, data and critique to explain why modern capitalist democracies around the globe are experiencing a slow economic melt-down the likes of which they have not seen since 1929. Automation, globalizing national economies and a new world-wide division of labour are the culprits. Neither free-market capitalism nor Keynesianism can stanch the outward flow of good jobs or save the middle class. After reading this book it is hard *not* to be a socialist.

Finally, Harrington's two autobiographies - *Fragments of the Century* (1972a) and *The Long-Distance Runner* (1988a) – are crammed with reminiscences of personalities, events and crises on the US left from the 1950s to the 1980s. It is all very entertaining, but readers also quickly sense the contradictions of being socialist and American, painfully experience Harrington's breakdown, and then discover the inner strength and compassion of this unique individual.

Notes

1. Harrington first used the term 'socialist capitalism' in *Socialism* (Harrington, 1970). Thereafter, he used this term and 'post-industrialism' interchangeably.
2. On the differences between 'social democracy' and 'democratic socialism', see Harrington (1970a: ch. 1; 1970b: 254; 1972b: 57).
3. Intraclass disputes pit large capitalists against small, multinational corporations against national corporations, old money against parvenus, and smart capitalists against stupid ones.
4. Harrington pointedly criticized Domhoff's popular instrumentalist view of the state for crudely ignoring capitalist politics (Harrington, 1976: 313–19).
5. In the 1970s, Harrington wanted to federalize AFDC. In the 1980s, with the federal debt skyrocketing, Harrington suggested increased federal funding and raised minimum standards, but no longer insisted on federalizing AFDC (Harrington, 1980: 253; 1986b: 617).
6. Unpublished letter from Harrington to John Simmons, 9 February 1979, Tamiment Library of New York University, DASA Collection, Michael Harrington Correspondence.

7. Harrington called this 'collective profit sharing' (Harrington, 1979b: 134).
8. Harrington called this the President's 'Report on the Future' (Harrington, 1968: 110–18). In *The Other America: Poverty in the United States* (1962: xxvi), Harrington called for an 'Office of the Future' attached to the Presidency, and a Joint Congressional Committee on the Future to receive, debate and modify or adopt the White House suggestions. The broad perspective of this 'Report on the Future' would be operationalized in the target dates and quantities of what Harrington termed (adopting A. Phillip Randolph's phrase) a 'Freedom Budget'. The latter would present a timetable for abolishing poverty and achieving full employment over a period of ten years. See Harrington (1968: 123–4).
9. Harrington, 'Private profit and the public good', unpublished manuscript, c. 1980, Tamiment Library of NYU, DSA Collection, Michael Harrington Correspondence, p. 4.

References

Chernow, R. (1977) 'An irresistible profile of Michael Harrington (you must be kidding)', *Mother Jones*, **2**, 6, pp. 28–60 *passim*.
Harrington, M. (1962) *The Other America: Poverty in the United States*, New York: Macmillan.
Harrington, M. (1966) 'The politics of poverty', in Howe, I. (ed.), *The Radical Papers*, Garden City, NY: Doubleday.
Harrington, M. (1968) *Toward A Democratic Left*, New York: Macmillan.
Harrington, M. (1970a) *Socialism*, New York: Saturday Review Press.
Harrington, M. (1970b) 'Why we need socialism in America', *Dissent*, **17**, 3, pp. 240–303 *passim*.
Harrington, M. (1971) 'I am not a Marxist, I am Marx', *Nation*, **213**, 22, pp. 694–6.
Harrington, M. (1972a) *Fragments of the Century*, New York: Simon and Schuster.
Harrington, M. (1972b) 'Soaking the poor', *Commonweal*, **97**, 3, pp. 57–60.
Harrington, M. (1974a) 'Grass-roots needs', *Nation*, **218**, 3, p. 68.
Harrington, M. (1974b) 'Welfare capitalism in crisis', *Nation*, **219**, 22, pp. 686–93.
Harrington, M. (1975) 'Our proposals for the crisis', *Dissent*, **22**, 2, pp. 101–4.
Harrington, M. (1976) *Twilight of Capitalism*, New York: Simon and Schuster.
Harrington, M. (1978) 'Full employment and socialist investment', *Dissent*, **25**, 1, pp. 125–36.
Harrington, M. (1979a) 'The new class and the left', in Bruce-Briggs, B. (ed.), *The New Class?*, New Jersey: Transaction.
Harrington, M. (1979b) 'Social retreat and economic stagnation', *Dissent*, **26**, 2, pp. 131–4.
Harrington, M. (1980) *Decade of Decision*, New York: Simon and Schuster.
Harrington, M. (1981) 'The virtues and limitations of liberal democracy', *The Center Magazine*, **XIV**, 2, pp. 50–3.
Harrington, M. (1982a) 'A path for America: proposals from the democratic left', *Dissent*, **29**, 4, pp. 405–24.
Harrington, M. (1982b) 'A path for America', *Dissent*, **29**, 4, pp. 405–24.
Harrington, M. (1984) *The New American Poverty*, New York: Holt, Rinehart and Winston.
Harrington, M. (1985a) 'What socialists would do in America', in Harrington, M. (ed.), *Taking Sides*, New York: Holt, Rinehart and Winston.

Harrington, M. (1985) 'If there is a recession – and if not', *Dissent*, **32**, 2, pp. 139–44.

Harrington, M. (1986a) *The Next Left*, New York: Holt.

Harrington, M. (1986b) 'Progressive economics for 1988', *Nation*, **242**, 60, pp. 601–19.

Harrington, M. (1988a) *The Long-Distance Runner: An autobiography*, New York: Holt.

Harrington, M. (1988b) 'The first steps – and a few beyond', *Dissent*, **35**, 1 pp. 44–55.

Harrington, M. (1989a) *Socialism: Past and future*, New York: Arcade.

Harrington, M. (1989b) 'Markets and plans', *Dissent*, **36**, 1, pp. 56–70.

Long, M. (1988) 'Paradise tossed – visions of utopia', *Omni*, **10**, April, pp. 36–108 *passim*.

Schor, J.B. (1992) *The Overworked American*, New York: Basic Books.

Part IV

Marxists

Introduction

Like all the other ideologies discussed in this book, Marxism is a form of both analysis and prescription. It is an attempt to explain both how society functions and how it should ideally be constructed. The ideal society prescribed by Marx has always been hazy to the extreme in both its socialist and communist forms because of his dislike of blueprints for a social organization that was in the distant future. It was up to the socialists of a particular country to decide the details of socialist structures, so long as these were within the broad parameters that he laid down. The trouble is that these parameters were so broad that they could be interpreted in very different ways.

What concerns us most in this part of the book is the relevance of Marxism as a form of analysis because of the implications this has for the welfare state. Despite numerous criticisms, the Marxist explanation of social change in capitalist societies, with its emphasis on the significance of material factors, has a lot to commend it. Although it does not ignore the importance of ideas and of individuals, it does set their significance within the material environment that they find themselves in.

Most Marxists consider the welfare state as a form of capitalism and they would prefer the term 'welfare capitalism' to the 'welfare state' for it is a more accurate portrayal of its origins and functions. Indeed, the term 'welfare state' is seen as a form of mystification designed to portray the capitalist class in benevolent terms. The truth, according to Marxism, is quite different. Welfare reforms have been grafted on to capitalism by a class state either as a result of working-class pressure or as deliberate measures introduced by a capitalist state in order to improve the profitability and legitimation of the capitalist system. These reforms confer as many benefits on the upper class as on the working class, and only a service-by-service analysis will show the exact benefits accrued by each class. On the whole, however, social reforms reinforce rather than undermine capitalism. Strangely enough, Marxists are more in accord with writers from the middle way than with democratic socialists, who, as we saw, view reforms as undermining capitalism.

The notion of class which is so central to the Marxist analysis of the development and functions of the welfare state has recently come under severe criticism from various directions. There are many, including some Marxists, who find the classical Marxist typology of working class versus capitalist class too simplistic in advanced industrial societies. They prefer a more detailed typology that acknowledges the conflicts of interests between the various sections of both the working class and the capitalist class. Many feminists, too, take a dim view of the Marxist neglect of gender as a structural tool for analyzing both the development and the functions of the welfare state, as we shall see later. Classical Marxists will accept that there are such divisions, but they will insist that on the central issue of the transformation of capitalism to socialism the two main classes are in deadly opposition to each other. Their interests are diametrically opposed.

O'Connor's work was a major departure from this classical Marxist perspective on the welfare state. His contribution was to show that in advanced industrial societies high levels of public expenditure presented a catch-22 situation for the capitalist system. Such expenditure, although necessary to improve legitimation and accumulation for the capitalist class, also presented that class with the very real problem of how to raise enough funds to pay for it. The dilemma faced by that class is that it cannot win whether it chooses to reduce expenditure or whether it decides to levy the necessary heavy taxes. It is this which he called the 'fiscal crisis' of the state, discussed in detail by Gough in the following chapter. Offe took a similar line with his claim that while capitalism cannot do without the welfare state, neither can it live with it indefinitely. They are, indeed, unnatural bedfellows.

Despite these and other failings, Marxism provides a better explanation of the development and functions of the welfare state than most of the other ideologies discussed in this book. It certainly provided a much-needed corrective to the social conscience thesis, which attributed the development of the welfare state to altruistic and charitable individuals. Its major weaknesses have been: first, its support for the use of violence to achieve political ends; second, its promise of a utopia which is not only beyond the horizon of most people, but which is based on an ultra-altruistic human personality in consumerist societies; and third, its sometimes overdeterministic stance on political developments, which led to a neglect of the need to win public support for Marxist ideals. European communist parties have tried hard to divest themselves of these features, but it is difficult not to suspect that the current crisis of Marxism as a form of prescription may eventually prove fatal to the entire doctrine. Caution, however, is needed in such predictions, for, as adherents of the New Right will testify, ideologies have their ups and downs in history.

12 O'Connor

Ian Gough

Brief biography

James O'Connor was forty-three when *The Fiscal Crisis of the State* was published in 1973. He grew up and was educated on the East Coast of the USA, completing a doctorate in economics in 1964. In 1966 he moved to California, where he has lived and taught ever since, first at San Jose State and from 1976 onwards a little further south at the University of California, Santa Cruz. He is now Professor Emeritus of Sociology and Economics, as befits someone whose education and work straddles at least these two disciplines. He is the author of almost a hundred separate books and articles, very many of them translated and republished. He is especially well known and respected in Italy, Spain, Latin America and Japan.

However, Jim O'Connor is no closet academic. He has been politically active in a variety of causes throughout his life, including several with a direct relevance to welfare issues: work with the National Association for the Advancement of Colored People (NAACP); participation, arrest and acquittal in the second Freedom Ride in Florida; founding with others an alternative school in San Francisco; work with public sector unions. This is not to mention the organization of the Medical Aid for Cuba Committee; Professors Against the War and other anti-Vietnam War mobilizations; solidarity work with South Africa, Nicaragua and El Salvador; founding the Environmental Project on Central America; and more recently, anti-Gulf War struggles.

Frequently, the academic and the politically active side have come together, as in the San Francisco and San Jose State strikes in the late 1960s. O'Connor also helped found *Socialist Revolution*, was co-founder of *Kapitalistate* in 1973 and, in 1988, founded *Capitalism, Nature, Socialism: A journal of socialist ecology*, the major focus of his work in recent years. Jim O'Connor is the archetypical American, radical, Marxist academic and activist.

Main ideas

O'Connor's writings can be grouped under five main headings:

- *The Origins of Socialism in Cuba* (1970) and other work on imperialism and socialism in the Third World.
- Essays on the theory of capitalist development, some of which were brought together in *Corporations and the State* (1974).
- *The Fiscal Crisis of the State* (1973), other contributions to 'fiscal politics' (1969) and empirical updates of the book (e.g. 1981).
- Work on crisis theory in the 1980s, notably *Accumulation Crisis* (1984) and *The Meaning of Crisis: A theoretical introduction* (1987).
- More recent writings on Marxism and ecology in *Capitalism, Nature, Socialism* (e.g. 1988, 1991) and elsewhere.

All of these works are explicitly Marxist or neo-Marxist, terms which O'Connor has never disavowed. His most common self-description is 'neo-Marxist', which he defines as 'work within a deeply reformed Marxist paradigm ... containing revisions of orthodox or classical Marxism which "neo-orthodox Marxists" generally find unacceptable' (O'Connor, 1987: 2). Although sometimes using the term 'post-Marxist', O'Connor has more recently distanced himself from the pluralism and relativism which this entails (O'Connor, 1988: 34–8). The collapse of a socialist model in Eastern Europe and the triumph of capitalist individualism have led him to refashion but not reject the concepts and corpus of Marxism.

All five themes listed above clearly have some relevance to 'social policy' broadly defined, notably the last three. For example, O'Connor's analysis of social, political and personality crises has links with Habermas and Offe. In particular, his recent work on Marxism and ecology has implications for a green approach to social policy, considered in Part VI of this volume. He argues that ecology and socialism need each other, despite much present hostility between them. World capitalism and its recurrent crisis have pressured corporations to cut costs at the expense of the environment, and thus have accelerated the imbalances in nature. Socioeconomic justice and ecological responsibility go hand in hand, but this requires that both socialists and greens rethink some of their fundamental concepts.

However, in this chapter I shall concentrate almost exclusively on *The Fiscal Crisis of the State*, for several reasons. First, it has a *direct* relevance for understanding social policy today. By 1993 the British budget deficit had reached £50 billion, or about £1,000 of government borrowing for each person in the UK. Substantial tax increases and spending cuts were announced to help bridge this fiscal gap. Understanding the fiscal crisis of the state remains of first-rank importance to all students of social policy.

Second, the book has become a classic, translated into seven languages including Japanese and Korean. It was one of the earliest contributions to the development of a more open, sophisticated and empirically aware school of Marxist political economy. It had a special impact on the study of social policy.[1] Third, *Fiscal Crisis* was written in dialogue with orthodox economics, in a way that makes it readable and relevant today when neo-classical and neo-liberal analyses are so pervasive. It also brings together theory and empirical data (mainly about the United States) in a compelling and attractive way. Fourth, it is a readable and accessible book. Much of his more recent theoretical work (not his more popular pieces) is written in a closed, impenetrable style reminiscent of fundamentalist Marxism (e.g. 1984, 1988). *Fiscal Crisis* is more open perhaps because in it O'Connor is wrestling with other perspectives.

The Fiscal Crisis and its relevance to welfare

The Fiscal Crisis of the State contends that the modern capitalist state tries to fulfil two, often contradictory, functions: to aid capital *accumulation* and to buttress the *legitimation* of its social relations. Corresponding to these functions, state expenditures have a twofold character, labelled *social capital* and *social expenses*. Expenditures on social capital are required for profitable private accumulation. They in turn consist of two categories: *social investment* expenditures, which increase the productivity of a given amount of labour, and *social consumption* expenditures, which lower the reproduction costs of labour power. Either way these state activities are indirectly productive of surplus value and hence profits. On the other side are social and military expenses required to maintain social harmony, which are not even indirectly productive of surplus value and profits.

O'Connor points out that many expenditures will contain more than one of these three elements. For example, 'welfare' payments (in the American sense) are a social expense to control the 'surplus population' (O'Connor's early label for what some now term the underclass), whereas social insurance is an investment in the productive sector of the labour force. Education and training embrace elements of social investment, social consumption and social expenses. Nevertheless he considers that each domain of public expenditure has a major function.

Using this framework, O'Connor seeks in the book to answer two questions. What has determined the growth of the state, notably the US state, in the twentieth century? And what are the fiscal and political consequences of this growth? In a nutshell his respective answers are: the expansion of monopoly capital, and a 'fiscal crisis' – the tendency for government expenditures to outstrip revenues.

The growth of the welfare state

The answer to the first question depends on O'Connor's analysis of American capitalism, developed in chapter 1. Modern America consists of three sectors, each employing about one-third of the paid labour force: a monopoly sector, a competitive sector and the state sector. The first is distinguished from the second by such factors as a large scale of production, a faster rate of growth of productivity, higher and more regular wages, and greater density of unionization. The third, state sector, is rather oddly defined to include those industries from which the state procures goods and services, such as arms manufacturers and construction contractors, as well as government departments and public agencies. It combines features of the other two sectors, exhibiting a low rate of growth of productivity, but with security of employment and wage levels closer to the monopoly sector. This represents an early statement of the 'dual economy' thesis with the added merit that the state sector is recognized as distinctive in its own right.

How does the interrelation between these three sectors generate tendencies to rising state expenditures and fiscal crisis? Briefly the process is as follows. Due to the increasing social character of production in modern capitalism, state investment and consumption are more and more necessary to ensure profitability and hence private accumulation. Examples would include public investment in communications and transport, education and training, research and development. This public spending raises total demand and income, which benefits the monopoly sector. Yet despite this, O'Connor argues that demand for monopoly-sector products does not grow as fast as capacity, resulting in surplus capital and a surplus population. These in turn call forth higher state expenses: the surplus capital necessitates a growth in military spending to protect overseas markets, and the surplus population necessitates more programmes of welfare relief. The net result is that all three types of expenditure rise in parallel as the state tries to secure both accumulation and legitimation.

Yet this is too simplistic and 'functionalist' an account of O'Connor's book, suggesting as it does that the state necessarily undertakes various activities simply because the consequences of not doing so would be harmful to monopoly capitalism. Alongside these 'structural' explanations there is also a political dimension, developed in chapter 3, which considers the actual mechanisms that transform these 'needs' into state services. Here O'Connor develops a standard Marxist account of the state which combines its structural location within the capitalist relations of production alongside a recognition of the political means by which interests are represented within the political system. To represent the collective interests of capital as a whole, rather than the particular interests of industries or regions or whatever, a 'class-conscious political directorate' is needed. It is the executive branch of government which provides this directorate, and O'Connor analyzes its growth and development in the United States in an uncontroversial way. One feature of this which he highlights is the centralization of the budgetary process in an attempt to manage particularism and to strengthen class politics. This chapter offers a detailed account of aspects of the United States' political and budgetary process, with some recognition that other countries differ in certain respects.

In Chapters 4 to 6, O'Connor applies this framework to explain the expansion of state social investment, consumption and expenses in modern America. In each case, a variety of structural and political factors are deployed. Structural factors which necessitate state social investment include the growing interdependence of production, the riskiness of investment, and the 'free-rider' problem, that individual firms will always underinvest in training and skills in the context of a free labour market. State social consumption has to offset the decline of family, private aid and mutual benefit societies. Welfare programmes are required to modify and control the surplus population, which is growing due to the inequality and disequilibrium of capitalist growth. Other state expenses include the military costs of global policing and the need for public anti-pollution policies to clear up the mess occasioned by private capital accumulation. In places in *Fiscal Crisis*, these structural influences appear to be over-determining, as when O'Connor writes: 'The welfare-warfare state is one single phenomenon, and military and civilian expenditures cannot be reduced significantly at the expense of one another' (1973: 236).

However, alongside these structural factors which predispose the state to develop its role O'Connor also examines the political pressures for it to do so. These include special-interest industrial lobbies, such as highway contractors and the military–industrial complex, as well as benefits to keep the self-employed and small businesses sweet. Social insurance is mainly advocated by the organized working class, but it is actively supported by monopoly capital because it lowers the reproduction costs, and hence the relative money wages, of these workers. In the case of 'collective' social consumption (things like schools, urban renewal and housing subsidies), there is an interesting account of the political split between suburb and city, and its implications for the American welfare state. In the suburbs, social services are well developed and meet the preferences of local citizens; in the cities, they are of poor quality and are introduced to control the population. The drift of the more affluent to the suburbs accentuates these inequalities and results in what O'Connor calls 'the exploitation of the predominantly working-class city by monopoly sector workers and middle-class and capitalist-class suburbanites' (1973: 129).

The upshot is an analysis which combines class and sectoral aspects: alongside class exploitation there is also the exploitation of the competitive sector by the monopoly sector. In the United States, at least, political interests are fractured along both lines and this shapes the pattern of welfare services provided. So the expansion of the modern capitalist state, and *ipso facto* of the welfare state, is explained by a combination of structural predispositions and political pressures. With a well-functioning political directorate the two can be aligned. However, in American reality the demands of the executive are built on top of the host of special-interest demands on Congress, so that a further twist is given to the rising spiral of state expenditures.

The fiscal crisis

'The fiscal crisis of the capitalist state is the inevitable consequence of the structural gap between state expenditures and revenues' (1973: 221). Clearly before we can make sense of this we need to consider the revenue side of the public accounts. There are only three sources of finance for the public sector – taxes, borrowing, and the surpluses of state enterprises of various sorts – and chapters 7 and 8 of *Fiscal Crisis* are devoted to these. State enterprises and productive activities are weakly developed in the United States but much more extensive in Europe, as O'Connor recognizes. However, even in countries like Italy he claims that they contribute little to government revenues, since their prime purpose is to subsidize private capital through the provision of cheap inputs like electricity and transport. State borrowing is not a long-term alternative, since interest payments add to future expenditure. It is adopted only in 'abnormal' times as when the United States faced popular hostility to raising taxes to finance the Vietnam War.

This leaves taxation. The growth of the welfare/warfare state is also the growth of the modern tax state. Taxes can be levied on expenditure, income or capital, and on corporations or households. The conflict over the distribution of this burden is just as much a part of class struggle as the conflict over wages and profits – indeed, 'the oldest form of class struggle' according to Marx. The result, according to O'Connor, is that rising taxation cannot match rising spending. To simplify the argument in chapter 2, higher taxes mean, on the one hand, a lower growth of real incomes or higher unemployment, especially for competitive-sector workers, which engenders further calls for state welfare expenses. On the other hand, they generate a tax revolt and more industrial conflict with the organized, monopoly-sector workers, who have to be bought off with higher social consumption. So taxation is part of the problem and cannot be viewed simply as a solution.

One 'solution' to the fiscal crisis of the state would be the development of a 'social–industrial complex'. This is a shorthand for making state expenditure more *indirectly* productive by transforming unproductive state expenses into productive state capital. It entails developing more 'rational' social policies to train workers, develop a national health insurance scheme, invest in urban renewal and so on – the sort of policies advocated by successive Democrat challengers for the Presidency, but rarely implemented. The reason is that the social–industrial complex requires a new balance of forces between classes, sectors and the state, and this is unlikely to develop in the United States. Monopoly capital must develop a more cohesive, class-based outlook, competitive capitals who oppose it must be weakened, and the trade unions must be co-opted but prevented from appropriating all the gains from this strategy. It is an American version of corporatism.

In places in chapter 2, the 'social–industrial complex' also appears to refer to the *direct* improvement of productivity in state services, through such means as intensified management control of work patterns and what we would now call 'quasi-markets' to replicate market pressures within the state sector. However, this too is claimed to exacerbate class conflict in the public sector.

In the absence of this, another scenario is a tax revolt: resistance to 'tax exploitation', 'when those on whom the burden falls feel that the tax structure is inequitable and/or when the purposes of state expenditures are rejected' (1973: 228). But this too is counterproductive in the longer run, and is likely to divide the working class. O'Connor does not consider the possibility that this could set up a reinforcing cycle, whereby the state divests itself of social functions while the middle classes exit and go private.

The last alternative is that movements of state workers and state clients will grow to challenge the fiscal crisis and argue for more radical solutions. The book offers an early examination of the specific features of public-sector workers, especially in the social services. On the one hand, they are educated to value the needs of clients, and their work requires a degree of professional autonomy. On the other hand, they are the immediate victims of the fiscal crisis, whether social workers in New York or teachers in country school districts. Moreover, their work situation is increasingly rationalized as they are proletarianized: 'A contradiction arises between the formal and informal requirements of their employment' (1973: 241). The roots of public-sector radicalism lie here.

At the same time, clients of state services are also victims of the cuts and restructuring. Most are in a weak position to respond, but in so doing they are forced to raise qualitative issues and avoid crude economistic demands. In this way, their interests begin to ally with those of state-sector workers. This perspective is taken further in later writings on the democratization of the state, where O'Connor distinguishes between struggles to establish *de jure* democratic control over hitherto appointed state bodies, and *de facto* democratic control by the users over these elected representatives (O'Connor, 1978). The last chapter of *Fiscal Crisis* and these other writings reflect O'Connor's activist struggles alongside various public-sector and welfare client groups.

It will be apparent that there are several similarities between O'Connor's neo-Marxist theory of fiscal crisis and that of the New Right surveyed elsewhere in this volume (Pierson, 1991: 147–52). Yet they differ in at least three respects. First, the New Right explains the fiscal crisis in terms of rising expectations coupled with the pursuit of self-interest within the political arena. There is no recognition, as there is in O'Connor, that rising state expenditure is a response to systemic requirements flowing from modern developments in the economy, the family and civil society. Second, the welfare state for O'Connor is not necessarily unproductive, ineffective and despotic (Pierson, 1991: 48). Part of it is and part of it is not; his is a more nuanced approach. Third, the ultimate cause of the fiscal crisis for several neo-conservative and neo-liberal writers is modern democracy, whereas for O'Connor it is monopoly capitalism. The ultimate solution therefore is not a constitutionally bounded domain of popular choice, but socialism.

An assessment

Fiscal Crisis has contributed to our intellectual understanding of the welfare state and to our political understanding of social movements in and around the state. Against this, O'Connor's work has encountered a series of problems centred in particular around his concept of crisis. Let me consider its positive and negative impacts in turn.

Fiscal Crisis serves as a model of a mature *political economy* analysis of the welfare state. O'Connor moves beyond the divisions between economics, sociology and political science and makes a genuine attempt to synthesize their insights. The economist would stop at the prediction of a public-sector borrowing requirement, the political scientist at the analysis of government coalitions, and the sociologist at growing sectoral divisions in modern capitalism. But O'Connor relates each of these to the other. Attempts to cut public spending to balance the budget may stimulate social divisions and tensions which change the balance of political pressures on the state and call forth more welfare spending. This may not only interfere with the original economic policy goal, but also undermine economic performance by substituting unproductive for productive state programmes; and so on. The book forced, and still forces, students of social policy to locate their work in a broad perspective. It forestalls spurious claims that social policy can assert intellectual autonomy from other disciplines.

Second, *Fiscal Crisis* represents an early attempt to develop a Marxist theory of welfare state development which avoids the twin problems of functionalism and idealism. O'Connor's Marxism interprets the 'welfare' state as the product of emerging capitalist relationships and their constraints. There is little room here for an idealistic view of social policy as a collective response to human need, or for the role of pioneering social reformers. Yet, O'Connor skilfully avoids (much of the time – see below) the opposite danger of a functionalist account of welfare state development where the state responds – always and appropriately – to the 'requirements' of the capitalist system as a whole. Politics plays a role, and O'Connor is alive to the specific features of the American political system which influence its public policy responses. The *Fiscal Crisis* is a rather eclectic but invigorating mix of Marxist theory and North American radical social science, drawing *inter alia* on Galbraith, Piven and Cloward, and Baran and Sweezy. The analysis is both integrative and nuanced, wide ranging and detailed.

Third, and perhaps most important, the state is not interpreted simply as an unproductive incubus on the capitalist economy, a feature of much orthodox Marxism up to that time,[2] and of much neo-classical economics even today. The welfare state is not only a means for managing aggregate demand, redistributing income and promoting legitimation; it can and does make a productive contribution to the accumulation of capital and thus to overall economic performance. Here O'Connor goes beyond Keynesian theory to argue that the *form* of state intervention is important. It matters whether the state sets people to work digging holes and filling them up again (an example of Keynes), building missile systems, teaching skills or paying the dole. The productive contributions of these activities differ. Put another way, the modern state must pay attention to the supply-side as well as the demand-side aspects of its activities. It is interesting that the 'efficiency' aspect of the welfare state is increasingly appreciated now in orthodox economic theory (Barr, 1992). O'Connor made sure that Marxists could no longer overlook the productive contribution of social policies to modern capitalist development.

Fourth, this process, O'Connor contends, is not a smooth one. The state activities generate a fiscal crisis, which is at the same time a political and social crisis. All the available solutions to this crisis generate further problems. The welfare state is not a neutral, technical fix, but part of the problem itself. The 'crisis' in this second, broader sense is an ongoing historical phenomenon, the outcome of which cannot be foreseen because it depends on the struggle between classes. In this way, it helps us to understand the emergence of Thatcherism and Reaganism in the 1980s (although O'Connor does not explicitly argue this himself). The New Right in both countries can be interpreted as a successful counter-mobilization against the power of unions, 'social democracy' and the new social movements. But neither offered a solution to the problems of economic failure and lack of competitiveness because they were blind to the positive productive role of state action. The resulting policies were maladapted to the requirements of modern capitalism, and paradoxically they both worsened the original fiscal crisis (see Gough, 1991).

Nor should we ignore the practical impact of O'Connor's work. In 1981 he wrote:

> *The Fiscal Crisis of the State* was intended to be a practical and theoretical intervention into the debates and social struggles raging in the US in the late 1960s and early 1970s. Practically, *Fiscal Crisis* was meant to help shift the American left's focus from industrial workers to the radical possibilities of state worker and state client organizations and actions. (O'Connor, 1981: 43)

His predictions of a growing public-sector militancy and social movements in and around the welfare state were prescient. His analysis of the way that social service workers must perforce augment traditional trade union demands with more qualitative issues centred on their work relations was important in combating crude economistic views about class struggle in the public sector. His thinking on the 'democratization of the state' contributed to the theory and practice of participatory democracy and bottom-up struggles within the welfare field.

If I move on to some problems, these should not be divorced from the merits and positive impact of his work discussed above.

One problem arises because the *Fiscal Crisis* appears to take for granted the underconsumption model of the capitalist economy of the Monthly Review School, notably of Baran and Sweezy (1968). A central argument of O'Connor is that the demand for monopoly-sector products does not grow as fast as capacity, which results in surplus capital and surplus population (O'Connor, 1973: 24–5). This then calls forth, as we have seen, rising military and welfare spending; together the result is the Marcusian warfare/welfare state and further fiscal crisis. Quite apart from the functionalist overtones of arguments like this, why should monopoly-sector capacity expand faster than demand? O'Connor's answer is that its capacity is enhanced by state capital which socializes the cost of some investment, while its demand is hampered by the slow growth or stagnation of competitive-sector wages. No evidence is given for this last stage in the argument.[3] Later on he refers to 'the unfortunate "functionalist" formulations of the basic thesis of *Fiscal Crisis*' (O'Connor, 1981: 47) and stresses the historical and conjunctural role of class conflicts. Nevertheless, in his later work he adopts a more uncompromising, capital-centred approach without the tempering effect of detailed empirical analysis (O'Connor, 1984, 1988).

Second, an implication of the above argument is that the social expenses of legitimation increase faster than accumulation expenditures under advanced, monopoly capitalism. Now this is not borne out when the composition of postwar state spending in the USA and other capitalist nations is explored. In an early attempt to do this I concluded that 'an increasing proportion of ... [state expenditures] are *productive* expenditures' (Gough, 1975b: 80). Since then Miller (1986) has made a careful analysis of US public spending from 1952 to 1980. He plausibly allocates different items of state spending to O'Connor's categories: Medicare, Medicaid, public assistance, unemployment insurance and other social welfare are regarded (along with non-welfare items like military defence) as social expenses, while social security, education, labour training, housing and health expenditure are regarded as social capital. The share of unproductive social expenses for legitimation fell from 72 per cent of total public spending in 1952 to 56 per cent in 1960 and to 47 per cent from 1972 to 1980. He concludes: 'According to O'Connor's analysis, the ability of the state to support accumulation in the 1970s should never have been greater' (Miller, 1986: 246).

A third critical point concerns the origins of the fiscal crisis. Why, if borrowing is only a sporadic solution to funding state spending in modern capitalism, is there a chronic tendency to fiscal crisis? Why, in a context of economic growth, cannot rising spending be matched by rising taxation? His main answer is that a tax revolt develops, chiefly because of the conflicting interests of monopoly-sector and competitive-sector workers. This is an interesting insight with relevance to modern economies beset by a growing dualization in the labour market. Yet there is plenty of countervailing evidence that in many countries the tax levy on households has grown *pari passu* with state spending without engendering a tax revolt. In the USA, Miller argues, the 'tax exploitation of the working class' has risen since the early 1950s. Following O'Connor's comments on the incidence of various taxes between labour, or households, and capital, Miller shows that 'labor's share of the tax burden has *not* remained constant, but has, in fact, steadily increased over the post-war period' (Miller, 1986: 243). In other words, there appears to be no systemic barrier to financing the welfare state out of higher taxes, which moreover are levied on wages and consumption, not profits and capital.

Fourth, more general criticisms have been levied against the very concept of a fiscal crisis. Moran (1988) provides a lucid survey of crisis theories of the welfare state, including O'Connor's. He distinguishes three usages of the term 'crisis': catastrophe (a crisis caused by an external blow), turning point (crisis as a moment of resolution of difficulties), and contradiction (crisis as a situation of being trapped between conflicting imperatives). O'Connor's use of the term has varied, although his core idea is of fiscal crisis as an ongoing contradiction within capitalism. Moran concludes (1988: 412): 'There is no crisis of the welfare state ... Welfare states have proved resilient in the capacity to command popular support, to mobilise resources and to weather economic storms.' The genuine fiscal difficulties of 1975–81 were the result not of an underlying contradiction, but of external shifts in the global economic system. Capitalism has notably demonstrated that it can adapt and learn from past problems. According to Taylor-Gooby (1991: 1): 'In the event, the predicament of welfare capitalism was resolved and growth restored through a policy mix of welfare cuts, industrial protection and fiscal discipline varying from country to country.'

Once we move away from a reliance on crude expenditure figures, it is apparent that national responses in the 1980s diverged between retrenchment, restraint and maintenance. This is borne out in a study of welfare statism in five countries since the mid-1970s by Pfaller, Gough and Therborn (1991, ch. 8). This shows that in the USA and the UK there were both direct attacks on social programmes and a deterioration in welfare outcomes; in France and Germany there were few reductions in social programmes, but some worsening of welfare outcomes due mainly to rising unemployment; while in Sweden, neither programmes nor welfare outcomes deteriorated. Interestingly, these different responses correspond to the three 'welfare regimes' identified by Esping-Andersen (1990): English- speaking liberal, Continental corporatist, and Nordic social democratic. Since he explains the development of these regimes in terms of class coalitions, this offers some indirect support for O'Connor's view that the resolution of the fiscal crisis depends on the class balance of forces.

However, the main implication of this theoretical and empirical work for *Fiscal Crisis* is that it undermines its generality. Most of O'Connor's work is specific to the USA and cannot be directly applied to all advanced capitalist nations. Now, O'Connor is often clear about this, and sometimes signals that things may be different elsewhere. But he also writes that 'many of the ideas presented can be adapted to the experience' of other advanced capitalist countries' (O'Connor, 1973: 6). A comparative analysis of advanced capitalist economies qualifies and rejects some parts of his work. It forces us to reinterpret what is a rich and insightful treatment of state expenditure in the USA in the late 1960s into a more general, but necessarily comparative, theory (Gough, 1975a, 1975b).

Fifth, a still more general problem has been raised by some: it is that fiscal crisis tendencies are not specific to capitalist states, but apply equally well to communist or state socialist countries (Bell, 1976). Moreover, Campbell (1993) shows that they also exist in the post-communist states after 1989. This has been put most forcefully by Klein (1993) in 'O'Goffe's tale', a conflated caricature of the main ideas of O'Connor, Offe and myself. Klein writes:

> The same conflicts, contradictions or crises afflicted the Communist welfare states as the Keynesian welfare states. The real difference lay in the fact that while the capitalist societies of the West were able to cope with the supposedly irreconcilable contradictions, the communist regimes of the East collapsed under their weight. (Klein, 1993: 9)

He draws from this the lesson that a statement purporting to be about a class of societies must be tested against a counter-factual to avoid solipsism. This is especially the case since industrialization theories, such as Wilensky's (1975), provide alternative explanations which apply to all developed societies, capitalist and state socialist.

With Klein's accusation of an untheorized neglect of the non-capitalist world, I, speaking only for myself, could agree. But it is less plausible to argue that communist and capitalist welfare states faced the same contradictions and crises. Rather, the official economy in the Soviet bloc was so inefficient that there was much less surplus for the socialist state to appropriate, while the underground economy could not be legally recognized and therefore taxed (see Campbell, 1993). And, whatever the consensus which emerges as to why the state socialist systems collapsed so precipitately, I can think of nobody who would lay the whole burden of the explanation on the fiscal crisis of the state. Klein's attempt at a demolition job is in turn too determinist and all-embracing. There is still a need for a theory of the fiscal limits to social policy in *capitalist* societies, albeit one which pays attention to the great differences within this group of nations.

In conclusion, O'Connor is immune to several recent critiques levied against representatives of 'neo-Marxism', well summarized by Pierson (1991). Neo-Marxism is accused of overlooking the centrality of gender and race issues, and the green critique of social policy. O'Connor's work has always shown an awareness of gendered and racial oppression, and a concern to integrate accounts of such oppression into more traditional class-based Marxist categories.

Above all, in recent years O'Connor has pioneered a new journal of socialist ecology and made a major attempt to integrate analysis of labour and the family, the urban space, and nature and the environment. In an essay on socialism and ecology (1991), O'Connor argues that each needs the other, despite recent divisions between reds and greens. It is world capitalism which creates the basis for an effective linking of the two philosophies and social movements. Through economic pressures, it has forced corporations to externalize their social and environmental costs of production, which exacerbates the degradation of nature. And through its globalizing tendencies, it requires solutions to be addressed not only at the local level, as favoured by the 'deep greens', but at regional, national and international levels too. The solution is, however, both traditional and vague – a 'democratic state'. Much of this work is valid and some is inspiring, but unfortunately there is not the space here to debate it.[4] His recent and ongoing work reveals how O'Connor is continually open both to new theoretical challenges and to the potential of new social movements.[5] He has made *Capitalism, Nature, Socialism* into one of the foremost red-green-feminist journals in the world, with significant practical impacts on, for example, the policies of the PT in Brazil. It is a living exemplar of two of O'Connor's favourite precepts: 'criticise everything' (Marx) and 'commit yourself, then see'.

Key texts

The Fiscal Crisis of the State (1973) argues that the state must try to fulfil two basic and often contradictory functions: accumulation and legitimation. It must maintain or create the conditions in which profitable accumulation of capital can take place, and at the same time the conditions for social harmony. Corresponding to these two functions are two categories of state expenditure: social capital, which is indirectly productive for private capital; and state expenses, which are not. Welfare spending comprises both kinds, although the balance may change. Both sorts of state spending increase in the present age of monopoly capital, and this generates a fiscal crisis of the state: a tendency for government expenditures to outrace government revenues. Various solutions to this dilemma are considered, but they all face other problems. The modern state is thus saddled with a systemic tendency to fiscal crisis, and this has social and political aspects too – it is not simply an economic problem. The book contains many references and insights into modern American 'fiscal politics', but these are illustrative of more general tendencies in the advanced capitalist world at large.

Accumulation Crisis (1984) links the crisis of American capitalism since the late 1960s to its dominant ideology – individualism. Contemporary capitalism commodifies needs,[6] a feature of the domination and alienation of modern life common to much critical and neo-Marxist analysis. However, O'Connor goes on to claim that this generates, first, economic militancy among the working class and the salariat, as workers seek to extend their consumption levels, which in turn threatens profits and creates an 'under-production crisis of capitalism'. Second, new social movements appear to protest in various contexts against the narrow individualism and the commodification of life; they contribute to the social crisis of modern American life and pressure governments to buy them off with higher state spending, which again threatens accumulation. The book favours a future development which is local, populist and democratic, building on the new social movements. O'Connor essays a wide-ranging integration of material across disciplinary boundaries and a synthesis of cultural and economic analysis of a new kind. If the attempt does not come off, the book remains a rich source of ideas and material for others to mine. The book develops out of a quotation of Stokely Carmichael, cited at the end of *Fiscal Crisis*: 'individualism is a luxury we can no longer afford'.

The Meaning of Crisis (1987) delineates four approaches to crisis theory:

1. Bourgeois economic theory, which focuses on exchange or market relationships.
2. Neo-orthodox Marxist theory, which privileges the production and circulation of capital.
3. Neo-Marxist theory (among which O'Connor includes himself, Offe and Habermas), which broadens its scope to include capitalist social relations and their disintegration.
4. Social-psychological theory, concerned with personality disintegration in contemporary capitalism.

The third, neo-Marxist approach reflects the politicization of economic life analyzed in *Fiscal Crisis*, while the fourth theory relates to the crippling of inner life as a result of excessive commodification, analyzed in the previous book. None of these theories are more correct than the others, but moving from the first to the fourth, O'Connor contends, takes us to more concrete, less deterministic approaches.

These two later works contribute little to the understanding of social policy. Despite the focus on ideology, the framework of the former is orthodox, capital-centred Marxism. Moreover, as the themes become more grand, the empirical foundations on which they are built narrow. Above all, there is no clear definition of the explanandum – what is this 'crisis' which we need to explain? In *Fiscal Crisis* it referred to the 'tendency for government expenditures to outrace revenues'. In *Accumulation Crisis* it is the slowdown of economic growth in the US after the early 1970s. By 1987 it has become a term 'soaked with social, political and cultural meanings, and the connections between economic crisis, consciousness and social action are mediated by these social concepts at many different levels of human experience' (O'Connor, 1987: 126).

Capitalism, Nature and Socialism: A journal of socialist ecology was founded by O'Connor in 1988 and is now published four times a year. It is an international red/green journal of theory and politics which promotes the ideals of ecological socialism and feminism. O'Connor has contributed several key articles as well as shorter pieces. The 'second contradiction of capitalism' develops the argument that capitalism threatens itself by destroying its conditions of production (O'Connor, 1988). These include not only nature and the environment, but also human labour power and urban, collective conditions of production. The only hope lies in new social movements organized around all three conditions of production. *Capitalism, Nature and Socialism* is linked to the Center for Ecological Socialism (also founded by O'Connor), and the address for both is: CNS/CES, PO Box 8467, Santa Cruz, CA 95061, USA. Tel: 408-459-4541. Fax: 408-459-3518.

Acknowledgement

I am indebted to Jim O'Connor and Paul Wilding for helpful comments on an earlier draft of this chapter. Neither of them, least of all Jim, will agree with all of it or should be held responsible for any of it.

Notes

1. Perhaps this is the place to record the debt I owe to O'Connor's book and the influence it had on my own work (Gough, 1975a, 1975b, 1979). Now Klein (1993) has humorously yoked us together, along with Claus Offe, in 'O'Goffe's tale', discussed below.
2. I have discussed the Marxist concept of productive and unproductive labour and its relationship to state services elsewhere (Gough, 1972, 1975b and 1979: ch. 6 and appendices B and C). O'Connor's subsequent contribution to this topic (O'Connor, 1975) I do not find particularly clarifying – he redefines all labour as simultaneously productive and unproductive – and it reveals some inconsistencies which surface in *Fiscal Crisis*, notably where he conflates selling costs and taxation as equivalent unproductive claims on the surplus (e.g. O'Connor, 1973: 232).
3. It is true that in the USA the wage share has fallen and real wages have stagnated since the early 1970s, which would appear to be a vindication of O'Connor's argument. However, this stagnation did not occur in most other western countries. What was hypothesized as a general feature of advanced capitalism turns out to be a particular feature of US capitalism.
4. Again I would argue that, in his treatment of the economic crisis and its ecological impact, O'Connor generalizes from the highly specific productive forms in the USA. Lipietz (1992: 147–88) provides an alternative analysis of a similar range of issues and from a similar perspective. He recognizes, however, that the Rio summit exposed significant differences between the environmental interests of American capitalism on the one hand, and of European and Japanese capitalism on the other.
5. However, in my view, this open-mindedness exists despite, not because of, his reliance on a conceptual framework derived from Marxist value-theory and capital-centred analysis. It would take too long to summarize the debates over Marx's labour theory of value which took place in the 1960s and 1970s. The upshot, according to the majority of protagonists, was to undermine confidence in the value of value analysis and to destroy Marx's theory of a tendency for the rate of profit to fall. For a simple demonstration of these points, see Steedman (1975).
6. I would substitute 'wants' for 'needs' here, in order to retain the latter term for the universal, objective preconditions for successful human participation (Doyal and Gough, 1991: chs. 3–4).

References

Baran, P. and Sweezy, P. (1968) *Monopoly Capital*, Harmondsworth: Penguin.
Barr, N. (1992) 'Economic theory and the welfare state: a survey and interpretation', *Journal of Economic Literature*, **30**, 741–803.

Bell, D. (1976) *The Cultural Contradictions of Capitalism*, New York: Basic Books.

Campbell, J.L. (1993) 'The fiscal crisis of post-communist states' *Telos*, Fall, pp. 89–110.

Doyal, L. and Gough, I. (1991) *A Theory of Human Need*, London: Macmillan.

Esping-Andersen, G. (1990) *The Three Worlds of Welfare Capitalism*, Cambridge: Polity.

Gough, I. (1972) 'Marx's theory of productive and unproductive labour', *New Left Review*, **76**, 46–72.

Gough, I. (1975a) 'Review of *The Fiscal Crisis of the State*' *Bulletin of the Conference of Socialist Economics*, **11**, Summer, pp. 3–7.

Gough, I. (1975b) 'State expenditure in advanced capitalism', *New Left Review*, **92**, pp. 53–92.

Gough, I. (1979) *The Political Economy of the Welfare State*, London: Macmillan.

Gough, I. (1991) 'The United Kingdom', in Pfaller *et al.* (1991).

Klein, R. (1993) 'O'Goffe's tale', in Jones, C. (ed.), *New Perspectives on the Welfare State in Europe*, London: Routledge.

Lipietz, A. (1992) *Towards a New Economic Order: Postfordism, ecology and democracy*, Cambridge: Polity.

Miller, J.A. (1986) '*The Fiscal Crisis of the State* revisited', *Review of Radical Political Economy*, **18**, 1–2, 236–60.

Moran, M. (1988) 'Crises of the welfare state', *British Journal of Political Science*, **18**, pp. 397–414.

O'Connor, J. (1969) 'Scientific and ideological elements in the economic theory of government policy', *Science and Society*, **33**, 4, pp. 385–414.

O'Connor, J. (1970) *The Origins of Socialism in Cuba*, New York: Cornell University Press.

O'Connor, J. (1973) *The Fiscal Crisis of the State*, New York: St Martin's Press.

O'Connor, J. (1974) *Corporations and the State: Essays in the theory of capitalism and imperialism*, New York: Harper and Row.

O'Connor, J. (1975) 'Productive and unproductive labor', *Politics and Society*, **5**, 3, pp. 297–336.

O'Connor, J. (1978) 'The democratic movement in the United States' *Kapitalistate*, **7**, pp. 15–26.

O'Connor, J. (1981) '*The Fiscal Crisis of the State* revisited: economic crisis and Reagan's budget policy', *Kapitalistate*, **9**, 41–62.

O'Connor, J. (1984) *Accumulation Crisis*, New York: Blackwell.

O'Connor, J. (1987) *The Meaning of Crisis: A theoretical introduction*, New York: Blackwell.

O'Connor, J. (1988) 'Capitalism, nature, socialism: a theoretical introduction', *Capitalism, Nature, Socialism*, 1, pp. 11–38.

O'Connor, J. (1991) 'Socialism and ecology', *Capitalism, Nature, Socialism*, 8, pp. 1–12.

Pfaller, A., Gough, I. and Therborn, G. (eds) (1991) *Can the Welfare State Compete? A comparative study of five advanced capitalist countries*, London: Macmillan.

Pierson, C. (1991) *Beyond the Welfare State: The new political economy of the welfare state*, Cambridge: Polity.

Steedman, I. (1975) 'Value, price and profit', *New Left Review*, **90**, pp. 71–80.

Taylor-Gooby, P. (1991) *Social Change, Social Welfare and Social Science*, London: Harvester Wheatsheaf.

Wilensky, H. (1975) *The Welfare State and Equality*, Berkeley, Calif.: University of California Press.

13 Offe

Hartley Dean

> I would challenge anyone's right to monopolize definitions of
> Marxism and its limits.
>
> (Offe, 1984:254)

Brief biography

The intellectual climate in which Claus Offe's thinking first developed was that
of the Free University of Berlin in the early 1960s, followed by the University
of Frankfurt (as a contemporary of Jürgen Habermas) in the late 1960s. From
such foundations, Offe went on to the United States with a visiting fellowship
to Berkeley and Harvard between 1969 and 1971, returning to work (again with
Habermas) at the Max Plank Institute in Starnberg. He later became Professor
of Political Science and Sociology at the University of Bielefeld and, since the
late 1980s, at the University of Bremen. The range of Offe's writing has been
considerable, although it has only erratically and tardily been translated into
English. The main works of his to be published in English are *Industry and
Inequality* (1976), *Contradictions of the Welfare State* (1984) and *Disorganized
Capitalism* (1985a). At least one critic of Offe's work has pointed to the difficulty
in distinguishing 'what was original at the time it was written from the common
pool of ideas to which it has contributed and on which it draws' (Klein, 1984:
486). It is perhaps because of the way in which Offe's work has been presented
to English-speaking audiences that there is some truth to this observation. This
is unfortunate because it obscures the extent to which Claus Offe has been
responsible at different times for innovative syntheses between German Marxism
and American functionalism; between critical theory and systems theory; and
between competing strands of Marxian thought. Although broadly characterized
as a Marxist thinker, Claus Offe draws on several theoretical and methodological
perspectives and is first and foremost to be regarded as a sociologist.

Main ideas and themes

The diversity and complexity of Offe's ideas makes him an especially difficult thinker to write about. If one attempts to reduce his main ideas to a simple list of propositions, the outcome appears almost banal, even self-contradictory. Thus it may be said that, according to Offe:

1. Advanced capitalism as a *system* is sustained through a self-regulating complex of economic, administrative and normative sub-systems.
2. But this system is unstable and tends to *crisis*.
3. *Social policy* contrives to manage the system's crises through the regulation of wage labour and the promotion of commodity production.
4. But the welfare state also tends to *paralyze* capitalism.
5. Capitalism has lately become increasingly *disorganized*, in the process of which the role of social provision through the state has been brought into question.

Although we shall return to give greater depth and semblance of meaning to these propositions, it is important first to situate them within the broader scope of Offe's work, the central social scientific focus of which can best be described as the relationship between form and content. There is a sense in which, for Offe, the sociologist takes over where the philosopher leaves off:

> Two plus two *equals* four; person x and person y have *equal* access to higher education. It is not just playing with words if we start with the observation that the relationship of 'equality' is both a logical and a sociological one ... What matters is ... the conclusions we can draw ... regarding the degree of conformity between sociological and logical equality. In this sense it is its critical function that makes sociology interesting. (Offe, 1985a: 170)

According to Offe, sociology is only necessary or indeed possible under liberal-capitalist social formations, where form (the normative liberal equation, 'all people are equal') is *contradicted* by substance (the empirical facts regarding substantive inequality).

To this extent, Offe's notion of social scientific inquiry involves a questioning of the false 'common sense' by which capitalism is sustained (Keane, 1984: 12). The approach is unequivocally Marxian in its conception of the *contradiction*. 'Liberal' or bourgeois theorists may describe the structural problems and conflicting pressures which advanced capitalist societies exhibit and define them in terms of 'dichotomies' or as 'dilemmas'. Offe, however, regards such contradictions as destructive tendencies which undermine the preconditions upon which the very survival of capitalism depends (Offe, 1984: 130–2).

In the context of this general project, Offe has pursued three overarching themes relating to three dimensions of life under capitalism: work, welfare and politics.

Work

The necessity for all societies to enter into a 'metabolism with nature through labour' is arguably the fundamental assumption or 'social fact' within both bourgeois and Marxist sociology (Offe, 1985a: 129), and much of Offe's own empirical research throughout his career was focused on labour markets and associated employment and training policies. One of his earliest preoccupations was with the distribution of status and reward that is associated with the ways in which work is organized (Offe, 1976).

According to Offe, the so-called 'achievement principle' model of society, by which inequality may be justified with reference to differences in occupational work performance, is now discredited. First, he says, the actual distribution of life chances under advanced capitalism is demonstrably at variance with performance criteria. Second, an achievement-oriented pattern of distribution is in any event neither logically nor morally justifiable under a system which, to sustain itself, requires decreasing levels of labour input and increasing levels of social consumption. Third, the concept of performance is being progressively displaced by 'regulatory norms': the distribution of roles and status through work 'is turning into a disciplinary technique which rewards loyalty to the dominant interests and forms of life' (1976: 138).

In later writings, Offe goes further and questions the validity not only of the 'achievement principle', but of the labour market concept itself. Drawing particularly on the work of Karl Polanyi, Offe argues that the notion of labour as a commodity can be no more than a fiction (Offe, 1984: 263; 1985a: 53). Living labour does not – *without coercion* – behave as a genuine commodity. In any event, the strategies of actors in the labour market, through for example the formation of trade unions, can constrain its functioning as a 'market'. What is more, structural economic and technological change renders the labour market increasingly obsolete as a mechanism for distributing labour power on the one hand, or for satisfying the consumption needs of wage-earners and their households on the other.

Ultimately, therefore, Offe writes of the end of 'work society'. Acknowledging the ideas of both critical theorists like Habermas and post-structuralists like Foucault, he points to the 'implosion of work's power to determine social life' (1985a: 150). By accepting that in western societies it is 'increasingly misleading to equate the development of productive forces and human emancipation' (1985a: 149), Offe ostensibly abandons Marxist orthodoxy. None the less, in his writing on democratic socialist politics (see below), there is a strong sense in which he continues to adhere to an essentially Marxian enlightenment project and a vision of a 'welfare society'.

Welfare

Offe is undoubtedly best known to English-speaking audiences for his writing on the welfare state, and it is to this aspect of his work that we shall return at greater length. For the time being, however, it is important to note the sense in which the welfare state has been central or pivotal to his theoretical enterprise.

Probably the most frequently cited quotation from any of Offe's writings is his following statement: 'The contradiction is, that while capitalism cannot coexist *with*, neither can it exist *without* the welfare state' (Offe, 1982: 11). This formulation, repeated by Offe in other works (Offe, 1974: 54), indeed encapsulates his position. Out of context, however, it also oversimplifies that position, not least because it fails adequately to convey the particular significance and depth which Offe attributes to the term 'contradiction'.

For Offe, the welfare state is central because it both sustains and threatens the existence of capitalism. His concern therefore is with the *limits* of the welfare state (Keane, 1984: 12). He regards the welfare state neither as the ambiguous product of an unequal class struggle (cf. Miliband, 1969), nor as the unqualified achievement of fully developed social citizenship (cf. Marshall, 1963). His view is in part functionalist, resting heavily on a reinterpretation of non-Marxist systems theory, especially the work of Niklas Luhmann. This, however, is not a simple functionalism. It is informed by a Marxian dialectic which takes the welfare state as contradiction or, using Esping-Andersen's metaphor, as 'a Trojan horse that can penetrate the frontier between capitalism and socialism' (1990: 11). This, however, is a metaphor not for the kind of self-conscious strategy which Fabians or social democrats might adopt, but for the way in which the economic, political and cultural sub-systems of the welfare state contribute to rather than resolve capitalism's self-paralyzing tendencies.

It follows that the welfare state is not merely a technical institution, but a political phenomenon. Offe detects in the actions of the welfare state an 'unresolved tension between bureaucratic and system rationality' which calls into question the supposed disjuncture between policy and administration (Offe, 1985: 304). Most significantly, the welfare state politicizes the citizen. The ordering and intervention functions of the state demand the consensus or even the participation of the individual subject.

Politics

So it is that, in his later work, Offe is concerned less with systems theory and welfare policy, and more with a political sociology grounded in a social and political conflict perspective. None the less, work and welfare remain as central themes, and Offe himself dismisses the idea that there is some disjuncture within his work. He suggests that the conceptual tool of systems theory corresponds with the ways in which the managers of our political, economic and cultural sub-systems themselves see the world (Offe, 1984: 257).

Offe's concern is to analyze, first, the 'matrix of social power' which has superseded the class anatagonisms of classical Marxism, and second, the question of 'institutionalized political authority' as it has unfolded through the development of the modern (or post-modern?) capitalist state (Offe, 1985a: Introduction). His fundamental thesis is that the mediating links and channels of communication between social power and political authority are failing to *organize* the sociopolitical systems of welfare state capitalism. Borrowing a term coined by Scott Lash (see Lash and Urry, 1987), Offe describes an age of 'disorganized capitalism'. The precarious balance between the components of a market economy, political democracy and the welfare state has, he suggests, been destabilized.

The ascendancy since the 1970s of New Right or neo-conservative thinking has ironically given currency to certain of the very criticisms which Offe himself has made of welfare capitalism, specifically its tendency to government overload and fiscal crisis. What is more, the consequences of economic restructuring and social change have provided fertile ground for a popular anti-statist backlash. The formal mechanisms of dissent allowed to individuals by political democracy can demonstrate an inherent propensity, Offe argues, for undermining support for the substantive benefits of collective welfare provision (Offe, 1987; see also Offe, 1980). Rejecting the prescriptions of the New Right, Offe addresses the political alternatives. These he identifies as corporatism and democratic socialism.

Corporatism bypasses the mechanisms of parliamentary democracy by drawing élite representatives of capital and labour into state-supervised processes of negotiation and covert forms of policy making. Where it has occurred, the shift to corporatism has been calculated to revive the commodification process *in spite* of the welfare state. The consequences according to Offe are threefold. First, corporatism generates new patterns of conflict because of the inherent class bias which tilts tripartite arrangements in favour of capital. Second, corporatism blurs the boundary between civil society and the state, so further eroding the legitimacy of the liberal-democratic state, whose capacity to sustain capitalism rests upon its formal separation from the spheres of the market, the household and social relations of power. Third, corporatism creates a society which is dependent upon a degree of political repression on the one hand, and upon continuous economic growth on the other, since these become the preconditions of social and political equilibrium (Offe, 1982: 14; 1984: 291–2; see also Keane, 1984).

The democratic socialist alternative to welfare state capitalism – an egalitarian 'welfare society' – is achievable in Offe's view only through an alliance between trade unionists and the new middle class. In this respect, Offe identifies a pivotal role for the new social movements, such as feminism, environmentalism and pacifism; middle-class movements which are themselves a symptom of the erosion of mass loyalty to the capitalist welfare state, but which yet hold out the possibility of a new socially oriented politics (Offe, 1985a: ch. 9; 1985b). Offe himself was a founder member of the Green Party in former West Germany.

Relevance to welfare: critique of the capitalist welfare state

The starting point in Offe's analysis of the welfare state is distinctive: 'The conservatives ... are partly correct in their assessment of the welfare state as "creeping socialism", not because it is socialism but because it creeps' (Offe, 1972: 485). At a time when other commentators seemed preoccupied with the differences in the levels of welfare provision in different capitalist societies (and most notably between the residualist welfare regime of the USA and the more developed systems in Europe), Offe was at pains to point out that such differences were merely quantitative. Advanced and backward welfare states alike presided over greater or lesser extremes of affluence and poverty, reflecting 'the coexistence of the logic of industrial production for profit and the logic of human need' (1972: 480). What struck Offe was that the welfare state has emerged as a universal feature of capitalism; not, he believed, as the outcome of ideological struggle, but as a technocratic and potentially authoritarian attempt to compensate for new problems generated by the nature of advanced capitalism.

Offe drew attention to the extent to which state 'welfare' was often directed to the benefit, not of the poor, but of capital profitability through direct and indirect subsidies to industry. As he was often to do, he also endorsed right-wing assertions (such as those by Friedman: see Offe, 1972: 485) that state welfare bureaucracy could create more problems than it solved.

Here we return to the five propositions crudely outlined near the beginning of this chapter.

Capitalism as a self-regulating system

Having concluded that the capitalist welfare state does not promise equality and security for all, Offe moved on to consider the 'capitalist' nature of the welfare state, and how that nature is guaranteed (Offe, 1974; see also Mishra, 1981: 78–80). His object was to transcend the instrumentalist or 'influence' theories of Miliband and the structuralist or 'constraint' theories of Poulantzas, and to explain the 'systematic' basis on which the state can function as if indeed it were, in Marx and Engels' classic phrase, 'an executive committee of the bourgeoisie'. This is the point at which Offe begins to call upon systems theory. Class rule, he argues, does not result from the direct influence upon decision making by members of a ruling class, or from the structural constraints imposed by capitalist relations of production and exchange. The class nature of state institutions results from their systematic selectivity; from the way in which certain events are excluded, while others are permitted. This selectivity succeeds, on the one hand, in promoting the collective interests of capital (in ways of which short-sighted, self-seeking individual capitalists are incapable) and, on the other, in repressing anti-capitalist interests.

The class character of state governance results not from political domination, but from internal structures and filtering processes. Such processes function on at least four levels: at the level of *structure*, which determines the limits of state jurisdiction and the rights of the citizen; at the level of *ideology*, which determines what is culturally and intellectually possible within the orbit of state affairs; at the level of *process*, which determines bureaucratic rules and procedures; and at the level of *repression* and the ultimate sanction represented by the state's monopoly of force. Social order is therefore achieved neither through conspiracy nor by accident, but systematically. The problem, however, is that an abstractly drawn systems theory of this nature is, even in Offe's own estimation, difficult to verify, precisely because the selectivity of state institutions disguises the realities of class conflict. The essence of bourgeois democracy, as Offe puts it, is that 'sovereignty has been functionalized' (Offe, 1974: 46; see also Offe, 1975: 127): the political–administrative 'sub-system' denies the reality of class power.

The true nature of the welfare state, Offe surmises, is therefore to be revealed by demonstrating, first, the *concurrence* between policies which safeguard the interests of capital accumulation and the 'flanking strategies' which generate public consensus in support of such policies; second, the *incongruity* between the functions of state policy and the motives mobilized to engender such consensus; and third, the growing 'credibility gap' or 'legitimation deficit' which opens up as welfare states develop. For example, intervention by the state to remedy unemployment occasioned through a crisis of the market may in time generate public expectations of the state and a redefinition of unemployment as a political–administrative problem. The class conflict inherent in the original causes of unemployment is disguised, but when the capacity of state policy to contain unemployment is exhausted, the conflict appears in a new and politicized form. The state may respond by seeking to expand or contract the scope of its welfare functions, but ultimately the 'systemic interest' of capital must seek to bridge the contradiction between social production and private appropriation. The consequence of the selective mechanisms by which this is achieved is to give political form to the class content of that contradiction: capitalism needs the welfare state, but it also stands to be undermined by it.

The tendency to crisis

In developing his application of systems theory, Offe attempted what might properly be called a 'post-Marxist' theory of the contradictions of capitalism (see Pierson, 1991: 58). The fundamental contradiction identified by classical Marxism is that between the social organization of labour and the private accumulation of capital. The 'crises' predicted by such theories are economic in nature (resulting, for example, from the posited tendency for the rate of profit to fall). The fundamental contradiction identified by Offe is between three competing organizational 'sub-systems' of capitalism: the economic, the political–

administrative and the normative systems (Offe, 1984: ch. 1). The crises predicted by Offe are 'second order' crises (1984: 51): they arise 'Not [through] the self negation of the exchange principle but [through] its restriction and questioning by the other two organizational principles' (1984: 38).

At one level, Offe was no more than restating neo-Marxist orthodoxies about the 'relative autonomy' of the state and of normative institutions such as the family. At another level, however, he was going much further. His appropriation of systems theory meant that he looked upon the 'crises' of advanced capitalism not as foreseeable events determined (in the last instance) by economic contradictions, but rather as violations of the 'grammar' of social processes (1984: 37): violations, that is, of the selectivity which permits some events and prevents others (see above). The flanking sub-systems of the capitalist economy (i.e. the political–administrative and normative sub-systems), instead of remaining subordinate to the principles of capitalist exchange relations, and instead of managing the crises of such relations, have a tendency to undermine those principles and to redefine such crises. The phenomenon, therefore, is of a crisis of crisis management.

If this sounds perverse, it none the less draws attention to the phenomenon which Offe sought to explain: not the success of the welfare state in managing capitalism, but its failure. Over the longer term, the irreversible trend in advanced capitalism has been towards 'decommodification': that is, towards the provision of goods and services by the state, rather than through the market. The consequence, according to Offe, is a decline in the share of labour time available to the market sector and in the organization of civil society, and an associated rise in the functional relevance of the state sector and in the intensity of political conflict. To hold the line against such tendencies, the balance which must be struck 'depends on the organizational linking and mutual insulation of three "sub-systems"' (1984: 52). The *economic* system depends on the *political–administrative* system to regulate its malfunctioning, while at the same time providing the tax revenues upon which the political–administrative system depends. For its part, the *political–administrative* system supports the expectations, demands and claims of the *normative* system through the provision of welfare services and appropriate repressive functions, while at the same time depending on the normative system for 'mass loyalty'. The political–administrative system therefore insulates the economic and normative systems one from the other, so preventing economic malfunctions from becoming political conflicts. It is the failure of this mechanism which constitutes the so-called 'crisis of the welfare state'. According to Offe, it is a crisis at three levels.

First, it is a fiscal crisis (cf. O'Connor, 1973), in which the fiscal inputs which the system demands exceed the capacity of the economy to deliver. Second, it is an administrative crisis, in which the services provided by the welfare state fail to be effective in relation to normative expectations and requirements (cf. Hadley and Hatch, 1981). Third, it is a legitimation crisis, in which the mass loyalty upon which the system depends is eroded through the effects of the fiscal and administrative crises (cf. Habermas, 1975). From this abstract formulation, a number of related strands of thought may be seen to emerge.

Social policy's regulating functions

Offe's critique of social policy intervention is founded in his view that its *content* or external function is contradicted by its *form* or internal structure. The emergence of the interventionist state and, in particular, of productive rather than merely allocative forms of state activity, occurs because 'the process of competitive accumulation becomes too fragile to regenerate itself' (Offe, 1975: 134). State production (of education, health care or housing, for example, or environmental, transport and communications infrastructure) is promoted to remedy the weaknesses of capital. It is provided, however, in the form of 'policy', subject not to the rules of market exchange, but to the rules of the political–administrative sub-system. The 'problems' which social policy purports to address therefore appear as substantive political–administrative issues, rather than as formal strategies of capital accumulation.

'Liberal' policy theorists, Offe suggests, are blind to the discrepancy between state functions and state structures. They criticize the unregulated market for its failure to compensate for external effects and social costs, for its inability to ensure stability of income and employment, and for its lack of social justice. However, the remedies they propose assume the state to be 'neutral'. Such theorists (and the charge would seem to be directed not only at figures such as Keynes and Beveridge, but also at Fabian socialist reformers) ignore the capitalist nature of the state and regard the problems that the state must solve as problems in its environment, rather than problems of the state itself: 'that is, its internal mode of operation' (1975: 135). This point Offe expresses in a number of ways. He argues, for example, that regardless of whether the state adopts bureaucratic, technocratic or consensual procedures, it cannot transcend its 'structure/function problem' (1975: 142). Regardless of whether social policy aims to prevent or relieve hardship, to institutionalize or enable the needy, to furnish expertly prescribed or democratically brokered solutions, it confronts a 'compatibility problem' (Offe, 1984: 104). 'Liberal' social scientists correspondingly face a 'twofold – methodological and political – dilemma' (1984: 91): their research into social policy fails, first, because it is governed by the normative presumptions of those who conduct it, and second, because its revelations that policies do not achieve what they 'ought' cannot (and do not) of themselves influence the outcomes of the political–administrative process.

The common theme here is the disjuncture between the *structural* level of the political–administrative system (the rules of which differentiate it from the economic and normative systems whose demands it must mediate) and the *functional* level of 'policy' (which must balance the substantive requirements of the capital accumulation process with those of labour). The point for Offe is that neither level on its own can provide a satisfactory explanation. The development of social policy can be solely explained neither in terms of the systemic and objective imperatives of capitalism, nor in terms of the contingent needs and interests of particular classes or social groups. *Both* have to be taken into account, although *each* may contradict the other (1984: 100–4). In Offe's conundrum, the welfare state represents the ambiguous fulcrum between his other theoretical interests: structural and political processes on the one hand; and work and the labour market on the other. His view of the *structural* contradictions of the welfare state will be considered in relation to his thesis concerning the paralysis of the commodity form, but for now we shall consider Offe's treatment of the *functional* significance of the welfare state.

Offe's central contention is that 'social policy is the state's manner of effecting the lasting transformation of non–wage labourers into wage labourers' (1984: 92). The historical emergence of wage labour did not result automatically from the dismantling of feudal social relations and the dull compulsion of economic necessity: 'The transformation of dispossessed labour power into wage-labour is itself a constitutive socio-*political* process' (1984: 96). To this extent, the success of social policy during capitalism's formative stages has been threefold. First, it has suppressed alternative modes of subsistence, such as begging, and promoted the norms of a wage-labour culture through the medium of education and training. Second, it has introduced qualitative controls which have sustained the organizational form of wage labour by way of health and safety protection, the provision of education, health care and housing, and the creation of administratively controlled 'catchment areas' outside the labour force, in which to maintain, not only a 'reserve army' of unemployed workers, but also students, disabled people and retired workers. Third, it has exercised quantitative controls to regulate the supply of labour from the above-mentioned 'catchment areas'. What distinguishes Offe's account of these processes is his assertion that 'The owner of labour power first becomes a wage-labourer as a citizen of a state' (1984: 99).

The paralysis of capitalism's commodity form

Capitalism is constituted through the production, distribution and exchange of commodities. Drawing upon Marx's classic account of the commodity form, Offe observed that 'the dynamics of capitalist development seem to exhibit a constant tendency to *paralyse* the commodity form of value' (1984: 22). It has been remarked (Keane, 1984) that Offe does not analyze this self-paralysis in any great detail, but I would suggest that, while the terms in which he does so do not always remain the same, it is in fact a central theme to his treatment of the welfare state. Offe's analysis of decommodification (the tendency for the state to take over the production of essential goods and services) needs to be understood in parallel with his analysis of the internal structure of the state (which is governed by political–administrative rules rather than the principles of market exchange):

'the state's attempts to *universalize* the commodity form require organizations whose mode of operation is no longer subject to the commodity form' (Offe, 1984: 127).

This paradox, however, is a reflection of that deeper contradiction, between 'differentiation or privatization of production *and* its politicization or "socialization" (in the Marxian sense). These two strategies thwart and paralyse each other' (1984: 83). From such theoretical premises, Offe is able with self-conscious irony to share ground with public choice theorists and certain neo-conservative critics of the welfare state.

Offe acknowledges that the commodity form as the essence of capitalism is compromised by the welfare state in at least three ways: first, because the provision of welfare services absorbs taxes and labour power at the expense of the market economy; second, because the development of welfare services involves ever-expanding forms of production not governed by the rules and disciplines of market exchange; and third, because the availability of welfare services threatens to erode the culture of 'possessive individualism' which drives the market (1984: 126–8). What is more, Offe's conception of the structural contradictions of the capitalist state is such as to allow him to endorse the 'ungovernability thesis' of the New Right: that is to say, the view that political democracy has allowed parties and interest groups to 'bid up' the size of the welfare state, and to generate claims and expectations which it is beyond the power of the state to meet. In Offe's terms, the 'steering capacity' of the political–administrative sub-system is limited, and is increasingly overburdened by the demands of the normative sub-system (1984: 67–73).

The crisis of the welfare state descried in the 1970s by left and right alike was attributable in Offe's view to the state's growing incapacity to mediate the conflict 'between the political reproduction demands of labour power and the private reproduction strategies of capital' (1984: 77).

Disorganized capitalism and the future of welfare

In his more recent writings, Offe's view of the welfare state appears to have undergone a change. On closer examination, however, this would seem to be a change of emphasis rather than substance. In the elaborate theories outlined thus far, Offe portrays the welfare state as a dynamic and contradictory phenomenon, but it is made none the less explicit that the welfare state has 'in a certain sense, become an irreversible structure' (Offe, 1982: 11). Yet Offe was soon to observe 'that the welfare state as we know it as a major achievement of post-war Western European societies is rapidly losing its political support' (Offe, 1987: 528). What he detected was not so much the final realization of the crisis of crisis management as an unravelling of the systems through which capitalism is organized. Pierson (1991) has equated Offe's notion of *dis*organized capitalism with the more widely discussed idea of 'post-Fordism'. Certainly, the concepts are similar, each being cognizant that the global economic restructuring of capitalism in the late twentieth century has been accompanied by trends away from mass production and centralized administration, and towards dual labour markets and new 'matrices' of social power.

In his earlier formulations, Offe had foreseen that attempts to remedy the paralysis of the commodity form might be pursued through a variety of strategies: by inaction (a *laissez-faire* approach calculated to restore the principles of market exchange); by extending the welfare state even further (a social democratic approach calculated to achieve a new balance between the market and the state); or by a process of 'administrative recommodification' (an approach which he appeared to identify with neo-corporatism) (Offe, 1985a: 123–5; see also Offe, 1982). In the event, under disorganized capitalism Offe perceived in several western European countries a tendency to authoritarian anti-welfare state populism fuelled in part at least by *laissez-faire* ideology; the disappearance of the structural basis for labour-centred collectivist statism in the social democratic tradition; and a tendency to corporatism and/or to processes and alliances which deform political democracy by privileging certain social groups and marginalizing others (Offe, 1987: 508–14).

Underpinning this normative erosion of the welfare state have been funda-mental economic changes associated with new technology and new global patterns of capital investment. The effect has been to undermine the prospects for long-term full-time employment on which the Keynesian welfare state was built, and to divide the labour force into a secure 'core' and a vulnerable 'periphery' with different welfare interests. In this context, neo-conservative diagnoses – regarding the excessive cost of the welfare state, its tendency to 'crowd out' productive economic activity and its 'demoralizing' consequences for investment and employment incentives – are reflected in 'self-confirming' policy prescriptions which favour, not necessarily inaction and an end to state intervention in the organization and reproduction of labour power, but certainly a more minimalist, conditional and 'remoralizing' approach (1987: 503–8).

Offe therefore claims that there is a need to rethink the macrosociology of the welfare state using a synthesis of 'structural, phenomenological and rational choice approaches' (1987: 515). The sociological question to which he aims to return has to do with the very basis of citizenship.

The thrust of Offe's earlier argument had been that 'a supportive framework of non-commodified institutions is necessary for an economic system that utilizes labour power as if it were a commodity' (Offe, 1984: 263). This was the sense in which the wage labourer is first a citizen of a state, and this was the reason Offe had at one time rejected the theoretical schema of T.H. Marshall (1963). The latter had supposed that 'welfare' was a relatively late development within capitalist societies, whereas Offe argued that it had been a condition precedent for the transformation of dispossessed labour power into wage labour. None the less, Offe's rethink leads him to consider the ideological roots of citizenship and its origins in the political theories of liberalism, democracy and the welfare state;

theories respectively corresponding to the key 'civil', 'political' and 'social' dimensions of citizenship identified in Marshall's schema (see Chapter 6).

The essence of Offe's argument is that disorganized capitalism calls into question our understanding of the interrelationship between the civil, political and social dimensions of citizenship. The issue is whether that interrelationship is based on 'harmony, compatibility, even evolutionary mutual reinforcement', or 'strains, stresses, contradictions' (Offe, 1987: 503). Having reformulated the question in these sociological terms, he does not seem explicitly to resolve it. In his most recent writings, however, which have focused on issues as diverse as basic income proposals on the one hand and developments in eastern Europe on the other, Offe suggests that the future of citizenship's social dimension lies in 'non-productivist' policy designs (Offe, 1992) and in spheres of civil self-regulation which lie beyond either the market or the state (Offe, 1991).

Offe's influence

Offe's work has made a directly or indirectly formative contribution to the development of at least four theoretical approaches bearing upon the welfare state: the 'political economy', the 'legitimation crisis', the 'social corporatist' and the 'civil society socialist' approaches.

Prior to the 1970s, there had been little in the way of Marxist analyses of the postwar welfare state, Saville (1957/8) being probably the principal exception. The renaissance of Marxian and neo-Marxist thought in the late 1960s fuelled vigorous debates on the academic left as to the nature of the modern capitalist state, especially the much-scrutinized Miliband/Poulantzas debate. Offe's contribution, as outlined above, not only focused specifically upon the *welfare* functions of the capitalist state, but sought to transcend the instrumentalist/structuralist dichotomy. Additionally, Offe's writing captured the ambiguity of the welfare state: its capacity to serve the exploitative interests of capital, but also to bring real and lasting benefits to wage labour. Offe and O'Connor together furnished much of the basis for the political economy of welfare theoretical tradition exemplified in the seminal work of Gough (1979). This has been a sophisticated analytical approach which traces the flows and counterflows of resources and benefits supervised by the welfare state, and the substantive functioning of welfare services in the reproduction of the social relations of production, at both a quantitative and a qualitative level.

At more or less the same time, Offe's erstwhile colleague Jürgen Habermas sought to incorporate into the critical theory tradition ideas which it seems he and Offe had developed together at the Max Plank Institute. Habermas (1985), like Offe, posited the existence under advanced capitalism of three interacting systems: he called them the economic, the political and the sociocultural systems. He further suggested that interrelationships between these systems tended towards crisis and, in particular, a legitimation crisis, when the changing relationship between the political and the economic systems called for cultural legitimation of a kind which the sociocultural system could not produce. Habermas, however, was to take this analysis in a quite different direction, concentrating on the ways in which meanings are generated at the cultural level and, in later work, producing new insights into the impact of administrative surveillance upon the individual 'life world' of welfare citizens: insights later acknowledged and appropriated by Offe (see, for example, Offe, 1987: 506).

In a tangential or even negative way, Offe has also contributed to the debate about corporatism. During the 1970s, theorists of various persuasions paid renewed attention to the role played by interest groups and, most especially, the phenomenon in western industrialized polities of more or less formal tripartite negotiating forums created outside the democratic process between leading representatives of the interests of capital, labour and government. Offe argued that corporatism offered a rather less than desirable way to ameliorate the structural contradictions of the welfare state by short-circuiting democratic processes and safeguards. In the event, under the 'disorganized capitalism' of the 1980s, the representative organizations of both capital and more particularly labour fell into decline, and the concept of corporatism in some countries (especially the UK) began to seem anachronistic. In spite of this, there remains an older and richer corporatist tradition in other western European countries (Esping-Andersen, 1990) and, in *opposition* to Offe's perception of corporatism, writers like Esping-Andersen, Korpi and others (see, for example, Mishra, 1990) have envisaged a form of *social* corporatism which combines, as it were, the best features of highly corporatist welfare regimes (e.g. Austria) with those of highly developed social democratic welfare states (e.g. Sweden). They reject Offe's implication that corporatism necessarily co-opts and compromises trade union power, and suggest that tripartism can become 'a form of – and a moment in – the ongoing struggle between owners of capital and the working classes' (Mishra, 1990: 114).

In a more direct way, Offe has influenced the emergence of new forms of political thought best described as civil society socialism (though elements of this approach may also be described as 'eco-socialism'). Probably the best-known proponent to English-speaking audiences is Keane (1988). The project emerges, at one level, from Offe's insights into the interpenetration of state and civil society under welfare capitalism and, at another, from his speculations about the prospects for new alliances between new social movements and the 'traditional' left. Civil society socialism seeks to explore the possibilities of a democratized civil society in which modes of human co-operation would be neither dictated by the logic of capital accumulation, nor governed by administrative surveillance and control. Under such a social formation, the power of private capital, the state and white, male, heterosexual citizens would be curtailed. The state would be 'recast', becoming accountable to civil society as the mediator and guarantor of social needs identified or generated in the course of ecologically sustainable production and consumption.

Key texts

Most of Offe's writing has been in the form of essays and articles. Although this chapter has ranged across a variety of such materials, as already indicated, only three complete books by Offe have appeared in the English language.[1]

Industry and Inequality (1976) is the English translation of Offe's doctoral thesis (originally submitted in 1967). Based upon a study of occupational recruitment, mobility and income, the thesis represents a critique of explanations of social stratification based on the 'achievement principle'. However, the analysis clearly prefigures his later critiques of the welfare state by identifying the development of administrative state power as central to any understanding of the distribution of life chances under advanced capitalism.

Contradictions of the Welfare State (1984) is a diverse collection of essays and articles written over an eleven-year period. They are presented with an introduction by John Keane, the editor of the collection, and with the text of an interview with Claus Offe conducted in 1982 by John Keane and David Held. This is in my view the most significant single volume of Offe's writings, since it encompasses aspects of both his early systems theory and his later social power-based writings. The interview, entitled 'Reflections on the welfare state', is especially illuminating.

Finally, *Disorganized Capitalism* (1985) is similarly an edited collection of essays and articles from a period which overlaps with those in *Contradictions of the Welfare State*. However, the focus, as the title implies, is less upon the welfare state and more upon the development of labour markets and politics in the emerging era of 'disorganized capitalism'.

Klein has suggested that the theoretical schema advanced in such texts is 'too grand, too vague and too general' (Klein, 1984: 487). Certainly, Offe is often guilty of overgeneralization and of an approach which cannot easily take account of different experiences in different countries. Keane (1984) points out that Offe's analysis suffers from being very much restricted to the dimension of the *nation*-state, and fails therefore fully to account for international economic and political dimensions. Recent developments, moreover, such as the creation in the UK of 'quasi-markets' in state-financed health care, education and social services, would clearly demand a significant recasting or refinement of Offe's explanatory framework.

None the less, Offe's was a bold project. He aimed to set aside the 'false image' which the welfare state creates – that is to say, the artificial separation between work and politics – and he sought thereby to understand society 'as a coherent totality to be changed' (Offe, 1982: 13). To this extent, Offe's writings reflect a democratic socialist ideal, the achievement of which he frustratingly but characteristically admits will require 'new concepts, goals and strategies whose outlines today remain largely uncertain' (Offe, 1987: 535).

Acknowledgement

The author wishes to thank Ian Gough, Rob Page, Vic George and Marc-Phillipe Cooper for helpful comments upon an earlier draft of this chapter, but none the less accepts sole responsibility for any errors of fact, omission or interpretation.

Note

1. A fourth text, written by Claus Offe and Rolf G. Heinze, *Beyond Employment: Time, work and the informal economy* (Cambridge: Polity), was published in 1992. This has not been discussed above because joint authorship makes Offe's specific contribution impossible to distinguish. The work is in any event especially remote from the neo-Marxist theoretical tradition with which Offe has until more recently been associated. Discussion in the book focuses upon past experiments with non-monetary systems of exchange, and upon provocative new ideas for 'co-operation circles' functioning beyond the formal labour market. These ideas are presented as a 'supplementary microstrategy' rather than a thoroughgoing social reform, and they are linked to other eco-socialist/'green' demands for a shortening of working hours and the introduction of basic income.

References

Esping-Andersen, G. (1990) *The Three Worlds of Welfare Capitalism*, Cambridge: Polity.

Gough, I. (1979) *The Political Economy of the Welfare State*, London: Macmillan.

Habermas, J. (1985) *Legitimation Crisis*, Boston, Mass.: Beacon Press.

Hadley, R. and Hatch, S. (1981) *Social Welfare and the Failure of the State*, London: Allen and Unwin.

Keane, J. (1984) 'Introduction', in Offe (1984).

Keane, J. (1988) *Democracy and Civil Society*, London: Verso.

Klein, R. (1984) 'Review of Claus Offe, *Contradictions of the Welfare State*', *Journal of Social Policy*, **13**, 4, pp. 485–7.

Lash, S. and Urry, J. (1987) *The End of Organised Capitalism*, London: Verso.

Marshall, T.H. (1963) 'Citizenship and social class', in Marshall, T.H., *Sociology at the Crossroads*, London: Heinemann.

Miliband, R. (1969) *The State in Capitalist Society*, London: Weidenfeld and Nicolson.

Mishra, R. (1981) *Society and Social Policy*, London: Macmillan.

Mishra, R. (1990) *The Welfare State in Capitalist Society*, Hemel Hempstead: Harvester Wheatsheaf.

O'Connor, J. (1973) *Fiscal Crisis of the State*, New York: St Martin's Press.

Offe, C. (1972) 'Advanced capitalism and the welfare state', *Politics and Society*, **2**, 4, 479–88.

Offe, C. (1974) 'Structural problems of the capitalist state', in von Beyme, K. (ed.), *German Political Studies*, **1**, London: Sage.

Offe, C. (1975) 'The theory of the capitalist state and the problem of policy formation', in Lindberg, L., Alford, R., Crouch, C. and Offe, C. (eds), *Stress and Contradiction in Modern Capitalism: Public policy and the theory of the state*, Lexington, Mass.: Lexington Books, D.C. Heath and Co.

Offe, C. (1976) *Industry and Inequality*, London: Edward Arnold.

Offe, C. (1980) 'The separation of form and content in liberal democratic politics', *Studies in Political Economy*, **3**, pp. 5–16.

Offe, C. (1982) 'Some contradictions of the modern welfare state', *Critical Social Policy*, **2**, 2, pp. 7–16; reprinted in Offe (1984).

Offe, C. (1984) *Contradictions of the Welfare State* (ed. J. Keane), Cambridge, Mass.: MIT Press.

Offe, C. (1985a) *Disorganized Capitalism* (ed. J. Keane), Cambridge: Polity.

Offe, C. (1985b) 'New social movements: challenging the boundaries of institutional politics', *Social Research*, **52**, 4, pp. 816–68.

Offe, C. (1987) 'Democracy against the welfare state', *Political Theory*, **15**, 4, pp. 501–37.

Offe, C. (1991) 'Capitalism by democratic design? Democratic theory facing the triple transition in East Central Europe', *Social Research*, **58**, 4, pp. 865–92.

Offe, C. (1992) 'A non-productivist design for social policies', in Parijs, P.V. (ed.), *Arguing for Basic Income*, London: Verso.

Pierson, C. (1991) *Beyond the Welfare State*, Cambridge: Polity.

Saville, J. (1957/8) 'The Welfare State: an historical approach', *New Reasoner*, **3**, winter, 5, 6, 11, 12–17, 20–4.

Part V

Feminists

Introduction

Feminist ideas have been around for centuries, but feminism as a social movement and as an explicit ideology is fairly new. It dates back to the 1960s, that fertile short period which saw the rise of several social movements across the industrialized world.

All the ideologies discussed in this book contain several related strands of thought, and our choice of authors is intended to bring out these divisions. Feminism is no exception. Different authors have different lists of these strands but the three most important are the liberal, the socialist and the radical. What unites the various strands of feminism is the belief that women are exploited by men, and that the welfare state was devised by men for the benefit of men. What divides them is, first, the explanation given for this state of affairs and second, what the possible solutions to this problem are. The main division lies between radical feminism and other strands. The first attributes the inferior position of women in society to male dominance, and sees their emancipation in the creation of separate social structures. The other strands hold social factors responsible, either in whole or in part, and they believe that social changes can change the situation. To illustrate: women's low wages in relation to men's are seen by radical feminists as the result of exploitation of women by men; by socialist feminists as the result of the capitalist system that exploits weak groups in society, of which women are a major one, because of its patriarchal as well as its capitalist nature; and by liberals as the result of industrialization in a patriarchal world.

The claim that the welfare state developed along sexist lines is almost self-evident. In patriarchal societies where men held most of the positions of authority in society, it was inevitable that decisions about the nature of the social services would have been taken by men and would have been based on assumptions that were gender biased. This holds true irrespective of whether one adopts a class conflict, a pluralist, a functionalist or any other theoretical explanation of the development of the welfare state. In male-dominated societies, the development of the welfare state would have discriminated against women irrespective of whether this was by default or by design. Until very recently, women's role was seen as primarily that of mothers and wives, serving their children and husbands. Social services were developed with these two assumptions in mind, with the result that education was not considered as important for girls as for boys, entitlement to social security benefits for women in their own right was not considered necessary, home ownership was invariably registered in the husband's name and so on.

Over the years, the distributional effects of social policies were analyzed in terms of class, region, age and other such dimensions. The arrival of feminism forced a reconsideration of this, with the result that today gender has become one of the established dimensions that social scientists use to look at the effects of economic and social policy. Feminism has thus enriched our understanding of social policy, although in the absence of adequate data it is not always possible to disentangle the relative significance of class, gender and ethnicity. As societies become less sexist and racist, one would logically expect to see the declining significance of both gender and ethnicity in the distributional effects of the welfare state. This happy state of affairs, however, is a long way off.

Despite their critical stance towards the welfare state, most feminists feel that the welfare state would have the potential of promoting women's emancipation if it pursued a different set of policies. The provision of good-quality and affordable child-care facilities, the payment of benefits that took fully into account women's work at home, the enforcement of anti-discrimination legislation in the labour market, and the provision of home care leave for both fathers and mothers are just a few examples of the kind of welfare provision that would improve the position of women in society. For social policies to be feminist, they need to be based on the twin recognition that there are numerous socially constructed obstacles impeding women's equality with men, and that men should be encouraged to undertake activities which are traditionally considered as female. Such feminist social policies have the potential of changing sex roles not only in the public but in the private sphere too, for these two spheres are related and they are both, in essence, political. It is a moot point whether all these changes are achievable within a capitalist system, and a point on which the various strands of feminism strongly disagree. Liberals will answer in the affirmative, socialists will consider it impossible and will look towards socialism, while radicals will insist that only separate gender services and structures will achieve this, irrespective of whether the political system is capitalist or socialist.

Comparative and historical evidence suggests that a good deal can be achieved through welfare reforms, although not as much as the protagonists of the reforms envisaged. The proportion of women reaching higher education in all advanced industrial societies has increased, and in many countries it has reached parity with that of men. The gap between men's and women's earnings, however, has not narrowed all that much, if at all. These two examples show that progress is easier in some areas than in others, and how much more needs to be done before true equality of the sexes can be reached. Whether this provides grounds for optimism or pessimism is very much a matter of personal interpretation based on one's brand of feminism.

14 De Beauvoir

Mary Evans

Brief biography

Simone de Beauvoir was born in Paris in 1908, and spent the greater part of her adult life in that city. She died there in 1986, universally hailed as 'the mother' of twentieth-century feminism.[1] Her book on women, *The Second Sex* (1964b), had bought her global fame and, although de Beauvoir wrote widely on other subjects (including old age) and published numerous novels and essays, she has always been primarily identified as the author of *The Second Sex*. The book is informed, as is all de Beauvoir's work, by existentialist philosophy, which de Beauvoir, with her life-long companion Jean-Paul Sartre had done much to develop. Essentially, de Beauvoir argued that women constitute 'the other' in the social and political world, and are seldom able to seize for themselves the same possibilities of action and self-determination as men. This theme – of women's dependence and limited ability to act – runs through all de Beauvoir's work. She encouraged women to refuse conventional personal and social ties, and her radicalism about interpersonal relationships was matched by a political radicalism and a consistent commitment to left-wing politics both in France and elsewhere. In her later years, she became a leading figure in French feminist politics. De Beauvoir travelled widely throughout her life; at the end of the Second World War she became a full-time writer and in 1955 was awarded the Prix Goncourt for her novel *The Mandarins*.

Main ideas

Simone de Beauvoir was trained in the discipline of philosophy, and it was during her days as a philosophy student at the Sorbonne that she met Jean-Paul Sartre, with whom she formed a long-term personal and intellectual relationship. In her childhood and youth, de Beauvoir had been influenced first by the fervent Roman Catholicism of her mother (a commitment to Catholicism so strong that it had ensured that de Beauvoir was educated at Catholic primary and secondary schools) and subsequently by the idealism and social reformism of Robert Garric. Garric established Équipe Social, a social service institute with a strong Catholic orientation in order to aid the working classes in the more impoverished districts of Paris. Garric enlisted young middle-class people as teachers and role models, and de Beauvoir spent several years as a teacher of literature to working-class adolescent girls. In part, the commitment was one of convenience, in that it allowed her to escape from her family's (particularly her mother's) surveillance and enjoy a degree of personal autonomy.[2]

But commitments such as this disappeared once de Beauvoir met Sartre. Her life, and her work, are difficult to separate from his, and in some senses her novels, her essays and indeed *The Second Sex* represent a life-long dialogue with him and his ideas. Both read philosophy, both taught philosophy in French lycées (initially in the provinces, although subsequently in Paris) and both became known, in the years immediately after the Second World War, for their discussion and elaboration of the philosophy of existentialism. This set of ideas is organized around the central theme of freedom: put most baldly, it is the stated belief that everyone is equally free and that the circumstances for acting freely exist for everyone. Given the imperatives which are now widely recognized as constraints on human action, the idea seems to be absurd, yet its radicalism was the suggestion that people did not have to accept the givens of any particular situation. The ideas which dominated the bourgeois world in which de Beauvoir and Sartre had been born and bred – ideas of duty, fidelity and obedience, for example – were defined by existentialism as constraints on freedom, and as part of an external world which did not have to be obeyed. The philosophy, at its most extreme, does not recognize the problem of individual freedom for one person being the individual constraint for another; this is not a set of ideas which identifies social interdependence or community as important. Indeed, to an existentialist, these ideas would be seen as imposed limits on freedom.

What is striking, therefore, about existentialism in its purest – Sartrean – form is its individualism. In one of the first major texts of existentialism, Sartre's *Being and Nothingness*, he had argued that all freedoms are equal.[3] This had led Sartre to espouse his famous view that even the person about to be hanged is 'free' in the existential sense, since he (and it is a he who is the subject of the text) can live out, and in, that situation in different forms of freedom. De Beauvoir, in the pattern of much of her work, wrote an essay on *Being and Nothingness*, 'Pyrrhus et Cinéas', in which she attempted what she subsequently described as a reconciliation between her views and those of Sartre. Sartre, she pointed out, was arguing that all freedoms are equal, an idea which she could not accept entirely because for her 'situations are different, and therefore so are freedoms' (Bair, 1990: 270).

'Pyrrhus et Cinéas' unfolds as a dialogue, and a dialogue in which a number of figures (for example, Hegel, Flaubert, Kafka and Kant) appear as well as Sartre. The conclusion to the essay is one which remains entirely faithful to Sartre's construction of freedom, even though in the course of it de Beauvoir had given repeated indications that she had reservations about a theory of freedom which admitted no difference between the situations of individuals. The essay was published in 1944, and was followed in 1947 by 'The Ethics of Ambiguity', in which de Beauvoir suggested, again, that there were no universally valid 'rules' for behaviour; the only important 'rule' was that individuals must follow their own drives. She writes:

> any man who has known real lives, real revolts, real desires, and real will knows quite well that he has no need of any outside guarantee to be sure of his own goals; their certitude comes from his own drive. There is a very old saying which goes: 'do what you must, come what may.' (Bair, 1990: 322)

As a theory, let alone a prescription, for social action, this idea has its very obvious limitations to anyone educated in an era literate in psychoanalysis, not to mention knowledgeable about the social consequences of random and uncontrolled individual action. 'Real' desires, we would probably now assume, cannot be read in a neutral let alone a uniquely positive sense; they only become good or bad in terms of their impact on others and on the individual concerned. De Beauvoir herself was later to express considerable dissatisfaction with the views she expressed in 'The Ethics of Ambiguity'; she was, she wrote, too preoccupied with events in her personal life to think clearly when she wrote it.

But when she began her next non-fiction work, which was to be *The Second Sex*, she had clearly resolved, and come to terms with, many of the issues which had been troubling her at the time of 'The Ethics'. *The Second Sex* was published in two volumes in 1949, and it was written after de Beauvoir's own assertions of independence – a trip to the United States and a passionate and rewarding affair with the Chicago-based writer Nelson Algren. Difference, and distance, from Sartre had been achieved through both these actions, and the result was a monumental study which asserted the existence of another sex; the universal male subject of philosophy was effectively deconstructed by de Beauvoir in this work. Even so, the book still retains explicit allegiance to existentialism: the female subject is expected to attempt to achieve the same independence as men. But the step has been taken towards acknowledging that the central actor of all post-Enlightenment rationalist philosophy is not only a man, she may also be a woman.

Thus the major, and lasting, importance of *The Second Sex* is the assertion, within the context of that most abstract of bourgeois disciplines – namely, philosophy – that sexual difference exists, and that this difference has a formative impact on the experiences and life chances of individuals. Moreover, *The Second Sex* offered what few discussions of women had previously offered: a theoretical interpretation of the place of women in society. Other feminist writers, such as Mary Wollstonecraft and Charlotte Perkins Gilman, had written books which described, and indeed deplored, the social position of women. But these writers, and others like them, had been more concerned with the description of the subordination of women, particularly in the analytical sense, than its analysis. Gilman had offered an explanation of women's subordination (which she located in women's domestic responsibilities), but de Beauvoir was the first woman to offer, in the best masculinist tradition of modernism, a theory which attempted to explain women's universal material and cultural inferiority.

De Beauvoir based her explanation of women's universal subordination in culture and nurture. The second volume of *The Second Sex* opens with the famous statement that 'one is not born, but rather becomes, a woman' (de Beauvoir, 1946b: 249). Nurture and culture are held responsible for the emergence of the person who becomes female, and who occupies what de Beauvoir has described as the place of 'the other' in society. De Beauvoir argues (and in doing so helps to establish a tradition which many later feminists were to follow) that history was made, and written, by men. In short, the social world is a male construction and a construction which women find works to their disadvantage should they ever wish to challenge it; however amiable relations between wife and husband may be, and however apparently consensual their relationship, this consensus depends to a very large extent on the mutual goodwill of the two parties – particularly the husband towards the wife. Should that goodwill break down, or should the wife need to renegotiate her place within either the marriage or the social world, then she will very rapidly find that she is up against the entrenched institutional power of men.

In making this distinction, between the informal privileges and delights that some women may enjoy as a result of male goodwill and the general public powerlessness which all women experience within patriarchal systems, de Beauvoir asserts a fundamental principle of twentieth-century feminist thinking: that it is essential, in order to understand the position of women in society, both to acknowledge the existence of the public and the private spheres *and* to theorise the relationship between them. Bourgeois society, as de Beauvoir knew very well from her own experience and from watching the behaviour of her family and friends, made (and makes) sharp distinctions between the public and the private. Indeed, the 'private' is in many ways a residual part of the social world, in which the unacceptable can be kept. At the same time, bourgeois privacy has long been defended as a place of freedom and the legitimate location for behaviour that is deemed either unsuitable or unacceptable for the public space. But the effect of this rigorous distinction, in a social world which has entrenched gender distinctions, is to make the public world a male world, and the private world a female world, which men sometimes share. The isolation, the futility, the loneliness and the pettiness of the private world are all described by de Beauvoir with great rigour and force; having seen her mother live a *private* life, it was apparent that she would not entertain such a fate for herself or for other women.

So the freedom to move about a social world, to travel and to inhabit, as an autonomous person, an urban world, are all freedoms which, in 1949, de Beauvoir claimed for women. Subsequently, women have made repeated claims of the same kind; the campaigns organized around the slogan 'reclaim the night' are informed by exactly the kind of thinking which inspired *The Second Sex*: namely, that women should be free to inhabit the public world. Many of the constraints (particularly around clothing, manners and sexuality) which de Beauvoir described in *The Second Sex* have long since disappeared (rigid dress codes are a notable example), but access to the public, urban space is still contested, and still frequently difficult for women. De Beauvoir's father has often been described by her biographers as embodying *l'ésprit boulevardier* – the urban man who inhabited, and who gained his identity from inhabiting, a particular kind of leisured urban space. His daughter, as an adolescent girl in Paris in the 1920s, discovered that this space could never be hers in the same way and on the same terms. Even though Paris became, in 1940 and 1941, largely a city without adult men, women's experience of this environment remained, as de Beauvoir's did, largely marginal.

The nature of 'being in the world' which preoccupied both Sartre and de Beauvoir thus had a special and particular meaning for de Beauvoir, as she came to recognize that her 'being' in the world was mediated and organized in ways outside her control and in relationship to a general category – that of women – which she could not escape. The word 'trapped' as a description of how de Beauvoir presents the situation of women is scarcely too strong to convey the picture she presents of the containment of women in western society, and the degree to which their existence is organized for them by men. The problem of how to escape from this is inevitably a matter of interest for de Beauvoir: what can be done to liberate women from the private (even if sometimes comfortable) prisons which they inhabit?

The answer for de Beauvoir does not lie (as it did for Mary Wollstonecraft or Charlotte Perkins Gilman or many other groups of women) primarily in changes in social policy, most specifically in the education of women, on which so many feminists put so much emphasis. For de Beauvoir, the change was to be found, literally, in a change of mind: women have to learn, de Beauvoir maintained, to be their own free agents. What women have to do, she writes in the conclusion to *The Second Sex*, is to refuse immanence – to refuse the position which makes them passive *and* encourages them to use passivity and helplessness in a battle with men. She writes:

> The woman who is shut up in immanence endeavours to hold man in that prison also; thus the prison will be confused with the world, and woman will no longer suffer from being confined there: mother, wife, sweetheart are the jailers. Society, being codified by man, decrees that woman is inferior: she can do away this inferiority only by destroying the male's superiority. She sets about mutilating, dominating man, she contradicts him, she denies his truth and his values. But in

doing this she is only defending herself; it was neither a changeless essence nor a mistaken choice that doomed her to immanence, to inferiority. They were imposed upon her. An oppression creates a state of war. And this is no exception. The existent who is regarded as inessential cannot fail to demand the re-establishment of her sovereignty.

Today the combat takes a different shape; instead of wishing to put man in a prison, woman endeavours to escape from one; she no longer seeks to drag him into the realms of immanence but to emerge, herself, into the light of transcendence. (de Beauvoir, 1964b: 675)

Thus women, in the second half of the twentieth century, are ready to abandon the state of passivity and subjectivity which has been theirs for too long. The nature of the relationship between the sexes is one which, to de Beauvoir, imposes 'bad faith' and 'lack of freedom' on both parties. Women refuse to act independently, and in de Beauvoir's terms 'freely', because they are afraid of the consequences and costs of freedom. Men are only too aware of the lack of freedom of women, and thus cannot act towards them as equals: male/female relations are poisoned by the mutual knowledge, of both men and women, of the power of men over women.

So de Beauvoir, both in *The Second Sex* and elsewhere in her work, constructs a life-long battle against female passivity and female dependence. The conclusion of *The Second Sex* advocates a different form of socialization for girls, and a much greater social encouragement for women's active qualities – be they intellectual or physical. But although this conclusion speaks of an understanding of the general social arrangements of western society, de Beauvoir is essentially concerned with the development in women of the quality which can be best described as autonomy: a sense of personal, emotional independence. De Beauvoir is well aware that such independence is impossible without such social supports as an independent income, effective contraception which women can control, and social policies which do not distinguish between the civil rights of women and men, but she is also advancing an argument which is more radical than that of mere equal opportunities; it is an argument about taking and achieving personal responsibility and through it constructing a social and intellectual world which is informed by both women and men. It is an argument which fundamentally asserts the right of women to make decisions, and to act as citizens of the world. The 'other' is to become a fully emancipated inhabitant of a genuinely egalitarian social space.

In 1949 *The Second Sex* was hailed as innovative by its supporters, and as obscene by its critics. In the late 1940s to write of sexuality and reproduction in explicit ways still attracted attention, and to do so in a way which validated female sexual experience remained subversive. Nevertheless, even if in part due to its notoriety, *The Second Sex* became immediately a best seller and a widely influential book. It allowed de Beauvoir a platform on which to speak on other issues: she had, in fact, successfully entered the public world through a critique of women's exclusion from it. In the decades up to her death, she was to support many left-wing causes and in the 1970s to become actively involved in feminist politics. Indeed, her later life was to demonstrate a movement away from philosophical and abstract issues and towards an engagement with pragmatic concerns and very specific campaigns around such questions as male violence against women, and women's access to abortion.

She was also to publish, in 1970, a lengthy study of ageing, *Old Age* (1978). Adopting very much the same pattern as *The Second Sex*, she presented the old as, literally, another 'other', and documented this condition of 'otherness' in literature and history. She wrote in the conclusion to *Old Age* that 'Society cares about the individual only in so far as he is profitable' (de Beauvoir, 1978: 604). The book draws extensively on western (particularly North American) accounts of the treatment of the elderly, and as such it is a savage indictment of the way in which many old people are treated. A rich and insightful account, it is nevertheless perhaps most significant as a demonstration of de Beauvoir's own intellectual progress away from idealism: *Old Age* is as grounded in the realities of the social world as any social policy text. The real world, by 1970, had assumed a determining significance, and with it had a new understanding of ideas about constraint and freedom to the woman who had once argued that all people possessed freedom.

What is particularly striking about *Old Age* is the use which de Beauvoir makes of ageing as a creative process. Many Anglo-Saxon accounts of ageing (see, for example, Townsend, 1963) focus on the aspects of decline, decay and helplessness in old age. De Beauvoir does not deny these issues, but she does cite numerous examples of individuals who became more productive as they grew older. At the same time, the *ambiguity* of old age is emphasized in this account: in old age we know more, and may well be in a situation to reap what has been sown, but at the same time we may have less will to learn, and much less physical and mental capacity (and energy) to engage in new interests. What de Beauvoir recognizes is that old age, like other aspects of human life, is often an ambivalent state: a state in which we *may* enjoy existence and gain from it rich rewards, but at the same time its inevitable features (such as declining physical strength) make it more difficult to act freely in the social world.

In *Old Age*, de Beauvoir discusses a reality of existence which now confronts an increasingly large proportion of the 'northern' population. As people live longer, old age is no longer a brief state of difficult survival, but an extended period of human existence. As de Beauvoir recognized, those best able to age are those who have lived rich lives (particularly in the social and intellectual sense) in their maturity. Those who have been able to invest, both literally and metaphorically, are those best able to enjoy what has become for many people the last third of their lives. The model of the 'good life' of maturity which de Beauvoir invokes is essentially one of productive (particularly intellectual) and creative work. This acquired habit is the most likely to make later life interesting and rewarding. Whereas other writers about old age concentrated on its poverty and its social isolation, de Beauvoir (while she does not ignore these aspects of its condition) considers old age as a state of being – a state of the continuing possibility of human freedom and choice.

This makes *Old Age*, and de Beauvoir's other interventions on social policy (for example, on abortion and education policy), a fascinating and vital contribution to thinking about welfare, in that she deals not just with the material issues of a particular question, but with the human possibilities which may or may not be developed within a situation. She recognizes being old as a condition which brings with it infirmity and dependence, but she asks us to think of old age less as a fixed and a final state and more as part of a continuum in which individuals should still recognize (and have recognized) their capacity for action and choice.

De Beauvoir and welfare

In the previous section, de Beauvoir's transition from the extreme idealism of her youth to something approaching materialism in her maturity has been outlined. As she herself wrote in her autobiography, in the days just after her graduation she held to the view (as did Sartre) that there was no such thing as a Jew, or a woman, and that people had the liberty to define themselves. This extreme version of bourgeois individualism (which in de Beauvoir's case was entirely vindicated by her own successful transition from dutiful daughter to independent philosophy teacher) was rendered absurd by the Holocaust and by the events of the Second World War. Social power, constraint, and other people as enemies and foes, all entered a world which had previously appeared to be a matter of choice and personal preference. While even in her idealist youth de Beauvoir had supported socially progressive politics, such as paid holidays and improvements in education, it is apparent from her own work that she still maintained the view that in the construction of our lives we are all free agents.

The German invasion of France in 1940 shattered this belief once and for all. It was now clear to de Beauvoir that differences of opinion between herself and Hitler were very much more than academic; they were actually about to impose themselves on her very existence and that of Sartre. Freedom, she recognized as the Germans walked into Paris, is not absolute, and the world has to be seen in terms which allow for the existence of greater degrees of social power. The experience of living through the German occupation, of four years of hardship, surveillance and the loss of friends, shifted de Beauvoir's thinking to the point where she acknowledged the idea of the concept of woman as not just a category, but a *coercive* category. In that shift, and in that idea, there lies the first of the major contributions of de Beauvoir to thinking about welfare.

As is already perhaps apparent, it is difficult to look to de Beauvoir and find much detailed discussion of how society should be organized. On the other hand, it is entirely possible to turn to her work and find ideas which have been enormously influential in the theoretical analysis of the position of women in society, and in the welfare services in particular. De Beauvoir's understanding of the coerciveness of the idea of 'the feminine' and 'femininity' is one such idea, and through it generations of feminist writers have developed ideas about women's internalization of the (apparent) imperatives of womanhood. The sections of *The Second Sex* which deal with the married woman and the mother provided the framework in which feminist sociologists such as Hannah Gavron and Ann Oakley were later to produce studies of the housebound mother and the condition of maternity (Garron, 1968; Oakley, 1974, 1986). De Beauvoir's innovative analysis of the reality behind the myth of motherhood thus laid the theoretical foundations for later work which was to examine systematically the lived experience of being a mother and a housewife in western industrial society. When Ann Oakley wrote *The Sociology of Housework*, and named the tedium and repetition of doing housework, she was in effect bringing up to date an idea which de Beauvoir had first expressed in 1949 when she wrote:

> Woman wastes a great deal of time and effort in such striving for originality and unique perfection; this gives her task its meticulous, disorganized and endless character and makes it difficult to estimate the true load of domestic work ... The worst of it all is that this labour does not even tend towards the creation of anything durable. Woman is tempted – and the more so the greater pains she takes – to regard her work as an end in itself. She sighs as she contemplates the perfect cake just out of the oven: 'It's a shame to eat it!' (de Beauvoir, 1964b: 428)

In this passage, and the paragraphs which follow it, de Beauvoir captures some of the endless, endlessly destroyed, nature of housework. Writing on *The Second Sex* in 1989, Ann Oakley commented that, just as her work was informed by de Beauvoir so the writing of *The Second Sex*, and women's reactions to it, make de Beauvoir more consciously feminist than she had previously been (Oakley, 1989).

So the unknowing feminist who was the author of *The Second Sex* became a dominating feminist influence in the second half of the twentieth century. The message which de Beauvoir wished to communicate to women was one which was designed not primarily for institutional or political use, but as an attempt to change women's minds about their situation. As such, the message was one which advocated independence and autonomy for women, a discussion which did much to inform the ideas of feminism in the 1960s and 1970s about the dependence of women in marriage. Thus a particular way in which de Beauvoir developed the concept of femininity as coercive was through the power of the idea to persuade women to adopt an attitude of living through and by men. Critics have subsequently pointed out that much of de Beauvoir's analysis of this issue was drawn from material about the French middle class of the early twentieth century; as such its relevance to the situation of non-white and non-middle-class people is more than a little tangential. But it is equally possible to reply that the idea of female economic dependence in marriage has been generalized from middle-class experience to all other classes by a long tradition of male social reformers, many of them with apparently radical social commitments.

Yet what is so striking about de Beauvoir's analysis of dependence – and I would argue it is the aspect of her analysis which makes it so uniquely radical – is that, although she is concerned with women's financial dependence on men (whether as daughters, wives or dependent female relatives), she is also concerned with a form of dependence which goes much deeper, the kind of dependence which inhibits women from attempting or valorizing their own work. De Beauvoir rightly acknowledges the barriers and prejudices which can prevent women from entering the professions or higher education but again she is more concerned with the issue of internalized expectations of femininity – namely, the belief of women themselves that they should not attempt work of their own or develop their own interests and values. In some ways this idea can sound similar to the now commonly recognized 'fear of success' among women. What makes it different, and I would suggest in important ways, is that de Beauvoir does not locate 'fear of success' simply in terms of an occupational structure with particular hierarchies, but suggests a more insidious, and more general, phenomenon in which women refuse to value their own talents or make the development of those talents a legitimate goal. The case is best illustrated by the instance of one of the characters in *The Mandarins*, a woman named Paula. Paula is something of a stock character in de Beauvoir, in that she is a woman who has lived through a man, and now finds that the man in question (her lover Henri) is growing tired of the relationship. Unfortunately for Paula, Henri has begun to find that Paula's endless devotion is something of a burden. Despite the fact that she is a talented singer, Paula refuses to train or develop this skill; she maintains that she can only sing for Henri.

The absorption in private romance is, as suggested, a form of infantilism among women which de Beauvoir is particularly good at identifying. She wishes women, as many men have done, to be more like men in terms of independence and ability to act autonomously. The terrible costs, to women but also to men, of people who refuse responsibility for their own lives are very fully covered in *The Second Sex* and in de Beauvoir's fiction. As such, the ideas which she outlines still deserve consideration in societies in which femininity is constructed in diverse and obviously contradictory ways. The France which de Beauvoir wrote about in *The Second Sex* (largely non-urban and predominantly agricultural) has since altered dramatically, but in all western European societies, the impact of femininity still seems to be such as to inhibit women from playing a larger part in the social world. Again, this is not to interpret 'success' in terms of professional career structures, but it is to emphasize the part that women could play in the social and political world, and largely do not.

Thus what de Beauvoir's work informs is feminist debate about women and the public world. On the one hand, there are those who see the absence of women from the public world very much in terms of structural constraints: that is, hours of work, lack of child-care facilities, and direct and indirect prejudice all prevent well-qualified women from achieving adequate recognition. This thesis, which can easily be backed up by endless evidence about the way in which paid work is organized around male experiences and expectations, obviously lends itself to social engineering of diverse kinds and policies of equal opportunities. On the other hand – although the lines between the two groups often overlap – are those who see the contemporary constraints on women as being largely informal rather than structural: that is to say, women themselves are loath to part with what they construct as 'femininity' in order to become dedicated to particular tasks. In 1946 Mirra Komarovsky, an eminent woman sociologist and member of the Frankfurt School, published an article about women's fear of success as a loss of femininity (Komarovsky, 1946). She identified, like de Beauvoir, a culture about femininity which persuaded women that achievement (and, in the case of Komarovsky's sample, academic achievement) would make women less attractive to men. De Beauvoir and Komarovsky both identify, it should be emphasized, the culture as the problem. That point is important, since women's 'fear of success' has often been turned into a blame-the-victim argument about women and achievement.

That women *are* influenced by a western culture of femininity can be easily demonstrated by reference to studies which evaluate the achievements of similarly qualified women and men. Equally, a study of what women say about themselves and their achievements replicates thousands of times everything said by de Beauvoir (and Komarovosky) in 1946 and 1949. For example, Sylvia Plath's *The Bell Jar* (1966) is a vivid study written about precisely the kind of women, i.e. women students in higher education, whom Komarovsky studies. In *The Bell Jar*, the narrator, Esther Greenwood, goes to some lengths to disguise her intelligence; in an adolescent culture which emphasized the importance for women of being successful at 'dating', it was deemed politic for women to appear as non-threatening to men in terms of intellectual competence. 'Playing dumb', in the way described by Plath, was probably something which de Beauvoir never chose to do (although there is a good case for arguing that she underestimated her intelligence relative to that of Sartre), but what she did recognize was a pattern of deliberate under-achievement and learned incompetence which made women the apparently 'natural' victims of the male world. The sociology of education, particularly as informed by feminists, has taken up on both sides of the Atlantic the debilitating impact on women of perceptions about the 'unattractiveness' of intellectually successful women. The literature on the importance of role models, and of single-sex schools for girls, is all derived from a discourse about women and achievement which, although not derived from *The Second Sex* alone, is nevertheless much informed by it.

But the model of the social world which informs the social world of *The Second Sex*, and to a very large extent de Beauvoir's fiction, is that of the white, western middle class. She does not write about working-class people (except as passing, additional characters), nor does she assume (in a way which is perhaps derived from the specific homogeneity of much of French culture) a cultural pluralism within one society. Thus for her the problems of the working class are very much problems of poverty; like many other middle-class reformers before her, de Beauvoir did not know (either through experience or study) of social worlds outside her own. Clearly, this remains a problematic aspect of *The Second Sex*, and what it does is to reinforce the impression which de Beauvoir gives in the text of a dichotomous social world: that is, a world divided into male and female. It is a model which has been extremely influential, not to say formative, within contemporary western feminism, and by way of example we can cite two best-selling feminist tracts of the early 1970s, Kate Millett's *Sexual Politics* (1977) and Shulamith Firestone's *The Dialectic of Sex* (1979), which drew heavily on inspiration from *The Second Sex*. Both these authors presented a picture of the social world which was very much part of early 1970s western feminism – a world divided into men, who were misogynist and patriarchical in their thought and actions, and women, who were the victims of these oppressive systems of thought. An inevitable, and logical, development of this analysis was to advocate the withdrawal of women from relationships with men, and the establishment of a new matriarchy in which reproduction was accomplished through techno-logical intervention.

Thus while the strength of de Beauvoir's work (and *The Second Sex* in particular) is that it helped to establish the need for a philosophy, and indeed a politics, of gender relations, the weakness, or the problem, of the work is that it is based on a dichotomous view of women and men. Although de Beauvoir is not arguing, in *The Second Sex*, that the sexes are intrinsically different (as later French feminists such as Cixous and Irigaray were to suggest), she does present the existing social world as one in which sexual difference, and indeed sexual antagonism, is all present (see the discussion in Marks and de Courtivron, 1980). Obviously, she does not wish this state of affairs to continue. Her solution, as many critics have pointed out, is largely to make women more as she assumes men to be: that is, independent and self-defining. Added to this is a degree of social reorganization, in the mould of Engels, which suggests state responsibility for child care, improved contraception and more equitable legislation about marriage and divorce.

Most of the suggestions which de Beauvoir made about changes in legislation on sexuality and marriage have now been made, or are being actively negotiated, in northern societies. Debates over responsibility for child care continue, but what is now firmly on the agenda (again in the countries of the industrialized North) is the issue of child care, and indeed the gender politics implicit in care in general. But as discourses on the appropriate roles and responsibilities on the sexes have shifted, and have come to incorporate policies which suggest an acceptance of androgyny, so societies return to the issue of the origins of gender difference which de Beauvoir raised in *The Second Sex*. As we have seen, for de Beauvoir women were made, not born. By implication we must assume that the same is true of men. Thus what de Beauvoir did was to locate herself very firmly on the side of nurture in debates about the origins of constructions of femininity and masculinity. She was 'made' into a little girl, and then a young woman, in a culture which had relatively non-ambiguous understandings of these states of being. She could also observe a society in which adult gender roles were rigidly demarcated, policed and observed. Inevitably, the 'social' in this experience was not just significant, it was formative.

But what this prioritization of the social world did for de Beauvoir's analysis of the position of women, and for the feminist tradition which it did much to establish in the West, was to underestimate, in theoretical terms, the part which 'the personal' plays in social life. This issue is one of complexity, and fascination, in the history of the relationship between feminism and politics, since it is always a contested area. De Beauvoir, and feminism in general, advocate the increased participation of women in 'public' life. So far so good, but what then becomes contentious is the question of the value of what passes for constructed, institutional 'public' life. It is one thing to campaign for the increased voice of women in public life, another to wish to maintain the dichotomy between public and private and the consistent undervaluation of the private which accompanies this distinction. Thus the inherent value of the private, domestic space was one campaign which feminists after de Beauvoir fought. The Wages for Housework campaign, and debates about the socialization of child care, are both examples of areas where there were, and are, significant differences of opinion. In the case of the latter, many women have pointed out that schemes (such as those in place in eastern Europe prior to 1989) which automatically assumed the participation of mothers in paid work gave those women no choice about paid employment, and were anyway located firmly within a system of values that endorsed social production but did not value the individually organized care of children and dependants. Again, critics of what they would describe as 'coercive' child-care policies would point out that the paid work which the majority of women did in these societies was mundane, badly paid and of low status.

So the negotiation of the public and the private was, and remains, a contentious and contested area for feminism. In one way, there are considerable reasons to separate the interests of women and men; in general, if this is not done, the interests of women are usually subsumed under those of the general, universal person who is taken for granted as male. At the same time, this rigid distinction ignores the patterns of reciprocity, and shifts in priorities throughout individual lives, which do exist between women and men in all societies. The dichotomy between female and male bequeathed to feminism by de Beauvoir largely ignored this, in much the same way as her analysis refused the possibility of the complex blend of nurture and nature which makes up human beings. Largely refusing, as she did, the insights of psychoanalysis, de Beauvoir was at all times at pains to stress the rational and the role of reason. Entirely located within a post-Enlightenment tradition which believed in the all-encompassing power of reason, what de Beauvoir did not recognize was the degree of intellectual congruence between her theory of society and the technical–industrial society which had emerged (and was emerging in ever greater force after the Second World War) in twentieth-century Europe.

The impact of de Beauvoir on debates about welfare

The concern of de Beauvoir with questions about the organization of the social world can be divided into two periods. Before the Second World War there was little to suggest that de Beauvoir had anything except a cursory interest in politics or issues about the institutional organization of the social world. As she was freely to admit in her autobiography, Sartre was interested in political questions while she remained blithely unconcerned about political events in the 1930s. Her sympathies were always with the left, and she never entertained the slightest sympathy for fascism, but on the other hand neither did she develop political ties or affiliations with left-wing parties and organizations.

Much of this changed after 1939. The absolutely undeniable fact of the German invasion of France, the persecution of the Jews and the vendettas conducted against the Resistance all confronted de Beauvoir with the reality of political power. She and Sartre became involved in the politics of the Resistance, and although neither of them was ever engaged in military activity, both played a limited part in developing socialist agendas for the postwar world. As such, these agendas (which attempted to fill a socialist space without becoming formally allied to the Communist Party) emphasized issues about the political freedom of citizens and the theoretical nature of democracy. Postwar reconstruction, it should be emphasized, was not seen by either Sartre or de Beauvoir in terms of the reorganization and establishment of state welfare services. Indeed, the writing of both Sartre and de Beauvoir during the Second World War concentrated more or less entirely on philosophical questions about the nature of freedom. Sartre's play *Les Mouches*, which was produced during the war, was seen by the audience as an attack on the German occupation, and as such establishes credentials for Sartre as an anti-German writer. Equally, de Beauvoir's Resistance novel (which she was not able to publish until after the liberation) made little secret of the author's hostility to the Germans (de Beauvoir, 1966).

But hostility to the Germans did not, as members of the Communist Party and the Resistance noted about Sartre, actually contribute a formal, developed, political agenda. What became evident during the war was that neither Sartre nor de Beauvoir had any detailed interest in social questions; they were 'for' freedom, but in a way which was entirely compatible with a market economy. As they travelled, and encountered both the degrees of poverty and wealth in the United States and the terrible poverty of many Third World countries, they began to identify more firmly with socialist parties and socialist solutions to material deprivation. Sartre's relationship with the Communist Party was always tense, and one to which he devoted a great deal of energy. But essentially, the problem about the Party remained for him – as it did for de Beauvoir – the problem of the degree of freedom allowed to the individual.

After 1945, and in large part as a result of travel and wartime experiences, de Beauvoir's work gradually became more programmatic in terms of its discussions of social issues. *The Second Sex*, as we have seen, included demands for better education for women, access to contraception, child care and improved legal rights for women. In the 1950s, as de Beauvoir concentrated on writing fiction and autobiography, she had little to say about specific issues of social organization. However, what she did do, particularly in her travel books (*America Day by Day*, 1952, and *The Long March*, a study of the Chinese Revolution and the coming to power of Mao Tse-Tung, 1958), was to include social analysis in her account of her travels. She recognized that it was a particular form of largely unregulated capitalism which produced the urban squalor of much of the United States, and she powerfully condemned the country's explicit racism. What emerged, therefore, from *America Day by Day* is an account of both a very rich and a very poor society, a society in which the interpretation of freedom was such as to produce considerable hardship and suffering.

The experiences in the United States led de Beauvoir to take up the position of explicit support for China, and subsequently for socialist movements throughout the Third World. In terms of her own society, she generally took a dim view of the strengths of all the main political parties, and it was not until the Presidential elections which brought Mitterrand to power that she publicly endorsed any French politician. In any event, her attitude to domestic politics had been coloured by her opposition, throughout the 1950s, to French policy in Algeria. Determined to maintain direct political control in Algeria, the French government had savagely attacked the national liberation movement, and de Beauvoir's sympathies (publicly known and publicly expressed) had been entirely with the Algerian nationalists. Again, the issue at stake (as was the case during the Second World War) was the issue of freedom, and the extent of legitimate state power over the lives of its citizens.

Thus throughout the 1950s and the 1960s, de Beauvoir's political interests were generally for socialism (particularly in countries outside France) and against unregulated capitalism. In May 1968 both she and Sartre spoke on behalf of the students; again, the demands of students for a greater degree of control over their lives and a less authoritarian university structure not only were easily incorporated into de Beauvoir's view of the world, but had actually been formed by it. Hence in these political events, and in the feminism which emerged throughout Europe at the end of the 1960s and the beginning of the 1970s, de Beauvoir found that history was now being made partly by the influence of her ideas, and she was now having to take part in the active consideration of the relationship between her ideas and social reality. The 'force of circumstance', which was once seen by de Beauvoir as the impact of history on her, now became a history in which she was expected to play a major part.

And so, throughout the 1970s, the woman philosopher who had once kept something of a distance between herself and political intervention became involved in the politics of abortion, violence against women, the state provision of care for the mentally ill and the aged, and a number of other causes. De Beauvoir quite literally took to the streets in her politics and became a passionate critic of authoritarianism and patriarchy in state institutions. The theoretical ideas found not just one context, but a number of contexts, and through them de Beauvoir became involved in a new conception of politics – a conception which emphasized particular rights rather than universal ones, and the importance of local and non-hierarchical political organization. In this, de Beauvoir can hardly be said to have developed a theory of welfare; but what she did do was to lend her very considerable prestige and reputation to the idea, which she had done so much to develop, of the right of women to self-determination in social and political structures. The 'women-friendly' welfare state was never an idea which de Beauvoir explicitly recognized, yet it was only through the contribution of her analysis of women's second-class status that the idea developed. Long after formal and detailed blueprints on welfare have been abandoned (and will no doubt continue to be abandoned), de Beauvoir's systematic and coherent account of the constricted passivity of women remains central to discussions about the organization of the social world.

Key texts

A Very Easy Death (1964a) is an account by de Beauvoir of the death of her mother, Françoise de Beauvoir. The book has two themes. The first is the reaction of de Beauvoir to the death of her mother, and her articulation of her surprise at her sense of devastation and of loss. Relations between mother and daughter had often been difficult, although in later years some degree of *rapprochement* had occurred. Even so, de Beauvoir, by her own admission, had not expected to be significantly affected by her mother's death, and *A Very Easy Death* is in part a reaction to that sense of surprise. But the second theme – and one which has made the book of very general interest – is that of the apparent determination of western doctors to keep patients alive at all costs, even when it is apparent that they are going to die. The title of the book comes from a remark by one of the nurses: when de Beauvoir commented on the horror of her mother's death, the nurse replied that, on the contrary, it had been a 'very easy death'.

The first volume of de Beauvoir's autobiography, *Memoirs of a Dutiful Daughter* (1963; first published in 1958), is an autobiographical reconstruction of growing up in bourgeois France in the period just before, and after, the First World War. Born into a well-to-do bourgeois family, the young de Beauvoir had every reason to suppose that the world would remain, for her, a reliable and comfortable place, in which she would make a conventional marriage and live a life of prosperous ease. As it was, the loss of her parents' income, and the discord between them, dislocated this assumption and its way of life. The book is in part about the impact on a child of unexpected changes in experience and parental disagreement. Always identified as a clever child, she turned this identification to good use both as a retreat from her domestic world and as a means of escape from it. She became precociously successful at school, and subsequently at university, and in doing so freed herself from the claims of family and 'duty' and 'dutifulness'. In the latter part of the book, she contrasts what she sees as her escape from a stifling social world with the fate of her close friend Elizabeth Mabille, who died of an undiagnosed illness in the midst of a family dispute about a romance. The book remains a lasting testament to the struggles of women for higher education and personal autonomy.

A Woman Destroyed (1987) is a short novel originally published in France in 1968 under the title of *La Femme Rompue*, and is the definitive statement by de Beauvoir of one of the central (if not the central) themes of her work, that of the emotional dependence of women on men. The heroine of the brief novel is a married woman whose husband tells her of an affair he is having with a younger colleague. The novel, structured in terms of an autobiographical diary, describes the older woman's collapse into frantic despair and depression at the thought of the loss of the man around whom she has organized her life. Terse and economical in its telling, the novel essentially encapsulates de Beauvoir's continued determination to challenge women's emotional passivity and their refusal to act for themselves.

Jean-Paul Sartre was de Beauvoir's life-long companion and their relationship became one of the great relationships of history: a union between two powerful intellects which always allowed relationships with others, but which nevertheless appeared to remain central to both parties. It was, and remains, the stuff of which myth is made; all the more so since, after the death of both parties, many letters that they exchanged were published which presented both parties in a less than favourable light. But the demythologization of the relationship was begun by de Beauvoir in *Adieux: Farewell to Sartre* (1986). Originally published in 1981, just one year after Sartre's death it was a vivid account by de Beauvoir of Sartre's physical collapse in the last five years of his life. Although the book ostensibly was written to commemorate a friendship, and contains some memorable writing about the impact of Sartre's death on de Beauvoir, it was the beginning of deconstruction of the myth of the perfect intellectual relationship. The book raises questions about the ethics of revelation, and indeed about the motives and morality of divulging to the world in general information about the personal lives of others. It is, in a sense, a book by a survivor, but also a survivor who wished to claim ownership of a shared past.

Notes

1. The fullest biography of de Beauvoir is Bair (1990). Also interesting is Moi (1993).
2. See the account in Bair (1990: 109–11) and de Beauvoir's own discussion in the first volume of her autobiography, *Memoirs of a Dutiful Daughter* (De Beauvoir, 1963: 179–98).
3. Jean-Paul Sartre's *Being and Nothingness* was first published in France in 1943. It marked the beginning of the identification of Sartre and de Beauvoir with existentialism.

References

Bair, D. (1990) *Simone de Beauvoir*, London: Jonathan Cape.

de Beauvoir, S. (1944) *Pyrrhus et Cinéas*, Paris: Gallimard.

de Beauvoir, S. (1948) *The Ethnics of Ambiguity*, New York: Philosophical Library.

de Beauvoir, S. (1952) *America Day by Day*, London: Duckworth.

de Beauvoir, S. (1957) *The Mandarins*, London: Collins.

de Beauvoir, S. (1958) *The Long March*, London: Andre Deutsch.

de Beauvoir, S. (1963) *Memoirs of a Dutiful Daughter*, Harmondsworth: Penguin. First pubished 1958.

de Beauvoir, S. (1964a) *A Very Easy Death*, Harmondsworth: Penguin.

de Beauvoir, S. (1964b) *The Second Sex*, New York: Bantam. First published 1949.

de Beauvoir, S. (1966) *The Blood of Others*, Harmondsworth: Penguin. First published 1945.

de Beauvoir, S. (1978) *Old Age*, Harmondsworth: Penguin. First published 1970.

de Beauvoir, S. (1986) *Adieux: Farewell to Sartre*, Harmondsworth: Penguin. First published 1981.

de Beauvoir, S. (1987) *A Woman Destroyed*, London: Fontana. First published 1968.

Firestone, S. (1979) *The Dialectic of Sex*, London: The Women's Press.

Gavron, H. (1968) *The Captive Wife*, Harmondsworth: Penguin.

Komarovsky, M. (1946) 'Cultural contradictions and sex roles', *American Journal of Sociology*, **52**, 3, pp. 508–16.

Marks, E. and de Courtivron, I. (eds) (1980) *New French Feminisms*, Brighton: Harvester.

Millett, K. (1977) *Sexual Politics*, London: Virago.

Moi, T. (1993) *Simone de Beauvoir: The making of an intellectual woman*, Oxford: Blackwell.

Oakley, A. (1974) *The Sociology of Housework*, Harmondworth: Penguin.

Oakley, A. (1986) *From Here to Maternity*, Harmondsworth: Penguin.

Oakley, A. (1989) Chapter 6, in Forster, P. and Sutton, I. (eds), *Daughters of de Beauvoir*, London: The Women's Press.

Plath, S. (1966) *The Bell Jar*, London: Faber and Faber.

Townsend, P. (1963) *The Family Life of Old People*, Harmondsworth: Penguin.

15 Barrett

Fiona Williams

Brief biography

Michele Barrett was born in 1949. Her academic training was in sociology, and in 1989 she became Professor of Sociology at City University, London. Her main publications include *Ideology and Cultural Production* (1979) which she co-edited, *Virginia Woolf: Women and writing* (1979) which she edited and introduced, and, most importantly, *Women's Oppression Today: Problems in Marxist feminist analysis*. This came out in 1980 with a revised edition in 1988. She co-authored with Mary McIntosh *The Anti-Social Family* (1982) with a second edition appearing in 1991, and she co-edited with Roberta Hamilton *The Politics of Diversity: Feminism, Marxism and nationalism* (1986). Her most recent publications include *The Politics of Truth: From Marx to Foucault* (1991) and *Destabilizing Theory: Contemporary feminist debates* (1992), co-edited with Anne Phillips.

Themes and developments in Barrett's work

Apart from its particular intellectual concerns, Barrett's work is significant in two ways. First, it represents some of the key debates and discussions within and between contemporary Marxist and feminist theory. Much of Barrett's work attempts to articulate, dissect, understand and resolve the theoretical problem areas which British socialist and feminist political developments of the 1970s, 1980s and 1990s have exposed. Second, while her work represents particular concerns within specific areas of social and political theory, what nevertheless characterizes it is a capacity for self-criticism and an openness to change. Thus, although it may have been easy in the mid-1980s to fit Barrett's work into the category of Marxist or socialist feminism, today such categorization carries no clear meaning because of the ways in which the theory and practice of Marxism, socialism and feminism have themselves been challenged and have changed.

The contribution of Barrett's work to social policy is not a direct one. It is connected through the parallel development of a feminist scholarship within the discipline of social policy, and what Barrett's work and this scholarship share is the shifting contexts of feminist debates, campaigns and movements over the last fifteen years. The aim of this chapter is to examine this parallel development. The first section looks at a selection of Barrett's work in terms of three chronological and thematic phases. The focus of the first phase is the relationship between women, the family and the state as it is discussed in the first editions of *Women's Oppression Today* and *The Anti-Social Family*. The second phase looks at the significance of 'difference' (both as sexual difference and as difference between women). This draws upon discussions in two articles on 'race' and on the concept of difference (Barrett and McIntosh, 1985; Barrett, 1987), and the introductory essay in the second edition of *Women's Oppression Today*. These represent a link to the third phase, which concerns the development of post-structuralism and its impact upon subjectivity, ideology and materialism, and the relationship between universalism and difference. These are explored in *The Politics of Truth* and *Destabilizing Theory*. The next section of the chapter examines the ways these ideas and their development have found reflection in feminist social policy. A final section considers briefly the impact of feminist ideas and demands upon the discipline and making of social policy.

Capitalism, women and the family

The intellectual and political context of the UK into which *Women's Oppression Today* (1980) emerged was one which saw the decline of social democratic ideals amid a deepening economic recession and the rise to power of Margaret Thatcher's first New Right administration. Set against this was the relative confidence of an autonomous women's movement, which had begun to generate new approaches and new questions. This development fed into a wider questioning of the economism of Marxist theory and politics generated by the influence of the works of Poulantzas and Althusser. At the same time, the debates within the women's movement about the theoretical and strategic implications of these questions, especially the relative attachment to patriarchy or capitalism as the roots of women's oppression, were intense.

Women's Oppression Today sought to unpick and clarify the key problem areas in these debates within feminism as well as between Marxism and feminism. In the book Barrett asks: what are the relative merits of the analyses of patriarchy or of the reproduction of capitalism in understanding women's oppression? And how far is women's oppression an ideological process? She argues that a classical Marxist analysis, which explains women's oppression in terms of the needs of capitalism for labour power, reared and serviced through women's domestic labour within the household, is inadequate: it is functionalist and economically

reductionist, and it fails to explain many aspects of women's subordination pre-
and post-capitalism. Yet neither does patriarchy on its own offer a sufficient
account: it is both ahistorical and biologically determinist. Barrett offers instead
a historical analysis of the development of 'gendered capitalist social relations',
which highlights the struggles and relations of both gender and class. Added to
this, she stresses the importance of ideology in the construction of gender. Here
again she argues for the need to steer a path between an overemphasis on
ideological processes entirely dissociated from economic relations and a view
which can only understand ideology as the manifestation of the material conditions
and relations of capitalism. The clearest way Barrett connects ideology to
materiality is through the organization of the household. She identifies the division
of labour within the household, and the ideology of familialism associated with
this, as directly and historically related to the development of capitalism.

The theme of the family as 'the site of women's oppression' is elaborated in
The Anti-Social Family written with Mary McIntosh (Barrett and McIntosh,
1982.) Within the context of a neo-conservative government espousing 'family
values' and a fragmented left with no consensual politics of the family, Barrett
and McIntosh set out to deconstruct the family, to analyze it as a social institution
and as an ideology, and to develop strategies which link personal desires and
aspirations to political change.

Their strategies for change focus on two aims which connect the personal to
the political: for personal choice and diversity in household forms, and towards
a collectivism or a socialization of the unpaid work carried out within households.
The political changes centre upon challenging policies and practices which shore
up 'anti-social family' life: the reorganization of the relationship between work
and home life; the disaggregation of social security; the provision of allowances
sufficient to give mothers and carers the choice between caring and paid work;
more collective provisions for social and health care, with greater user-control;
flexible types of housing with secure tenure; changes in laws regarding divorce,
domestic violence and rape; and a reassessment of child rearing as a collective
as well as an individual responsibility.

The impact of difference

By the mid-1980s, feminist politics and theory began to face a variety of changes
and challenges. Two articles, 'Ethnocentricism and socialist-feminist theory'
(Barrett and McIntosh, 1985) and 'The concept of difference' (Barrett, 1987),
were a reflection and response to some of these challenges. The second of these
articles was an attempt to analyze the competing notions of difference used in
feminist theory and politics: difference as a form of experiential diversity (as
claimed through age, sexuality, disability, ethnicity); difference as used by
post-structuralists to indicate the relativity of meaning (signifier/signified); and
difference as in sexual difference between men and women. The substance of
the arguments in 'Ethnocentricism and socialist-feminist theory' were incorpor-

ated into commentaries for the second editions to *Women's Oppression Today* (1988) and *The Anti-Social Family* (1991) (see below). In her introduction to a long essay prefacing the second edition of *Women's Oppression Today* (re-subtitled *The Marxist–feminist encounter*), Barrett poignantly illustrates this shift in focus by pointing out that the meaning of each word in the title and subtitle of the first edition is now open to discussion with the exception of the word 'problems'.

First, the implicit homogeneity in the use of the category 'women' and the tendency to universalize from a white western experience have been subject to substantial critiques, perhaps most forcibly by black and Third World feminists who pointed to the ways in which 'race', ethnicity and racism can reconstitute the experience of both oppression and being a woman. Barrett and McIntosh (1985, 1991) recognize the implications of this for their work on the family in terms of the need, first, to provide more empirical detail of the impact of 'race', racism and ethnicity in information about households, education, occupational segregation and working conditions, and second, to re-examine the theoretical assumptions underpinning this work. Most contentious of these is the claim of the family as the 'site of oppression', for this occludes an understanding of the history of forced migration and the contemporary role of the state in breaking up black families – for example, through racist immigration laws – as well as the role of the family as a 'site of resistance' against violence, harassment and exploitation (for a discussion and critique, see also Bhavnani and Coulson, 1986).

Second, the concept 'oppression' could no longer represent the direction of feminist politics in the 1980s. This was away from an emphasis upon women merely as victims of patriarchal (or patriarchal capitalist) oppression, towards a celebration of the positive values which sexual difference brings for women – sharing, caring, and so on. For Barrett, this raised a number a new theoretical considerations: the need not to dispense with the significance of biology or the body as her earlier 'social constructionist' account of gender had implied, but to understand more the relationship between sexual difference and the construction of gender. This consideration brings with it a reassessment of the claims of essentialism (the notion that women are essentially biologically, culturally or psychically different from men): she suggests that, again, the point is not to deny the claims, but to be clearer about why they are made.

These paths lead her into the new 'corporeal feminism', which focuses on the body, to Foucault and to new areas of Lacanian psychoanalytic literature which explore subjectivity. The turn to these works is also the result of her increasing unease with the use in social and political theory of 'ideology', and the way in which the concept has been used to plug rather than to open up questions of agency and subjectivity.

This unease has been reinforced by the fate of 'Marxist feminist analysis' – the last problematic element in the original subtitle – 'an attempt to bring together two world-views that have continued to go their separate ways in spite of our efforts at marriage-guidance' (Barrett, 1988: i). At the end of the essay in the second edition of *Women's Oppression Today*, Barrett admits that, just as it is impossible not to attempt an integration of the issues of 'race' and ethnicity into theoretical work today, so too it is 'impossible to write in such a confidently materialistic vein' (1988, xxxiii). No surprise then that her publications in the 1990s deal with this unease through an exploration of the fate of Marxism and of the impact of post-structuralism on feminism.

Shifting the paradigm: from things to words

Barrett suggests that one of the unresolved theoretical problems in *Women's Oppression Today* is her application to *gender* relations of the Marxist concept of 'ideology', in which it is *class* that acts as both the determinant of ideology and its material base. In *The Politics of Truth*, Barrett subjects ideology to an interrogation which, in the end, leads her not to a reformulation of the concept, but to conclude that the concept has little value once stripped of its class-determinism. And furthermore, as she demonstrates, what we know about the history of social divisions – of gender and of 'race' in particular – means that we cannot stick with a Marxism which 'may have enabled bourgeois men to analyse society from the point of view of the industrial proletariat but has . . . occupied a position that was both masculinist in content and Eurocentric in context' (Barrett, 1991: 161).

So Barrett turns for support, via Gramsci and Althusser, to the post-Marxists and post-structuralists – Laclau and Mouffe and especially Foucault – all of whom provide new approaches to the understanding of social relations of power in society which rest neither on the primacy of class nor on the exposition of a fundamental historical truth. What characterizes their work (in different ways) is the use of the concept 'discourse' and their move away from seeing society as a bounded totality.

According to Barrett, the theoretical problem we are left with is the necessity to avoid universalistic pretensions without completely surrendering to particu-larism. She suggests three ways of moving on: first, 'to rethink old prejudices about relativism' – in other words, to be more explicit about the contingent nature of knowledge and the relationship between that contingency and existing power relations; second, 'to develop a more self-conscious interpretive stance'; and third, to counter the anti-humanism of much post-structuralism with 'a language of motivation to understand political agency' (1991: 161–5).

Apart from the critique of the class-primacy position, the argument for humanism is the only thread which ties this book to feminist politics. But the state of feminist theory and politics is pursued in *Destabilizing Theory: Contemporary feminist debates*, edited with Anne Phillips. In an introductory chapter, they outline what they describe as a 'paradigm shift' from the feminism that characterized the 1970s to that which characterizes the 1990s. The shift has been away from the search for a structural cause of women's oppression, away from the unitary, universal category of 'woman', away from the hierarchical binary oppositions (male/female; mind/body; nature/reason) inherent in western thought, towards an assertion of the instability of female identity and the significance of differences, and towards an equality that can acknowledge differences. Along with this has been a shift 'away from the social sciences' preoccupation with things . . . towards a more cultural sensibility of the salience of words' (Barrett, 1992: 205).

In her contribution to *Destabilizing Theory*, Barrett explores the overlap between recent developments in feminism and in post-structuralism. Apart from common subject areas, what feminism and post-structuralism share is a critique of the meta-narrative, of theoretical universalism, of economic determinism, and of modernity's faith in science, rationality and truth. While, as Barrett suggests, there is no need for a wholesale abandonment of the social sciences, the shift nevertheless opens up possibilities for shaking off the old disciplinary paradigms and for searching for new and better accounts of subjectivity, identity and political agency. Again, unlike post-structuralism, what feminism offers is a humanist perspective, but one which is critical of its modernist progenitors. And feminist political strategy? Barrett and Phillips propose that 'Forging a commonality across difference now figures as a goal rather than as a given: a process . . . of engagement rather than discovery' (Barrett and Phillips, 1992: 9).

The relevance of Barrett's work to social policy

In order to examine the relevance of Barrett's work to social policy, I want to look at some of the ways in which her ideas find reflection in the development of feminist social policy, following the three thematic phases outlined above.

Women, familialism and the welfare state

In Barrett's work on women's oppression and the family (Barrett, 1980; Barrett and McIntosh, 1982), three issues – the capitalism/patriarchy debate, the importance of ideology, and the family as a site of oppression – are all developed in the earlier feminist critiques of welfare. The relationship between women's oppression and capitalism was developed around an understanding of the state. So, for example, both Elizabeth Wilson (1977) and Mary McIntosh (1978) identify the state as maintaining a particular family form (often in a contradictory way) which is primarily beneficial for capitalism, but also oppressive for women. By the mid-1980s, however, feminist social policy writers were inclined to give greater weight to the patriarchal nature of the state: Gillian Pascall (1986) for example, saw the state as meeting capital's needs, but in a predominantly patriarchal manner. Hilary Rose used a 'dualist' analysis of capitalism and patriarchy as interlocking systems to explain the welfare state – 'an accommodation between capital and a male dominated labour movement' (Rose, 1986: 81).

Rose's reference here to the role of the organized male working class in reproducing women's subordination (largely through their financial dependency) was an important part of a developing feminist critique, and is best represented by the analysis of the 'family wage' system developed in Barrett's work (1980) and elsewhere (Barrett and McIntosh, 1980). This system assumes a male-breadwinner model of the family. Not only does this model (often more myth than reality) underpin many welfare policies – especially social security – historically it has been a central plank in trade union bargaining practices. Barrett and McIntosh's analysis suggests that the system represented a coincidence of interests of the organized male working class and capital.

This analysis provided a pivotal argument in the development of feminist work on gender inequalities in social security and the critique of Beveridge (Land, 1976; Wilson, 1977), as well as uncovering the myth of the male breadwinner and the assumption that the male wage is shared equitably within the household (Pahl, 1980). It also provided the basis on which to examine critically the Marxist conceptualization of the welfare state representing a truce between the interests of capital and the working class, and the assumption of a unitariness in these interests (Williams, 1989).

If social security policies could be seen as directly upholding gender inequalities and the family form which exacerbated these, then the ideology of familialism was seen to permeate all areas of state provision – health care, education, social work, housing policy, community care policies – which, in different ways, reinforced ideologies of femininity and masculinity through their assumptions of a norm of able-bodied, heterosexual nuclear families where a woman's primary role was as housewife and carer. In this way, the welfare state played a distinctive role in the social construction of gender and the perpetuation of gender inequalities. In turning to look at the family itself and its relation to the state, feminist analysis and campaigns also converted the inequalities of the personal and the private into political issues – domestic violence, in particular, but also reproductive rights, rape and later child sexual abuse. It should be said that these campaigns which exposed the darker side of idealized family life were initiated as much, if not more, by radical feminists operating with an analysis in which it was patriarchy and patriarchal social institutions (the family, the state) which were at the heart of women's oppression, as by the 'gendered capitalist social relations' described by Barrett.

In spite of its role in reproducing gender inequalities, the welfare state was nevertheless, for the women's movement of the 1970s and 1980s, central to demands and strategies for women's emancipation. Almost all the political strategies developed in The *Anti-Social Family* focus on reforming and expanding public state provision: not only policies to create women's financial independence and sexual autonomy, but a more socialized and collectivized approach to the care of dependants (coinciding also with the cutting back on public provision). This tension between endorsing and criticizing the welfare state, explained partly by the commitment of socialist feminists to both class and gender inequalities, was reflected by a strategic tension of a different sort: whether to push for demands based on a conception of women as equal or as different. In other words, how far, by demanding immediate or short-term practical improvements in benefits and support for carers, better access to ex-husband's pensions or to maintenance for children after divorce, do we perpetuate women's financial dependency and their responsibility for caring (and incidentally the dependency of those for whom they care) and undermine arguments for longer-term equality? Indeed, how far, by demanding the socialization of women's domestic and care work, do we merely shift a private sexual division of labour to a public sexual division of labour (where women's unpaid work becomes women's low-paid work) and leave untouched the question of a more equitable distribution between men and women of domestic and emotional labour? This tension between equality and difference struck a chord in the late 1970s which was to resonate more loudly through the feminisms of the 1980s and 1990s.

Accounting for difference

The publication of *The Heart of the Race: Black women's lives in Britain* (Bryan *et al.*, 1985) expressed most clearly and directly what other black feminist writers (Carby, 1982; Amos and Parmar, 1984; Mama, 1984) had been articulating: that black women's experiences of the state and the welfare state were mediated through a shifting interrelationship of 'race', gender and class, and were historically constituted within the development not simply of gendered (and patriarchal) capitalism, but of a racially structured (or imperialist) gendered capitalism. This work and the campaigns which spawned it (against racism within education, social work and health particularly) forced a reappraisal of the history, operation and theorization of the welfare state (see Williams, 1989).

It would be wrong to overestimate the extent to which 'race' and racism have been taken on board within either feminist social policy or the discipline in general. However, within feminist social policy writing, the exploration of women's differences has developed more than in Barrett's writing. Work from disabled feminists (Morris, 1991; Begum, 1992) and writings from and about older women (Evers, 1984) have highlighted disability and age as mediators of women's experience, particularly their experiences of welfare provision (see also Langan and Day, 1993). The issue of caring which was initially explored by feminists from the perspective of the carer (caring being seen as an example of taken-for-granted and unpaid welfare work performed by women) has faced substantive critique from the perspective of those who are cared for (see Morris, 1991). It has been pointed out that such research fails to acknowledge that the majority of the people in need of care are themselves women, and that collectivist strategies aimed at providing residential care in order to relieve the carer often take no account of the interests or agency of the cared-for person.

Interestingly, this challenge to analyses of caring by disabled feminists also highlights three other issues that feature in Barrett's critical reappraisal of *Women's Oppression Today*. The first is her move away from an exclusive 'social constructionist' account of gender towards more of an engagement with biology or the reality of 'the body'. A similar development can be traced within analyses of disability. A central argument within the disability movement is that disability should be seen not as a medical condition but as a condition created by the social, economic and environmental aspects of able-bodied society. However, Jenny Morris comments:

> Such a perspective is a critical part of our demand for our needs to be treated as a civil rights issue. However there is a tendency within the social model of disability to deny the experiences of our own bodies, insisting that our physical differences and restrictions are entirely socially created ... A feminist perspective can help to redress this, and in so doing give voice to the experience of both disabled men and disabled women (Morris, 1991: 10)

The second issue raised by Barrett that this quotation illustrates is the increasing significance given to subjective experience as a guide to understanding difference. However, this issue of the significance of identity and subjectivity can also be illustrated by turning back to the feminist research on care of which Morris was critical. One way in which this research attempted to break down some of the paradigmatic limitations of the discipline was by bringing together an understanding of the material and ideological aspects of caring with a psychoanalytic understanding of the development of masculine and feminine identities. For example, Hilary Graham argues for the two areas of knowledge to be brought together to show 'that caring defines both the identity and the activity of women in Western society' (Graham, 1983: 30). Similarly, Clare Ungerson's study of carers ends with a consideration of Carol Gilligan's psychoanalytic work on the development of women's moral framework, in which 'they define themselves in a context of human relationships but also judge themselves in terms of their ability to care' (Gilligan, 1982: 17; quoted in Ungerson, 1987).

The third issue illustrates the tension around competing meanings of difference discussed by Barrett in 'The concept of difference' (1987). In this case it is the tension between difference as a form of oppression and difference as a reason for affirmative pride or celebration. The title of Jenny Morris's book is *Pride Against Prejudice* and the cover bears an illustration of a banner which reads 'Celebrate the difference'. This shift to a positive reappraisal of women's attributes was also reflected in welfare provision through the development in the 1970s and the 1980s of women-only services – run by women for women, initially outside the state or local state: refuges for women escaping domestic violence, rape crisis centres and well-woman clinics. Many of these services were characterized by principles of organization which stood in marked contrast to traditional welfare services. They attempted to be non-hierarchical, to share specialist knowledge and to offer users control. These principles can be seen, on the one hand, as an alternative to the paternalism of welfare services and, on the other, as an attempt to put into practice 'woman-centred values'.

What these developments also marked was a move towards an easing of the tension between strategies based on difference and those based on equality. For some, difference led to an exploration of the psychoanalytic theory to explain women's 'special nature'; for others, it became the focus for celebration and organization. For yet others, it represented an alternative way of life which, if taken on by malestream society, could create the conditions for equality, as Anne Phillips suggested: 'Why not a new approach? If the needs of the children do not fit with the demands of full time work, then the jobs must be changed' (Phillips, 1983: 5).

A post-structuralist feminist social policy?

So far it is clear that there were common developments in Barrett's ideas and feminist social policy. But what of feminism's turn to/overlap with post-structuralism? What of its apparent rejection of structures and material things in favour of moments, discourses and words? Where does that leave feminist social policy? If society is no longer a bounded totality, how do we understand the state? Barrett's background is in literature as well as social sciences and this enables her to ride the crest of the paradigm shift, but what of those whose bread and butter involves making sense of the General Household Survey or trends in poverty or shifts in patterns of employment?

Barrett's observation of the shift in analysis from an emphasis on things to an emphasis on words need not be read as an either/or (as has been the tendency by extreme protagonists of post-modernism or materialism or empiricism). Rather the shift can be seen to provide the possibility of a more complex inquiry into the relationship between identity, agency and welfare discourses, and how these combine in different ways to shape the materiality of people's lives. The exploration of discourses is not new to social policy (in notions of the deserving and undeserving poor, or the way discourses of motherhood intermesh with class, 'race', sexuality and disability). But what has been less common is an attempt to develop an understanding of the relationship between welfare discourses, discursive practices, forms of difference and individual action. One reason for this is that social policy's development of concepts of agency and action is fairly limited. Individuals and their welfare needs have traditionally been understood as passive objects within categories of researchers', providers' or policy-makers' own making (socio-economic groups, children at risk, disabled, old, etc). In so far as individuals' own needs and strategies have been studied, such studies have tended towards a pathological view of poverty, ill-health and so on. And while the individual pathology type of explanation has been rejected by many within the discipline of social policy, it has not been replaced by an alternative understanding of the subjective perceptions of individuals' needs and problems, and the strategies they adopt to meet or overcome these.

The political economy of welfare introduced the notion of human agency into welfare through the notion of class struggle. Subsequent feminist critiques of this perspective have refined and differentiated the understanding of agency and drawn attention to its multifaceted nature, but the notion of human action still tended to be theorized in terms of collective action.

Other feminist studies have concentrated on this question of subjectivity by investigating individual perceptions, experience and motivations, and have attempted to tie these accounts to structural forces and welfare needs. Many of these are excellent (see, for example, Evers (1984) on older women's perceptions of dependency), although unlike Graham and Ungerson's work noted earlier, they often operate theoretically only at the level of structural theory and interpretation, not at the level of a compatible theory of subjectivity. An example of a move in another direction is Janet Finch's work on *Family Obligations and Social Change* (1989). Using Giddens' structuration theory, she develops a more general theory of human action involved in the negotiations and obligations around providing family support for older kin (although her conceptualization of gender remains relatively undifferentiated).

I am suggesting that we need to understand the social positioning of individuals in both political and subjective terms, and not simply consider individuals as members of discrete administrative or methodological categories. However, just understanding this subjective meaning is not enough, at least not for social policy. We need to recognize the often conflictive relationship between the meaning given to a particular category by the forces that construct it (social, economic, environmental forces) and the meaning given to it by an individual within that category. An example from disability can illustrate this conflictive relationship. Using a questionnaire from an OPCS survey of disabled people in the UK (quoted in Martin *et al.*, 1988), Mike Oliver demonstrates how the questions reinforce an explanation of disability caused by personal or functional limitations (e.g. 'Do you have a scar, blemish or deformity which limits your daily activities?') He presents a reformulation of the questions in a way which locates the disabling process outside the individual (e.g. 'Do other people's reactions to any scar, blemish or deformity you may have limit your daily activities?') (Oliver, 1990). In this example, the focus for social policy analysis would be the relationship, or struggle, between the different and contested meanings caught up in political, administrative and subjective discourses of disability.

At the same time, the move away from binary oppositions (male/female; black/white) requires policy researchers to have a far more dynamic understanding of the social categories they study. Rather than seeing people (or indeed ourselves) as fixed within a single category, we need to be able to understand the complex interplay of social positions and identities shifting over time and space.

If we were to follow this kind of analysis, what would it mean for our understanding of the state? Given the range of differences now in play, do we add more adjectives to our description of the state – capitalist, patriarchal, etc. – constantly qualifying this with 'and contradictory'? Rosemary Pringle and Sophie Watson are two feminist writers who have attempted to draw, like Barrett, on the ideas of Laclau and Mouffe and Foucault to present an analysis of the state (Pringle and Watson, 1990, 1992). Their aim is to move away from a monolithic notion of a state with coherent policies and practices, yet to avoid a liberal pluralist view of a neutral state. This process involves jettisoning the idea of 'contradiction': 'The discourse of contradiction implies a unity of state form which then surprises us when it appears to act in unexpected ways. We argue that the state is erratic and disconnected rather than contradictory' (Pringle and Watson, 1990: 237). In these terms, then, the state is the 'site of a number of discursive functions' (1990: 237). Similarly, the effects of policies can be expected to be uneven and diverse: 'The outcomes of particular policies will depend not purely on the limits placed by "structures" but in the range of discursive practices and struggles which define and constitute the state, and specific interest groups, from one moment to the next' (1990: 237–8).

Whether such an approach which favours moments and discourses over patterns and structures might serve to obscure some of the more unambiguously oppressive practices of some states – for example, ethnic cleansing programmes – is a moot point. Nevertheless, this sort of analysis can be helpful in pointing up the complexity of conflicting forces (or 'discursive struggles') in current British social policies. Take the 1990 NHS and Community Care Act. This can be understood as the outcome of a variety of competing discursive struggles and practices: the assertion of family values and the responsibilities of families to look after their own; the assertion of carers' rights; the development of a particular type of mixed economy of the welfare sector with the residualization of the state sector and the marketization of all welfare institutions; public expenditure cuts, increased needs and increased targeting; the managerialization of welfare and of welfare professionalism; deinstitutionalization and independent living; consumer sovereignty; and welfare citizenship.

A sensitivity to the complexities of difference also raises questions about the sources available to investigate and interpret material issues. For example, in a review of research literature on the circumstances and coping strategies of mothers in low-income households, Hilary Graham draws attention to some of the limitations of the data given our greater awareness of both gender-specific inequalities and differences which cut across gender. Much of the general data eclipse 'race' (and this too may be ethnically differentiated) and other dimensions of difference, such as diverse family forms. Therefore, Graham suggests, we can present only a partial picture of patterns of survival in lower-income families: 'provisional insights, understandings in the process of revision. They are likely to be revised as the circumstances of mothers' lives change through the 1990s ... [they] are also likely to be re-worked as poverty research engages with feminist debates about diversity and difference' (Graham, 1992: 224).

Empirical research can also point to the ways in which differences can be intensified. For example, recent information on wage differentials suggests significant changes not only between women and men, but also between women themselves. Marjorie Mayo and Angela Weir (1993) suggest that these changes provide evidence of an increasing polarization between full-time, professional women, on the one hand, and women trapped in women's work which has become lower paid, part time and casualized, on the other. In addition, marriage, or specifically the creation of a two-earner professional or managerial household, sharpens these advantages (even though these advantages may be spread unequally within a household, or be of a temporary or fragile nature).

But what are the implications for welfare strategies of this emphasis upon and evidence of difference? If no fixed category of 'woman' exists, does that rule out the possibility of welfare demands that can unite women? Not necessarily, but it does highlight their more contingent nature, as Joan Scott observes:

> Political strategies will then rest on analyses of the utility of certain arguments in certain discursive contexts without, however, invoking absolute qualities for women or men. There are moments when it makes sense for mothers to demand consideration for their social role, and contexts within which motherhood is irrelevant to women's behaviour, but to maintain that motherhood is womanhood is to obscure the differences that make that choice possible. (Scott, 1992: 262–3)

In their analysis of feminist social policy, Mayo and Weir say that the exploration of diversity need not undermine the goal of commonality:

> arguing the importance of acknowledging diversity is not at all the same thing as arguing that there are no key common interests which can be shared amongst feminists with fundamentally different perspectives. On the contrary, in fact, without suggesting that there is unanimity, there would seem to be a relatively widespread agreement on a core set of social policies which relate to women's rights to legal and economic independence from men, access to jobs and training without discrimination and the right to control their own bodies and their sexuality. (Mayo and Weir, 1993: 51)

This illustrates the relevance of Barrett's point that the political and theoretical problem that we now face is how to maintain a critique of universalist pretensions without surrendering totally to particularism and difference. It also points to a central tension in the theoretical and political development of welfare policy, and not just specific to women: how to develop consensual and universal welfare policies which are diverse and not uniform, reflecting people's own perceptions of difference, yet challenging of unequal forms of differentiation (Williams, 1992). In this I agree with Anne Phillips who, while stressing the need to expose false universalism, still maintains the importance of an aspiration towards universality, for this is 'the impulse that takes us beyond our immediate and specific difference' (Phillips, 1992: 28). Indeed, some of the movements and campaigns within welfare around specific differences have also had the effect of raising more forcibly universal welfare demands, most notably the issue of transforming provider–user relations and creating democratic control of services (Williams, 1989). The exploration of this tension between the universal and the particular is also marked by the intervention of feminist social policy writers in the debate on citizenship (e.g. Lister, 1993).

The impact of feminist social policy

Finally, how far have those ideas of Barrett's which find reflection in feminist social policy influenced the wider discipline of social policy, and how far has feminism influenced policies themselves?

In terms of policy, the picture is contradictory (or uneven). As well as the legal advances of the Equal Pay Act, and the Sex Discrimination Act, and specific victories such as the granting of the Invalid Care Allowance to married women, some of the issues raised by earlier feminist research and campaigns and proposed in *The Anti-Social Family* have found their acknowledgement in mainstream policy and practice. Domestic violence, rape and child sexual abuse in particular now receive far greater acknowledgement in legal and welfare institutions than they did twenty years ago. In addition, the development of equal opportunities units and policies in local authorities and social work, education and health care has been significant, as has the development of anti-discriminatory strategies in relation to gender, 'race', disability and occasionally age and sexual orientation. In addition, attempts to restrict the accessibility of abortion have been defeated by cross-party alliances.

However, these influences need to be set against three other developments. First, there is the commitment of the New Right to 'traditional family values', illustrated by the moral panic around young single mothers (Murray, 1990) and the attempt to shift their financial dependency away from the state and back on to the fathers of their children through the 1991 Child Support Act (though it should be said that this legislation also has some feminist support for different reasons). Second, there have been attempts to discredit anti-discriminatory policies: the disempowerment of local authorities has had the effect of under-mining the units, committees and funded voluntary groups which had attempted to put anti-discriminatory and equal opportunities policies into practice. There have also been moves through the National Curriculum to replace anti-sexist and anti-racist developments with a more traditional approach. Third, the combination of an international restructuring of employment with cutbacks in public expenditure and the reorganization of welfare have all contributed to an increasing polarization between the comfortably-off and the poor. The point about these effects of socioeconomic disadvantage is that they are deeply underscored by existing gender, 'race', age and disability inequalities. In general, it could be said that feminism has had greater influence in generating those policies which address individual rights rather than those which promote collective provision or counter structural inequalities (Mayo and Weir, 1993). At the same time, social and economic changes have altered the contours of family life, particularly through the rise in lone mothers, divorce and involvement of women in the labour market, so that the needs for appropriate socialized forms of care envisaged in *The Anti-Social Family* are as necessary as ever.

In terms of the discipline, while gender and other issues of difference are now less marginalized at the empirical level in local research and area-related texts than ten years ago, there is still a gap at the conceptual level. For example, Glendinning and Millar (1992) point to ways in which the conceptualization of poverty and the subsequent data on poverty often obscure women's poverty. As far as 'race' is concerned, this invisibility still operates at both conceptual and empirical levels. Perhaps the best way of illustrating this conceptual gap is by pointing to new areas of research in the discipline.

Until recently, the theoretical core of the discipline lay in the analysis of different political approaches to welfare in the UK. By the late 1980s, feminist writers had effectively shown the failure of the theoretical core to include any reference to feminist critiques (Pascall, 1986; Williams, 1989). In the meantime, the theoretical core of the discipline has moved to a less nation-bound analysis of different welfare regimes operating within the industrialised West, best exemplified by Esping-Andersen's *Three Worlds of Welfare Capitalism* (1990). Accompanying this has been the exploration of the dimensions of a 'new welfare order' (Taylor-Gooby and Lawson, 1993) or a post-Fordist welfare state (Hoggett, 1991), or a Schumpeterian Workfare State (Jessop, 1991). All these are helpful and insightful analyses which enable us to disentangle policies of the New Right government in the UK from the impact of global economic changes, to compare these policy responses with those of other countries, and to put the organizational changes within local welfare (markets, managers, consumers, choice) into perspective. Yet, of all the works I have referenced none attempts to incorporate the sort of gendered analysis articulated by *Women's Oppression Today* into the processes it is describing. So, for example, central to Esping-Andersen's understanding of the welfare state are the concepts of 'decommodification' and 'stratification', but they are used in a way that generalizes from a male experience of production and reproduction (for critiques, see Shaver, 1990; Lewis, 1992; Orloff, 1992; see also Ginsburg, 1992, for a comparative study which brings in gender and 'race'). Jessop's analysis of the crisis of Fordism and the implications for state welfare also centres upon changes in production and class/capital relations. The notion of gender is subsumed under references to changes in the family or to an implicit future role for the 'new social movements' (for a critique, see Williams, 1994). In those studies which have initiated important work in the development of post-Fordism within the organization of welfare, the concepts of 'core', 'periphery', 'managerialism', 'markets', 'fragmentation' and 'choice' also remain profoundly ungendered – empirically, theoretically, and at the levels of both agency and structure. Yet, from what we know of the postwar welfare state, it would not be wild to suggest that social relations other than class may well be implicated in the new welfare order.

Conclusion

Michele Barrett stands as one of the major intellectual figures in British feminism. *Women's Oppression Today* was, and is, a key text for women's studies courses which developed in further and higher education from the 1970s. Her particular influence as an academic with political experience in socialist and feminist organizations is a characteristic of an important strand of British feminism. What most characterizes her work is a capacity for honest and careful reflection and, from that, an ability to develop and move on.

Barrett's work has been both timely and of its own time and place, yet sometimes it does not make for accessible reading. In some ways this is unfair criticism because these are not textbooks. However, part of the inaccessibility is to do with the fact that you have the feeling that the debates that Barrett conducts are with a close (or closed) group of fellow-travellers. This is not to say that many from the same generation are not travelling a similar journey, but it has been along different tracks. The epistemological journeys that Barrett describes do not attempt to call out to others on nearby paths – to those who have been influenced by, say, utopian socialism or anarchism, or the writings of Raymond Williams, Franz Fanon or C.L.R. James.

The more policy-oriented strategies of *The Anti-Social Family* also, I feel, suffer from a narrowness of acceptable personal strategy. Partly this can be explained in terms of time-warping (which the authors admit in their second edition). But also there is an over-attribution of change to socialist and feminist ideas, and an under-acknowledgement of some of the more complex influences on women to find ways of living other than the conventional male-breadwinner model. In addition, there was a certain irony and lack of intergenerational awareness in the calls for people to be both tolerant and accepting of diversity, but 'to avoid oppressive relationships' (which could have made hermits of most of us) and to refuse the institution of marriage. However, their analysis of the centrality of familial ideology to policy discourse is as relevant today as it was ten years ago.

It is clear that Barrett's work is important in itself and for feminist social policy. Her ability to swim so strongly in different theoretical currents makes her an important role-model for feminist writers. And because her ideas have developed from a critical or marginal position within the social sciences, they lend themelves more easily to self-criticism and to the capacity to keep pushing against the old assumptions and complacencies in knowledge. This, too, is the role of feminist social policy within its own discipline: not simply to present a particular perspective, but to keep pushing ahead with new ideas, using feminist studies as the bridge to cross into new approaches, new insights and new disciplines.

Key texts

Women's Oppression Today (1980) provides an analysis of the theoretical, historical and strategic relationship between women's oppression and capitalism. Three questions are posed at the beginning of the book. How far is women's oppression independent of capitalism? What is the relationship between the economic and ideological processes of women's oppression? Can women's emancipation be achieved within capitalism or only with its overthrow? The answers to these questions are developed, first, through an examination of the three central but most troubling and imprecise concepts in the Marxist–feminist debate – patriarchy, reproduction and ideology. This examination exposes some of the theoretical inadequacies of existing Marxist and feminist theories. On its own, the concept of patriarchy tends towards a biologism and a universalism, and cannot provide any conceptual bridge to link it to either class or capital. On the other hand, while reproduction can explain some of the ways in which women's oppression is tied into the needs of capitalism, it cannot explain all these aspects, nor can it explain why *women* are oppressed in these ways. Thus it tends towards a functionalism and an economic reductionism. While ideology seems to offer a way out, there are problems when ideology is used to explain everything and is therefore detached from the economic base, but also problems when it is seen as simply being determined by its economic base. Instead Barrett suggests that an understanding of women's oppression needs to examine and provide evidence for the historically specific ways in which it is experienced and produced at both cultural/ideological and material levels.

The book pursues this examination in six areas: the construction of femininity and its understanding in psychoanalytic thought; the production and reproduction of gender ideologies in cultural practices; gender and class divisions in education; gender inequalities in the division of labour; gender relations and the family; and the role of the state. Central to Barrett's analysis of women's oppression is an understanding of the organization of the household and the ideology of familialism. The revised edition, published in 1988, contains an introductory essay evaluating some of the ways in which significant political and theoretical developments in the 1980s changed or challenged the original discussion – particularly the issues of 'race', ethnicity and the development of post-structuralism.

The Anti-Social Family (written with Mary McIntosh, 1982) takes up the theme of the centrality of familial ideology and practice to women's oppression. While acknowledging the appeal of the family, Barrett and McIntosh present an analysis of the family as the transmitter of economic and class inequalities, as a mechanism for the creation and reproduction of gender inequalities, as a place where privacy may mean lack of freedom or vulnerability to violence and abuse, and, through its promotion as a self-sufficient unit of consumption, as a counter to the values of altruism, community and the pursuit of public good. In addition, the privileging of a particular family form (the nuclear, heterosexual, male-breadwinner family) marginalizes the needs of those increasing numbers of people – old, single, gay and lesbian – who do not belong to this idealized unit.

Their analysis also examines the dual way in which familial ideology works – both through the social construction of the 'family' and through the familialization of society in which familial meanings are attributed to non-familial events and relationships (residential or religious institutions). A final chapter elaborates strategies aimed at meeting social needs and personal desires in a less oppressive way (see above, p. 257).

In a postscript to a second edition published in 1991, the authors describe how policies through the 1980s intensified the inequalities within and between families. At the same time, the decline of the legitimacy of socialism following the break-up of Eastern Europe and the former Soviet Union means that notions such as 'collectivism' have lost their currency. Developments in feminist politics and social theory suggest greater acknowledgement be given to the interaction of 'race' and ethnicity with issues of familial ideology and practice. Finally, they propose that Foucault's analysis of the discursive construction of things by words offers a helpful framework for a deconstruction of 'the family' and an understanding of familial ideology.

Foucault is a key player in *The Politics of Truth: From Marx to Foucault* (1991). Here Barrett revisits the problem which worries its way through *Women's Oppression Today*: the concept of ideology and its usefulness in explaining social oppression. She dissects and examines the use of ideology by a variety of Marxist and post-Marxist philosophers (Marx, Lukács, Gramsci, Althusser, Derrida, Laclau, Mouffe and Foucault) and concludes that the concept is too tied to a class-determinist model to be helpful in the analysis of social inequalities. In addition, the understanding of ideology as 'the mystification that serves class interests' implicitly posits the existence of a real knowledge, or truth, which ideology mystifies. These problems take Barrett through an unresolved discussion of agency and subjectivity in Marxism and psychoanalysis and towards an appreciation of Foucauldian theories of knowledge and power as more fruitful tools of analysis.

Acknowledgement

I am very grateful to John Clarke, Bob Deacon, Hilary Graham and Ruth Lister for their pertinent comments to a first draft of this chapter.

References

Amos, V. and Parmar, P. (1984) 'Challenging imperial feminism', *Feminist Review*, 17, pp. 3–19.
Barrett, M. (ed.) (1979) *Virginia Woolf: Women and writing*, London: The Women's Press.

Barrett, M. (1980) *Women's Oppression Today: Problems in Marxist feminist analysis*, London: Verso.

Barrett, M. (1987) 'The concept of difference', *Feminist Review*, 26, pp. 29–41.

Barrett, M. (1988) *Women's Oppression Today: The Marxist/Feminist Encounter* (2nd edn), London: Verso.

Barrett, M. (1991) *The Politics of Truth: From Marx to Foucault*, Cambridge: Polity.

Barrett, M. (1992) 'Words and things: materialism and method in contemporary feminist analysis', in Barrett and Phillips (1992).

Barrett, M. and Hamilton, R. (eds) (1986) *The Politics of Diversity: Feminism, Marxism and nationalism*, London: Verso.

Barrett, M. and McIntosh, M. (1980) 'The family wage: some problems for social feminists', *Capital and Class*, 11, pp. 51–72.

Barrett, M. and McIntosh, M. (1982) *The Anti-Social Family*, London: Verso.

Barrett, M. and McIntosh, M. (1985) 'Ethnocentricism and socialist-feminist theory', *Feminist Review*, 20, pp. 23–47.

Barrett, M. and McIntosh, M. (1991) *The Anti-Social Family* (2nd edn), London: Verso.

Barrett, M. and Phillips, A. (eds) (1992) *Destabilizing Theory: Contemporary feminist debates*, Cambridge: Polity.

Barrett, M., Corrigan, P., Kuhn, A., and Wolff, J. (1979) *Ideology and Cultural Production*, London: Croom Helm.

Begum, N. (1992) 'Disabled women and the feminist agenda', *Feminist Review*, 40, pp. 70–84.

Bhavnani, K. and Coulson, M. (1986) 'Transforming socialist-feminism: the challenge of racism', *Feminist Review*, 40, pp. 81–92.

Bryan, B., Dadzie, S. and Scafe, S. (1985) *The Heart of the Race: Black women's lives in Britain*, London: Virago

Carby, H. (1982) 'White woman listen! Black feminism and the boundaries of sisterhood', in Centre for Contemporary Cultural Studies (eds), *The Empire Strikes Back*, London: Hutchinson.

Esping-Andersen, G. (1990) *The Three Worlds of Welfare Capitalism*, Cambridge: Polity.

Evers, H. (1984) 'Old women's self-perceptions of dependency and some implications for service provision', *Journal of Epidemiology and Community Health*, 38, 4, pp. 306–9.

Finch, J. (1989) *Family Obligations and Social Change*, Cambridge: Polity.

Gilligan, C. (1982) *In a Different Voice: Psychological theory and women's development*, Cambridge, Mass.: Harvard University Press.

Ginsburg, N. (1992) *Divisions of Welfare*, London: Sage.

Glendinning, C. and Millar, J. (eds) (1992) *Women and Poverty in Britain in the 1990s*, Hemel Hempstead: Harvester Wheatsheaf.

Graham, H. (1983) 'Caring: a labour of love', in Finch, J. and Groves D. (eds), *A Labour of Love: Women, work and caring*, London: Routledge and Kegan Paul.

Graham, H. (1992) 'Budgeting for health: mothers in low-income households', in Glendinning and Millar (1992).

Hoggett, P. (1991) 'A new management in the public sector', *Policy and Politics*, 19, 4, pp. 243–56.

Jessop, B. (1991) 'The welfare state in the transition from Fordism to post-Fordism', in Jessop, B. *et al.* (eds), *The Politics of Flexibility*, Aldershot: Edward Elgar.

Land, H. (1976) 'Women: supporters or supported?', in Allen, S. and Barker, D. (eds), *Sexual Divisions and Society*, London: Tavistock.

Langan, M. and Day, L. (1993) *Women, Oppression and Social Work*, London: Routledge.

Lewis, J. (1992) 'Gender and the development of welfare regimes', *Journal of European Social Policy*, **2**, 3, pp. 159–73.

Lister, R. (1993) 'Tracing the contours of women's citizenship', *Policy and Politics*, **21**, 1, pp. 3–16.

Mama, A. (1984) 'Black women, the economic crisis and the state', *Feminist Review*, 17, pp. 3–20.

Martin, J., Meltzer, H. and Elliot, D. (1988) *The Prevalence of Disability Among Adults*, London: Gower.

Mayo, M. and Weir, A. (1993) 'The future for feminist social policy', in Page, R. and Baldock, J. (eds), *Social Policy Review 5*, Canterbury: Social Policy Association.

McIntosh, M. (1978) 'The state and the oppression of women', in Kuhn, A. and Wolfe, A. (eds), *Feminism and Materialism*, London: Routledge and Kegan Paul.

Morris, J. (1991) *Pride Against Prejudice: Transforming attitudes to disability*, London: The Women's Press.

Murray, C. (1990) *The Emerging British Underclass*, London: Institute of Economic Affairs.

Oliver, M. (1990) *The Politics of Disablement*, London: Macmillan.

Orloff, A.S. (1992) 'Gender and the social rights of citizenship: state policies and gender relations in comparative perspective', paper presented to the Conference on Comparative Studies of Welfare State Development, Bremen.

Pahl, J. (1980) 'Patterns of money management within marriage', *Journal of Social Policy*, **9**, 3, pp. 313–335.

Pascall, G. (1986) *Social Policy: A feminist analysis*, London: Tavistock.

Phillips, A. (1983) *Hidden Hands: Women and economic policies*, London: Pluto.

Pringle, R. and Watson, S. (1990) 'Fathers, brothers, mates: the fraternal state in Australia', in Watson, S. (ed.), *Playing the State: Australian feminist interventions*, London: Verso.

Pringle, R. and Watson, S. (1992) ' "Women's interests" and the post-structuralist state', in Barrett and Phillips (1992).

Rose, H. (1986) 'Women and the restructuring of the welfare state', in Owen, E. (ed.), *Comparing Welfare States and their Futures*, Aldershot: Gower.

Scott, J.W. (1992) 'Deconstructing equality-versus-difference: or, the uses of post-structuralist theory for feminism', in L. McDowell and R. Pringle (eds), *Defining Women: Social Institutions and Gender Divisions*, Cambridge: Polity.

Shaver, S. (1990) *Gender, Social Policy Regimes and the Welfare State*, Social Policy Research Discussion Paper, No. 26, University of New South Wales, Australia.

Taylor-Gooby, P. and Lawson, R. (1993) *Markets and Managers: New issues in the delivery of welfare*, Milton Keynes: Open University Press.

Ungerson, C. (1987) *Policy is Personal: Sex, gender and informal care*, London: Tavistock.

Williams, F. (1989) *Social Policy: A critical introduction*, Cambridge: Polity.

Williams, F. (1992) 'Somewhere over the rainbow: universality and diversity in social policy', in Manning, N. and Page, R. (eds), *Social Policy Review 4*, Canterbury: Social Policy Association.

Williams, F. (1994) 'Social relations and the post-Fordism debate', in Burrows, R. and Loader, B. (eds), *Towards a Post-Fordist Welfare State?*, London: Routledge.

Wilson, E. (1977) *Women and the Welfare State*, London: Tavistock.

Part VI

Post-industrial Greens

Introduction

Greenism comes in two contrasting shades: light versus dark or shallow versus deep greenism. Light greenism is now generally acceptable to all types of governments, to industry and business, and to the general public. Its main message is that increased economic growth and consumption are to be encouraged, but they must be pursued in environmentally friendly ways. Consumerism as a way of life is here to stay, but it must, as far as possible, take into account the needs of the environment. Dark greenism finds this message unacceptable, for it believes that it is not possible to emphasize both increased economic growth and environmental protection. The two are mutually exclusive. However much one tries, increased consumerism will destroy the environment. Only modest rates of economic growth and consumption are compatible with the safeguard of the environment. Indeed, advanced industrial societies already exhibit unacceptably high rates of consumption, although, of course, this is not the case with the Third World, which harbours three-quarters of the world's total population and where consumption is often below physiological requirements. Dark greenism is not only different from light greenism, but its central message is in conflict with that of all other ideologies discussed in this book, for they all value increased rates of economic growth, although they disagree on the methods of distribution.

It is with dark greenism that we are concerned here and, before we examine its main claims, it is worth looking briefly at its two main divisions. The first brand of dark greenism, usually referred to as deep ecology, considers animal and sometimes plant life as being of equal worth as human life. It, therefore, rejects anthropocentrism of any kind, and its adherents are quite willing to defend nature, violently if necessary, against human actions that they consider unacceptable. The second main brand of dark greenism, known as social ecology and best represented by Bookchin, takes into account social factors both in the ways that they affect the environment and in the ways in which society should be organized in order to achieve green objectives. It emphasizes equality, non-hierarchical structures and public participation as the hallmarks of a green society based on modest levels of consumption. While, for example, deep ecology blames all humans for pollution, social ecology will attribute it mostly to institutions, business and profit making.

Current rates of economic growth, according to dark greenism, pose several interrelated threats to the survival of the planet. First, there is the real danger that both renewable and non-renewable resources will be exhausted at some time in the future. It is simply not possible, for example, to provide every family in the world with one car, let alone two, without running the oil fields dry. Even water, a renewable resource, may prove insufficient if current rates of use by agriculture, families and tourists continue unabated.

Second, current methods of production pollute, in both direct and indirect ways, the environment – the soil, the rivers, the lakes, the seas and the atmosphere – with detrimental consequences for the survival of the planet. The depletion of the ozone layer, acid rain and global warming are three vivid examples of the threat that the planet is under from current rates and methods of production. Others may well be in store and a prime suspect is the storing of nuclear waste in the oceans and the earth. Greens find the reassurances of the nuclear industry too weak to take seriously.

Third, the insistence of the affluent world to carry on consuming regardless sends a clear message to the governments of the Third World that they have a duty to go for fast rates of economic growth so as to improve the living standards of their people. It is no surprise, for example, that Third World governments find the pleas of the rich world to save Third World forests for the benefit of humankind as nothing more than outright hypocrisy and a concealed form of eco-imperialism, since the latter rejects any serious proposals for redistribution of resources.

Fourth, intensive exploitation of the planet has destroyed and will continue to destroy many species of animal and plant life. This is unacceptable not only in economic self-interest terms, but for ethical reasons as well. Many, though not all, dark greens maintain that the animal world has as much right to be on this planet as humans. They reject current forms of industrial and agricultural production as anthropocentric, for they place the welfare of humans always above that of the animal world.

These and other threats to the planet cannot, according to the dark greens, be avoided by technological fixes. Some of these threats, such as the extinction of the animal world, can be avoided only by radical changes in attitudes and lifestyle. Others may well be avoided by improved technology, but in so doing other current threats to the environment are exacerbated and new threats may be created. There are also instances where it is impossible to know how much technology can do, although greens are, on the whole, not very hopeful.

This mounting pressure on world resources is exacerbated by current rates of population growth. It is, therefore, imperative that they be reduced substantially, not only in Third World but in other countries as well.

The two authors we have chosen for this section belong to the social ecology school, and more particularly to its post-industrial wing. Their major message is that the current division between paid employment and other types of equally useful but unpaid work is dehumanizing and unsustainable. Technological advances will create high rates of unemployment for which there is no humane solution under orthodox economic strategies, whether of the Keynesian or the monetarist kind. The only lasting sustainable solution is to recognize all types of useful work and to provide payment for them of a fairly egalitarian type.

All radical ideologies face the problem of how to find general support for their messages. Greenism faces this problem more acutely than other ideologies, for its utopia is so much at variance with current ways of life. Green political parties in affluent countries have thus had to moderate their message in order to gain popular support. It is for the same reason that many committed Greens have left green parties in outrage. Judging from the experience of the past twenty years, the general public has no appetite for the dark green view that only reduced rates of production and consumption are sustainable, or for the views of the post-industrials on work and remuneration. The affluent public favours the light green view that we can continue consuming as much as we can afford and still save the environment. It is a much more comfortable message because it allows the affluent to have their cake and eat it! For the general public in the Third World, concern for green issues is a luxury it can ill afford, for it has a much more pressing problem – how to scrape a living.

16 Gorz

Michael Kenny and Adrian Little

Brief biography

Born in Austria in 1924, Gorz's earliest intellectual influence was Sartrean existentialism, which he imbibed in postwar Paris. Here he was also introduced to the work of Hegel and Marx. In 1961 Sartre appointed him political editor of the journal *Les Temps Modernes* (Davies, 1988). From this platform he became a well-known journalist on the French left and a leading strategist for an increasingly militant workers' movement.

Like Sartre, Gorz was disillusioned by the failure of the workers' and students' uprising of May 1968, and was particularly discouraged by the hostility towards the insurgents of the French left, most of all from the Communist Party. Thereafter he broadened his political perspective, advocating a strategy of workers' control through factory councils and focusing his analytical attention on the process of production (Gorz, 1976). In the 1970s, the ecological crisis increasingly absorbed his intellectual energies. Like many former New Left activists, Gorz turned to the environmentalist movement as an alternative source of radical political vision.

Gorz has consistently eschewed formal political allegiances, continuing to work, until the mid-1980s, as a journalist and critical observer of political events and social change. He now lives in the heart of the Burgundy countryside, from where he continues to produce stimulating analysis of French politics, the changing labour process and environmental degradation.

Social theory

Gorz's distinctive contribution to social theory stems from his critique of the Marxist tradition, his interest in the nature of the labour process within capitalism, and his emphasis upon the emancipation of the individual. These commitments have shaped his theoretical work, which has ranged widely across the social and political terrain. In this section, the following themes will be elaborated: his concept of the neo-proletariat within contemporary society; his interest in technology, particularly the possibilities it offers of a reduction in labour time; his division of social activities into distinct spheres of social action, and the implications of his celebration of one of these spheres (autonomy) as the platform for an emancipated society; his analysis of the logic of economic reason, the spread of which constitutes the principal obstacle to radical social change; and his imaginative fusion of socialist and ecological ideas.

Gorz's immanent critique of the classical Marxist tradition constitutes the starting point for any analysis of his ideas. His recent work reveals how far he has moved from this perspective, although he retains the use of some Marxist concepts. In *Farewell to the Working Class* (1987b), he surveyed class relations in advanced capitalist societies and questioned the Marxist emphasis upon the industrial proletariat as the single revolutionary subject. He highlighted the existence of different constituencies within contemporary society which were already detached from the ethos of the industrial process and therefore more likely to rebel against the dictates of the existing economic system. For Gorz, the existence and size of this grouping – the neo-proletariat (the 'non-class of non-workers' (Gorz, 1987b: 66–74)) – illustrated the limitations of the Marxian emphasis upon proletarian consciousness. This tradition failed to address the social diversity and complexity of contemporary society. The 'neo-proletariat', made up of the long-term unemployed and those employed on a casual and/or part-time basis, as well as the young and elderly, did not constitute a class in the Marxist sense. Socialism was therefore inadequate in its interpretaion of the contemporary social structure, and misguided in its perception of the proletariat as the primary agent of social emancipation. Gorz turned instead to the emergence of new social and political movements – the women's movement, the environmentalist lobby and tenants' groups, among others – as vehicles for the articulation of the interests and outlook of these marginalized and dispossessed groups.

The work process in advanced capitalism has provided the key site for the development of Gorz's critique of Marxian ideas. The evolution of his thought encapsulates the analytical shift among Marxist theorists, over the last thirty years, from an ethic of collective proletarian liberation in the sphere of production to concern for the microsocial relations of the workplace and a recognition of the importance of other spheres of social life. In *Strategy for Labour* (1964), he argued for a system of worker self-management as central to the socialist case. After 1964, as he turned to consider the production process in more detail, he began to stress the emancipatory potential of modern technology. If the ethos behind the contemporary industrial system was replaced by one of co-operation and mutual support, technology could be put to more socially beneficial uses (Gorz, 1989a: 87–8). In particular, technology promised to reduce dramatically the amount of socially necessary labour undertaken by the individual. Without the accompanying shift in culture and social organization which he advocated, however, Gorz foresaw technology contributing to social degeneration and more acute division. He identified the dominant trends within the economies of advanced capitalism towards the 'creation of an increasing pool of long-term unemployed workers juxtaposed against a diminishing élite of skilled workers. More recently he has stressed that full employment is an impossible goal in advanced capitalist societies, as it runs counter to the dominant trends of the contemporary economy (Gorz, 1989a).

In his later work, Gorz has developed these conclusions in a more concrete fashion. He now celebrates the subversive potential of the development of free time, and has attempted to categorize the tasks that individuals perform within different spheres of social action as the basis for an alternative society (Gorz, 1989b). His analysis of current trends critically informs his projection of a possible future.

He has divided individual activities into three separate realms of social activity:

1. *Macrosocial activity*. This area encompasses all the work that individuals must perform to ensure the well-being of society. This is the realm of heteronomous necessity, and includes a variety of largely unpleasant tasks from which individuals derive little satisfaction. Recognizing that this realm cannot be wholly abolished, he suggests that macrosocial tasks should be shared as equitably as possible among adults, thereby minimizing the impact of such heteronomous activity upon individual lives. Indeed, individuals should determine when they perform this labour, having only to dedicate a certain number of hours over the course of their lifetime.

2. *Microsocial activity*. This sphere involves individual 'work for oneself'. Recognizing that individuals perform many tasks in the process of self-mainten-ance – cleaning, cooking and child care, for instance – Gorz suggests that these activities should be performed by the individuals whom they affect most directly. He therefore rules out the employment of others to perform one's own domestic and menial tasks.

3. *Autonomous activity*. This realm is paramount for Gorz and needs to be elevated in status above macro- and microsocial activity. Autonomous activity consists of freely ordained deeds in the pursuit of the satisfaction of the wide variety of fundamental human needs – creative, cultural, aesthetic and erotic. These needs transcend those of mere survival. He suggests that the realm of autonomy should dictate the organization of human time, so that individuals are temporally free to dedicate themselves to the development of their own particular mode of autonomous expression (Gorz, 1989a: 164–9).

At present, these spheres are neither clearly delineated nor balanced in a socially acceptable manner. Within advanced capitalism, the realm of necessity, the macrosocial sphere, dominates the autonomous lives of individuals. Mean-while, many microsocial tasks, such as child care, are commodified and hence turned into labour for a wage in the macrosocial sphere. An emancipated society,

Gorz argues, would be based upon the separation of these spheres and supported by a guaranteed minimum income. Assured of an income over the course of their lifetime, individuals could prioritize the satisfaction of existential needs, freed from the burdens of heteronomous activity. Above all, they could organize their time and activity autonomously, outside the dictates of economic reason (Gorz, 1992).

Economic reason, for Gorz, describes the process whereby the logic of growth, accumulation and individual consumption increasingly dominate the life-world of individuals (Habermas, 1987). This logic provides the dominant framework for policy formation in nearly all aspects of social existence, even in 'religious, ethical or existential matters' (Gorz, 1989b: 3) where its functioning is, in his view, singularly inappropriate. He continues to assert that many aspects of life cannot be reduced to the terms of cost/benefit analysis, or quantified a market exchange. Human need and social well-being constitute the ethical foundations for his rejection of the dominant order and advocacy of an alternative future.

Gorz's break with Marxism can be traced back to his early intellectual development. He has always prioritized concern for individual emancipation above other goals, such as proletarian liberation. This theme provides much of his analytical originality. Inherited from his existentialist forebears, the liberation of the individual works as an organizing principle for many of his political ideas, leading him to view social liberation as dependent upon the analytically prior goal of individual autonomy. Significantly, while the environmentalist dimension of his thinking has become more pronounced since the mid-1970s, Gorz has retained the belief that the liberation of nature depends upon the emancipation of the individual (Hirsch, 1982: 227).

His fusion of socialist and ecological arguments prefigured the arrival of red/green political alliances throughout western Europe in the 1980s. While Gorz has challenged the left to recognize the enormity and salience of the environmental crisis facing modern industrial society, he has also confronted ecologists with uncomfortable ideas. Refusing to prioritize nature over humanity, Gorz attempted to synthesize the existentialist concern for individual emancipation and the holistic outlook of ecology (Gorz, 1987a). This singular combination explains why his ideas sit uneasily with other political orthodoxies. He has come to view the processes of technology and automation as potentially emancipatory, for instance, because these might liberate the time of individuals and eradicate overproduction. This argument runs counter to the belief of many Greens that technology constitutes an epiphenomenal manifestation of the central drives of industrial society (Dobson, 1990: 97–102).

Gorz's distinctive contribution to social theory is the product of his radical interpretation of contemporary society and picture of a more environmentally secure and socially equitable future. The integration of the goal of individual autonomy with the social and ecological dimensions of human existence constitutes the most fruitful and troubling dimension of his theoretical project.

Gorz and welfare

Gorz is not primarily a theorist of welfare. His ideas do have implications, however, for a number of different social fields. His theoretical concerns lead him to reject both the Keynesian policy framework and the standard model of welfare provision in western Europe. These positions have occasionally led him to focus on specific aspects of social policy, and to intervene within debates about welfare provision.

In general terms, he rejects the welfare state as an appropriate model for securing social equity and equality, reiterating the Marxist claim that it is ultimately 'aimed at correcting and smoothing the workings of capitalist economies' (Gorz, 1987c: 5). He believes, like several thinkers of the New Right, that the welfare state undermines individual self-reliance and autonomy, resulting in a culture of dependency upon the state.

This perspective inspired one of his theoretical ventures into the realm of social policy, an assessment of the workings of the medical profession (Gorz, 1987a: 149–91). His analysis of this particular field highlights many of the key themes within his social and political thought. Drawing upon the work of the American theorist Ivan Illich (1976), Gorz subjected modern medicine to a swingeing critique several years before medical provision and the hierarchical structure of the welfare state became a major issue for the left. Gorz argued that the major causes of death and disease in advanced capitalist societies are associated with the specific social and environmental conditions which predominate in these countries. Despite their relatively abundant resources, medical practitioners in the developed world have been unable to prevent or cure these maladies. In fact, 'by treating illnesses as accidental and individual anomalies, medicine masks their structural reason, which are [*sic*] social, economic, and political. It becomes a technique for making us accept the unacceptable' (Gorz, 1987a: 150).

According to Gorz, medicine functions, paradoxically, to accentuate the dependency of the population on experts and specialists. This dependency undermines individual autonomy in the realm of self and communal care. Relying so heavily on medical expertise lowers the illness threshold of society as a whole. Dependency is further reinforced by the arrogation of resources for care by the medical profession, buttressed by the state. The everyday discourses of health, in which luck and accident are stressed more strongly than social background and economic resources, further legitimate the role of the doctor as the dispenser from above of expert advice and medical resources.

Gorz therefore emphasizes the notion of individual hygiene as the key to the maintenance of health. Individuals must be allowed to take responsibility for their own well-being, following the dissemination of medical knowledge throughout the population. While he does not envisage the complete abolition of the institutions of medical care, Gorz believes that illnesses which are perceived as curable only by particular medicines could be treated or prevented within the community, without the involvement of specialist professionals.

Medicine, he asserts, can accentuate illnesses rather than curing them, because it 'forgets that in the final analysis people are damaged in body and soul by our way of life' (1987a: 152). Illness is as much an existential as a biological problem. Reliance on external authorities prevents the individual from coming to terms with physical and biological existence. The nodal points of life – sexuality, birth, pregnancy – have been ruthlessly medicalized. Somewhat dramatically he contends that:

> Those in charge of this intervention have persuaded people that in order to live, survive, get well, or bear their illnesses, they need to live inside a kind of therapeutic bubble in which they are drugged, antisepticized, tranquilised, stimulated, regulated, and permanently controlled. (1987a: 160)

The problems facing the welfare state will not be solved by the provision of more resources or the more careful allocation of those already present. Gorz calls instead for a fundamental shift in conceptions of health policy. The myths of medicine need to be laid bare and expertise challenged. Doctors, for instance, should be encouraged to take a more critical approach to pharmaceutical products. Emphasis should be shifted from insurance for medical care to the adoption of working and living conditions which obviate medical treatment (1987a: 166).

At present, medical practitioners deal with individuals whose problems arise because they are unable to play their 'normal' role in society. Yet the system which allots this role causes existential, and hence physiological, anxiety because it is incapable of satisfying the real needs of these individuals. Gorz therefore advocates a fundamental shift in the rationale of medicine. Doctors should become 'enablers' within the community, aiming to make individuals as self-reliant as possible in matters of health. Ultimately, the attainment of a healthy society will require the abolition of work for wages. Time and needs must be liberated from the technical interest of advanced capitalism (Habermas 1976), so that individuals can regain control of all aspects of their lives, in particular their bodies. Only through a new politics of time can individuals assume responsibility for their own hygiene and seek to redress the wider social and political forces that foster a society of ill-health.

These ideas illustrate the uneven and unconventional nature of Gorz's theorizing particularly well. Combining theoretical elaboration with occasional empirical reference, he develops a cogent reading of this area of social policy in line with his distinctive theoretical principles. Compared with other critical theorists, Gorz refers far more frequently to concrete social behaviour. This gives his work a less cohesive philosophical appearance and has resulted in the, sometimes inaccurate, appropriation of his ideas by specialists in the different policy fields he addresses. In the case of medical provision, many of his ideas have since achieved mainstream status in debates about community care.

Gorz also believes that the welfare states of western Europe constitute failed responses to the crises experienced by the political and economic regimes in these countries. Like Habermas (1976) and Offe (1984), he views the advent of welfarism as an indication of a deepening of these crises as well as an attempt to sustain the legitimacy of advanced capitalism. The welfare state was designed to bolster economic growth after the Second World War and to redistribute economic resources across different social classes. In particular, welfare was intended to support the income levels of the working population, a key element in the strategy for economic growth. Yet welfare capitalism has failed to sustain growth largely because of contradictions within the system of personal consumption that it fosters. For Gorz, individual consumption fails to address the social needs of individuals and generates a number of adverse environmental consequences:

> the system was not able to meet those basic needs which cannot express themselves as effective individual demand for purchasable goods and services, or which originate precisely in the growth of individual consumption: the need for breathable air, living space, light, silence, drinking water, prevention of illness, preservation or reproduction of natural resources, good public transport, time, meaningful work and opportunities to use disposable time meaningfully. (Gorz, 1987c: 6)

Modern welfare policies are therefore inextricably linked to the contemporary economic system and ethos of growth. This connection undermines the welfare state on several grounds. First, the institutions of welfare co-exist uneasily with the contemporary, technical division of labour. This process involves the widening gap between a skilled élite of workers, on the one hand, and the unskilled and deskilled majority, on the other. For the former group, the disparity between the high levels of technological expertise they acquire but cannot employ outside the workplace leads to frustration and disillusion, thereby further undermining the political and social system. This divisive process, the 'South Africanization' of society (Gorz, 1989a: 71, 205), renders the provision of health policy on a universalist and egalitarian basis increasingly difficult. Second, welfare institutions, the health services especially, have been affected by the changing age profile of the population, the increase in the numbers of the long-term unemployed, and the fiscal crises which developed in the polities of western Europe in the late 1970s (Gorz, 1987c: 7). These developments sap the resources of the welfare state. As the overall number of workers shrinks, so does the tax base of the nation and, consequently, the resources available to sustain existing levels of personal consumption.

Therefore he concludes that the left needs to present an alternative programme for welfare, developed outside the framework of neo-Keynesian policy and committed to detaching social policy from economic reason (Gorz, 1989a). A key part of this strategy involves the provision of a minimum wage. While some commentators view a basic income as a means of shoring up consumption levels in the face of the social and economic crisis that Gorz identifies, he supports it for very different reasons. In particular, he envisages a social wage which would be paid to individuals in return for their performance of an agreed amount of labour over the course of their lifetime. Each individual would decide when they would perform this labour, without loss of income during periods when they choose not to work (Gorz, 1992).

Gorz remains adamant that his vision runs counter to conservative and neo-liberal versions of the basic income (Gorz, 1985: 40–2). While some thinkers from the latter tradition envisage the replacement of existing social and collectivist institutions by the basic income, he regards the social wage as a way of alleviating divisions within contemporary society and introducing autonomy into the expanded social sphere. This income would be set at a rate well above mere subsistence, providing the means for the satisfaction of basic needs and the pursuit of autonomy. Individuals may, for instance, choose to work to supplement this income, although extra income would be taxed at a high rate. The social wage ensures that, unlike the present system, all individuals are socially inserted into civil society and can achieve a measure of respect and identity in the public sphere (Gorz, 1992: 182). Anticipating accusations of utopianism, he has attempted to quantify this vision, arriving at a figure of between twenty and thirty thousand hours of socially necessary labour over each individual's lifetime (Gorz, 1989a: 210).

In terms of welfare, this programme would free individual time for the benefit of the community. It would encourage the deprofessionalization of a whole series of activities, health care especially (Illich, 1976). As individuals rediscover the time and space to take an interest in those around them, and provide care if necessary, social fragmentation and individual alienation would be directly redressed. A central feature of this process, according to Gorz, involves the replacement of many of the functions of the institutions of welfare by voluntary community services, unburdened by the bureaucracy of the welfare state and more cost-effective in their delivery of assistance (Gorz, 1992: 180). Gorz's perspective, shared by other radical social theorists (Stoesz and Midgley, 1991: 30), approximates most closely to the New Right on this point, as critics have observed (Sayers, 1991). He remains distinct from neo-liberals, however, by insisting on a role for the state in funding and overseeing the work of voluntary organizations, and maintaining that a shift to voluntary provision must be accompanied by a reduction in the individual's work time (Gorz, 1989: 232–6).

Responding to the criticisms that his system would inevitably involve cumbersome bureaucratic regulation and be practically impossible to implement, Gorz concedes that the construction of this post-industrial society will require a decade at least. His 'transitional period' involves the gradual reduction in working time and the institution of the social wage. These changes would form part of a larger social plan with targets which are 'no less feasible than setting target dates for new and more stringent pollution standards in industry and transport' (Gorz, 1987c: 11). This plan would also involve training and education to ensure that individuals are equipped to exercise their autonomy. Working time would be gradually reduced, beginning with a system of job sharing. The basic income would be funded by a taxation system operating in a similar fashion to value added tax: a levy would be imposed on goods in inverse proportion to their social and environmental usefulness (1987c: 14). Here the ecological dimension of his thinking is apparent; he calls, for instance, for the construction of durable domestic appliances which would be replaced more rarely (1987c: 15).

On the practical level, this scheme is problematic. Critics have pointed out the unfeasibility of these proposals on a number of grounds, not least because they obscure the difficulty of mobilizing popular support for such a radical shift in lifestyle and experience. The suspicion remains, for some commentators, that despite Gorz's celebration of individual autonomy, the conditions under which his vision of autonomy can be pursued may be created only by a *dirigiste* state. In this context, the authoritarian undertone of his most specific picture of post-industrial society, his fictional sketch in *Ecology as Politics* (Gorz, 1987a: 42-50), may be significant.

Yet the implications of Gorz's ideas elude a purely literal reading of his programme for radical social change. Indeed, his fictional sketch has been overemphasized and misread by commentators (Keane, 1987: 85-7). For Gorz, contemporary society provides an unstable and untenable environment for individuals faced with difficult life-choices and wrestling with their existential dilemmas. He attempts, therefore, to challenge the social assumptions of his readers by presenting a vision of an alternative future, thereby enabling critical reflection upon present circumstances. His 'utopian' theorizing is thus motivated by the wish to overturn present realities and the belief that change will occur when individuals are no longer intellectually and morally constrained by contemporary society. His uneven and idiosyncratic thought is best understood as an attempt to unshackle the imagination of his audience (Geoghegan, 1987: 128).

In terms of social policy and the agenda of welfare, Gorz proffered a radical critique of the framework of Keynesianism at a moment when few on the left challenged the assumptions of this system. He anticipated, moreover, the crisis and dissolution of the Keynesian consensus within western Europe, warning socialists of the need to rethink their political ideas even though they were, on the whole, unwilling to listen. Given the tacit acceptance by the political élites in many countries that unemployment is now a permanent feature of economic life, the erosion of the universalist ethos which inspired the foundation of welfare systems, and the increased levels of criticism of professional bodies and bureaucracies, his ideas have proved remarkably prophetic. Above all, he attempted to occupy the political space which the New Right colonized in the late 1970s with his social critique and sketched alternative. Ironically, the hegemony of neo-liberal ideas and policies, which he opposed vehemently, rendered his ideas more topical and influential than ever before.

Impact on welfare policy

Gorz's ideas have had little direct impact upon policy formation in the realm of welfare, yet he has influenced the thinking of Greens and, more recently, social democrats on several related questions. More generally, he has contributed to the rethinking of welfare on the left by challenging the assumptions of the Keynesian policy framework.

Several of Gorz's critics have suggested that his greatest impact, in policy terms, lay in preparing the ground for the ideological onslaught unleashed by the New Right on the welfare state in the late 1970s (Sayers, 1991). Clearly, the comparison between his ideas and those of neo-liberals is controversial. It is supported by his hostility to the state provision of social goods and his concern for the individual in modern society. In Gorz's view, collectivist policies deny human autonomy, reproduce capitalist imperatives through the public sector of the economy, and ensure that key areas of human existence, such as health care, are subjected to the tyranny of self-interested and élite professional groups. His celebration of voluntary activity in this sector resembles the policy recommendations of thinkers such as Hayek and Friedman (Stoesz and Midgley, 1991: 37–8).

On closer inspection, this similarity recedes. Whereas Hayek opposed state planning and the universal provision of social and economic goods on the grounds that they encroached upon the rule of law, interfered with the process of spontaneous social evolution, and incorporated a dangerous commitment to equality (Barry, 1979; Tomlinson 1990), Gorz has criticized the social goals embodied in the welfare state for their limited nature. Real social emancipation involves provision for the flourishing of individual autonomy in conditions guaranteed by the state. Consequently, individuals should be released from the need to participate in the market if they so desire, in order to commit themselves voluntarily to working for others as well as to their own autonomous activity. This vision involves the state provision of a social wage and the overseeing of the dualization of society, combined with individual participation in social tasks (such as health, education and nursing) and autonomous activity. In this sense, it differs fundamentally from the New Right's outlook. However, both projects can be seen as responses to the unfolding crisis of welfare economics and the erosion of the social and political assumptions which underwrote western European societies after the Second World War. Gorz approximates to the New Right because of the vehemence of his rejection, from the early 1970s, of Keynesian ideas.

He is by no means the only radical theorist to pursue these themes. Claus Offe, in particular, has been more rigorous in theorizing the role played by the state in advanced capitalism. On the basis of his analysis of the capitalist state's attempt to secure the goals of capital accumulation and bourgeois legitimation, Offe has increasingly viewed welfare as an inherently contradictory component of the state's strategy of crisis management. This political crisis is manifest in three areas: 'a fiscal crisis of the state, a crisis of administrative rationality, and a crisis of mass loyalty' (Jessop, 1982: 109). It can be resolved in various ways, most obviously through the 'administrative recommodification of economic and social life' (1982: 110), whereby the state rolls back the public sphere of the economy and secures the conditions for market exchanges to predominate once more. The comparison of Offe with Gorz is instructive: both share the belief that the welfare state constitutes a response to a deep-seated crisis of capitalist social relations (Kellner, 1989). They also agree that the conditions which were in place at the advent of the welfare state no longer pertain (Offe, 1992). Offe categorizes his own and Gorz's ideas as 'left-libertarian', a tradition concerned with the concepts of citizenship, work, autonomous activity and basic needs, unlike the dominant orthodoxies of the left. Like Gorz, Offe argues that the link between the establishment of a basic income and work performed for employers must be broken, and that a post-Keynesian, socialist welfare policy must reject the goals of full employment and economic growth (Offe, 1984: 1992).

Their differences are, however, also important. Gorz retains a more explicit, existentialist concern than Offe for the alienation of genuine needs in contemporary conditions. This emphasis has made Gorz's work attractive to many green activists and thinkers. His influence upon the thinking of Greens can be discerned in the calls for a drastic reduction in working time which several green parties have made (Green Party of Ireland, 1989). Yet despite the incorporation of an ecological dimension in his work, Gorz sits uneasily within mainstream environmentalist thought. In this context, his ideas approximate most closely to the tradition of social ecology and the ideas of Murray Bookchin in particular. Like Gorz, Bookchin rejects the belief of many Greens that changing the relationship between human society and nature should take precedence over changes *within* human society. Both are sensitive to the inequalities and exploitation that characterize the human realm, and stress the fusion of social and ecological goals.

Two fundamental differences divide them, however, with particular repercussions in the field of welfare provision. First, Bookchin's hostility to the state, in all its manifestations, encourages a marked hostility towards the institutions of welfare. Gorz, as we have seen, remains far more ambivalent in this area. His concern for individual autonomy and his rejection of corporatist and collectivist strategies for change means that he regards welfarist politics as an inadequate basis for human liberation. Yet he remains loyal to his socialist origins in the sense that social goals, inadequately realized at present in the welfare states of western societies, need to be embraced by radicals. He differs from Bookchin and other Greens, therefore, in discerning the traces of future liberation in present practices, however far from his ultimate goal these may be.

Gorz's second major difference with Bookchin concerns his critique of collectivist strategies for change. Here his ideas strike a chord with many Greens. He shares their belief in the renewal of individual responsibility within contemporary politics and the importance of developing autonomy within modern life. Existing ideological traditions, even if fused with ecological beliefs as in the

case of Bookchin's eco-anarchism, do not incorporate these aspects of emancipation. In one of his few references to Gorz (a hostile review of *Ecology as
Politics*), Bookchin (1980–1) ironically developed a similar criticism of Gorz: he
detected in the latter's work a residual and unacceptable commitment to an older
ideological orthodoxy – Marxism.

This criticism is unconvincing. Gorz has exerted some influence over sections
of the left, as well as the environmentalist movement, because of his theoretical
location on the border between socialist and ecological thought, not because of
a commitment to Marxism. In fact, his hostility towards many aspects of socialism
ensured his popularity with revisionist socialists in the 1980s. His concern to
refashion the left's ideological universe appealed to those who remained outside
the orthodoxies of social democracy and classical Marxism. His writings were
popularized in the UK, for example, by journals such as *Marxism Today* and
the *New Statesman* in the 1980s (Hall, 1988; Murray, 1988; Gorz, 1988, 1989c).

Some of Gorz's ideas have recently proved attractive to social democratic currents
in western Europe. In the UK, for instance, Patricia Hewitt, Neil Kinnock's policy
co-ordinator from 1988 to 1989, cites Gorz to substantiate her argument that
unemployment may be a semi-permanent feature of social life and can best be
combated through 'flexible working' (Hewitt, 1993). In addition, the left-leaning
think-tank, the Institute for Public Policy Research, foresees changes in the patterns
of an individual's working life which necessitate a new approach to the question
of time. The authors (including Hewitt) of a recent Institute report advocate 'time
banking', a system in which employees would be given the option of 'saving up
for paid time off, or taking part of their wage rise in the form of time bank
contributions. Employers should match such contributions and pension schemes
could run the time banks' (Institute for Public Policy Research, 1992: 15).

The appropriation of Gorzian ideas, which provide part of the inspiration for
such schemes, remains problematic. This perspective assumes the value of the
social democratic goals of economic growth and full employment. Hewitt favours,
for example, 'implementing European Commission proposals for a maximum
forty-eight hour week' (Hewitt, 1993: 23), partly as a route to securing higher
levels of employment. She also envisages a balancing of priorities for the employed
between 'work and the family' (1993: 23). Gorz rejects both the limited nature
and the political direction of such an approach. He calls instead for the liberation
of the individual's time so that she or he may move freely between the different
spheres of society, and benefit from the subjugation of work. The rigid boundary
between the public and private spheres, taken for granted by social democratic
thought, would be replaced by a more fragile one. Moreover, the 'time banking'
proposal outlined above involves a key role for benevolent employers, especially
in the funding of 'paid leave' (Institute for Public Policy Research, 1992: 15).
Gorz bypasses this corporatist approach with his combination of individual
self-determination and community control in the form of the social wage. In his
scheme, autonomous time would be granted to individuals in return for socially
necessary work for the maintenance of the community's overall interests.

While some of Gorz's ideas look attractive for social democratic parties in policy terms, they are ultimately grounded in a vision which remains inimical to the political assumptions of these bodies. Even among the radical intelligentsia, unburdened by the pressures of policy making and electoral calculation, Gorz has failed to acquire the status enjoyed by other thinkers. This can be explained by the idiosyncratic nature of his work, particularly his tendency to remain out of step with contemporary intellectual fashions. In the UK, many radicals believed that the hegemonic aspirations of Thatcherism and the connected demise of the left necessitated the rethinking of Marxist ideas. Yet Gorz has retained a more complex and problematic relationship with socialist and Marxist orthodoxy. While he clearly rejects much within these traditions, he continues to find inspiration in Marxian ideas, often borrowed untransformed from their original context. Additionally, he remains wary of the development of new orthodoxies which threaten to replace social and economic relations with ideology in their understanding of the political world.

The question of Gorz's relationship with other thinkers and political currents is therefore paradoxical. His work overlaps closely with that of other contemporary critical theorists (O'Connor, 1984), especially Offe. In addition, he has found favour with many Greens and, more recently, with social democratic parties searching for new ideas following the discrediting of Keynesianism. Nevertheless his ideas do not fit into any single political tradition. His eclectic intellectual origins and disdain for orthodox political commitments continue to ensure that his work touches on a number of conventionally separate disciplinary fields, and remains attractive to various political perspectives.

Key texts

Gorz has produced a large number of articles and books throughout his career (Little, 1993). While he was more concerned in his early work with the development of philosophical themes within existentialism, he is best known for several of the texts he produced after 1970.

Ecology as Politics (1987a) brings together articles that Gorz wrote in the early 1970s. More diverse in scope than his later books, it begins with a general critique of the dominant trends within contemporary capitalism. Gorz juxtaposes with this analysis a fictional sketch of a 'possible utopia', a society organized on an ecologically sustainable basis. This utopia appears to take place the day after the revolution. The goals of the new society are set out in the central event of this sketch – a television broadcast by the President and Prime Minister, setting out the philosophy of the revolution: 'we shall work less' (1987a: 44), and 'we shall consume better' (1987a: 45). A number of environmentally and socially pro-gressive measures are proposed, in a somewhat authoritarian manner: for instance, 'to encourage the exercise of the imagination and the greater exchange of ideas, no television programmes would be broadcast on Fridays or Saturdays' (1987a: 50). As one commentator has observed, this vision contains 'an uncomfortable mix of authoritarian/centralist and libertarian/pluralist ideas' (Geoghegan, 1987: 129). The remainder of the book is concerned with the social aspects of ecology, and investigates the relationship between poverty and affluence and the dangers of the unchecked growth of the world's population.

Gorz's most popular work, *Farewell to the Working Class* (1987b), includes a swingeing attack upon the classical Marxist tradition. He rejects, and possibly parodies, Marx's conception of the industrial proletariat, and challenges the reliance on the myth of collective appropriation of the means of production. Departing from this perspective with a multidimensional analysis of power relationships within contemporary society, he proceeds to highlight the existence of the neo-proletariat in contemporary society. This 'non-class' will play a key role in the development of a post-industrial alternative.

This book laid many of the foundations of his later work: in particular, the critique of Keynesianism which he developed in *Paths to Paradise* (1985). Written in the form of twenty-five theses concerning the present nature of capitalism and the tasks facing socialists, this text provides a commentary upon and critique of the influence of neo-Keynesian assumptions upon the parliamentary left in western Europe. He particularly rejects the assumption that infinite economic growth is possible and desirable. An alternative future must be built upon the destruction of present-day 'living-dead capitalism' (1985: 35), a system sustained by a technocratic élite of professional workers. In the book's second half, Gorz fleshes out this alternative future, outlining his proposals for a 'citizen's wage' based upon roughly twenty thousand hours of work performed by an individual over the course of his or her lifetime.

Gorz's most sophisticated and important work, *Critique of Economic Reason* (1989a), provides an historical account of the labour process within capitalism, and challenges previous ideological representations of the nature of work. The modern organization of work and the technical division of labour, in his view, lead to social disintegration and division. Both factors contribute to the hegemony of economic reason, which has spread to non-commodity areas of the social world where its dominance is inappropriate. In conclusion, he sets out his proposals for a reduction in work time, and reiterates his belief that the right to work has to be balanced by the individual's right to an income independent of work. This text places him alongside the most eminent social theorists of his generation.

Acknowledgement

The authors would like to thank Bob Eccleshall for his help in preparing this chapter.

References

Barry, N. (1979) *Hayek's Social and Economic Philosophy*, London: Macmillan.

Bookchin, M. (1980–1) 'Review of A. Gorz, *Ecology as Politics*', *Telos*, 45, pp. 177–90.

Bookchin, M. (1990) *Social Ecology*, Montreal: Black Rose.

Davies, H. (1988) *Sartre and 'Les Temps Modernes'*, Cambridge: Cambridge University Press.

Dobson, A. (1990) *Green Political Theory: An introduction*, London: Unwin Hyman.

Geoghegan, V. (1987) *Utopianism and Marxism*, London: Methuen.

Gorz, A. (1964) *Strategy for Labour: A radical proposal*, Boston, Mass.: Beacon Press.

Gorz, A. (ed.), (1976) *The Division of Labour*, Hassocks: Harvester

Gorz, A. (1985) *Paths to Paradise: On the liberation from work*, London: Pluto. First published 1983.

Gorz, A. (1987a) *Ecology as Politics*, London: Pluto. First published 1975.

Gorz, A. (1987b) *Farewell to the Working Class: An essay on post-industrial socialism*, London: Pluto. First published 1980.

Gorz, A. (1987c) 'Reshaping the welfare state', *Praxis International*, 6, 1, pp. 5–16.

Gorz, A. (1988) 'Making space for everyone', *New Statesman/Society*, 25 November, pp. 28–31.

Gorz, A. (1989a) *Critique of Economic Reason*, London: Verso. First published 1988.

Gorz, A. (1989b) 'World of no workers', *Weekend Guardian*, 9 December, pp. 1–6.

Gorz, A. (1989c) 'A land of Cockayne? (Interview with J. Keane)', *New Statesman/Society*, 12 May, pp. 26–31.

Gorz, A. (1991) *Capitalisme, Socialisme, Ecologie*, Paris: Galilee.

Gorz, A. (1992) 'On the difference between society and community, and why basic income cannot by itself confer full membership of either', in Van Parijs, P. (ed.), *Arguing for Basic Income: Ethical foundations for a radical reform*, London: Verso.

Green Party of Ireland (1989) *Communism and Capitalism – one down, one to go: Towards a sane economy*, Dublin: Green Party of Ireland.

Habermas, J. (1976) *Legitimation Crisis*, London: Hutchinson,

Habermas, J. (1987) *The Theory of Communicative Action: The critique of functionalist reason*, Vol. 2, Cambridge: Polity.

Hall, S. (1988) 'Brave new world', *Marxism Today*, October, pp. 24–9.

Hewitt, P. (1993) 'Time's up for 9 to 5', *New Statesman/Society*, 15 January, p. 23.

Hirsch, A. (1982) *The French Left: A history and overview*, Montreal: Black Rose.

Illich, I. (1976) *Medical Nemesis: The expropriation of health*, New York: Pantheon.

Institute for Public Policy Research (Blackstone, Cornford, Hewitt and Miliband) (1992) *Next Left: An agenda for the 1990s*, London: IPPR.

Jessop, B. (1982) *The Capitalist State: Marxist theories and methods*, Oxford: Martin Robertson.

Keane, J. (1988) *Democracy and Civil Society*, London: Verso.

Kellner, D. (1989) *Critical Theory: Marxism and modernity*, Cambridge: Polity.

Little, A. (1993) 'The political theory of André Gorz', Ph.D. thesis, Queen's University, Belfast.

Murray, R. (1988) 'Life after Henry (Ford)', *Marxism Today*, October, pp. 8–13.

O'Connor, J. (1984) *Accumulation Crisis*, Oxford: Blackwell.

Offe, C. (1984) *Contradictions of the Welfare State* (ed. by J. Keane), London: Hutchinson.

Offe, C. (1992) 'A non-productivist design for social policies', in Van Parijs, P. (ed.), *Arguing for Basic Income: Ethical foundations for a radical reform*, London: Verso.

Sayers, S. (1991) 'Gorz on work and liberation', *Radical Philosophy*, 58, pp. 17–26.

Stoesz, D. and Midgley, J. (1991) 'The radical right and the welfare state', in Glennerster, H. and Midgley, J. (eds), *The Radical Right and the Welfare State: An international assessment*, New York and London: Barnes and Noble/Harvester Wheatsheaf.

Tomlinson, J. (1990) *Hayek and the Market*, London: Pluto.

17 Robertson

Michael Cahill

Introduction

Green social and political thought emerged as the new ideology of the late twentieth century, challenging existing conceptions of self and society and conventional forms of political and economic organization. The growing realization of resource scarcity and environmental damage has prompted rethinking among adherents of all the major perspectives in social and political philosophy. For the last twenty years, the English writer James Roberston has been an important contributor to green thinking and debates in the western world. True, his books are not nearly as well known as such gurus as Ivan Illich or E.F. Schumacher, from whom he gained much of his early inspiration, but taken together they articulate an important response to the problems which late-twentieth-century societies are facing. Unlike the majority of thinkers discussed in this volume, Robertson is not an academic, although for short periods he has been attached to university departments. This is not surprising: the green perspective is one that has been formulated and debated for the most part outside of universities and the academic world. It has no well-heeled think-tanks, its conferences tend to be spartan affairs, and much of the debate takes place in fringe journals. In this sense, the greens are heirs to an honourable tradition of dissent across western Europe and the United States of America.

Over the last twenty years, Robertson's work has had a distinctively utopian cast, with an espousal of a sane, humane and ecological society which has been expanded and amplified in his later work. This is not work which is exercised with the question 'how?'; rather it seeks to provoke and inspire. Robertson is writing from within the green movement to the wider society. His work is a product of the alternative thinking on ecology, economy and society which has proceeded on the margins of British society over the last two decades.

Brief biography

James Robertson was born in 1928 and attended Sedbergh School in Yorkshire. After a degree at the University of Oxford, he spent a short time in the Royal Horse Artillery and then a period working for the Sudan government. He joined the Colonial Office as an administrative civil servant in 1953. He was following in the footsteps of his father, Sir James Robertson, who after many years working for the colonial service in the Sudan ended his career as Governor-General for Nigeria in the run-up to independence. This era marked the end of Britain's Empire and could not fail to have a major impact on both Robertsons, father and son. In this regard, it is interesting to note that in his work James Robertson refers on a number of occasions to the need for decolonization, applying the term to the need for professionals to share their expertise and knowledge (Robertson, 1978). In 1960 he moved to the Cabinet Office, where he worked with Sir Norman Brook, later Lord Normanbrook, then Head of the Home Civil Service and Secretary to the Cabinet. From here Robertson transferred to the Ministry of Defence, where he resigned his career as a civil service high-flyer in 1965. Robertson writes that he had become disillusioned with the world of central government, seeing it as a labyrinthine maze which stifled effective decision making and good government:

> It was a profound shock to discover after ten years of rewarding – indeed exciting – work in Whitehall that so many of the stock criticisms of it were justified. There appeared to be literally thousands of people – real, live, individual people like oneself, many of them potentially able or once able – whose energies were being wasted on non-jobs (most of which would be done all over again by someone else and most of which would in any case make no difference whatsoever to anything of importance in the real world), whose capabilities and aspirations were being stunted, and who were gradually reconciling themselves to the prospect of pointless work until retirement. (Robertson, 1971: 141)

After working for a firm of management and computer consultants in 1968 Robertson was appointed Director of the Inter Bank Research Organization. At this time he wrote his first book, *Reform of British Central Government* (1971). Parts of it had already appeared as evidence to the Fulton Committee on the future of the civil service. In 1973 Robertson left the Inter Bank Research Organization and became a freelance writer and consultant. Essentially, his writing from this point on is the concern of this chapter.

Main ideas

Once Robertson left the establishment world of government and finance, his thinking quickly evolved along lines which had already been hinted at in his book on the reform of British government, allied to his perception that society was now moving into a post-industrial phase which would have to take account of the scarcity of resources. Daniel Bell's *The Coming of Post Industrial Society* had just appeared (Bell, 1973), while the Club of Rome report on *The Limits to Growth* was published two years earlier (Meadows *et al.*, 1971). There were any number of signs that the consensual world of the 1950s and 1960s was coming to an end: the oil price rise overnight enriched Arab oil states and threw the western nations into crisis, while at home the inconclusive general elections of 1974 marked the emergence of party dealignment, with Labour and the Conservatives receiving a much lower share of the vote because of the gains of the Liberals and the nationalist parties.

The first book by Robertson to reflect this new turn in his thinking was *Profit or People? The new social role of money* (1974), which originated in a series of articles for the *Sunday Times*. It is a plea for a 'socially responsible free enterprise' (1974: 20). In his first book, Robertson had advocated a thorough-going reform of political institutions so that the processes of Whitehall and Westminster would become much more visible and accountable. In *Profit or People?* he urged a parallel process of openness for the private sector, in which a company's board of directors would be overseen by a governing body which would ensure that the idea of social responsibility was being taken seriously by the firm. His message was aimed primarily at large public companies, where he felt that the centrality of profit needed to be displaced by self-management, customer orientation and the philosophy of the small businessperson. He envisaged that a much greater proportion of the profits of the firm should go to the workers in the enterprise.

Similarly, a reform of the financial institutions was necessary, for they were ossified and tended to operate in self-perpetuating ways which inhibited the growth of enterprise and encouraged the pursuit of individual self-advantage rather than the collective good. Perhaps Robertson's most radical proposals related to his belief that income taxation should be abolished and replaced by a tax on wealth and consumption taxes. The wealth tax would be progressive and take an annual form. His belief was that the fiscal system should reflect the way in which people make demands on the system through their spending and their capital accumulation, rather than the way in which they contribute to the system through their work. Such a reform of taxation would give an opportunity to people to pass on money and make gifts in a variety of ways without the intervention of the state. As for the benefits system, he advocated universal, flat-rate payments to meet the needs of the population. At the heart of the book is Robertson's belief that money itself needs to be overhauled as a procedure which would provide for an efficient accounting of the activity of society. There had to be a reformed, fair and open money system which would then secure legitimacy in the eyes of the general public.

James Robertson returned to this theme with *Power, Money and Sex* (1976), a title which sounds like a blockbuster paperback in search of a mini-series. The book represents the next stage in the development of Robertson's thought towards an 'alternative' or 'New Age' perspective. (He uses the term 'New Age' in the introduction to the book.) Whereas *Profit or People?* had been about the reform of institutions, this book is an examination of the ideologies which inform the workings of society. As he explained, the ideas outlined in his earlier book had put him into contact with many people who were committed to lifestyle change and alternative projects. Robertson felt that this was important. Some key 'New Age' ideas are present in the book: we have to live in harmony with the planet, change is necessary in hearts and minds, and there is a primary emphasis in the book on lifestyle change: 'The only way in which individuals can recover personal autonomy and balance will be to reject the personal ethic prevailing today, that sets such a high standard on material consumption' (1976: 59). Robertson was now of the view that there was an inherited genetic programme which underlay the drive for material consumption, power, money and sex. This was exhibited in the behaviour of males, and Robertson accepts the feminist claim that society is organized as a patriarchy in which these values are dominant.

It is in this book that we see the gist of Robertson's ideas on work and wealth, which became central to his thinking in the 1980s. Here he remarks that the market is not necessary for an economy, and discusses some societies in Africa and other parts of the Third World where the economy is not organized on a monetary market basis. Robertson felt that work had to be rescued from the association with paid employment, and that each of us should expand the time given to housework and caring work. In this way, as more forms of work are liberated from the cash economy, work will become less alienating and divisive (1976: 38). The employment crisis in the industrial societies in the 1980s has kept this perspective to the fore as of, necessity, the boundaries between work and leisure have been renegotiated.

In *Power, Money and Sex*, Robertson provides a discussion of organizations and institutions which draws on the work of radical critics, pre-eminently Ivan Illich. By now Robertson had renounced his earlier credentials as an institutional reformer. We find the former mandarin writing: 'by their nature institutions and organisations are prone to malfunction' (1976: 68) and 'I am now convinced that large organisations cannot reform themselves from within' (1976: 74). His critique of organizational life is more wide ranging, for he feels that institutions have disempowered us in large areas of our lives, and that no way has been found of making them socially responsible. We send our children to schools, we rely on hospitals and a bureaucratized health-care system for our health needs, increasingly our food comes from large food stores. If *Profit or People?* was a radical book written by the former head of the Inter Bank Research Organization, then *Power, Money and Sex* can be viewed as the first in the *oeuvre* of James Robertson, the New Age thinker.

In *The Sane Alternative: A choice of futures* (1978), Robertson outlined the essentials of his world-view: his vision of the future is the SHE society: Sane, Humane and Ecological. The book stems from work which Robertson had been doing at that time on the future of industrial society for the Anglo-German Foundation for the Study of Industrial Society, the Stanford Research Institute, and the International Foundation for Social Innovation, among others. Robertson was committed to the belief that post-industrial society was going to be a far superior place in which to live. For him a 'paradigm shift' was taking place in the values of our society, which he described as the transition from a scientific and economic view of nature to an ecological and spiritual view (Robertson, 1978). The SHE future which Robertson embraces is one where the limits to growth and to economic life are observed and the forms of expansion are social and psychological. The economy is decentralized and systems of production are organized locally.

Despite the growing ecological and economic crisis of the late 1970s, Robertson pointed out that there were those who believed that the future was to be a continuation of certain trends in the present or, as he terms it, 'business as usual'. Three assumptions underlay this perspective: that the state would continue to be the political unit; that welfare state services would continue as mass services staffed by professionals; and that manufacturing would continue to be the basis of economic activity. In addition, there would continue to be a distinction between work and leisure, and work and home (Robertson, 1978: 21). Then there was the 'disaster' scenario in which population explosion, ecological damage and food shortages all interact and provide the setting for the collapse of democracy because, as a system of government, it proves itself incapable of meeting these monumental challenges. One response to this from a minority of the green movement has been to espouse authoritarianism: given the selfish predilections of populations, the only way that the planet can survive is by a centralized, authoritarian form of government. Finally, there is the 'hyper-expansionist' prospect: the view that the industrial system can provide enough wealth to weather the crises and existing trends towards an expansion of consumerism, and that economic growth will continue abetted by techno-fixes which will prevent environmental disaster.

In the 1980s Robertson turned his attention to the nature and extent of work, the central problem for western economies as they adjust to deindustrialization, the rise of the Pacific Rim as a serious industrial competitor, the globalization of markets and the impact of information technology on industrial processes. In *Future Work* (1985), Robertson expanded on the propositions about work which he had outlined in *The Sane Society* in the context for a Sane, Humane and Ecological (SHE) society. Acknowledging the immense impact that industrialization has had upon the lives and aspirations of people in the advanced societies over the last two centuries, Robertson predicts that the post-industrial revolution will have a similar impact, but here his emphasis is different from many of the other post-industrial writers: 'the breakthrough will be primarily psychological and social, not technical and economic. It will enlarge the human limits to human achievement, it will simplify our capacity to develop ourselves as human beings, together with the communities and societies in which we live' (1985: 5).

In *Future Work*, Robertson outlines the contribution that 'ownwork' will be able to make to the emerging scenario, where full employment has come to an end. Ownwork is defined by Robertson as 'activity which is purposeful and important, and which people organise and control for themselves. It may be either paid or unpaid' (1985: x). Because the prevailing definition of work as employment – paid work – has come to an end, there are millions of people without work. Yet although the economy cannot produce the full-time-for-life jobs that were available in the past, employment is still the way in which we characterize work. There is the paradox of mass unemployment, but much work left undone in homes, neighbourhood care, social welfare and other sectors of the economy. In a consumer society where access to money is the passport to participation, paid work gains an exalted status. Housework, child care and caring in families are undervalued, with the result that much of this work is not performed or, as in the case of the middle class, is done by others as waged work: nannies and cleaners enable middle-class parents with children to engage in full-time work.

Robertson argues that our conception of work as paid employment is one which is inextricably linked with industrialization. Coupled with this has been the urbanization of work, such that most people expect to leave their home and their family in order to work. Robertson claims that the power structures of the modern world are based upon the assumption that employment is the dominant form of work: the organized labour movement, the financial system, and government and politics. He sees the labour movement as originating in a defensive effort to protect the interests of working people as they were moved into the era of industrialization. Those initiatives to provide work outside of the industrial system were forgotten, such as the Owenite experiment at New Lanark in Scotland in the 1830s, where workers could purchase goods directly from the community store using their own currency (see Offe and Henze, 1992: 71–3). Unfortunately, this defensive stance, understandable in the past, is a hindrance in the present as it means that the labour movement is wedded to an industrial conception of work as employment which is fast fading and resulting in unemployment for many trade union members. More generally, Robertson sees employment as producing a dependency in the population such that rights become a dominant form of discourse: 'We depend on shops to provide us with food, on the education profession to provide our children with learning, on the medical profession and the drug industry to provide us with health, on the state to provide us with welfare – and on employers to provide us with work' (Robertson, 1985: 117–18). Robertson wants these bureaucracies to wither as more of us begin to meet our own needs.

In an industrial society, the primary motivation to work, although not the only one, is financial reward. In moving to a pattern of work where ownwork was much more prevalent, what would happen to this linkage with money? Robertson is at pains to point out that there would still be paid employment, although its role would have been reduced. Indeed, money will be paid to every citizen regardless of their work status through the Basic Income Scheme. In this way, those who do ownwork such as child care or housework will be given a financial recognition. But the Basic Income will be paid to every citizen regardless of whether they are in paid employment or not – at a standard rate which it will then be for the citizen to decide whether they wish to supplement. Money roles will need to change to accommodate the demands which ownwork will impose. Robertson envisages that community economic enterprises will require capital to sustain their endeavours. Smaller, local forms of savings institution will need to be created so that capital can be supplied for local schemes. Robertson sees the existing financial institutions, building societies and banks as too remote and only interested in producing the highest reward for their investors. In fact, what Robertson suggests is nothing more than a return to the early days of these institutions when they were locally controlled and run. Money should be directed to local schemes: this is for Robertson preferable to banks and building societies taking millions of pounds and merely investing them for the best return.

In *Future Work*, Robertson returns to a very old English radical theme, the taxation of land. He wants more people to be able to work the land, and to this end he wants to see the mechanism of a land tax introduced which would penalize those landowners who did not work the land, but who merely wanted to profit from the increase in land prices. The land tax is designed to bring more land into cultivation, and Robertson's belief – shared by most Greens – is that the land needs to see more people working it, growing crops and raising livestock, in order that they can provide more of their own needs. The hope is that the land tax will free up more land so that many more people will have a chance to work it.

Technology will have an important part to play in the ownwork agenda. But it will be technology which will be designed to help with local, small-scale problems, and the acid test for it will be

> whether the new material, or equipment, or process, or system is likely to enlarge the range of competence, control and initiative of the people who will be affected by it, or whether it is more likely to subordinate them to more powerful people and organisations, and make them dependent on bureaucracies and machines which they cannot themselves control. (1985: 180)

To the reasonable question 'how will this ownwork future be brought about?', Robertson's answer would appear to be that self-activity will gradually persuade others of the validity of this way of life. *Future Work* was written, in large part, to persuade people to change their way of working and to outline an alternative – the book concludes with a questionnaire which encourages readers to reflect on their own work. Robertson's hope, expressed on the last page of the book, is that there will be a gradual conversion, a conversion which will be abetted by the way in which the older forms and notions of employment are proving inadequate as we move into a post-industrial age.

In the mid-1980s James Robertson was one of the founders of The Other Economic Summit (TOES). The Other Economic Summit was held at the same

time and in the same place as the G7 economic summits between the leading
industrial nations. (For a selection of papers from these meetings, see Ekins
(1986).) By this time, alternative or 'new economics' had achieved a certain
standing in the green movement, although perhaps not in the world of
conventional economics. In *Future Wealth: A new economics for the 21st century*
(1989), Robertson reviews the major themes of the 'new economics'. Wealth
creation must be about the well-being of people, asserts Robertson. Like all of
his books since *The Sane Alternative*, it is written for people who think as he
does and for those whom he wishes to persuade; it is not a theoretical or an
academic text on green economics such as that of Jacobs (1991).

The economic development which he outlines in the book has four main
themes: it should be enabling; it should be conserving of resources and the
environment; the world's economy should be seen as a one-world system with
self-governing but interdependent parts; and it should be supported by up-to-date
economic ideas. The extraordinary population growth we are currently experiencing in the world will make enormous ecological impacts which will seriously
threaten the future of the planet. To help to reverse this process, Robertson
judges that we need to dispel the notion that economic growth equals social and
economic progress (Robertson, 1989: 3). People need to become more self-reliant,
and central to this process is seeing the home and the household in a new light.
Until the industrial era, the household economy was of great importance, but
the movement of work out of the home into the factory and the office has
diminished its significance. Likewise, conventional economists are blind to the
work of household labour, assigning no value to it whatsoever. The informal
economy needs much more acknowledgement and strengthening, so that tasks
and activities can be shared between households and between neighbours and
friends.

Local economies must become more self-reliant and make sure that more of
their wealth stays within the community rather than seeping away to other places.
To this end Robertson advocates local needs being met by local resources and
local work, a greater proportion of local income circulating locally, and local
savings being invested in local enterprise. Robertson highlights what he calls 'a
socio-economy', by which he means ventures such as community advice centres,
housing associations, self-help health promotion schemes, and education and
leisure projects which are not seen as formal economic activity, but are in fact
a mixture of social and economic projects. It is not surprising that, given this
local emphasis, he sees a dominant role for the local economy being played by
local authorities, much the same role in the national government plays in the
national economy today: as banker, economic development agency and tax-
collector (Robertson, 1989: 49–50).

It might be thought that the world capitalist economy would defeat these
proposals, but here too Robertson is optimistic, calling for controls on the activities
of transnational corporations via taxation. He envisages a reform of world
economic institutions such as the World Bank and the International Monetary

Fund, so that they can become agencies which help to stimulate and promote the kind of local economic and sustainable development he advocates. Among the reforms envisaged are: taxes on ocean fishing and sea bed mining, pollution taxes, taxes on imports between one country and another, and a uniform international currency exchange tax. The book is more than one man's contribution to the debate about the economics of the environment, for it also serves as a summation of the position of the New Economics Foundation, the body established to promote the ideas behind The Other Economic Summit. Taken together with Ekins *et al.* (1992), it represents the thinking of the 'new economics'. What distinguishes this new school is its emphasis on values: the economy is shaped by the society of which it is only one part, along with ecology, and there can be no separation between social and economic policy.

Relevance to welfare

James Robertson has not written a book entitled *Future Welfare* – although does he need to when, on the first page of *Future Wealth*, he declares that he wants to use the word 'wealth' in its original meaning of well-being? The applicability of his ideas to welfare and social policy are clear enough. I will examine three themes from his work which bear upon welfare: the welfare state and the role of professionals; the extent to which ownwork is a feasible option; and the ways in which income and work can be combined.

   Welfare states are, for Robertson, part of the industrial pattern of society, large-scale institutions established to distribute benefits and services to a mass population. As such they are liable to the same criticisms that writers such as Illich have made of state bureaucracies – they provide opportunities for professionals to self-aggrandize and to deskill clients of their potential to help themselves. Yet it is possible to share the 'disabling professionals' critique of Illich and still move beyond this towards partnership between worker and user (Illich *et al.*, 1977). Doubtless many instances of 'user empowerment' do not go far towards this aim, but there are examples to show it can be done. Robert Holman's neighbourhood work in urban communities has given a valuable lead in this respect, which exemplifies the remarks of Gorz to the effect that society needs professionals but there is no necessity for their privileges and status (Holman, 1981, 1986; Gorz, 1985: 55–6).

   For Robertson, welfare state bureaucracies are themselves obstacles on the path to a post-industrial future in which we will be able to create our own welfare based on self-help and voluntary social service (Robertson, 1982). This will be part of the move to much more localized forms of self-government and economic activity than at present. The twin emphasis is upon self-reliance for the individual and greater participation by individuals in their communities. At this point, Robertson's underlying commitment to personal development comes through when he acknowledges that the path to what he calls post-welfare development will need a combination of individual growth (becoming better people) and social progress (becoming a better society). This combination of personal and community development will replace the need for social service and welfare state bureaucracies. Professionals are at fault because they tend to turn their clients into passive consumers of welfare rather than self-determining individuals. Robertson acknowledges that the problems with which social workers have to deal are created by conditions which are outside their control. Equally, he is persuaded that the cash-nexus has eroded our capacity for spontaneous, mutual support for one another – everything is measured in terms of the monetary cost.

Essentially, then, Robertson argues for those with emotional difficulties to make use of the wide variety of alternative therapies – at some points he quotes with approval humanistic psychology – rather than rely on state professionals. Yet this is to ignore the extent to which social workers, psychologists, doctors and others have themselves been influenced by the alternative therapies and have attempted to incorporate them into their own practice. In some ways, the mushrooming of alternative therapies is an example of ownwork, yet it is not without its own drawbacks. These can be seen with counselling where, because of the absence of state regulation, anyone can at present set up as a counsellor whether they are qualified or not. Likewise counselling can induce dependency in of some its users, although it is not a state-regulated profession.

Robertson proposes a linking of the concerns of social policy, community development and the voluntary movement. Central to his thinking is the new definition of work which he offers – work as ownwork – and from this much else follows. Ownwork will usually be local, will be often done in or around the household, and will be carried out in the neighbourhood. If this is to entail a revaluation of caring and household work, then all these facets of ownwork will mean that there are going to be more people living and working at home. If this shift to ownwork were to take place in a context in which fossil-fuel-burning transport became much more expensive, it can be appreciated that many more people would be living and working in their own locality. There are developments in employment patterns which already point in this direction: teleworking and other forms of homework are increasing rapidly (Cahill, 1994: 140–4).

But what Robertson does not acknowledge is that there are many other forces working against the idea of ownwork. In the late-twentieth-century UK, exposed to decades of consumerism, many people have become deskilled as home workers. Cooking, knitting and sewing are now associated with a much devalued role of housewife. Two trends have contributed to this: the spread of consumer capitalism, which encourages us not to make do and mend, but to throw away and spend; and feminism, which has encouraged a dissatisfaction with the traditional role of housewife and mother staying at home while the man is the breadwinner. Most occupations are still organized today to fit a male workforce, with no thought of parenting responsibilities. Employers are still clinging to hours of work and types of work organization which are hangovers from the days when the male-breadwinner role was the norm.

We are in one sense talking here just as much about time as work. Jobs and careers which demand very long or anti-social hours are not compatible with running a family or caring for children. This positively disadvantages parents, or they have to employ a number of people who will care for their children as they are unable to because of the demands of their career. There has been no revolution in the world of work to enable parents, whether they be male or female, to combine parenting with a commitment to their career (Hewitt, 1993; Leach, 1994). Recently, Penelope Leach cited research which suggests that the total amount of time that children and parents spend together has dropped by 40 per cent in a single generation (Leach, 1994: 258). Part of the reason why parenting has changed is, as Etzioni has pointed out, that it takes parents away from work which will earn money, and in a society where the cash-nexus has become increasingly powerful, parenting and children have suffered (Etzioni, 1993).

Robertson described the social change associated with the new pattern of working in this way:

> we have become dependent on paid work and other work outside the home to give us a sense of identity, a social role, that the diminished functions of our households and immediate neighbourhoods can no longer supply. Most of us need such work to enable us to meet people, and to provide us with a way of structuring our time – needs which the isolated, unproductive homes of late industrial society have become less and less able to meet. (Robertson, 1985: 29)

As a result of this development in many middle-class, dual-earner families, many of the essential household tasks are now part of the cash economy, due to the employment of nannies, cooks and cleaners. As employment patterns change in the economy, there are more and more part-time jobs, which appeal to women who have child-care responsibilities. Robertson does not take these facts into account when outlining his vision of a SHE future. Instead he acknowledges that there are trends which are not moving us into a sustainable future – on the contrary – and these are put into his Hyper Expansionist future of a small group of well-paid experts and professionals, and the great majority of the population either unemployed or doing the housework and child care of the élite. Although the 1980s media fascination with yuppies and workaholics was overplayed, it none the less pointed to an underlying reality in which work had become a central form of identity for many people: many people as well who by no stretch of the imagination could be confused with young upwardly mobile professionals.

Impact on policies and debates

Given the seeming inability of the UK economy to produce sufficient employment for those who seek it, there are a number of possible responses. The reduction of working hours for those in employment is advocated by André Gorz (Gorz,

1989), but as Wiesenthal points out, there are insuperable problems in getting trade unions and employees to agree to this rather than an increase in wages (Wiesenthal, 1993: 186). The way in which the part-time employment sector has grown may well accelerate the reduction of working hours: two-thirds of jobs created in the 1980s were part-time (Balls and Gregg, 1993). But it is no good simply shortening the hours of paid work if it is still regarded as distinctively superior to the unpaid work that we all have to do. If, on the other hand, there were systems of exchange apart from money, then the shortening of work hours might become more attractive to employees. This is where the introduction of moneyless exchange schemes become important, such as Local Employment Trading Schemes or Co-operation Circles, where members exchange services for mutual assistance and can use some of the extra time they have gained in earning credits to purchase services previously available only by cash payment. These local exchange schemes, which originated in North America, have now spread to Australia and Europe (see Robertson, 1989: ch. 12; Offe and Henze, 1992).

In the UK, the trends seem to be working against Robertson and others like him who think that post-industrial society could usher in a new philosophy of work. During the ten years since he wrote *Future Work*, Robertson's fears that Hyper Expansionism might prevail in this sector have been borne out: 'many essential activities which people still do today unpaid – such as parenting, housekeeping, comforting, preparing meals, looking after children and elderly people, providing hospitality at home to friends – will be transformed into paid work' (Robertson, 1985: 129). Quite so: spending on domestic services has risen five times in the last decade to over £3 billion in the UK (*Demos Quarterly*, 2, 1994).

In contrast to the reduction of hours, the idea of Basic Income advocated by Robertson and most members of the green movement is much more attractive. The payment of an income to all citizens, regardless of their status, has the advantage, as Robertson sees it, of enabling some payment to be made (and hence, in our society, some recognition to be given) to those who perform vital but undervalued work, such as housework, caring and looking after children. In addition, the Basic Income would allow some people to take up low-wage jobs, thereby benefiting many community and voluntary schemes. Yet in order to administer such far-reaching social security measures, a greater degree of centralization would be needed than some Greens might wish (Dobson, 1990: 115). Needless to say, there is the important question of how the Basic Income Scheme is to be paid for: land and pollution taxes are advocated by Robertson (Robertson, 1994).

In focusing on work, the Greens are highlighting one of the major sources of discontent with capitalist industrial society – its inability nowadays to deliver on the promise of full employment, and its toleration of mass unemployment. The focus on the nature of unpaid work in the home will be less welcome for many who might see it as a concealed attempt to revive women's guilt at leaving their children with nannies or childminders, or their decision to employ a cleaner to do the housework. However, unlike Edward Goldsmith, who has traditional views on the role of women and the family (Goldsmith, 1988), Robertson accepts feminism and the claims of women to do paid work on an equal basis to men, and is attempting to revalue informal, unpaid work, which in common with many other people he regards as of great importance. It is noteworthy in this respect that there are no reliable statistics as to how much unpaid work is carried out in the home (Anderson, 1991: 57–8).

In part, what Amitai Etzioni and Penelope Leach in their recent work on the losses for children in a consumerist, privatized society are highlighting is the triumph of materialism over personal relationships. Robertson would appear to be unduly optimistic about the power of the ideas he advocates to win support. Some trends in the western industrialized nations in the past decade, not just the diminished status of child care, make one question the extent to which his Sane, Humane and Ecological society can have a great appeal. Globalization is recognized as one of the most important forces inducing social and economic change planet-wide. The media play an important part in this new scenario of one world, but they are media which are saturated (and indeed controlled by) western economic interests. There is increasing evidence that the global media are having a powerful influence on the countries of the South, inducing their populations to want western consumer goods. This major change in the aspirations of millions of people in the poor world is occurring at just the same time that Greens are trying to persuade the inhabitants of the rich world to live more simply.

The western consumerist lifestyle is the butt of Greens because it is expensive, exploitative and unsustainable. Robertson advocates a change in lifestyle in the here and now. He is one of the supporters of the Lifestyle movement, which has as its aim a more thoughtful, sharing and responsible way of life. In practice, its members aim to live more simply, consume less and make things last. It can be made to seem an eccentric way of life, but it is sobering to reflect that from necessity this is the way of life for most of the world's population outside of the rich world and, indeed, it was the culture of the working class until the age of affluence emerged in the postwar period. This Lifestyle movement is just one part of the green movement to which Robertson belongs, but it emphasizes an important point. The Greens are political activists, but activists who want to see personal change now. This has been one of the major tensions within the UK Green Party, between those who think that the party should act like other political parties, and those who think that the only real way to achieve change is to change one's life and work now, and that the building of the party is secondary to this. There is a parallel to be found one hundred years ago with the dispute among those who advocated the spread of socialism by personal conversion and creating a socialist culture, and the proponents of an electorally successful party (Pierson, 1979). Robertson's books are handbooks: they are meant to be used, and are primarily for activists. Any critic of his work is wise to heed this admonition:

The whole range of activities involved in compiling, studying, researching, analysing, assessing, evaluating, criticising and discussing, but not taking part in, what other people are trying to do, is typical of late industrial society. If we genuinely want to go down the post-welfare development path towards a SHE society, we should be more concerned with how we propose to act ourselves than with discussing the activities of others. (Robertson, 1982: 34)

The work of Robertson and others in the green movement has been important in popularizing Local Economic Trading Schemes (LETS), Basic Income and local alternative economic development. Some of this work has also influenced more mainstream academic thinking. Although in the 1990s more attention has been paid to environmental economists such as David Pearce who attempt to put a value on the environment using neo-classical methodology, important work from the 'new economics' on quality of life and the concept of needs has gained considerable attention (Pearce *et al.*, 1989; Ekins and Max-Neef, 1992). One promising development has been the formulation of alternative measures to gross national product (GNP), which is flawed in that it ignores unpaid work, and hence considerably underestimates women's contribution to the economy, and it takes no account of environmental impact (Anderson, 1991). It is sobering to note that, as we move into the post-industrial society, the latest endeavour by the New Economics Foundation to measure environmental and social as well as economic factors using the Index of Sustainable Economic Welfare developed by Daly and Cobb in the USA concludes that the quality of life in the UK is worse in the 1990s than in the 1970s (Daly and Cobb, 1990; Jackson and Marks, 1994).

Robertson's work – his radical critique of the organization of work and wealth – puts him firmly in the camp of the dark Greens: he wants an end to industrialism and its present phase of consumer capitalism, for it is destroying the earth and hence the chance for millions of people in the future to sustain a livelihood. Robertson has championed and publicized the many practical alternatives to consumer capitalism – trading schemes, co-operatives, health-care alternatives. This is no mere utopianism, but an espousal of policy proposals and practical alternatives which point towards a fairer and more sustainable society. The difficulty with the exercise is that it fails to connect with a wider movement in its own terms because in the UK the myriad of green projects and groups have still to find a popular political expression. It must be said that there is an idealism about Robertson's political strategy:

the post-industrial revolution will be brought about primarily as a non-violent transformation of society in which there will be a constructive role for almost everyone to play ... There is no need to try to destroy the present system or take it over. It will be enough to withdraw support from it ... (Robertson, 1983: 122)

Yet this emphasis on lifestyle change and ownwork can only influence a minority of the population. The majority of the population of the industrialized western countries are too physically and materially involved in the structures of those societies to be able to opt into alternative forms of economic organization which will pay them less and hence prevent them purchasing the status symbols prized by consumer capitalism. It is the institutions which encourage the ceaseless pursuit of ever higher material standards which will need to be controlled: the global media and the transnational corporations. In achieving this new political form, the work of James Robertson will be essential in enabling us all to see the problems of the planet from a new perspective.

Acknowledgement

I am grateful to Vanessa Cahill and Paul Fox-Strangways for comments on a draft of this chapter.

Key texts

The Sane Alternative (1978) outlines the possible scenarios for the economy as it confronts environmental destruction. The book contains the essence of Robertson's world-view, with material on the SHE economy and paradigm shifts, and an outline of his strategy for achieving change.

Future Work (1985) explores the future for work, how people's perceptions of work have changed, how work has been viewed by economic theory, how the concept of employment has dominated discussion of work, and how ownwork can be realized.

Future Wealth (1989) is a straightforward guide to the 'new economics', with discussion of the world economy, the role of money, taxes and an agenda for the 1990s. An appendix sets the book in the context of Robertson's previous work.

References

Anderson, V. (1991) *Alternative Economic Indicators*, London: Routledge and Kegan Paul.
Balls, E. and Gregg, P. (1993) *Work and Welfare*, London: Commission on Social Justice.
Bell, D. (1973) *The Coming of Post Industrial Society*, New York: Basic Books.
Cahill, M. (1994) *The New Social Policy*, Oxford: Blackwell.
Daly, H.E. and Cobb, J.B. (1990) *For the Common Good*, London: Green Print.
Dobson, A. (1990) *Green Political Thought*, London: Unwin Hyman.
Ekins, P. (ed.) (1986) *The Living Economy: A new economics in the making*, London: Routledge and Kegan Paul.
Ekins, P. and Max-Neef, M. (eds) (1992) *Real Life Economics: Understanding wealth creation*, London: Routledge.
Etzioni, A. (1993) *The Parenting Deficit*, London: Demos.
Goldsmith, E. (1988) *The Great U-turn: Deindustrialising society*, Bideford: Green Books.
Gorz, A. (1985) *Paths to Paradise: On the liberation from work*, London: Pluto.

Hewitt, P. (1993) *About Time: The revolution in work and family life*, London: Institute of Public Policy Research/Rivers Oram Press.

Holman, R. (1981) *Kids at the Door*, Oxford: Blackwell.

Holman, R. (1986) *Resourceful Friends*, London: Children's Society.

Illich, I., Zola, I.K., McKnight, J., Caplan, J. and Shaiken, H. (1977) *Disabling Professions*, London: Marion Boyars.

Jackson, T. and Marks, N. (1994) *Measuring Sustainable Economic Welfare: A pilot index: 1950–1990*, London: Stockholm Environment Institute/New Economics Foundation.

Jacobs, M. (1991) *The Green Economy: Environment, sustainable development and the politics of the future*, London: Pluto.

Leach, P. (1994) *Children First: What our society must do – and is not doing for our children today*, London: Michael Joseph.

Meadows, D.H., Meadows, D.L., Randers, J. and Behrens, W. (1971) *The Limits to Growth*, New York: Universe.

Offe, C. and Henze, R.G. (1992) *Beyond Employment: Time, work and the informal economy*, Cambridge: Polity.

Pearce, D., Markandya, A. and Barbier, E.B. (1989) *Blueprint for a Green Economy*, London: Earthscan.

Pierson, Stanley (1979) *British Socialists: The journey from fantasy to politics*, London: Harvard University Press.

Robertson, J. (1971) *Reform of British Central Government*, London: Chatto and Windus/Charles Knight.

Robertson, J. (1974) *Profit or People? The new social role of money*, London: Calder and Boyars.

Robertson, J. (1976) *Power, Money and Sex: Towards a new social balance*, London: Marion Boyars.

Robertson, J. (1978) *The Sane Alternative: A choice of futures*, Ironbridge, Shropshire: James Robertson. 2nd edn 1983.

Robertson, J. (1982) 'What comes after the welfare state? A post-welfare development path for the UK', *Futures*, February.

Robertson, J. (1985) *Future Work*, London: Gower/Maurice Temple Smith.

Robertson, J. (1989) *Future Wealth: A new economics for the 21st century*, London: Cassell.

Robertson, J. (1994) *Benefits and Taxes: A radical strategy*, London: New Economics Foundation.

Wiesenthal, Helmut (1993) *Realism in Green Politics: Social movements and ecological reform in Germany* (ed. by J. Ferris), Manchester: Manchester University Press.

Part VII

Race/Anti-racism

Introduction

Racism, ethnic prejudice and discrimination are endemic features of contemporary societies, although their intensity and form vary according to historical, cultural and socioeconomic factors. In the worst cases, they are compounded by religion, nationality or colour, and they are sometimes sanctioned by the legal system of the country. Affluence, education, travel, mass communication and other such features of today's world do not seem to have made much difference. Indeed, the collapse of eastern European socialism has reawakened nationalistic sentiments and with them bitter ethnic conflicts in parts of Europe where such animosities were thought to have been a thing of the past.

Generalizations can be both misleading and illuminating. The attitudes of governments in all advanced industrial societies towards 'the strangers in their midst' since the end of the last world war have been pretty similar. To begin with, the emphasis was on assimilation: immigrant communities were to be fully absorbed into the host society. When it became evident that this was not possible because neither the host society nor the immigrant community were too keen on the idea, the emphasis switched to integration. Certain aspects of immigrant life were to be made similar to those of the host society, while others were to stay unaltered. The crucial point would be mutual understanding and tolerance between the two sides. It was not long before ethnic communities found to their cost that in practice mutuality was a one-way process and worked against them. Understandably, many ethnic communities began to emphasize separateness but under the more appealing slogan of cultural diversity – a pretty impossible policy, if taken literally. Now as ever, relationships between ethnic communities and the rest of society are in varying degrees of animosity where racism, prejudice and discrimination are rife. There is no doubt that, in white societies, black people suffer more from racism than other ethnic groups.

There is abundant evidence that employment opportunities and earning levels of many immigrant groups are below those of the rest of society, even when educational standards are taken into account. It is well documented that the educational achievements of children from some ethnic backgrounds are lower than those of other children for a variety of reasons: socioeconomic conditions of the family, neighbourhood values towards education, and school factors relating to teachers' attitudes and curriculum content. Housing conditions are inferior, health conditions worse and mortality rates higher. These and other disadvantages are well documented, generally agreed and need no further elaboration here.

What is in dispute is the explanation of and the solution to these disadvantages. Happily, the days are past when they were attributed by many academics to such ethnic group characteristics as low intelligence, lack of effort or initiative, anti-social values and other unsavoury features. Blaming the victim is now a minority academic exercise. The main explanations today are structural, either in Weberian or in Marxist terms. Weberian explanations stress the interminable conflict between various income, occupational, housing and other such groupings. Ethnic groups tend to lose out in such conflicts because one disadvantage leads to another, particularly when officialdom acts in discriminatory ways. Marxist explanations emphasize the central significance of the role of the capitalist state as an ideological and repressive apparatus in perpetuating racism, prejudice and discrimination in society. Weberian explanations claim that the abolition of prejudice and discrimination is possible, though extremely difficult, in capitalist societies. Progress will result in the declining significance of ethnicity and the corresponding rise in the significance of class, defined in Weberian terms, in the distributional practices of society. Marxist approaches consider this a contradiction in terms. Harmonious and egalitarian ethnic relations are possible only in a socialist society. Socialism does not necessarily lead to ethnic harmony, but it is an essential prerequisite.

Anti-racism, whether defined in Weberian or Marxist terms, is not merely a defensive ideology and strategy. It is also a positive, forward-looking approach for the creation of harmonious multiethnic societies. It is true that it seeks to expose and remedy the many injustices committed against ethnic groups in society, but it also attempts to show that a multiracial society built on egalitarian ethnic relationships is a far better society than societies riven by ethnic strife. Like all other radical ideologies, anti-racism is faced with innumerable, and some would say insurmountable, obstacles in pursuing and achieving its objectives. Radical ideologies are in varying degrees utopias for they reach out for the seemingly unattainable. History, however, shows that the utopias of today can sometimes become the realities of tomorrow.

18 Hall

David Denney

Brief biography

Stuart Hall was born in Jamaica in 1932. He won a Rhodes scholarship to Oxford University in 1951. For two years he taught at a secondary school in Brixton, and from 1961 to 1963 he was a lecturer in Liberal Studies at the Chelsea College of Science. Hall was then to become Research Fellow at the Centre for Contemporary Cultural Studies (CCCS), University of Birmingham, and from 1972 to 1979 Director. Since then he has been Professor of Sociology at the Open University. Hall has made important contributions to the *New Left Review* and *Marxism Today*.

Hall's career is unusual in a number of important respects. First, he was able to become a leading black academic in the 1960s and 1970s in what was even more of a white middle-class enclave than it is today. Second, he is one of the few British academics who have been able successfully to use the media, particularly television, to bring theoretical ideas to a wider audience. This has been particularly evident in his television work, most notably for the Open University. Hall's writing has been influential in social science over a period spanning almost thirty years.

Main ideas

Hall can be regarded as developing 'core' concepts in relation to 'race', racism and the state. His distinctive approach to the analysis of the concept of 'race' was developed through the 1970s, although his more descriptive programmatic writings can be traced to the mid-1960s (Solomos, 1986).

Hall claimed that sociological accounts of race and racism had hitherto failed to take into account the historical, economic and structural features of societies which enabled racism to be reproduced. He thus moved beyond a simplistic form of Marxist analysis, which reduces all social relations to the productive process offering in the seminal *Policing the Crisis* (Hall *et al.*, 1978) what Barker has referred to as 'A case study of relatedness without reduction' (Barker, 1992: 85).

Race and class

The nature of this relatedness can be seen most clearly in Hall's analysis of class, 'race' and racism. The relationship between these concepts, as suggested by Weberians like Rex, and by other Marxists, had hitherto been dominated by an undiluted form of economic reductionism. Cashmore and Troyna, when summarizing the work of Oliver Cox, encapsulate the reductionist approach:

> People are encouraged to think in terms of race, and therefore, inherent inequality because it benefits capitalism. This system is based on a basic split over the ownership and means of production: the owners, capitalists, continually need to exploit the nonowners, workers on whom they depend for labour. Their remaining in power as owners is contingent on their ability to maintain their grip over the workers and this is best done if those workers don't perceive their common exploitation, unite and present opposition. So it becomes necessary to keep them divided into fractions, if possible by introducing and perpetuating antagonisms between them. The race issue performs the function perfectly. (Cashmore and Troyna, 1990: 43)

In *Policing the Crisis*, although class fractioning is acknowledged, the conceptualization of 'race' and class, and the relationship between these two concepts, is developed beyond the simple 'ruling class' need to divide an homogeneous grouping. 'Race' is conceptualized as a 'modality in which class is lived'. In other words, class constitutes the manner in which black people 'live', experience and make sense of the social structures of which they form a part. It is through what Hall refers to as the 'modality' of race that black people comprehend, and begin to resist, the exploitation which is an objective feature of their class situation (Hall *et al.*, 1978).

Following Gramsci, Hall argues that there is no homogeneous social formation 'the working class' or the 'ruling class'. It is the conceptual connection, or in Hall's words the 'articulation', between race and class which is of analytical importance, not their existence as separate entities (Hall, 1980b). Under specific historical conditions, alliances between different fractions of classes are formed. The apparatuses of the state, including welfare agencies, enable 'blocs' or 'ensembles' of relations between class fractions to form. It is through such alliances that social authority is exercised within the state (Hall *et al.*, 1978: 204). In calling for a new theoretical approach to racism, Hall overcame the reductionism which had dominated many Marxist writings on 'race'.

Throughout his work, Hall has retained an interest in the media representations of reality, and particularly representations of black people. He suggests that television disseminates messages through relatively autonomous processes of production, circulation and reproduction (Hall, 1980a). Populist modes of media communication constructed both the 'crisis' and the remedy, which during the 1980s became a populist demand for more law and order. Mass communication techniques have their own structure of dominance, reflecting the imprint of dominant institutionalized power relations. It is not simply economic conditions or the machinations of the media which create the 'crisis', but more importantly the efforts made by the state to defend the status quo (Hall, 1983). The radical right created a discourse which emphasized the need for law and order, economic discipline and authority, in the face of a crisis constructed in terms of a conspiracy by the enemies of the state, the onset of social anarchy, and the dilution of British stock by 'alien black elements'. What emerged was a form of 'authoritarian populism' which is described by Hall as 'An exceptional form of the capitalist state which unlike classical fascism has retained most (though not all) of the formal representative institutions in place, and which at the same time has been able to construct around itself an active popular consent' (Hall, 1983: 22).

The movement towards authoritarianism was not temporary or recent, but had its roots in the imperialist crisis of the 1880s and 1890s. It developed out of social anxieties and tensions generated by Britain's changing place in the world order, and was tutored by a social philosophy which sought to restore social harmony through 'traditionalist morality' and an 'unqualified respect for authority'. The economic decline which followed the post–Second World War boom was compounded by oscillations between recession and recovery, with a steady tendency towards deterioration throughout the 1960s. This destroyed the remnants of the Wilsonian 'radical programme' of social reform which had re-emerged in 1964 following thirteen years of Conservative government

The economy had slipped into 'slumpflation' by the Heath years of 1971–4: 'By the mid 1970s the economic parameters wrere dictated by a synchronisation between capitalist recession on a global scale, and the crisis of capital accumulation specific to Britain – the weak link in the chain' (Hall, 1988: 24). Domestic politics were dominated by government clashes with organized labour. The repertoire of government policy during the 1970s was, according to Hall, incomes policy first by consent and then by imposition, while towards the end of the decade the imposition of the socal contract was intended by the Labour government to mark a reconciliation between capital and labour. The Labour Party in the late 1970s, according to Hall, effectively became the party of social democracy.

Hall's early work has been crucial in the development of ideas about racism and anti-racism within welfare. Miles argues that the empirical evidence available relating to racial discrimination gives support to Hall's argument that

> Racism is not a set of mistaken perceptions ... it arises because of the concrete problems of different classes and groups in society. Racism represents the attempt

ideologically to construct those contradictions and problems in such a way that they can be dealt with and deflected at the same moment. (Hall, 1978: 35, quoted in Miles, 1989: 82)

In other words, as Miles points out, racism can

successfully (although mistakenly) make sense of the world and thereby provide a strategy for political action for sections of different classes. It follows that to the extent that racism is an attempt to understand a specific combination of economic and political relations, strategies for eliminating racism should concentrate less on trying exclusively to persuade those who articulate racism that they are 'wrong' and more on changing those particular economic and political relations. (Miles, 1989: 82)

The development of anti-racism

Hall's work has enabled anti-racism to be formulated at a number of conceptual levels. Feuchtwang (1990) has described the 'politics of anti-racism' as being essentially based on the achievement of the right not to be discriminated against on the basis of 'race'. Anti-racism must address itself to the distribution of labour power, the structuring of jobs themselves, the allocation of housing, the assessment of health, and the potential for education and training. In all these areas, anti-racism requires an elimination of discrimination on 'grounds of origin'.

The second major concern which defines anti-racism is for Feuchtwang cultural, encompassing diet, dialect, language, body image, marriage and other customs of life. Anti-racist practices require the elimination of discrimination in both these areas (Feuchtwang, 1990). Gilroy (1992) has noted the recent failure to connect anti-racist policies with the everyday lives of black people. The creation of an undifferentiated notion of the black community has for Gilroy been the calamitous result of some forms of anti-racism. What was once an anti-racist movement has now been enveloped in a 'catastrophe' characterized by the absence of mass mobilization around anti-racist aims and a crisis of political language, images and cultural symbols. Anti-racism has thus been responsible for black people being conceived of as victims and not an active force 'working in many different ways for our freedom from racial subordination' (Gilroy, 1992: 60).

Through his conceptualizations of 'race', racism and the relationship between discrimination and the state, Hall has clarified and developed concepts which provide a theoretical base for those formulating social policy in both the 'public' and the 'cultural' domain, while taking cognizance of the concerns expressed by Gilroy.

Hall's early contribution was to insist on a more critical and multidimensional approach towards anti-racism which could inform strategies for challenge and change. In an important paper entitled 'Race articulation and societies structured in dominance' (Hall, 1980b), racism is centrally positioned within economic, political and ideological relations. Hall, by clarifying a number of concepts, has created the basis for an anti-racist strategy. His analysis also combines an understanding of racism with the workings of the state of which welfare is an integral part.

A Marxist account of racism

According to Solomos, Hall has provided a Marxist account of racism which can form the basis for anti-racism in three ways. First, there is a rejection of the idea that racism is a general feature of all societies. What does exist are differing forms of racism or racisms, each of which are related to specific historical conditions. This must be appreciated if the complex nuances of racism are to be understood and tackled by any welfare organization.

The second principle is based on the idea that, although racism cannot be analyzed in isolation from other forms of social relationship, it is relatively autonomous from other economic, political and ideological relationships. Relative autonomy, although having its roots in the work of Marx and Engels, was developed by Hall in the late 1970s and throughout the 1980s to encapsulate a study of racism. It effectively means that there is no monolithic correspondence between racism and specific economic or social relations like class. Other writers have utilized this idea to argue that the working class cannot be conceived of as a continuous historical subject, since black people can constitute themselves as an autonomous social force in politics (Solomos, 1986; Gilroy, 1992).

The third proposition develops from the second in that, while race is relatively autonomous from class, it is impossible to understand one in terms which are completely separate from the other. Class has a reciprocal relation with race, and it is the 'articulation' between the two, not their separateness, which is important for analysis.

The relevance of Hall's ideas to welfare

Since Stuart Hall's work tends towards theoretical analyses of ideology and dominant forms of discourse, the direct relevance of his work to welfare is more often generalist than specific. It is sometimes difficult, therefore, to find specifically developed analyses of particular services in his work.

Hall argues that, by the 1960s, the whole impulse had come near to reshaping in a fundamental way public attitudes and public philosophies in the UK, towards creating a commonsense view among the majority of the population in favour of a socially redistributive public philosophy. However, Hall is not incognizant of the weaknesses of the welfare state when he argues that the 'welfare state was often bureaucratic, inflexible, resistant to the needs of other people, defensive, inward looking' (Hall, 1989: 6).

According to Hall, the undermining of welfare was central to the spread of the 'authoritarian populism' which dominated British politics throughout the 1980s. The notion of 'equality' on which the welfare state and anti-racism were based, he argues, was replaced with the notion of 'freedom'. The state no longer represented the caring society, but was transformed by a celebration of institutionalized individualism and selfishness. During the period of drift into what Hall refers to as a 'law and order society', the need to develop theoretical perspectives which defended threatened welfare services was paramount.

Cultural deficit models and welfare provision

The earliest sociological writings on race and race relations were assimilationist in orientation, appearing to view black people as 'dark strangers' who had the responsibility to adapt to the customs and habits of the 'host community' (Patterson, 1971). The literature relating to welfare provision with some notable exceptions virtually ignored the presence of black people throughout the 1960s. The isolated pieces of literature that did emerge in this period appeared to condone an assimilationist position, blaming black people for inappropriate use of welfare services (Fitzherbert, 1967). White perceptions were inherently superior to the black person's view of the world, since the white social worker could function more effectively in society.

Hall's work during this period, although essentially descriptive, provided an antidote to the dominant ethnocentric cultural deficit model of social need. His early writing in the area of education, for instance, although tending towards the descriptive, offered vivid accounts of what life was like for young black people in the inner city. Discrimination was conceptualized in terms of practices which precluded black people from gaining access to sources of power. The role of the teacher was to assist white people in understanding the needs of vulnerable black people, and to help them through adversity (Hall, 1967).

Liberal pluralism

During the 1960s, some of Hall's concerns were not that dissimilar to those of the liberal pluralist, a paradigm which came to dominate welfare discourse during the early 1970s. Within this framework, society is conceptualized in terms of competing groups deriving their power from a variety of sources, military, religious and economic. Discrimination in these terms can be seen as emanating from the practices which exclude black people from gaining access to sources of power (Cheetham, 1972). The reality of multiple deprivation is acknowledged by the liberal pluralist as affecting black people differentially. Corrective action is seen as being required within existing systems of welfare provision in order to correct the balance. The role of welfare is seen in terms of assisting black people through the inevitable difficulties which they experience in attempting to utilize welfare services for their own advancement.

Policies with the stated aim of giving black people access to equal educational opportunity have been an important feature of liberal pluralism. Full entitlement to services, with the creation of clearly stated equal opportunities policies, is also emphasized in relation to housing and social work services. All policies should have the aim of reducing inequality. Understanding individual problems and developing relationships with black people who need help provides an essential bridge between black people and the white population. The overall race relations goal for the pluralist is a complex blend of integration and assimilation.

Integration, a concept much beloved of politicians throughout the 1970s and 1980s, implied that a certain amount of responsibility lay with the white 'host' community to adapt to a situation in which black people were a permanent part of many communities. In 1965 the then Home Secretary Roy Jenkins in a major speech noted the end of assimilationist policies and the beginning of policies which aimed towards integration, which he described 'not as a flattening process of assimilation but equal opportunity combined with cultural diversity in an atmosphere of mutual tolerance' (quoted in Jones, 1977: 148). The most important feature of the pluralist paradigm was that it was dominated by white academics and policy-makers, who set the policy agenda without reference to the perceptions of black people or the need to analyze the nature of racism and other forms of discrimination within welfare institutions.

Hall, while constantly drawing attention to both the relatedness and the relative autonomy of race and class within his analysis, is careful to see the significance of the shift from assimilation to the pluralist form of integration. Although he distances himself from pluralism as his Marxist analysis develops throughout the 1970s and 1980s, he clearly views the liberal position as having importance in the development of policies towards black people.

This point can be illustrated in relation to Hall's reaction to the Scarman inquiry into the Brixton disturbances of 1981. Here he argued that Lord Scarman's report, which in many respects can be regarded as an exemplar of the liberal pluralist perspective, needed to be seriously analyzed and not dismissed out of hand. He viewed Scarman not simply as a well-intentioned liberal ultimately serving the capitalist mode of production. The 'forces of law and order', Hall argued, regarded Scarman as a 'wild irresponsible radical in wig and ermine' (Hall, 1982: 67). Despite Scarman's 'liberalism', Scarman 'perfectly' understood the roots of the disorders in the material deprivation of black people, and incisively described how long-term conditions and short-term contingent factors trigger unpredictable events. The main distinction between Hall and the position taken by Scarman and others was the liberals' failure to grasp the fact that oppressive policing is not simply a set of fortuitous events, but a 'structural condition'. Scarman is thus unable to recognize the structural bases of racist practices, which marks the 'one limit-point to his reformism' (Hall, 1982: 68).

Cultural pluralism

Another strong theoretical current which emerged during the 1970s, and to some extent has re-emerged in the 1990s as a counter to the total absorption suggested by the assimilationists, is cultural pluralism. Here there is an attempt to demonstrate how the understanding of several ethnicities can ameliorate the worst injustices created by a society in which positions of power are occupied by white people (Ballard, 1979; Khan, 1979). While recognizing 'ethnic diversity', an essentially consensus-oriented view of society is taken, although the cultural pluralist would emphasize the appreciation of cultural differences and the potential strength that emanates from cultural identity as being the key component in the planning and delivery of welfare services. Culturalism has been a powerful force within both multicultural education and the provision of personal social services. Teachers during the late 1970s and early 1980s were required to reflect a multicultural society in the development of curricula, while social workers needed to form specialist sections staffed by 'ethnic minorities' in order to offer culturally sensitive forms of assistance (Tomlinson, 1984; Ely and Denney, 1987).

Some black writers have conceptualized multiculturalism as a misguided attempt to study not the relations between race as defined by colour, but the relations between ethnic groups as defined by their culture. British society was to be viewed not as some sort of homogeneous cultural monolith (as had happened in the past), but as a multicultural, multiethnic society, and the business of the ethnic school was to ameliorate, mediate and buffer the injustices of white society. All that black people needed to do was to 'pull themselves up by their ethnic bootstraps' (Bourne and Sivanandan, 1980: 343).

Hall has made it conceptually possible to combine a structuralist critique with the notion of cultural resistance. He has pointed to some of the dangers associated with a hegemonic conception of ethnicity that encapsulates the Thatcherite notion of 'Englishness', which is closed, regressive and exclusivist. Hall has also observed that 'The term ethnicity acknowledges the place of history, language and culture in the construction of subjectivity and identity, as well as the fact that all discourse is placed, positioned, situated, and all knowledge is contextual' (Hall, 1992: 257). Hall calls for a more appropriate, non-reductionist analysis of ethnicity as forming the basis for a new cultural politics which engages rather than suppresses difference, and which is dependent on the construction of new identities. He is also quick to emphasise the importance of 'decoupling' ethnicity from its function within the dominant discourses of nationalism, imperialism and racism.

In more recent work, Hall has argued that national cultures should be thought of not as being unified, but as constituting what he refers to as a 'discursive device' representing identity. All modern nations are, as far as Hall is concerned, 'cultural hybrids'. Culture, ethnicity and race cannot therefore be associated with nation in any unified sense (Hall, 1992). This theoretical approach enables services to be developed which are sensitive to cultural differences, while also locating racism within the structure of dominant institutions.

The binary proposition between multiculturalism and anti-racism has recently been called into question. Rattansi, writing on education, has argued that 'Although both movements have made important contributions, my judgement is that their frameworks and policies share significant and disabling weaknesses' (Rattansi, 1992: 39). Hall moves beyond such limiting conceptual barriers, which trivialize struggles against racism by isolating the concept from other political antagonisms (Gilroy, 1992). He thus enables his work to be useful to the development of ideas which are relevant to people on the streets, while also placing race and racism at the forefront of his analysis.

The emergence of structural and black perspectives in welfare

The structuralist analysis of welfare services which emerged in the late 1980s had its base within various forms of Marxist analysis, locating institutional racial subordination in a state which exists for the sole purpose of supporting capitalism. Racism was conceptualized in terms of being an ideology which not only excludes black people from service provision, but also ensures that they are overrepresented within the state's more punitive institutions (Denney, 1992). Welfare services should work to remove racially structured subordination, while providing black consumers of welfare and the black community with more material resources. Writers within this perspective would not direct attention towards personal problem-solving capabilities and cultural differences, but would focus on identifying groups which suffer structurally based discrimination, to whom resources should be transferred.

Although Hall is frequently associated with the development of such a perspective, his work has enabled black perspectives to develop. Singh warns against conflating a black perspective in relation to welfare services into one monolithic concept. Black identities never remain the same, but are, as Hall would argue, historically contingent fields of contestation within the nature of a hierarchical, racialized and gendered society (Singh, 1992). In a much-quoted passage, Hall claims that the word 'black' itself 'was coined as a way of referencing the common experience of racism and marginalisation in Britain and came to provide the organizing category of a new politics of resistance amongst groups and communities with in fact very different histories, traditions, and ethnic identities' (Hall, 1992: 252).

Hall's writing reflects a range of experiences of racism, and a commitment to ensure that black people gain the power to have a voice in formulating policies which are of direct relevance to their needs. His analysis of particular aspects of welfare reflects this commitment.

In the area of 'criminal justice', Hall's collaboration with Clarke, Critcher, Jefferson and Roberts resulted in the seminal *Policing the Crisis*. The authors describe how a series of moral panics culminated in the 'black mugger' becoming the condensed symbol of everything that was going wrong in Britain (Barker, 1992). Young black school-leavers were constructed by various arms of the media as 'an ethnically distinct class fraction – the one most exposed to the winds of unemployment' (Hall *et al.*, 1978: 332). Policing black people threatened to combine with the problem of policing the poor and the unemployed in the 1970s. Such a perception of crisis required black people to be successfully depicted by government and media as a threat to essential Englishness, and to cherished values enshrined in such institutions as the family and the sanctity of the home.

The construction of the black mugger at a particular historical moment challenged the view that the relation between news and crime is a simple one. The writers argue that definitions of crime and in this case black crime are socially constructed officially by agencies responsible for crime control, the police and the courts being the 'primary definers of crime'. Such definitions reflect the selective attention of journalists and the routine practices of news gathering and presentation, while official definitions of crime are transformed into the vigorous public language of popular journalistic rhetoric. The public definition of crime is therefore dependent on the official and media definitions of crime (Hall *et al.*, 1975, 1978).

Similarly, by the 1980s Hall had identified education as being a fundamentally important site of struggle against the New Right. The ascendancy of 'progressive education' had been halted by the creation of a right-wing moral panic relating to a fall in standards of school-leavers. There were allegations of creeping mass illiteracy and innumeracy created by progressivism in schools, and that such problems were bound to affect the efficiency and productivity of the nation. Such was the new logic created by the 'three popular ventriloquist voices of the radical right, the *Mail*, the *Sun* and the *Express*' (Hall, 1985: 53).

The welfare state was one of the founding principles of the postwar political settlement, marking the boundaries of a consensus within whose limits both the major political parties agreed to contend (Hall, 1979). What Hall describes is the steady undermining of welfare and welfare rights, particularly with regard to black people. In the 'social market', welfare is a rigidity from which free-thinking and free-market-minded men and women seek to escape, according to Hall. It is clear that, in 1979, Hall envisaged not the restructuring of the welfare state, but the 'substantial destruction of the welfare state which is now on the cards' (1979: 5). Four years later, Hall took the argument even further by asserting that the New Right had 'savaged public expenditure and the welfare state' (Hall, 1983: 12).

Although the results of this shift in policy had been felt by all poor people, black people had been differentially affected. Even to raise the question of welfare rights and the rights of black people to be free of discrimination had become 'tantamount to declaring oneself a subversive' (Hall, 1979: 4). Hall continues by arguing that

We are now in the middle of a deep and decisive moment towards a more disciplinary, authoritarian society. This shift has been in progress since the 1960s; but it has gathered pace through the 1970s and is heading, given the spate of disciplinary legislation now on the parliamentary agenda, towards some sort of interim climax. (1979: 3)

Impact of Hall on welfare policies and debates

It is within his analysis of what he regards as the creeping authoritarianism of the state that Hall has made a particularly important impact on 'race and institutionalized racism'. His position opened up debates with Weberian socio-logists of 'race relations' like John Rex and with other Marxists. Although Hall was concerned with the way in which racism functioned and was produced and reproduced within societies, he was equally interested in other substantive areas, most notably the relationship between racism, class, gender and other social relations.

Such concerns to some extent contrasted with the Weberian conclusions drawn by Rex and Moore from their classic study of the Sparkbrook area of Birmingham (Rex and Moore, 1967). Here it had been argued that an individual's life chances are determined not simply by the relationship that an individual has with the means of production. On the contrary, there are numerous other possible areas of conflict not directly connected with the means of production.

Rex and Moore argued that the housing market or 'housing class' constitutes a separate site of struggle for scarce resources. Housing, they claimed, creates unique constellations of conflicts in which black people are discriminated against. Health, education and other areas of welfare would also constitute discrete examples of complex competitive battles for scarce resources. Explanations of racism cannot therefore be reduced to the productive relation alone. Such writing departs from what Rex has referred to as a 'crude' focus on the mode of production (Rex, 1986), recognizing that 'class theory can and should be supplemented by the theory of ethnicity' (1986: 81). There may be ethnic situations where there is no conflict based on class interests.

Hall has also attempted to move the concepts of 'race' and ethnicity away from the reductionism which characterized some forms of analysis on the left. In his reconceptualization of 'race', he to a degree supports John Rex in his critique of oversimplified reductionist Marxist analyses of racism (Hall, 1980b). Rex acknowledges that, although he and Hall come from different classical sociological positions, there would appear to be some level of theoretical convergence. 'Stuart Hall', Rex writes, 'has taken on board many of the criticisms that I have made of Marxist analysis, arguing that structural issues which I raise are not incompatible with a more sophisticated form of Marxism' (Rex, 1986: 68). Hall also recognizes that some aspects of his own analyses – in particular, the notion of 'structured in dominance' – are not dissimilar to Rex's account of racism in South Africa and the Caribbean (Hall, 1979). Hall supports Rex in describing a number of Marxist explanations of race and racism as overdetermined and reductionist.

Although Hall's work lacks a detailed engagement with specific policy measures, his ideas, along with the ideas of other prominent black academics, have had an impact on various aspects of social welfare provision (see, for example, Mullard, 1991). In the field of education, Hall advocates a pedagogical approach which emphasizes the understanding of racism as an ideology and the distinctiveness of race and class relations in different social formations at specific points in history. He calls upon all educators to frame questions to students in such a way as to enable them to make correlations between economic movements and race relations legislation (Hall, 1981). Teaching strategies should not simply be about changing prejudiced attitudes and putting 'good' attitudes in their place. Education should deconstruct the obvious, and demonstrate that students' life experiences are not 'just like that'. The teacher and student have to undermine the obvious in order to show how social and historical processes operate. Students must be taught to understand that social reality is not 'written in the stars' in order that the process of questioning can begin. A central role for the educator, according to Hall, is to question 'illusion' (Hall, 1981).

In a few isolated cases, the impact of the theoretical thrust of which Hall is a part have been felt. In social work education, for instance, anti-discriminatory practices are integrated and tested areas of competence to be developed on all Diploma in Social Work courses (CCETSW, 1991a, 1991b).

Hall's concerns relating to the differential treatment of black people by state agencies has led him towards a consideration of welfare and welfare rights. The right to welfare rights is what Hall calls the 'core' of the 'social contract', which has 'made it possible for the popular classes and the poor to consent to be governed as they are within a class-divided society' (Hall, 1979: 5). Hall notes two dominant tendencies that point to the changing role of the law in a number of areas which threaten to erode or destroy those rights in relation to specific groups. First, the police and particularly police chiefs are not only policing, but formulating ideas which are related to criminal justice policy. In the late 1970s and early 1980s, this was most obvious in the policing of industrial disputes. Second, there is an unprecedentedly high profile in relation to the policing of black people. In 1979 the pervasive application of 'arrest on suspicion' and the introduction of 'Special Patrol Groups' provided examples of the 'drift' into a social formation dominated by law and order.

While Hall is right to emphasize the changing role of the police and its associated implications, it should be remembered that the 1948 Criminal Justice Act, which was introduced by the Labour government at the point at which the welfare state was being constructed, also represented a drift into further law and order before the emergence of 1980s authoritarianism. This Act introduced the punitive detention centres which were designed to create a 'disciplined' environment for the young offender. Such ideas were echoed in the 'short sharp shock' which heralded the 1982 Criminal Justice Act. Also the notion of abolishing capital punishment was abandoned in 1948, while the minimum age for imprisonment was reduced from sixteen to fifteen (Gilroy and Sim, 1985; Brake and Hale, 1992). The move towards more overt authoritarian forms of state intervention cannot therefore exclusively be associated with a government of the New Right.

Hall's powerful critique of the New Right has ensured that his ideas have not played a central part in policy formulation since 1979. If anything, recent government statements on law and order have turned Hall's critique on its head and blamed collectivism for, in Hall's terms, the negative results of Thatcherism. Although recent government policy with regard to all aspects of welfare provision would appear to affirm many of Hall's ideas on the diminishing role of welfare in penal policy, the impetus created by the ideas of critical academics like Hall appears on occasions to have had some tangible effect. Although section 95 of the 1991 Criminal Justice Act is vague and to some extent open ended, it does require the Secretary of State to publish information that she or he considers expedient for the purpose of enabling people involved in the criminal justice system to avoid discrimination on the grounds of race, sex or any other improper ground (Home Office, 1992). It would be difficult to sustain the case that Hall's work has practically impacted on the successful struggle to include section 95 in the 1991 Criminal Justice Act, while it is undeniable that the position taken by black lawyers and the National Association of Probation Officers who fought for its inclusion in the Act was not dissimilar to that taken by Hall.

Hall's critics have characterized his analysis as emphasizing the political and ideological levels, which has resulted in the inhibition of constructive strategic thinking. The result of this has been a tendency to homogenize Thatcherism into a 'monstrous monolith', while failing to examine government programmes in detail (Jessop *et al.*, 1984).

Hall's analysis of welfare and the position occupied by black people within welfare and coercive apparatuses has also been characterized as rhetorical. It is only through a more specific analysis of government policy that Thatcherism can be understood, it is argued. Hall has thus been accused of overlooking important contradictions and tensions within Thatcherism and the process of policy formation (Jessop *et al.*, 1984).

An alternative interpretation to that of Hall suggests that, far from being destroyed by Thatcherism, the welfare state has been preserved between 1979 and 1987: 'Contrary to popular perception, indicators of welfare inputs, outputs and outcomes in key areas such as education, health care and community care had either remained constant or had actually risen over the period, even when changes in needs were taken into account' (Le Grand, 1992: 3). Current government rhetoric celebrates the rights of citizens to high-quality market-tested services, not, it is argued, the wholesale destruction of services. It is important to note, however, that Hall is not closed to other positions in his analysis of welfare policy.

Key texts

In selecting the most important contributions made by Hall, one is faced with three immediate problems: first, the sometimes bewildering extent and complexity of his contributions; second, as was said at the outset, the wide time span of his work; and third, the fact that Hall, like many prolific writers, has developed ideas which have been influenced by numerous intellectual themes which have changed over time.

In selecting *Policing the Crisis*, it is hoped to capture the culmination of Hall's ideas before the election of the Thatcher government in 1979, and his critique of the ideology which emerged after 1979. Both of the texts considered below are concerned with aspects of race and racism.

Policing the Crisis (Hall *et al.*, 1978) was a major intellectual achievement which still has an enduring influence in social science. The book is centrally concerned with the media presentation of mugging, and the centrality of mugging at a specific historical moment in British politics. The writers trace events which transformed 'mugging' into a 'general crisis in hegemony', the development of a postwar consensus, the establishment and disintegration of an extensive 'hegemony' and the failure of the political parties claiming to represent the interests of working people. All this resulted in 'the resumption of more manifest forms of class struggle' (Hall *et al.*, 1978: 219) The welfare state, having failed many working people is seen by the authors of *Policing the Crisis* as an attempt to 'manage' capitalism in a manner which backfired on the Labour government. The Labour government's policies enabled the ideology of the New Right to be constructed in terms of a force which could reclaim essential values like thrift, unity, the family and nationhood.

'Race articulation and societies structured in dominance' (Hall, 1980) is significant since it clearly establishes the distinctiveness of Hall's approach to the study of race and racism, while also influencing the development of Marxist thought. Hall makes his analytical framework clear, in that racism had to be located within social relations which were historically specific. A number of fundamental questions set a new agenda for the study of race and race relations. Hall focused his attention in this paper first on the relationship between racism and social structures within capitalist forms of social organization. His second set of questions as Solomos (1986) has pointed out, concerned the way in which racism directly influenced social relations within capitalist societies, with specific reference to class and gender. It was also in this paper that Hall made explicit the relative autonomy of race and class, while arguing for the development of a new Marxist paradigm which sought to overcome the lack of historical specificity and reductionism that had characterized other forms of Marxist analysis. The ideas expressed in this paper formed the basis for further work which took place within the Centre for Contemporary and Cultural Studies throughout the 1980s.

Conclusion

It has been argued in this chapter that Hall is not a Marxist polemicist who will reduce all forms of analysis of welfare to the contradictions within the capitalist mode of production. Neither is his work relevant to analysis only at the level of ideology. It would be difficult to overestimate the importance of Hall's contribution during the last three decades. His ability to offer clear analysis has ensured that a corrective voice has been continually present in the face of attempts to erode all forms of state welfare provision. Even his most thoughtful critics acknowledge that he has been a 'powerful force in rethinking traditional relations between economy, polity, class and party, structures and strategies' (Jessop *et al.*, 1984: 60).

On questions concerning 'race', racism and anti-racism, Hall has extended the understanding of the structural nature of racism at specific historical points, by breaking down false conceptual barriers. His work in the area of culture, media, theories of the state, and racial subordination has facilitated the understanding of racism at individual, collective, historical and institutional levels. He has also clarified the interrelationships between oppression based on race, class, gender, disability, sexuality and age. His analysis provides the basis for a process of transformation by focusing on the contradictory historical forces and interests which have shaped these forms of oppression.

References

Ballard, R. (1979) 'Conflict, continuity and change: second generation South Asian', in Khan, V.S. (ed.), *Minority Families in Britain*, London: Macmillan.

Barker, M. (1992) 'Stuart Hall, *Policing the Crisis*', in Barker, M. and Beezer, A., *Readings into Cultural Studies*, London: Routledge.

Bourne, J. and Sivanandan, A. (1980) 'Cheerleaders and ombudsmen: the sociology of race relations in Britain', *Race and Class*, 21, pp. 331–52.

Brake, M. and Hale, C. (1992) *Public Order and Private Lives*, London: Routledge.

Cashmore, E. and Troyna, B. (1990) *Introduction to Race Relations* (2nd edn), London: Falmer.

CCETSW (1991a) *One Small Step Towards Racial Justice*, London: Central Council for Education and Training in Social Work.

CCETSW (1991b) *DipSW Rules and Requirements for the Diploma in Social Work*, London: Central Council for Education and Training in Social Work.

Cheetham, J. (1972) *Social Work with Immigrants*, London: Routledge and Kegan Paul.

Denney, D. (1992) *Racism and Antiracism in Probation*, London: Routledge.

Feuchtwang, S. (1990) 'The politics of equal opportunities in employment' in Cambridge, A. and Feuchtwang, S. (eds), *Antiracist Strategies*, Aldershot: Avebury.

Fitzherbert, K. (1967) *West Indian Children in London*, London: Bell.

Ely, P. and Denney, D. (1987) *Social Work in a Multiracial Society*, Aldershot: Gower.

Gilroy, P. (1992) 'The end of antiracism', in Donald, J. and Rattansi, A. (eds), *Race, Culture and Difference*, London: Sage.

Gilroy, P. and Sim, J. (1985) 'Law, order and the state of the left', *Capital and Class*, 25, pp. 15–51.

Hall, S. (1967) *The Young Englanders*, London: Community Relations Council.

Hall, S., Clarke, J., Critcher, C., Jefferson, T. and Roberts, B. (1978) *Policing the Crisis*, London: Macmillan.

Hall, S. (1979) *Drifting into a Law and Order Society*, London: Cobden Trust.

Hall, S. (ed.) (1980a) *Culture, Media, Language*, London: Hutchinson.

Hall, S. (1980b) 'Race articulation and societies structured in dominance' in UNESCO, *Sociological Theories, Race and Colonialism*, Paris: UNESCO.

Hall, S. (1981) 'Teaching race in the school in the multicultural society', in James, A. and Jeffcoate, R. (eds), *The School in the Multicultural Society*, London: Harper and Row/Open University Press.

Hall, S. (1982) 'The lessons of Scarman', *Critical Social Policy*, 2,2, 66–72.

Hall, S. (1983) 'The great moving right show', in Hall, S. and Jacques, M. (eds), *The Politics of Thatcherism*, London: Lawrence and Wishart.

Hall, S. (1985) 'Authoritarian populism: a reply to Jessop *et al.*', *New Left Review*, 151, pp. 115–24.

Hall, S. (1988a) 'The crisis of labourism', in *The Hard Road to Renewal: Thatcherism and the crisis of the left*, London: Verso.

Hall, S. (1988b) *The Hard Road to Renewal: Thatcherism and the crisis of the left*, London: Verso.

Hall, S. (1989) *The Voluntary Sector Under Attack?*, London: Islington Voluntary Action Council.

Hall, S. (1992) 'New ethnicities', in Donald, J. and Rattsani, A. (eds), *Race Culture and Difference*, London: Sage.

Hall, S., Clarke, J., Critcher, C., Jefferson, T. and Roberts, B. (1975) 'Newsmaking and crime', Stencilled Occasional Paper, Birmingham Centre for Contemporary and Cultural Studies.

Hall, S., Clarke, J., Critcher, C., Jefferson, T. and Roberts, B. (1978) *Policing the Crisis*, London: Macmillan.

Home Office (1992) *Section 95: Race and the criminal justice system*, London: Home Office.

Jessop, B., Bonnet, K., Bromley, S. and Ling, T. (1984) 'Authoritarian populism: two nations and Thatcherism' *New Left Review*, 147, pp. 32–64.

Jones, C. (1977) *Immigration and Social Policy in Britain*, London: Tavistock.

Khan, V.S. (ed.) (1979) *Minority Families in Britain*, London: Macmillan.

Le Grand, J. (1991) 'Quasi markets and social policy', *Economic Journal*, 101, 1256–67.

Le Grand, J. (1992) 'Paying for or providing welfare?' in Deakin, N. and Page, R. (eds) *The Costs of Welfare*, Aldershot: Avebury.

Miles, R. (1989) *Racism*, London: Routledge.

Mullard, C. (1991) *Towards a Model of Antiracist Social Work*, London: Central Council for Training and Education in Social Work.

Patterson, S. (1971) *Immigration and Race Relations in Britain* 1960–1967, London: Institute of Race Relations/Oxford University Press.

Rattansi, A. (1992) 'Changing the subject: racism, culture and education', in Donald, J. and Rattansi, A. (eds), *Race, Culture and Difference*, London: Sage.

Rex, J. (1986) 'The role of class analysis in the study of race relations: a Weberian perspective', in Rex, J. and Mason, D. (eds), *Theories of Race and Ethnic Relations*, Cambridge: Cambridge University Press.

Rex, J. and Moore, R. (1967) *Race, Community and Conflict*, London: Institute for Race Relations/Oxford University Press.

Singh, G. (1992) *Race and Social Work from Black Pathology to Black Perspectives*, Bradford: Department of Social and Economic Studies, University of Bradford.

Solomos, J. (1986) 'Varieties of Marxist conceptions of "race", class and the state: a critical analysis', in Rex, J. and Mason, D. (eds), *Theories of Race and Ethnic Relations*, Cambridge: Cambridge University Press.

Tomlinson, S. (1984) *Ethnic Minorities in British Schools: A review of the literature 1960–1982*, London: Heinemann.

19 Rex

Floya Anthias

Introduction

John Rex has made a pathbreaking contribution in the areas of sociological theory and the study of race and racism in the UK. Rex's *Key Problems in Sociological Theory*, published in 1961, was a major theoretical contribution to British sociology and arguably has had a profound influence on later developments. It particularly interrogated positivistic, empiricist and functionalist sociology. It called for a return to a concern with conflict and inequality in society, and heralded the demise of the Parsonsian domination over sociology in the UK. For the first time, the work of Marx, and its tremendous sociological insights, was incorporated into a new synthesizing approach to social relations.

John Rex's passionate hatred of all forms of inequality is best illustrated by his concern with racism, or what he called 'race relations' situations. The engagement with this issue, theoretically, was pioneering within British sociology. It is no exaggeration to regard Rex as the founding father of the theoretical study of race and ethnic phenomena in the UK despite the many criticisms, some unjustified, of his work. He was able to identify racist exclusions as central and malignant forces in modern industrial societies, and linked them to economic and political inequalities more generally. He was also less than optimistic about the capacity of the liberal democratic and welfare state to deliver society from the inequalities that reproduced racist ideas and actions; hence the enormous weight he gave to class and ethnic mobilization as forms of struggle. John Rex has also contributed centrally to the debate on the relationship between research, politics and social policy.

Sociological debates and research around race and racism in fact highlight some central issues relating to the link between the academy, politics and social policy. The liberal democratic state is dedicated to the cohesion of social forces, to consent, compliance and legitimation. The terms of the agenda of any specific state at any moment may also be seen as a product of the forces of challenge and contestation within the state and civil society. Policy on immigration and race relations, as in other areas, is state led, although the product of contestation and negotiation. The state is centralized even though the workings of the local state (Ball and Solomos, 1990) are also relevant. Moreover, its personnel are highly professionalized, including experts and quangos. The state's role is ambiguous *vis-à-vis* the desire to control and the desire to know and accomplish the social good.

The relationship between the state and research and the academy is crucial in answering the issue of the extent to which researchers can set the agenda for policy-makers. The positivistic notion of knowing as objective ignores the role of the researcher in constructing the object that is to be known. It is not possible to see research as just an information-gathering exercise. It is important to see how the researcher and researched interact, and how racism features in the research process where studies of racism are concerned. This raises the issue of the aims of research and the construction of objects rather than subjects in the research process (for a critique of the role of white social scientists, see Amos *et al.* (1982)).

Criticisms of race relations research abound in radical journals like *Race Today* and *Race and Class* as well as in work from radical black writers (e.g. Centre for Contemporary Cultural Studies, 1982). There has also been a debate about whether research should be on the cultures and values of the groups themselves, or on the processes that give rise to racism and the institutional structures of the state in European societies.

Research on racism has tended to take an objectivist stand and has stressed information gathering that could then be used by policy-makers (e.g. Smith, 1977, 1981; Brown, 1984). This is a position countered in the work of John Rex, probably the most influential writer on issues of race and politics in Britain.

The work of John Rex

John Rex's contribution to British sociology cannot be easily pigeon-holed. His work spans four decades and incorporates work on social theory as well as work, both theoretical and empirical, on ethnicity and race.

Broadly speaking, John Rex is a Weberian theorist who has drawn heavily on a Marxist-influenced conflict theory, and indeed has developed what in the early 1970s was called a radical or conflict approach in sociology. He rejected, however, some of the more dogmatic and what he felt to be untenable aspects of Marxism in favour of a more reflexive and subject-centred sociology.

In his influential book *Key Problems in Sociological Theory* (1961), he developed a critique of empiricism and functionalism, rejecting approaches that merely sought to establish statistical relationships without looking at their implications for class conflict. He rejected the idea that societies were characterized by the existence of consensual normative systems. He argued that advanced industrial capitalism was characterized by the imposition of dominant values – that is, the exercise of power by a ruling class – and concomitantly of subcultures of resistance. Such societies were therefore essentially conflict societies: conflict being primarily between ruling-class values and those of subordinate groups. He espoused the possibility, following Marshall (1950), that a new value consensus could emerge out of this conflict as a kind of truce which rested on a balance of power in the emerging welfare state.

Class conflict and class consciousness were central notions in his approach. These were derived from an earlier humanist Marxism that stressed the role of collective actors (Lukács, 1971) although his interest was in producing a Weberian analysis of class identities: a kind of Weberianized Marxism (Rex, unpub. paper).

Rex rejected the kind of totalizing theories that were embodied in the work of both structural functionalism and structural Marxism. He espoused an interactionist perspective which was historically and empirically informed. In addition, he favoured a Weberian methodology for empirical and historical investigation.

His empirical and theoretical work on race has served to fuel debates in the UK around a range of important issues: the role of colonialism in structuring what he called race relations situations; the nature of class relations and the notion of housing classes (Rex and Moore, 1967); black colonial immigrants as an underclass and the Marxisant debate on the links between race and class; disadvantage and inequality and the existence of working-class racism as a response to the threats felt by indigenous workers from black immigrants (and the role of the heritage left by colonialism in this); the importance of autonomous ethnic organization and ethnic mobilization for the attainment of a more equal share in resources by immigrant groups; the development of a schema or general approach regarding race relations situations that purport to have general theoretical application; delineation of the features of racism; and the concept of a multicultural society.

The contributions made in books such as *Race Relations in Sociological Theory* (1970), *Race, Colonialism and the City* (1973) and *Colonial Immigrants in a British City* (1979) – the latter co-written with Sally Tomlinson – as well as a number of other publications will be the focus of much of this chapter.

Research and policy

Rex is one of few writers that has a clear position on the relationship between research into race and racism and social policy. Put simply, he accepts the Weberian position that sociologists must avoid political engagement in the research process at all costs.

Sociologists deal with social problems, however, which leads them to the area of social policy. Rex, following Weber, believes that sociologists should clarify what it is that all the parties are actually asking for. His view is that intelligent policy-makers should look at the roots of their own values.

He believes that sociologists should resist the attempt to absorb the study of race relations questions into social policy discussions (as well as absorbing them into a general theory of social stratification (Rex, 1973)). Moreover, social policy must be seen in the context of societies (metropolitan/capitalist) being conflict ridden, where élites attempt to impose views from above: policy cannot be neutral. His view of the state is that it is the place where élites act out their struggle for dominance, and not the place where subordinate groups get represented. This explains largely his belief in the importance of autonomous ethnic mobilization to protect ethnic or other disadvantaged groups.

He also queries the kind of 'liberal' recommendations made by the PEP and other surveys: a sociological study of the question he reminds us rightly would necessarily involve considering the political forces which permit or prevent the implementation of recommended policies. Rex's critique of social policy is linked to his notion of government and social conflict as well as his disillusion with the practical outcomes of race relations industry and policy.

John Rex was concerned (following Myrdal, 1969a) with how ideological aspects of race inform much analysis. He also criticized research that works with assumptions of the inadequacies of the culture and family structure of black and Asian immigrants in the UK. He formulated ideal types of race relations situations believing that heuristic tools can be devised that guard against bias and distortion. He attempted to develop a reflexive sociology of race relations. Writers very rarely examine the difficulties of disengagement on the field and their own experiences during the research process. Espousing C. Wright Mills's edict for self-reflexivity (1970) seems the least a researcher can do in the circumstances. We can locate this debate within the broader framework of value neutrality also.

Before he arrived at his position about social policy, Rex held views which derived from his early experience of Britain and the coming to power of the Labour Party in 1945. The Beveridge dispensation (1942) constituted for Rex a huge step forward not only because it introduced a system of social insurance. The most important right in industrial society is the right to a job (Rex, 1988). Marshall (1950) in talking about the first stage in the struggle for working-class rights saw social rights as comprising full employment, the acceptance of trade union bargaining, and a range of social rights. Rex saw the Marshall dispensation as a truce. Where Marshall saw this as a transition Rex saw it as dependent on the deployment of power by oppressed groups. Changes were seen not as a development of humane ideas in British government but as resulting out of class struggle.

In Myrdal's view (1969a), those who commission research must have their value goals clarified. Myrdal says that we are bound to have a value starting point and chose 'The American Dilemma' (1969b) for his own work. The equivalent for Rex is to take Butskellism as a manifestation of Marshall. But he saw that the reality contradicted it, given the positions of all the various classes. He has made an important contribution to conflict theory on this, reminding us that the recognition of plurality does not mean an equal balance of power;

overriding this are particular power relations. A group which was oppressed would be in a situation of severe conflict if bidding for power. Power is seen in terms of resistance, suggesting a theory of the state as a site of struggle.

Rex (1988) has argued that reliance on legislation and legal rights is problematic, and that all relations between oppressed groups and the state have to take account of co-optation and corporatism. Groups need their own independent organization because they cannot depend on the beneficence of the state. He is almost Gramscian in his view of historic compromise. His own version is to say that compromise will exist as long as there is mobilized power to defend it. Mobilization is central to class struggle, compromise, consensus, and the welfare state.

According to Rex, it is ultimately through political action by minority rank and file that racial discrimination and racism will be defeated (1988: 50). He criticizes a system of welfare which could only, through the Beveridge dispensation, provide a broad framework for policy. This was placed under considerable strain even in times of relative prosperity (1988: 10) but could not 'take the strain which recession and developing racial conflict imposed' by the late 1970s (1988: 13). He criticizes the *ad hoc* nature of policy developments and the poor resourcing of legislation throughout.

Rex wants to distance himself as a sociologist from political engagement. He holds on to what some have seen as a simplistic separation between theoretical concepts (or ideal types, as he prefers to call them) and political values (Back and Solomos, 1993). He sees himself simply as a 'sociologist' who draws on Marx and Weber.

The study of race and ethnicity

Rex has been associated with, and criticized for, adopting a race relations problematic, and he stands in opposition to two writers of different theoretical positions who reject the race relations paradigm: Miles (1982, 1989, 1993) and Banton (1983, 1987, 1988).

Rex's work provides a bridge between the ethnic studies and race relations approach and a Marxist approach that sees ethnic and race categories as essentially economic and class categories. John Rex is a Weberian, concerned with class as it relates to the differential access to resources (at the level of distribution) rather than to production (Weber, 1969). His work on race is specifically concerned with the position of 'black' groups, but he posits a general theory related to colonialism and class exclusion that is clearly also applicable to all ethnic groups in a migrant context.

In order to locate his work, I will first look at the British context of research into race and immigration.

The dominant approach to the study of ethnic minorities in the UK focuses on the relations between ethnic groups. It is possible to distinguish between, on the one hand, an ethnic studies and, on the other hand, a race relations problematic. The problematic of the ethnic studies tradition is that of interaction between distinct cultural groups (Jeffery, 1976; Watson, 1977; Wallman, 1979). Race/racism or racial prejudice/discrimination are considered complicating variables with regard to questions of cultural maintenance, adaptation or progress of an ethnic minority. Often it is argued that these processes differ for 'white' and 'black' groups given the special disadvantages accruing from colour visibility, racial stigmatization or 'black' categorization, which generally means a slower progress towards assimilation or integration for 'black' groups and indeed a possible backlash through the development of resurgent or emergent ethnicity. Within American sociology, this tendency finds expression in the enormously influential debate around social assimilation processes which may or may not be seen to exclude black groupings (Glazer and Moynihan, 1965, 1975).

The race relations tradition, on the other hand, is more centrally concerned with racialized categories, generally defined with regard to colour, and the interaction between 'white' and 'black' populations within a unified nation-state, where the white is in a dominant 'host' position and the black is in a subordinate one as colonial migrant. The main emphasis is on racial stigmatization and its effects on 'race relations'. Social policy recommendations are often made. There are various tendencies within this tradition, ranging from empirical studies of black groups, and their economic and housing deprivation in an urban sociology context, to studies of white racism or of the conflict areas within which 'race relations' are played out (Rex and Moore, 1967; Rose and Deakin, 1969; Van den Berghe, 1978; Rex and Tomlinson, 1979; Brown, 1984).

Marxist approaches, on the other hand, contain a number of distinct tendencies, although Miles (1982) has argued that many of the positions share the race relations problematic with Weberians like John Rex (1970, 1973). The most important attempt seeks to understand racism as a constituent of the development of capitalism, and its ongoing effects in modern societies despite its origins being located in slave society or colonial experience (Cox, 1970; Sivanandan, 1976, 1982). Ethnic and 'race' phenomena tend to be reduced to class phenomena (Anthias, 1990). Another tendency is the attempt to theorize processes of migration from the point of view of the structural requirements of the mode of production, and especially with regard to the role of migrants as categories of labour within developed capitalist nation-states (Castles and Kosack, 1973; Castells, 1975; Nikolinakos, 1975; Phizacklea and Miles, 1980). The Marxist approaches share the problem of resolving the question of the distinct effectiveness of racial/ethnic categories and locating ethnic and 'race' processes within the constituent elements of the capitalist mode of production.

A more synthetic and critical approach that draws from cultural studies can be identified in the recent work of Stuart Hall (1988a, 1988b) and Paul Gilroy (1987, 1993). Finally, a recent trend has been the development of a post-Marxist or post-modernist tendency which rejects the possibility of a general framework within which racisms can be understood (e.g. Cohen, 1988; Bhabha, 1990).

Conceptualizing race relations

Rex's work on race stems from his early involvement with the UNESCO committee which rejected 'race' as denoting a valid scientific taxonomy but which used the term 'race relations situations' to characterize a field of conflict in society. In *Race Relations in Sociological Theory* (1970) Rex gives a definition of a race relations situation.

1. A situation of differentiation, inequality and pluralism between groups.
2. The possibility of clearly distinguishing between such groups by their physical appearance, their culture or occasionally merely by their ancestry.
3. The justification and explanation of this discrimination in terms of some kind of implicit or explicit theory, frequently, but not always, of a biological kind (Rex, 1970: 30).

In 1986 in his book *Race and Ethnicity* Rex revises this somewhat, referring to 'situations of severe conflict, exploitation, oppression and discrimination going beyond what is normal in a free labour market' (Rex, 1986: 20).

In addition to delineating the specificity of race relations situations in such terms, Rex offers, in a number of places, a schematic list of the different types of situation that historically these can embrace while avoiding a systematic typology; they are offered as illustrative of the enormous diversity of such situations (Rex, 1970, 1973, 1981).

Rex has developed an analysis of the social relations of what he terms 'colonial societies', drawing from the work of Furnivall (1939) and M.G. Smith (1965). He relates ethnic groups in colonial societies to the means of production rather than to the absence of a 'common will' (Furnivall, 1939) or to 'differential incorporation' (Smith, 1965), although accepting with Smith the context of legal and political institutions within which such class struggle takes place.

His delineation of colonial society from metropolitan society (advanced industrial society) is in terms of the implications of the transportation of immigrants from the one to the other. His argument is that the importation of workers from colonial society to the metropolitan centre was affected centrally by the position of the groups established under colonialism, and was therefore structured by colonial relations. He posits the existence of two classes, the colonial immigrants and the indigenous working class, who inhabit a differential and unequal position in the labour market. He uses the notion of the 'underclass' to conceptualize colonial immigrants whose position is structured not only by their actual inferior economic placement in the sphere of distribution of resources, including those of housing, but also by their status. Their valuation and honour position *vis-à-vis* the native working class is linked to the degree of race prejudice and inferiorization they face in British society. This is a result of their colonial heritage and being identified with a colonial population.

Rex is against the view of racism as just a system of ideas that can be dealt with by race awareness policies. He sees racist ideas as rationalizations and justifications of class exploitation. Strictly racist justifications are only one of the possible forms of justification, and the use of ethnic and cultural difference can play the same role as biological arguments about inferiority. In *Race Relations in Sociological Theory* (1970) he suggests that other forms of justification have emerged, such as religion. It is therefore necessary to specify the different ways in which inferiorization of groups takes place.

Racism is more than biological determination for Rex. But it is clear that he retains the kind of 'Rexism' found in his threefold definition of a race relations situation: the specificity of a so-called race relations situation is given by severe conflict, competition and exploitation between groups, recognizable by signs regarded as unalterable and rationalized by some deterministic theory (Rex, 1973: 203).

The problem with this is that Rex focuses on relations between groups rather than structural and ideological factors that provide the context for intergroup conflict. However, if we look at the analysis further (1973: 213) we find that Rex is keenly aware of the role of what he calls 'the structural forms of metropolitan societies'. The problem becomes redefined as one of 'the transfer of the immigrant from a colonial society to one in which he has to play a role in metropolitan society' (1973: 213). He notes a divided working class made up of immigrants and natives (1973: 214). Immigrants share this position with other contingents of 'the new poor' but he sees the underclass as a 'structurally distinct element' from the established 'native class'.

Race relations involve the ascription of roles which justify as well as explain inequality (1973: 218). However, Rex stresses the role of colour (see my discussion on blackness later). He is also keen to delineate a special sub-field of social relations that he calls 'race relations', seeing them therefore as essentially produced by ideas of race difference, rather than the ideas of race difference being mediating factors in a broader kaleidoscope of social relations. However, it is difficult to disentangle these as it could be argued that the focus should be on the different constellations of inequality found within social formations. Rex, on the other hand, assumes a given ontological space for race, which produces particular forms of social relations.

According to Miles (1982), Rex's race relations problematic reifies the notion of race, constructing it as a real social relation. However, it is clear from Rex's earliest book *Race Relations in Sociological Theory* (1970), that he is referring to those situations that have been socially defined as resulting from race difference. He does not accept the category of race as signifying a real taxonomy. It is a term used in popular discourse rather than a scientific concept. A more valid critique of his conception of race relations situations is the centrality Rex gives to the empirical study of intergroup relations. He fails to look at the context of ideological, political and economic relations, which may allow us to identify problems of racisms as being those of the relations between perceived races.

Attention should be given to the study of the production of racisms as discourses, practices and outcomes.

Rex sees immigrant workers as having a separate class position based upon a different relation to the means of production, because the terms for the sale of their labour are different and structured through racism. Interestingly, this is a position that Phizacklea and Miles (1980) refer to with their deployment of 'class fraction' (for a critique see Anthias, 1990, 1992c). They see black migrants as a racialized fraction of the working class.

Rex emphasizes the functionality of deterministic ideologies of race difference: in other words, that they function as systems of justification or legitimation of inequalities around supposed race lines. Racisms are not merely sets of false ideas about the necessary social and cultural outcomes of supposed generic stock difference (as Miles (1989) asserts), but they are produced first and foremost in order to justify and legitimize the political projects of exclusion and subordination. He is closer here to Oliver Cox (1970) than to Miles (1982, 1989). The view that racisms justify and rationalize exploitation and oppression is, however, linked to his notion of the ruling class. One problem with this conception is that it fails to note the ethnic nature of class phenomena and the interpenetration of class dominance by ethnic and 'race' dominance. This is a feature of his work that keeps him within an earlier, fairly economic determinist, Weberianized Marxism.

Rex is not actually promoting a race relations problematic, in the strict sense of seeing the relations to be really structured by visible colour differences, although much of the actual empirical referents stem from situations where colour visibility exists. This presents a rather incoherent picture of his approach which I take up later in the discussion of the black working class.

Like Miles (1989), Rex wants to confine racisms to ideologies, not being happy about the extension of racism found in the term 'institutionalised racism'. This appears confusing within the overall schema, since he defines race relations situations as those of inequality and exploitation: he must then be seeing this inequality as an outcome of ideologies rather than structures. He espouses a type of relative autonomy approach to racist ideology, with the idea that it comes from situations of colonialism and is transported (hence becoming relatively autonomous from structure) to metropolitan societies. Racism then functions as a justification of colonial relations, as an ever-playing record in a new setting. Racism in the UK, for example, is not explained with reference to the actual structure of British society. The place of immigrants is seen as the result of an ideology arising in colonialism, but continuously reproducing itself in the present.

Classes and the notion of the underclass

In the notion of colonial immigrants as an underclass, Rex is presenting something distinct from the notion of sub-proletariat (compare Castles and Kosack, 1973). Such a group does not lie outside the class structure because it is marginalized and excludes paupers, the unemployed and social outsiders. It lies within the class structure itself, but at the bottom. This subordinate position within the working class refers to economic position (black immigrants as the new poor), but also to the valuation that black immigrants receive from metropolitan society. Colonial status is crucial in constructing the latter, and this is signified by colour visibility, which allows the individuals to be accurately recognized, evaluated and placed in the stratification system. However, blackness becomes meaningful when it represents another difference which is seen as inalienable; that is, visibility is socially constructed. For Rex, the significance of colour is given by the colonial situation.

The notion of the underclass, for Rex, does not imply one cohesive class grouping. His position is that there are a number of underclasses. More recently, Rex has preferred to abandon the term and talk about class and ethnic mobilization instead.

It is not clear in this, as I have argued elsewhere (Anthias, 1982, 1990), whether it is the valuation of individuals by the indigenous working class that produces them as an underclass, or whether these valuations are themselves a product of low economic position. Rex has not clarified theoretically the mechanisms of interaction and causality between structural position and social status evaluation. This part of his work remains deeply ambiguous.

The notion of housing classes in his earlier work used Weber's notion of class (Rex and Moore, 1967) relating it to the differential distribution of resources and the marketplace. Class struggle was seen in terms of domestic as well as industrial property. There have been myriads of critiques of this from Marxists, who conceptualize class not in terms of the distribution of resources, but in terms of production (e.g. Miles, 1983). For these critics, housing is a phenomenon that is linked to the distribution of resources and not the production process. The notion of a housing class was therefore to be rejected.

Struggle around housing (Rex and Tomlinson, 1979) was relatively independent of industrial class struggle. Housing was, however, an arena within which issues of class (in the sense of struggle over the distribution of resources) could take place. In this sense, Rex is a precursor to those post-modernist or New Times positions which locate struggle within broader social movements. These struggles over resources are undertaken in non-class terms (eg Hall and Jacques, 1988). The main difference is that Rex deploys the concept of housing classes to argue the case for the continuing importance of class, rather than abandoning it entirely.

Rex distances his use of the underclass notion from its association with 'the culture of poverty' thesis. This involves the idea that people are totally demoralized, and that there exists transmitted deprivation. His own interest is in the rights people have in the economic and political system, and how they are forced to fight for their rights.

For Rex, the 'underclass' nature of colonial immigrants (note that he does not use the term 'migrant labour') consists in their inferior position within the working class, and in the fact that they are politically separate from the organized labour movement. However, factors which structure the position of colonial immigrants within the market and politically (he conceptualizes ethnic (Black) politics in terms of defensive confrontation) are never clearly specified, and conflate the economic requirements of capital with discrimination practices by human actors.

One criticism that has been made of Rex's deployment of the term 'underclass' is that it is theoretically loose and that there is little attempt to distinguish it from the working class/proletariat (Gilroy, 1980). Another criticism is that it is Weberian, referring to a differential access to resources (at the level of distribution) rather than related to production (Phizacklea and Miles, 1980). This is clear in his early work on 'housing classes' which were defined by their access to the scarce resource of housing and worked within an urban sociology problematic. The accusation of Weberianism cannot in itself be a valid critique if it is merely made by writers whose theoretical standpoint is different. The major difficulty is in Rex's insistence on devising a hybrid Weberianized Marxism that leads to some ambiguity about the deployment of concepts in his work.

One of the most pressing problems for John Rex is the shifting of theoretical interest and levels of abstraction. Rex and Moore (1967) are concerned with racial disadvantage, how it is experienced by actors, their response to it, and social policy recommendations for its elimination. Race and ethnicity are then reduced to advantage/disadvantage, and the specific question concerning the links between race/ethnicity and class as modes of differentiation is never addressed. This conceptual problem is reflected in the use of the term 'immigrant' by Rex and Moore, despite the rejection of an immigrant-host framework. Phizacklea and Miles' (1980) main objection to this is that it implies that immigrants are permanent settlers, but their economic orientation and desire to return to their country of origin as Dahya (1974) notes for Asians and Anthias (1982, 1992c) for Cypriots, indicates that they must be treated both as migrant labour and in terms of the ideology of return. The term 'immigrant' subsumes too many concerns and is descriptive rather than analytic, as are the concepts of black, Asian and Cypriot.

In an article in *Racial and Ethnic Studies*, Rex replies to his Marxist critics. Race relations, he argues, have always been conceived by him as a 'set of situations of particularly severe economic exploitation and political oppression ... utterly dependent upon some form of class analysis' (1981: 1). However, in terms of his specification of the particular kinds of exploitation, oppression and conflict, Rex appears to use empirical rather than analytic categories – the theoretical class explanation is superimposed on empirical characteristics, but not sufficiently grounded in them.

According to Rex, 'race relations' are a category of class relations and not ethnic relations. While Rex seems to be reducing race to class, he also seems to be working with some notion of what ethnic relations might be that remains unspecified. Also, if 'race relations' are a category of class relations and race is about 'black' versus 'white' groups, then he is positing the existence of two classes, one 'white' and one 'black'. Class relations then come to signify relations between these two groups rather than relations between a capitalist class and a proletariat.

A central difficulty for Rex is to account, on the one hand, for his depiction of 'race relations as a category of class relations' and, on the other hand, for race relations problems as 'relating to the transfer of individuals and groups, whose structured position has previously been defined in colonial terms of some kind, to positions as workers or traders into metropolitan society itself' (Rex 1981: 17). Whereas the first depiction reduces race to class, the second focuses on the colonial origin of workers rather than their economic role. It is the valuation, then, of individuals with a colonial heritage that structures their underclass position rather than their actual placement. The colonial heritage is responsible for the stigmatization of black workers by the white working class, who consider them as outsiders or competitors. Rex is positing a political division between 'natives' and 'outsiders' within the working class. A further problem here is that he assumes a homogeneous indigenous class, not already divided.

Finally, although for Rex, class and ethnic organization become alternative bases for immigrant organization, he is unclear as to what provides the form of consciousness of ethnic organization and action, particularly in relation to the extent to which it is a particular form of class action or what its class effects are.

I have argued that Rex's depiction of race relations as class relations and the ways in which he privileges the colonial context in structuring racial stigmatization presents some theoretical difficulties. In addition, the stress on the stigmatization of groups through the prior seizing of state power by 'natives' assumes a homogeneous white working class and also a black/white divide. The final result is to reduce both race and class to the idealist representations of social actors. The structural location of migrants becomes reduced to the expression and effects of a racial ideology that has become a psychosocial mechanism for the pursuit of principles of economic rational interests by actors.

Colonialism and racism

As we have seen, Rex has contributed to the debate both on the links between colonialism and race and on the links between race and class, and can be read, despite his Weberianism, in terms of a tradition established by the black Marxist writer Oliver Cox (1970). This is a mode of argument that reduces races to false ideological categories constituted through the medium of class relations – racism becomes a medium for the rationalization and reinforcement of exploitation required by the economic system. A problem that is common to this tradition is that false racial stereotypes are left to the construction of individual consciousness (of capitalists for Cox and workers for Rex), in the absence of a mechanism by which the mode of production actually produces ideological effects (Gabriel and Ben Tovim, 1980). An additional problem is that any postulate of the origins of racism does not in itself adequately explain the structural conditions which account for its contemporary effectivity. It appears that its origin is presented as having ever present and ongoing effects to be continually reproduced at the level of the social formation. Rex's particular argument is that:

> Racial discrimination and racial prejudice are phenomena of colonialism. It was as a result of the conquest of poor and relatively underdeveloped countries by the technologically advanced nations during the 19th century, that new kinds of economy, new forms of social relations of production involving both conqueror and conquered, were brought into being. (Rex, 1973: 75).

It is the colonialist form that constructs ethnic stigmatization which is often justified in 'biological racist theories or some functional equivalent'. However, an additional element of Rex's thesis is that colonialism extends its influence into neo-colonialist or even internal colonialist structures so that he says: 'as the age of colonialism has passed ... colonial people have left their own countries to seek work in rich urban industrial societies of the metropolitan countries themselves' (1973: 76)

It is the colonial origin of the migrants that accounts for the development of social conflict between the indigenous working class and migrant groups. Rex considers as crucial the indigenous worker's perception of that origin as constituting the migrant as one variant of a non-free worker. Non-free workers are those who are not the working class of the industrial societies – the definition includes the indentured worker migrant in the compound, the domestic or farm servant, the peasant or share cropper on the semi-feudal estate, the peasant living by subsistence, and thus any worker who is in unequal power relations with the colonialist. Thus the definition is so broad that it becomes tautological – free workers are the organized working classes in the advanced world, unfree workers are all the others. Rex, in addition, is not clear as to whether it is the actual relations of inequality or power relations that are instrumental, or whether it is the perception by those within the countries of the advanced world that is crucial in defining 'race relations problems' as 'colonial problems'. Rex implies that the unequal power relations in the colony become transformed or expressed into idealist representations. The mechanism by which this occurs is not clearly specified.

Another problem with Rex's analysis is his supposition that the indigenous working class must stand 'in a different relation' from migrants to the capitalist classes of their own countries. This is linked to his notion of the 'free worker' who through trade union organization can dispose of his labour freely and is not the property of the employer. Rex's position rests on two grounds:

1. A separation of the *actual* class conditions of what he calls natives and immigrants. The first are not an oppressed class, but are 'free' to sell their labour how and when they choose. This freedom must be dependent on the exclusion of the migrant from these conditions for the sale of labour.

2. The exclusion is premised on the perceptions and delusions of the working class. Rex states that 'it is in the nature of free unionised labour that it will seek to strengthen or at least avoid weakening its market position and this will lead to adopting an anti-immigrant stand.'

It is the perception of immigrants as unfree workers through their colonial position that structures the behaviour of the working class. However, this cannot explain the structural position of immigrants in the labour market unless it is seen totally to depend on organized working-class activities and not on either the actual material character of migrant labour or the activities of capital in relation to it. Rex appears to consider trade union sectarianism as more powerful than the interests of capital in structuring the position of migrants. The material conditions of their colonial context have been represented in the subjectivity of the organized working class. Rex's argument posits the central role of the consciousness of human subjects, very much in keeping with a Weberian sociological standpoint.

Colonial immigrants and the black working class

In Rex and Tomlinson's *Colonial Immigrants in a British City* (1979), it is the emphasis on black disadvantage that is dominant. At times the caste-like barriers between whites and blacks are noted, which reinforces the notion that they are referring to an outclass, a group that is outside the dynamic of class relations and indeed structured by values and ideas.

The conceptualization of politics in this work is that of political actors within the organizational framework of the liberal democratic party structure, choosing to exclude black workers from their midst.

The terms we use are not only ways of classifying for juridical or for analytical purposes, but emerge out of discourses that include political and theoretical proclamation and contestation. Nor are they evaluatively neutral. Rex has consistently used the term 'black immigrant' in his analysis of ethnicity and racism in the UK. This does not mean that he is unaware of the need to look at class and other factors such as culture, but it does indicate that he sees the divisions in the UK to be those primarily of the racialization of inequality.

In the UK, we can find the term 'Black' used in four distinct although at times related ways:

1. Black as denoting those whose colour of skin is visibly darker: that is, Afro-Caribbeans, Africans and South Asians (now sometimes referred to as black and Asian with the former meaning those of African origin). This is usually a categorization from the outside rather than the inside, for individuals will not identify purely in terms of colour visibility.
2. Black as uniting those who experience racism irrespective of colour, ethnicity, identity or culture. This may be used both from the outside and from the inside.

3. Black as a positive political identification – as a reaction to negative attributions – as a means of converting 'otherness' to 'identity'. This is a form of identification rather than categorization.
4. Black as denoting those who share a common colonialist origin and who may also share a cultural origin. This is more a definition from the outside.

Black as a basis for solidary communal grouping has therefore been a shifting and confusing category, at times denoting both Asians and African Caribbeans or only the latter. Within the 'race relations industry', the black community is defined as an ethnic group with distinct needs, and is set up to compete with other groups like Asians and Cypriots for resources and funding.

The confusions around the notion are also found in public discourse on blackness, with the term being used in preference to country of origin or in addition to country of origin and ethnic identity where it was a shorthand for black skin. This is found in the ethnic-monitoring process of the former Inner London Education Authority, for example, and the ethnic Census question. A contradiction is also found between the aims and objectives of the various bodies which define 'ethnic minorities' as the object of intervention and social engineering (inclusive of Irish, Cypriots, migrants, refugees and so on), but which then somehow collapse them under the notion of black groups.

In some of the political divisions between Asians and African Caribbeans, there has been the accusation of privileged access to resources by both sides. For example, Asians have been seen to preponderate in formal positions as representatives of black groups, such as within the Commission for Racial Equality. African Caribbeans, on the other hand, are regarded as predominating in local authority race relations units (Modood, 1988).

The term 'colour racism' dichotomizes the victims of racism into all those who are black and who stand against the perpetrators, who are then all those who are white. It produces a unitary subject of racist intentionalities and effects. There are racists and there are victims. But a recognition of the contradictory articulations of racist discourse requires the abandonment of the notion of a unitary subject who is at the heart of racist society either as victim or perpetrator. Not only are working-class and middle-class racism different in the images they use, but these are never consistently expressed in everyday practices (Cohen, 1988).

But an even more important objection to the use of the term 'black' is that it cannot articulate processes of racialization in general or in their specificity. It is too limited because it excludes those who do not experience what can be called 'colour racism' (such as the Irish, Jews, Third World migrants, migrant workers and refugees). It is also too broad because it cannot tackle specific forms of racism, such as those against Asian women or African Caribbean youth, in the first case linked to gender and sexuality (e.g. the practice of virginity tests at immigration control) and in the second case linked to gender, generation and unemployment (criminalization). It reduces racism to a homogeneous set of experiences and practices organized around the centrality of skin colour as the visible marker of racist intentionality. Racism is therefore defined in intersubjective terms, being seen as exercised in and against subjects with particular ascriptive characteristics, rather than being a set of outcomes of a large range of legal, policy, institutional and discursive practices (Anthias, 1990).

Rex on ethnic mobilization and multiculturalism

In his recent writings, Rex prefers the term 'ethnic mobilization' to the depiction of immigrants as an underclass. According to this view, the guarantee of Jenkins' concept of 'diversity in equality' is to be found in ethnic mobilization. This espouses the view that an ethnic minority needs its own organization.

The formation of separate ethnic organizations for the expression of political interests, and the development of a solidary ethnic unit insisting on its own identity and claiming justice without absorption or assimilation is seen as a form of reactive ethnicity or defensive confrontation. The expression of class interests through this mode (as cultures of resistance) is thus denied. At times, Rex and Tomlinson seem unduly concerned with identity and its social pathology. Unlike some critics, I feel that there is a place for the discussion of the subjective dimensions of culture and disadvantage, for these have both individual and social effects. However, the concern with this should be separated from an analytic concern with the structure of ethnic and racialized groups and their import within society as central organizing ideological and material principles. An atomistic approach cannot grasp the social relations within a society, whether the starting point is the individual social actor or a discrete cultural response by a group (for example, identity crisis). To cite identity crisis as the real source of ethnic reaffirmation is to underplay the structural sources that may lead to political struggle.

There are major difficulties with the forms of representation of ethnic groups. For example, their leaders may be the most traditional and inegalitarian; this alone gives a space for anxieties over ethnic politics. Groups may be oriented to homeland politics, and some of this would be reactionary from the point of view of a non-sexist and non-racist participatory social democracy. While defending ethnic politics, Rex does recognize, to some extent, the dangers of co-optation (Rex, 1991).

Rex on multiculturalism

I want now to address Rex's writings on the concept of a multicultural society, a project he is currently engaged in working through.

In his essay on 'The political sociology of a multicultural society' (1991), Rex distinguishes the notion of a multicultural society from that of a plural society.

As first used by Furnivall (1939), the latter term described a society in which ethnic groups related only in the marketplace, marked by an absence of 'common will' between them. M.G. Smith (1965) saw the plural society as characterized by ethnic groups having their own institutions, but coexisting within a single political system dominated by a ruling group. Both emphasized inequalities between groups.

Rex also distinguishes the idea of a multicultural society from power-sharing states (such as Canada and Belgium), where two or more groups have their own separate political representation within a federal state structure.

In 1968 Jenkins put forward the view of 'cultural diversity, coupled with equal opportunity, in an atmosphere of mutual tolerance' (quoted in Rex, 1991: 56). Although this was not as radical as Marshall's (1950) view of social rights, it none the less set the terms of an agenda, like Marshall's, where citizenship rights involved a commitment to a shared political culture. However, what was not adequately explored was the potential conflict between a shared culture of the public domain and the rights to cultural difference which Jenkins had asserted.

The notion of two separate domains, those of a shared public domain and differentiated private cultural domains, did not take into account the difficulties in this depiction. Rex challenges the two domains thesis, both theoretically and practically. There appears no sociological validity to the view that two spheres of social life could exist without influencing each other. Nor can it be maintained that the various elements of one could be easily differentiated from the other. The question, for example, of what constitutes the shared public domain could be answered differently from different political or cultural positions. For example, some like Honeyford (1988) have identified the shared public domain as equivalent to an all-inclusive British national culture. But this is problematized by class differences as well as political differences. Feminists have also questioned the view that values and organization around gender and the family are private. They have argued for the breakdown of the dualism inherent in the distinction between the public and the private.

Practically, there are difficulties in locating, for example, the place of schools, for they are involved in socialization into both public and private values. Educational demands exist both in terms of the provision of equal opportunity for access to qualifications and jobs on the one hand, and for the preservation of communal values. There has been anxiety about the failure of schools to provide the latter for minority groups. The response of the Swann Report (1985) was to argue for policies to overcome racism in schools and for measures to educate all children into minority cultures or the infamous 'saris, samosas and steel bands'. Schools have been the main site of the conflicts inherent in the concept of a multicultural society according to Rex (1991).

There has also been confusion regarding the meaning of the term 'public cultural domain'. Some have equated it with the idea of British culture, rather than seeing it as a product of dialogue or negotiation. It is also difficult to distinguish between what is to be placed in the public sphere and what is to be placed in the private sphere. Commonly, religion is placed in the private sphere but this ignores the role that the Christian church still plays in the shared public domain, represented for example by blasphemy laws and religious worship in schools with regard to Christianity that do not apply to other religions. This issue has been brought to the fore by the Rushdie affair.

There is also the issue of those values – for example, around gender equality – that are seen to occupy the public sphere, but which some minority cultures do not endorse, or which in practice are not endorsed by many social groups. If the notion of a private cultural sphere is to be maintained, at what point are the rules within it around gender, sexuality or religion to be policed with regard to notions of public shared values. Extreme instances of this would be the practices of cliterectomy or polygamy.

In addition, as in the case of Islam, religious ideas do not always relate to private moral values, but involve a whole way of life, including public conduct. Finally, many minorities are committed politically to their homelands, and this problematizes the distinction found in the two domains thesis even further.

Rex concludes that the three possible outcomes are that over time the descendants of minorities will be less concerned with culture, or that there will be a continuation of conflict, or finally that there will occur dialogue and a renegotiation of the culture of the public domain. This latter appears the most positive prognosis for multiculturalism. But this assumes that there is no inherent conflict of universes of meaning to be found within culture. On the other hand, it recognizes, that culture is not static or fixed, but changes contextually and situationally.

Conclusion: the impact of John Rex on policy around race

There are contradictions in the ways John Rex's work has had a resonance in policy debates and how his work has been appropriated. Despite Rex's belief that the academy and politics and policy should be disassociated, intellectual ideas become disseminated and have an influence on activists. What has been disappointing is the way John Rex's ideas have been received by activists on the ground. Even though Rex makes a case for including excluded groups and has been a passionate advocate of participatory democracy, such groups have rarely placed him among their ranks. The reactions to the Handsworth book (*Race, Colonialism and the City*, 1973) were at times framed in terms of the problems of white researchers doing research on issues of race (Rex, interview, 1993). Such a position is formulated on the basis of a totalizing view of racism that treats all 'white' people as racist and makes a binary and rigid distinction between the perpetrators of racism (all whites) and the victims (all blacks). Such a position is laden with difficulties (see Anthias, forthcoming). In the USA, black people have used research to pursue legal cases, but this has never been the case in the UK.

In the UK, the terms of reference around 'race', from 1962 onwards, have been set within a liberal agenda, but the concern with individual rights was as a mechanism of social control of the population. Social incorporation was to be on the terms of the state's own agenda. This has involved the co-optation of groups that represent the least challenging face of immigrant groupings, and can be seen as a way of excluding them from mainstream politics (Anthias and Yuval Davis, 1992).

The anti-racist movement of the 1980s stressed the role of racism and promoted the idea of black autonomous organization, (such as black sections in the Labour Party), rather than targeting individual prejudice. The aim was to build an anti-racist society and culture. The stress was on race difference and awareness rather than the colour blindness promoted by liberalism: mixed race adoption was challenged and race awareness workshops were promoted, while ideas about black culture and identity and ethnic monitoring were fought for. Political resources were to be marshalled: through black councillors, black MPs, the role of blacks in the Labour Party, the funding of black groups and the presence of blacks in the media (see Hall, 1988). Equal opportunity policies were introduced, but they were not without their difficulties (see Anthias and Yuval Davis, 1992).

Rex's position has been used as an embodiment of the race relations tradition by both academics and activists (e.g. Miles, 1982; Gilroy, 1980). However, Rex has been opposed to a colour-blind approach and his work can sit happily with those approaches that argue for the importance of separate organization and mobilization. Nevertheless, such an approach is itself laden with the difficulties endemic in struggle formulated on the basis of ethnic commonality or identity politics. The current crisis in anti-racist strategies (Anthias *et al.*, forthcoming) is an indicator of some of these problems. But to recount these is to tell another story.

John Rex's work has been crucial to the development of British sociology. Despite some of the theoretical difficulties identified in his position, there is no doubt that he has made a seminal contribution to understanding the complex nature of 'race' and ethnic phenomena in modern society.

Key texts

In *Race Relations in Sociological Theory* (1970), Rex sets out to delineate the main characteristics of what he calls a 'race relations situation' in terms of a situation of differentiation, inequality and pluralism between groups; the possibility of clearly distinguishing between such groups by their physical appearance, their culture or occasionally merely by their ancestry; and the justification and explanation of this discrimination in terms of some kind of implicit or explicit theory, frequently, but not always, of a biological kind (1970: 30).

In his book *Race, Colonialism and the City* (1973), Rex collects together essays which conceptualize race relations as metropolitan urban problems and with regard to the exploitation of the 'Third World'. These range from a discussion of the role of colonialism in the construction of racism to looking at South African society from a comparative perspective.

In *Colonial Immigrants in a British City* (1979), co-written with Sally Tomlinson, a 'class analysis' is provided of Handsworth in Birmingham, as the subtitle of the book claims. The conceptualization of migrants is in terms of an 'underclass'. This book arose out of substantive empirical research in a local community, but sets out also to provide a significant class-related approach to migration and the settlement of black migrants in a British city.

Acknowledgement

This paper has benefited greatly from the interview that John Rex granted me in 1993. Any shortcomings in the interpretation of his work and its assessment remain strictly mine.

References

Amos, V., Gilroy, P. and Lawrence, E. (1982) 'White sociology, black struggle' in Robbins, D. *et al.* (eds), *Rethinking Social Inequality*, Aldershot: Gower.

Anthias, F. (1982) 'Ethnicity and class among Greek Cypriot migrants: a study in the conceptualisation of ethnicity', Ph.D. thesis, University of London.

Anthias, F. (1990) 'Race and class revisited: conceptualising race and racisms', *Sociological Review*, 38, 1, 19–42.

Anthias, F. (1992) *Ethnicity, Class, Gender and Migration*, Aldershot: Avebury.

Anthias, F. (forthcoming) 'Rethinking categories and struggles: racism, anti-racism and multiculturalism', in Anthias, F., Lloyd, C., Paterson, A. and Yuval Davis, N. (eds), *Rethinking Anti-racism*, Monographs in Ethnic Relations, University of Warwick, Centre for Research in Ethnic Relations.

Anthias, F. and Yuval Davis, N. (1992) *Racialised Boundaries: Race, nation, gender, class and the anti-racist struggle*, London: Routledge.

Back, L. and Solomos, J. (1993) 'Researching racism', *Economy and Society*, 22, 2, pp. 178–99.

Ball, W. and Solomos, J. (eds) (1991) *Race and Local Politics*, London: Macmillan.

Banton, M. (1983) *Race and Ethnic Competition*, Cambridge: Cambridge University Press.

Banton, M. (1987) *Racial Theories*, Cambridge: Cambridge University Press.

Banton, M. (1988) *Racial Consciousness*, Harlow: Longman.

Beveridge, W. (1942) *Report on Social Insurance and Allied Services*, Cmd 6404, London: HMSO.

Bhabha, H. (1990) *Nation and Narration*, London: Routledge.

Brown, C. (1984) *Black and White Britain*, London: Policy Studies Institute.

Castells, M. (1975) 'Immigrant workers and class struggle in advanced capitalism', *Politics and Society*, 5, 1, pp.34–66.

Castles, S. and Kosack, G. (1973) *Immigrant Workers in the Class Structure in Western Europe*, Oxford: Oxford University Press.

Centre for Contemporary Cultural Studies (1982) *The Empire Strikes Back*, London: Hutchinson.

Cohen, P. (1988) 'The perversions of inheritance', in Cohen, P. and Bains, H. (eds) *Multi Racist Britain*, London: Macmillan.

Cox, O. (1970) *Caste, Class and Race: A study in social dynamics*, New York: Modern Reader Paperbacks.

Dahya, B. (1974) 'The nature of Pakistani ethnicity in industrial cities in Britain', in Cohen, A. (ed.), *Urban Ethnicity*, London: Tavistock.

Furnivall, R. (1939) *Netherland India: A study of plural economy*, Cambridge: Cambridge University Press.

Gabriel, J. and Ben Tovim, G. (1980) 'Marxism and the concept of racism', *Economy and Society*, **7**, 2, pp. 119–50.

Gilroy, P. (1980) 'Managing the underclass: a further role on the sociology of race relations in Britain', *Race and Class*, **22**, 1, 47–62.

Gilroy, P. (1987) *There Ain't no Black in the Union Jack*, London: Hutchinson.

Gilroy, P. (1993) *The Black Atlantic*, London: Verso.

Glazer, N. and Moynihan, D. (1965) *Beyond the Melting Pot*, Cambridge, Mass.: MIT Press.

Glazer, N. and Moynihan, D. (eds) (1975) *Ethnicity: Theory and experience*, Cambridge, Mass.: Harvard University Press.

Hall, S. (1980) 'Race, articulation and societies structure in dominance', in Unesco, *Sociological Theories: Race and colonialism*, Paris: Unesco.

Hall, S. (1988a) 'New ethnicities', in Mercer, K. (ed.), *Black Film/British Cinema*, Institute of Contemporary Arts Document 7, London.

Hall, S. (1988b) 'New times', *Marxism Today*.

Hall, S. and Jacques, M. (1989) *New Times: The changing face of politics in the 1990s*, London: Lawrence and Wishart.

Honeyford, R. (1988) *Integration or Disintegration: Towards a non-racist society*, London: Claridge.

Jeffrey, P. (1976) *Migrants and Refugees: Muslim and Christian Pakistani families in Bristol*, Cambridge: Cambridge University Press.

Lukács, G. (1971) *History and Class Consciousness*, London: Merlin.

Marshall, T.H. (1950) *Citizenship and Social Class*, Cambridge: Cambridge University Press.

Marshall, T.H. (1975) *Social Policy in the Twentieth Century*, London: Hutchinson. First published 1965.

Marshall, T.H. (1981) *The Right To Welfare and Other Essays*, London: Heinemann Educational Books.

Mills, C. Wright (1970) *The Sociological Imagination*, Harmondsworth: Penguin.

Miles, R. (1982) *Racism and Migrant Labour*, London: Routledge and Kegan Paul.

Miles, R. (1989) *Racism*, London: Routledge.

Miles, R. (1993) *Racism after Race Relations*, London: Routledge.

Modood, T. (1988) '"Black", racial equality and Asian identity', *New Community*, **XIV**, 3, pp. 397–404.

Myrdal, G. (1969a) *Objectivity in Social Research*, London: Duckworth.

Myrdal, G. (1969b) *An American Dilemma*, New York: Harper and Row.

Nikolinakos, M. (1975) 'Notes towards a general theory of migration in late capitalism', *Race and Class*, **22**, 1, 5–17.

Parkin, F. (1979) *The Marxist Theory of Class: A bourgeois critique*, London: Tavistock.

Phizacklea, A. and Miles, R. (1980) *Labour and Racism*, London: Routledge and Kegan Paul.

Rex, J. (1961) *Key Problems in Sociological Theory*, London: Routledge and Kegan Paul.

Rex, J. (1970) *Race Relations in Sociological Theory*, London: Weidenfeld and Nicolson.

Rex, J. (1973) *Race, Colonialism and the City*, London: Weidenfeld and Nicolson.

Rex, J. (1981) 'A working paradigm for race relations research', *Ethnic and Racial Studies*, **4**, 1, pp. 1–25.

Rex, J. (1986) *Race and Ethnicity*, Milton Keynes: Open University Press.

Rex, J. (1988) *The Ghetto and the Underclass*, Aldershot: Avebury.

Rex, J. (1991) 'The political sociology of a multicultural society', *Ghandian Perspectives*, **4**, 1, 54–75.

Rex, J. (unpub.) 'A reply to my Marxist critics'.

Rex, J. and Moore, R. (1967) *Race, Community and Conflict*, Oxford: Oxford University Press.

Rex, J. and Tomlinson, S. (1979) *Colonial Immigrants in a British City*, London: Routledge and Kegan Paul.

Rose, E.J.B. and Deakin, N. (1969) *Colour and Citizenship*, Oxford: Institute for Race Relations and Oxford University Press.

Sivanandan, A. (1976) 'Race, class and the state: the black experience in Britain', *Race and Class*, **xxv**, 2, pp. 347–68.

Sivanandan, A. (1982) *A Different Hunger*, London: Pluto.

Smith, D.J. (1977) *Racial Disadvantage and Ethnic Minorities*, London: Policy Studies Institute.

Smith, D.J. (1981) *Unemployment and Ethnic Minorities*, London: Policy Studies Institute.

Smith, M.G. (1965) *The Plural Society in the British West Indies*, University of California Press.

Swann Report (1985) *Education for All*, Report of Committee of Enquiry into Education of Children from Ethnic Minority Groups, London: HMSO.

Van den Berghe, P. (1978) *Race and Racism*, Chichester: Wiley.

Van den Berghe, P. (1979) *The Ethnic Phenomenon*, New York: Elsevier.

Wallman, S. (ed.) (1979) *Ethnicity at Work*, London: Macmillan.

Watson, J. (1977) *Between Two Cultures*, Oxford: Blackwell.

Weber, M. (1969) *Economy and Society*, Vol. 1, New York: Bedminster Press.

Index